UNDERDOGS

www.**penguin**.co.uk

UNDERDOGS

Keegan Hirst, Batley and a Year in the Life of a Rugby League Town

Tony Hannan

BANTAM PRESS

LONDON • TORONTO • SYDNEY • AUCKLAND • JOHANNESBURG

TRANSWORLD PUBLISHERS
61–63 Uxbridge Road, London W5 5SA
www.penguin.co.uk

Transworld is part of the Penguin Random House group of companies
whose addresses can be found at global.penguinrandomhouse.com

First published in Great Britain in 2017 by Bantam Press
an imprint of Transworld Publishers

A CIP catalogue record for this book
is available from the British Library.

ISBN 9780593077498

Typeset in 11.5/15pt Minion by Falcon Oast Graphic Art Ltd.
Printed and bound by Clays Ltd, Bungay, Suffolk.

Penguin Random House is committed to a sustainable
future for our business, our readers and our planet. This book
is made from Forest Stewardship Council® certified paper.

1 3 5 7 9 10 8 6 4 2

For Paul

My brother

Sport, sport, masculine sport, equips a young man for society.
– *Keynsham*, Bonzo Dog Band, Liberty Records, 1969

I'm from Batley, for goodness sake. No one is gay in Batley . . .
– Keegan Hirst, August 2015

Contents

Prologue

MOUNTAINS ARE SACRED places. It has been so since mankind first gazed at their summits and thought them heavenly.

For it is on a mountain that a tribe stands closest to its gods; where divine breath might favour upturned faces.

And it is in their foothills that a human being might ponder his or her own brief mortality and significance in the universe.

Mountains mean stories. They speak of legends and heroic deeds – Mount Sinai, where Moses received the Ten Commandments; Mount Etna, beneath which Vulcan hammers in his Roman smithy; Mount Kailash, home of Hindu deity Shiva; Mount Olympus, of course, battlefield of the Titans, begetter of athletes and the Olympic Games, arena of Greek gods. Mountains attract devotees as shepherds gather flocks.

And where there are mountains, there are very often rivers, rivers of ice and fire and water, rivers of time.

In the town of Batley, in what used to be the West Riding of Yorkshire, it is to Mount Pleasant that the faithful come. Though no longer, it must be admitted, in any great number and with little expectation of paradise.

But then mountains are also there to be climbed.

Sunday, 20 September 2015; Batley v Hunslet, 60–12, the final game of the season

The mastodon bellow of an air horn brings exhaustion and relief. Keegan Hirst, 27-year-old captain of Batley rugby league club, feels it as much as anyone. Yet for the 6 ft 4 in. prop forward, what might have been the end of days instead heralds a whole new beginning.

The season just gone was gruelling and frustrating. Having spent most of it at the wrong end of the Championship table – rugby league's twelve-team second tier – survival had only now been assured. The Bulldogs went well in some games, not so well in others, but with Hirst leading from the front – literally – what had really made the job tougher was the sheer volume of narrow defeats.

That Batley, also known as the Gallant Youths, were in such a scrap at all owed much to the latest rugby league 'innovation' as the game moved into its so-called 'new era': a shake-up that to many was about as comprehensible as a quadratic equation. After twenty-three games, a three-way divisional split had taken place ahead of a seven-game mini-season, when the top eight teams in the northern hemisphere's elite competition, Super League, hived off towards play-offs and a high-profile Grand Final at Old Trafford. Super League's bottom four then joined the Championship's leading quartet in what were now to be known as the Qualifiers, or middle eight. For these clubs, the points-slate was wiped clean, as previously they'd competed in different competitions. Here, the top three returned to Super League in 2016, with a fourth promotion place up for grabs courtesy of a heavily hyped 'Million Pound Game' in which those finishing fourth and fifth participated.

Below that, in the bottom eight, Batley joined fellow remaining Championship sides Featherstone, Dewsbury, London, Workington, Whitehaven and cellar dwellers Hunslet and Doncaster – at least one of whom, in most other years, would by now have been demoted to League 1, the rebranded and geographically diverse 'third division' beneath the Championship. This year, though, the fight was still on to avoid those two relegation spots. And at the top of these 'after eights', a new trophy was on offer, the Championship Shield, though no one seemed overly excited about lifting it.

Come season's end, Doncaster, rock bottom on two points with only a solitary win, took the drop as expected. For Batley, however, the margin between them and the Mount's final visitors, Hunslet Hawks, had been far too close for comfort, Batley having ended the regular season in ninth on fourteen points, Hunslet eleventh on ten. At least it hadn't been as fraught as 2014, when only the overturning of a points-deduction for fielding an ineligible player kept Batley up and sent Keighley down instead.

To their critics, the Super 8s were ludicrously over-complicated – what was wrong with two up, two down? Yet as a replacement for a licensing system perceived as a failure on many levels, at least Championship clubs could now plot a course to the Promised Land, no matter how convoluted or unlikely the route. Not that anyone in Batley was for the moment concerned with that. They just wanted yet another interminable and disappointing campaign that had more latterly assumed cliffhanger proportions over and done with.

Back on August bank holiday Monday, Batley had viewed their trip to Featherstone's Big Fellas stadium as just another fixture to tick off the list, thinking themselves all but safe from relegation. By the end of that day, however, the trapdoor still gaped terrifyingly open.

Having kicked off the Super 8s four points clear of Hunslet, Batley had been beaten by Workington and Dewsbury in games one and two. The Hawks, though, mirrored those losses and failed to make up ground. So when the Bulldogs then went to already doomed Doncaster in game three, anything other than victory was unthinkable. A nervy win duly delivered, all they could do was wait. If the South Leeds side had lost in London, as seemed likely, the task was complete. Batley would hold a six-point advantage that, together with a vastly superior points difference and only eight points left to play for, would as good as see them home. And when the result reached local radio, they could indeed relax. Hunslet were losers in the capital, the Bulldogs confirmed safe.

But wait: this was Batley, wasn't it? When is anything so straight-forward in Batley? In a twist worthy of a dodgy soap opera, the bloke on the radio apologized. The Hawks hadn't lost in London at all. In fact, they had beaten the Broncos 41–24, for only their sixth win of the season. The four-point gap was retained: as you were. What came next would enter Mount Pleasant folklore.

A trip to Featherstone is seldom less than daunting, but given that Hunslet faced a long-haul trip to Whitehaven, defeat at the Big Fellas now seemed to matter little. By tradition, Cumbria is never an easy place to play and Haven had plenty at stake themselves. Surely at worst another weekend's fixtures would be crossed off and, with only three matches then ahead, fears of relegation calmed.

Batley, though, were not about to leave it to chance. Level at half-time, having dug in with resilience, their forward domination was such that they'd established a 26–6 lead with six minutes to go. But if a twenty-point margin over the eventual Shield winners wasn't enough of a surprise, with the clock counting down and the game almost up for the hosts, Rovers suddenly found their scoring touch. A trio of tries, two converted, and it was 22–26. Thrilling stuff but too little, too late, as the cliché goes. The hooter sounded just as Featherstone, a yard from their own line, hoofed the ball upfield, apparently to nowhere.

The kick was little more than defiance, a futile punt and hope. So when Batley's stocky left-winger Shaun 'Ainy' Ainscough pouched it on the bounce, that seemed to be that. A player of such talent and top-flight experience could manage this in his sleep. Find the nearest opponent and take the tackle, Ainy. Jog into touch. Heck, knock on and pick it up again if you must. At the next stoppage, the game and worry would be over.

In fact, about the only thing Ainscough ought not to have done is exactly what he did. In acres of space and under no pressure at all, he too kicked the ball wildly in the air – whether going for touch on the far side of the field or simply in joy, who knew? The end result was the same. In the time it takes a man to groan 'What have I done?', Rovers' winger Will Sharp had collected the loose kick and bounced over for a try in the corner.

There was still a tough conversion for Paul Sykes to negotiate. At that stage, Batley thought a draw would be enough. But as the kick sailed through the posts for a 28–26 home win and the clips on social media went viral, confirmation came through of the Hawks' 30–16 victory over Whitehaven. The pair of tries Ainy had contributed to an astonishing game were now forgotten in the fuss.

'I was just celebrating, wasn't I?' he would say later. 'I thought the whistle had been blown.' He had tried to leap on teammate Alex Brown, who said, 'Ainy, what are you doing?' and began to run. Going back into the changing room had been 'pretty bad'. Ainscough's rash kick could have proved disastrous. The incident would take him weeks to get over, though one day he might laugh about it.

This was, however, no time to panic. Three games left and two points in it, with that for-and-against ratio added security. Next week, though, playing Doncaster at home, Hunslet had a good chance to draw level in the table and Batley would face a desperate Whitehaven, thankfully at the Mount. How would that sickening late capitulation affect them psychologically? And with Hunslet meeting Featherstone, and Batley off to London after that, the stakes on the final weekend, when Hunslet were due at Batley, were set to be high.

Doncaster put up more of a struggle than expected but still went down, 25–16. Thankfully, with Keegan Hirst on the scoreboard, Whitehaven were walloped 50–0 and so the story continued. 'Never mind the Million Pound Game, we're heading for the Million Lira Game,' joked one online wag. But on the penultimate weekend the matter was finally, if not absolutely, put to bed. Despite another valiant display, Hunslet only just came up short against Featherstone on the Friday night, 18–10. Barring a mathematical miracle, Batley ought therefore to be safe, even though they then went down 50–16 in the capital. Whitehaven too were out of the mire. Upshot: the last game would now be a more relaxed affair, a points difference of about minus four hundred to minus one hundred saw to that. Not many games finish 150–0.

And lo, it came to pass that Hunslet made their short trip to Batley for a match watched by 737 spectators, the culmination of a season intended to revolutionize rugby league's appeal.

Mount Pleasant is a common enough name, with equivalents from Ballarat to Tennessee. There is even a Mount Pleasant on the Falkland Islands – in that instance an RAF base; its use is usually a clue that someone had a sense of humour. This particular Mount Pleasant, perched high over Batley town centre, is riddled with history, although its biggest fans would have to agree that the area has seen better days. During the Industrial Revolution perhaps, when, as with many a northern town and city, money was there to be made and workers were dying to make it in the region's mills, factories and coalmines.

Survival demanded ingenuity, brute force and mental and physical toughness amid the wind-blown craggy uplands and valleys of what is known, nostalgically, as the Heavy Woollen District. The chief industry by a distance was textiles. The area was famed for the manufacture of 'shoddy', rags recycled into coats, blankets and military uniforms, a business wherein fortunes were made. This was an age when, wherever you stood on Batley's then-cobbled streets, upwards of sixty mill chimneys muddied the sky.

The town motto: *floreat industria* – may industry flourish.

Batley's economic standing would never be higher. When the sun set on Victoria's empire, the town dwindled both in prestige and population to the 50,000 inhabitants of various religions and cultures it houses today. But wealth ought not only to be measured in finance. In areas like Skelsey Row, it was effluence rather than affluence that trickled down, such slum sites familiar with typhoid, scarlet fever, consumption, diphtheria and other such catastrophes, but strangers to sanitation, food in bellies and a decent living wage. Community spirit was the only affordable safety valve; there was a lot of it about.

Religion too was ever present, though not of the establishment type. With Dewsbury, Heckmondwike, Ossett and satellites such as nearby Birstall and Mirfield, Batley developed into a Methodist and Congregationalist stronghold. The district's hundred or more chapels – rather than churches – earned it a reputation for non-conformity, pragmatism and a fierce independent spirit: the ideal birthplace for a code of football that since 1895 has needed all of that and more.

Since December 2014, the Mount, a few hundred metres' steep climb out of the town centre, has been known as the Fox's Biscuits Stadium, thanks to the sponsorship of Batley's biggest employer. Having reached its peak, a visitor might take a seat in the Glen Tomlinson Stand.

Tomlinson, an Australian half-back, was a fixture here over a couple of stints from the early 1990s, sandwiching spells at top-flight Bradford, Hull and Wakefield. A popular figure, as having his name on the main grandstand attests, he scored a club record-breaking 124 tries in his two spells at Batley, before Craig Lingard – who is still around as assistant coach – surpassed that total in 2006.

But that's how it is here. Stand still for five minutes and they are apt to pop a little copper plaque on you, or bless a burger van in memory of your granddad. A commendable impulse, though a visitor could be forgiven for wondering if such heightened reverence for the past might not also betray deeper uncertainty about the future.

Today's opponents are strapped even more tightly to their historical life-support machine. In 1971, Hunslet's home since 1888, Parkside, fell prey to arson. The disaster heralded dissolution, then rescue, a tricky rebirth and years of precariousness thereafter. In 1980–81, Batley's centenary season, this year's relegation rivals were even forced to share Mount Pleasant for a while, having lost tenancy at Elland Road greyhound stadium. Since when, an undermining of the traditional industrial working class experienced right across England's north has ensured that it is survival, not glory, which keeps crowds nowadays numbered in hundreds rather than thousands nibbling at their admittedly cleaner fingernails.

Nevertheless, in defiance of such monumental forces of social upheaval, a thankless task goes on. Like Sisyphus pushing his rock, Hunslet RLFC is determined to endure. As the club song has it: *We've sailed the seas before, boys, and so we shall again.* Maybe, by sheer force of obstinacy or some sort of miracle, they will. Last year, after all, they gained promotion. Today, though, the rock will roll all the way down to the lowest level of the semi-pro game, money-spinning matches against Leigh, Bradford and Featherstone replaced by thankless trips to Oxford, Merthyr Tydfil and Gloucestershire.

Keegan Hirst wins the toss, so Batley play uphill, just as they like it. The tallest man on the field, he almost scores the opening try, but the offload from fellow prop Alex Rowe is deemed forward.

Given his height and stature, Hirst stands out; he is head and shoulders above everyone else, both physically and in performance. Physiology by Michelangelo, locomotive heart, he leads by example, hammering at Hunslet's middle defence repeatedly, the combination of ferocity and graceful handling remarkable in such a frame. In rugby league, men must be strong and men must be exceptional. Hirst is both. He is also currently the most famous man in a sport more usually starved of media attention, especially at this level.

Keegan: it's an unusual name for a Batley lad, brought up a fifteen-minute walk away. 'My mam says it's nothing to do with Kevin,' he says. 'It was in a book and she liked it. It's Irish. She thought it sounded nice.' Keegan has no Irish in him, so far as he is aware. *Nice.* Around here, it's important to be nice.

Prior to Sunday, 16 August 2015, when his homosexuality was revealed in the *Sunday Mirror*, 'Keegs' wasn't guaranteed recognition in the town of his birth, let alone the game he plays wholeheartedly. What reputation he had was of a solid journeyman prop in a division noticed by few. Another workhorse front-rower whose contribution even the most fanatical rugby league devotee might miss. Rugged, brave, dependable, yes, but then those are the qualities required of anyone brave or daft enough to step out on to a rugby field.

The reaction to his coming out, though, was extraordinary. When news broke on social media that an exclusive was on its way, the sport's followers went on the defensive – another hatchet job, no doubt. Yet the story was nothing of the sort.

'At first, I couldn't even say "I'm gay" in my head, let alone out loud,' said this northern working-class tough guy, product of a rough tough council estate, whose previous jobs included builder, nightclub doorman and factory worker. 'I feel like I'm letting out a long breath that I've hold in for a long time.' Over a two-page spread, the article revealed how the married father-of-two had finally 'found the words' to explain to wife Sara that they could no longer be together. He had told her he was gay a few weeks ago. 'She blamed herself when we separated but I knew she'd done nothing wrong. I couldn't bear it any more, the guilt of it all, of her not knowing why I left. It was eating me up.' Hirst explained how, when the couple met to discuss the matter at the kitchen table, his stomach was 'in knots'. He couldn't get his words out, felt like he was going to be sick. 'She didn't say anything at first. I explained why and how I felt; it was very emotional.'

Though Sara was 'surprised and angry' to begin with, she was now supportive about a 'weird situation' that Hirst confessed to having found liberating. It was good to be out of denial and not only from a personal point of view, going by an A-list celebrity response that included a telephone call from Elton John, who reportedly told Hirst he was 'fabulous'. The chattering social media class was swift to wish him well – Stephen Fry pitched in, as did *Harry Potter* actor Emma Watson. 'Courage is the choice and willingness to confront agony, pain, danger, uncertainty or intimidation,' she wrote. 'Physical courage is courage in the face of physical pain, hardship, death or threat of death, while moral courage is the ability to act rightly in the face of popular opposition, shame, scandal or discouragement.' Keegan Hirst, the UN Goodwill Ambassador concluded, had both.

But how would the testosterone-charged arena in which Hirst earned a chunk of his living take the news, this supposedly parochial pastime suitable only for hulking great northern brutes? This sport for real men, among the toughest – if not *the* toughest – team games in the world? Would he now be seen as a threat? Or be called a 'puff', a pervert or, worst of all, soft?

Would this courage so admired by Hollywood celebrities make him the target of taunts from the terraces and opposition players? Maybe even his teammates? And what about the club who paid him?

After all, as the man himself had wondered aloud, 'How could I be gay? I'm from Batley, for goodness sake. No one is gay in Batley.'

The answer wasn't long in coming. Hirst and Batley were to play Heavy Woollen rivals Dewsbury that same afternoon. Not only that, they would wear pink rather than the usual cerise and fawn, part of a 'Pink Weekend' breast-cancer awareness campaign organized by Beverley Nicholas, wife of club chairman Kevin, with the one-off outfits later sold to the highest bidders. The purely coincidental timing, Keegan would recall, left him 'absolutely mortified' – a boon to picture desks the world over, cringe-worthy. The Bulldogs also lost the game – their second loss in that end-of-season battle for survival. Otherwise, the reaction to the morning press was everything he'd hoped.

On the one hand: 'Well done'. And on the other: 'So what?'

The decision to talk to the papers had not been easy to take, though much easier than opening up to Sara and, not long after that, the teammates he went to war alongside every weekend. Hirst came out to his wife one Thursday, after training, and having done so his thoughts turned to his friends. Not unreasonably, he chose the three he was and remains particularly close to – James Brown, Alex Rowe and Joe Chandler, raw-boned rugby league forwards all.

How could he approach it, though? He tossed the possibilities over in his mind. 'Should I pull them over in training? Do I go round their houses? Do I get them to come to mine, go for a beer or whatever?' In the end, he settled on the latter. On Sundays, he, Rowey and Brownie always went for a drink at Priestley's Café-Bar in Birstall. Only on this particular occasion, Brownie wasn't there, so Keegs texted Chandler instead. 'I need to talk to you about something. Can we go for a coffee through the week?'

'It's all right,' said Joe, not working the next day. 'I'll come down.'

A few beers later, the trio ordered a pizza apiece and set off back to Keegan's. He'd just bought a new place, 'so it was like "come and have a look" or whatever'. Digging deep with Dutch courage, he thought, 'Fuck it, I'm telling them.'

Weeks afterwards, interviewed on ITV regional news show *Calendar* by the mate they'd shared a changing room and gym with for years, Rowey and Chandler sit like two rabbits in the headlights, recalling their reaction. 'To be honest,' Chandler tells his interrogator, 'I was happy. I felt good that you viewed us as good enough friends to tell us. It meant a lot to me, being the person you came out to.' But had he suspected anything, Keegan wants to know, his growl as deep and rough-hewn as Gaping Gill. 'I had a little bit of an inkling, if truth be known . . .' Chandler admits.

'How?' Keegan asks. 'Was it the hot pants?'

With these two aware, the rest of the team remained to be told, not that there would be any grand announcement. Keegs had said to tell whom they liked when they liked; little in rugby league stays secret long anyway. One by one the lads approached the big man to assure him it was fine, before enjoying a right good night out.

That was how the coaches heard. It was how the board heard too and also the Batley chairman Kevin Nicholas, who got in touch to tell the skipper that he had the club's absolute backing: 'Whatever you want to do . . .' And what he most wanted to do was get back to playing rugby.

Hirst had been in particularly towering form during that first coming-out encounter with Dewsbury. Yet despite the Bulldogs holding a 12–6 half-time lead, it was a game that finished 28–22 in the Rams' favour. At full-back, Johnny Campbell broke a leg – one of the worst injuries Batley's head coach John Kear had seen.

Five weeks later, in the season finale, the applause as Hirst is replaced after a full-blooded opening half hour against Hunslet speaks volumes. All that paper talk, the sniffing about of tabloid hacks, *the sensation* – it already seems such a long time ago. Nor has England's first openly gay rugby league player experienced any prejudice or abuse, home or away. Even the trip to Featherstone, a town Hirst has little affection for since he withstood an unhappy twenty-match endurance test there in 2014, passed without personal grief. If he would get stick anywhere, he thought, off players or fans, it would be at Fev: 'Although Ainy did take the pressure off by kicking that ball, didn't he?'

Having driven along Heritage Road past what's left of the Batley Taverners' social club, gutted in an overnight blaze a fortnight since, spectators are ushered towards the match-day car park, a scrap of land that doubles as a training paddock if all else is unavailable. 'Nah,' says an elderly attendant in a Hi-Vis jacket and flashing a toothless grin, he doesn't expect it will be busy. Once inside the stadium, the eye cannot fail to be caught by a dramatically sloping field. Corner to corner, over a diagonal easterly incline, it drops not far short of ten feet; at least forty minutes of every match is an uphill battle.

Along with three covered grandstands, the remaining vantage points are concrete terracing and walkways, rarely full, more often than not providing plenty of room in which to sprawl or huddle, depending upon prevailing climatic conditions. Today, the Met Office has predicted sunshine, though it never materializes and a chill breeze stiffens.

Two of those grandstands run parallel with each touchline, though neither for the entire length. The main Glen Tomlinson Stand is positioned to the right. The Kirkwood Hospice Community Stand – on the site of the fabled 'Long Stand' and soon to be renamed K2 – runs part way down the left, the area further along nowadays empty and littered with rubble.

At the bottom end, behind the posts and against a semi-rural backdrop of hills and houses across the valley, sits the Craig Lingard Terrace, twelve steps high, though with no sign to that effect. It blew away on a particularly windy day in the direction of Hanging Heaton.

The ground's largest edifice is a terraced Family Stand at the top of the ground, crush barriers and all. It is here that the followers of comparatively well-supported rivals like Featherstone, Bradford and Dewsbury – Hunslet no longer one of those – tend to congregate and make most noise. On its outside, it has a utilitarian feel, fronting a row of what might be taken for executive box windows but aren't; no one is allowed to get too far up him or herself here. Inside, along with much else, the building to which it is adjoined houses changing rooms and the players' tunnel – more accurately a corridor – that emerges beneath an advertisement for cider-brewing Championship sponsors Kingstone Press: 'Batley Bulldogs – Rugby to the Core'.

Nor is the Glen Tomlinson Stand devoid of extra-curricular activity. In the square at its rear, around which bottle bars, lounges and toilet blocks are positioned, a sign reads 'No Ball Games'. When the weather is kind, folk sit, chat and drink at tables here, beer-garden style, both sets of supporters mingling freely. Come half-time, they will do so again, in an atmosphere subdued but amiable. Among their number is a gang of teenage girls wearing Batley tops who, it transpires, are about to embark on a pioneering tour to Australia.

Before kick-off, pre-match entertainment. Former Eurovision Song Contest entrant Lindsay Dracass has driven all the way up from Sheffield to sing lustily on the back of a trailer. In 2001, in Copenhagen, the then fifteen-year-old Lindsay finished fifteenth out of twenty-three, earning twenty-eight points for the UK as against the 198 gathered by victors, Estonia. Her song 'No Dream Impossible' got to number thirty-two in the singles chart, the dawn of a glittering future. 'They could have Frank Sinatra up there and no one would notice,' sighs one sympathetic onlooker.

A seat in the stand itself offers an elevated view of a pitch in fine condition, given the time of year. 'It's better than my lawn, is that,' says one old boy, who claims to have played centre here in the early 1950s. To the left is the Roy Powell Terrace, upon which a small but rowdy away contingent is gathered, the Ron Earnshaw Terrace to the right. This latter looks over the notorious dipped end of the pitch known locally and colloquially as the 'nine 'oil'. And rising high above it all is the ground's single futuristic touch. Above the 'Doghouse' – Batley's club shop – turns a wobbly white wind turbine like some long-legged creation of H. G. Wells, sent on a mission from Mars.

This is the second oldest venue in professional rugby league, versions of rugby football having been played here since 1880. In fact, it is one of only four existing domestic venues to boast the distinction of having been there from the birth of what was initially the Northern Union in 1895, the other sites belonging to Leeds, Widnes and Wakefield, that latter the oldest, though all of those currently host Super League.

While few in number, Hunslet's fans are in excellent voice; they chant, *We hate Rhinos* on a loop. Their coach, too, isn't popular. Barry Eaton, when not at the Hawks an assistant at Leeds, has fielded over forty players under a controversial dual-registration agreement with Headingley, wherein anyone not playing for the Rhinos can have a run-out at Hunslet instead, judged fatal to team spirit and an affront to independence. He cops an earful en route to the dugout, his face a picture of disdain. Soon, relegation will confirm his departure, yet in just a few days he will celebrate an historic treble with Leeds at Old Trafford, the sort of scenario that might bring a sport into disrepute.

The home supporters are more reticent. There is little singing or agitation from them because there is nothing to get over-heated about. Scrum-half Scott Leatherbarrow's tenth-minute opener and Hirst's impressive stint puts the Bulldogs 20–0 up at the break; they are in complete control, destiny secure. A try from winger Wayne Reittie three minutes into the second half confirms that superiority and sparks another rendition from the Hunslet Hawks songbook.

Que sera, sera . . . whatever will be, will be . . . we're going to Coventry . . .

The only drama on the field in a game that finishes 60–12 goes unnoticed by most spectators. Forward Adam 'Gleds' Gledhill scores his first try of the season in its very last game, thereby avoiding a traditional naked run. A brief flutter of drama off it comes when the visitors on the Roy Powell Terrace release a couple of bright-green flares. The Bernabéu this isn't, though smoke does linger a while on the pitch.

As the hooter sounds, that smoke has long since dispersed and children race on to the field, several belonging to players headed in the opposite direction, coming to hug and acknowledge friends and relations in the Glen Tomlinson Stand. After which the weary soldiers turn and trudge back to the tunnel, where more applause awaits, John Kear sharing words with one Hunslet player in particular. His name is Danny Maun and as of this moment he is officially retired. A centre of distinction, not least with Batley, with whom he began and perhaps should have finished his first-team career after representing his hometown club in 254 games, his 34-year-old skeleton, muscle and brain have finally told him enough is enough.

'Congratulations, kid,' says Kear, patting him warmly on the back. 'You've done yourself and your family proud.'

Within twenty-four hours, one player was already on his way out of Batley: scrum-half Leatherbarrow, bound for London Broncos on a two-year contract. And on BBC Radio Leeds, Kear was forced to deny that his own tenure was under threat. 'The call before the game was about professional pride and finishing the season on a positive,' he told reporter Terry Crook, an ex-Batley player and coach himself. 'What we wanted to do was put on a bit of a show. We didn't want to be in this division on points difference, we wanted to be here by right. We are a bit disappointed we didn't get in the top four, as we felt we could have given the play-offs a shake-up.'

Since 15 February against Workington, his players had played every weekend but one. 'That's from lads who go to work and train on an evening. You've got to applaud them for that.'

Crook asked about recruitment for 2016. 'It's gone very well,' said Kear. 'When the fans get to see who we have brought in, they'll be very excited indeed. I'm excited and I think the board of directors are excited. I wouldn't know what to do if I wasn't coaching. It's just great fun, isn't it? I'm privileged to be part of this game and while ever I'm enthusiastic, I'll want to stay in it.'

In the Foothills

1

KEVIN NICHOLAS HAS his hands full. It is the evening of Friday, 13 November – lucky for some – and he and chief executive Paul Harrison are hosting a supporters' do.

Outside is darkness. It is a filthy night befitting a deep north of England winter. The road along the front of the stadium is lined with cars, engines purring, headlights glinting in the gloom. The drivers file their nails, check phones or listen to the radio, waiting to collect their children from soccer training nearby. A little further on, past the entrance to co-residents Batley Boys – or 'Young Peoples Club: Batley Boys, Girls, Ladies ARLFC' as it says above the door – are the large iron gates that give access to the square behind the Glen Tomlinson Stand, turnstiles nearby. Match-day admission: £17 adults, £12 concessions, juniors £3. Aside from the windmill creaking and whistling its inter-stellar signals on high, all is silence, the pitch beyond a nocturne in black and grey.

The venue for the supporters' night, Ron's Lounge, is reached via the front door – players and officials only on match-days – then along the corridor that doubles as the tunnel, past a handful of subterranean changing and treatment rooms and up two flights of claret-carpeted stairs to a brightly lit and utilitarian anteroom, or boardroom as it is grandly known. This is the hub of the club, its nerve centre, in which is found an assortment of chairs and circular tables, two small administrative offices and a kitchen. At one end, a large window extends from ceiling to floor, sentinel over the tunnel entrance below. At the other, a trophy cabinet is mounted on a wall.

Pride of place within the cabinet goes to the Champion of Champions Cup, won in 2011 for beating Halifax in a best versus best clash pioneered by the two clubs – Batley having won the 2010 Northern Rail Cup and their opponents that year's Championship Grand Final. 'We hoped it would be played for every year,' says John Miller, a third director. 'But no one else could be bothered, so we kept it.'

Otherwise, it contains little but framed photos, souvenir plates and salvers and old newspaper clippings, a porcelain bulldog crouched on top. Since winning the Challenge Cup three times prior to 1901 – including the very first in 1897 – there hasn't been much to polish. Alongside, three steps to Ron's Lounge. Just about every journey in these parts, large or small, involves a climb of some sort.

The predominant 'claret and cream' colour scheme is more accurately *rouge* cerise and *desert* fawn, a couple of variants on the club's traditional colours that, if rendered literally, would curse the place with bright-pink woodwork and yellow-tan walls.

Winter nights such as these are when rugby league used to be played. The game considers itself a summer sport now, if kicking off in February and concluding in November can truly qualify as such.

Behind a polygon of gold light at the top end of the field, chairman Kev, smartly turned out in black trousers and salmon shirt, reckons he will give it fifteen minutes. 'It's not a nice night,' he says, pint in hand. 'You wouldn't put a dog out, would you?'

Down to earth yet dapper, clipped moustache and reddish hair, this 56-year-old solicitor has the look of a light entertainer about him. A song and dance man, perhaps, but with the timing and material of a northern club comic. He bobs and weaves, handing out pieces of paper – last year's results in groups of eight, highlighted red, yellow and green. 'Nothing sinister.' He has brought a box of season tickets that the evening is designed to sell.

CEO Harrison, the club's only full-time employee, known to all as 'Iro' – no one including the man himself fully understanding why

– has his name above an entrance that marks the 249 appearances and 82 tries amassed here after a debut in 1994. Brother of John Kear's predecessor, former Great Britain international prop Karl Harrison, he joined from Hull, with whom he'd spent eight or so seasons before his decade at the Mount. His playing days long behind him, his right arm is in an elasticated sling. 'Unstable wrist,' he says, the diagnosis vocal gravel down a chute; golf injury no doubt. It won't stop him pulling pints. The two remaining Batley directors, Paul Hull and Andy Winner, muck in also, not a millionaire benefactor in sight.

Of the five, Nicholas holds the majority share in the club, 80 per cent. Winner holds 10, the remainder spread 'here and there'. The land on which the Fox's Biscuits Stadium sits, along with the adjoining cricket field and bowling green, is held in trust and therefore essentially owned by Batley RLFC, who rent it for one pound a year on a 999-year lease. Given that was agreed around 1880, it isn't running out soon.

But history, history is ubiquitous at Mount Pleasant. Every table, for example, has an engraved corner plaque, in memory of a contribution made. Next to the bar is a Great War Roll of Honour. Bygone days are clung on to here for dear life. Of the forty or fifty in tonight's congregation, most are of middle age and upwards, many over sixty.

Once the evening gets underway, the chairman – everyone calls him 'Kev' – outlines his ambitions to raise the Bulldogs' profile. A marketing team has been appointed, volunteers of course, and there are plans for the players – none present – to switch on the town's Christmas lights, 'although Cleckheaton have put a spanner in the works'. A new sound system is on its way, bartered down from £85,000 to a more appealing £7,000. 'It was bigger than Wembley's. They'd have heard it in Ossett.' Other necessary improvements include CCTV, Wi-Fi in the press box and better floodlights, vital if the club is to comply with Rugby Football League (RFL) regulations, 'if by some miracle we get into the middle eight'. Yet all of that needs brass. The lights alone will cost £30,000, a fair chunk of the £150,000 they are about to get from central coffers, a grant awarded on a sliding scale where teams highest up the table receive far more than those below them.

The club is trying to make season-ticket prices cheap and attractive but must be mindful of covering costs. A younger support base is needed, so Under-16s will gain free entry as long as they have a pass, price £2, that John Miller is 'taking care of as we speak, if he can get the camera working'. One youngster already has his, beaming with pride as he slides it into the little wallet handed to him by his dad.

'So,' Kev computes, 'fifteen games and the Blackpool Summer Bash costs £180, or £120 with concessions for students or over-sixties' – i.e. the vast majority. Most regular supporters, it emerges, benefit from one concession or other. He welcomes Batley Girls back from their Australian tour, the first such ever completed, and notes that their coach, Craig Taylor, has been voted 'Man of the Year' by the Her Rugby League Association, whose objective is to 'promote the game of rugby league by highlighting one of its greatest assets – its women'.

'It was between Craig and Keegan,' says Kev, adding that the girls won one game in four against a representative side selected from thirty Polynesian teams on the Sunshine Coast. 'There aren't thirty girls' teams in this country,' Taylor tells the assembly. At this point, Batley are the only British rugby league club to have a girls' section officially incorporated.

It's time for a break, during which Nicholas collects glasses and bottles before resuming his address. 'Our aim is to win twenty and lose ten, the reverse of last year,' he says. 'But that's a target, not a prediction.' The audience is referred to the sheet of paper received earlier. The three groups signify wins (seven in the regular season, three in the Championship Shield), losses by twelve points and upwards (eight in the regular season and two in the Shield) and crucially – as Kev sees it – defeats by less than seven points (eight in the regular season, two in the Shield). In summary, eight extra on-field points – and sometimes as few as two – in those latter ten matches would have meant a less stressful time all round. It may have even got them into the middle eight. So with that in mind, players have been bought who constitute 'a bit of a financial risk – though nothing that is going to endanger the well-being of the club'.

He puts a little more meat on the bones. The distribution of Championship money goes like this: the teams that were relegated into the competition from Super League ahead of 2015, Bradford and London, received £810,000 and £790,000 respectively. In 2016, that figure will drop to £700,000, the difference filtering a little further down the food chain, though £150,000 is still not £700,000, is it? Local rivals Dewsbury can thank a sixth-place finish for the extra £50,000 coming their way this term. Kev is not complaining about that: 'It's just the scenario we are in.' From the off, the hand is stacked against them in terms of attracting the quality of player required.

Batley, though, have been lucky, he reveals. Sheffield, who were third and made the middle eight last year, will now join Bradford, Leigh and London in becoming full-time. The upshot being that three members of their squad – Dominic Brambani, Pat 'Patch' Walker and James Davey – each of whom have good jobs and no desire to relinquish their part-time status – have chosen to come here instead. For what it's worth, Kev thinks the Eagles have made a mistake but is pleased to capture a trio of 'very useful and experienced players', particularly as it was in their positions that Batley were often found wanting last season.

The signings haven't come about through great management, he admits, but recommendation. Prop Alex Rowe played a big part in sell-ing the club, having once been at Sheffield himself. 'A lot rests on them; we are putting our hope in them.' To that end, an extra £30,000 has been spent, 20 per cent more than was spent on wages last season. The squad currently has twenty-three members, the majority familiar faces. A couple of centres, too, are on their way. One is a nineteen-year-old Leeds Beckett student, Zack McComb. The other is Chris Ulugia, a Samoan from Sydney via Bradford. That latter signing is particularly exciting, though his visa still needs approval from the RFL. He already has one to play with Bradford in 2016, but they don't want him and a new employer has to apply again. He has to have played 75 per cent of the games he was eligible for to get one. 'In many ways, he is our marquee signing.'

There is, though, another potential worry. Ulugia has just had an operation on a shoulder dislocated at the start of last season. 'He came back too soon – daft or brave, I don't know.' He's enthusiastic and disappointed he can't stay full-time at Bradford, 'a lad I'm sure will not give us any problems. He's very quiet, but very tough.'

In every position, the chairman is confident they now have plenty of cover, again not the case before. 'We are having a go at achieving something this year,' he says, before admitting that there is a further financial nettle to be grasped. Given how, by Nicholas's own calculation, £30,000 is the most the club can afford to run with, what if they do win more games? At this level, in a part-time environment, a player's eventual income is based on win, lose or draw. There would be bonuses to pay.

Voila: the Bulldogs' War Chest. Sponsoring the club for £5 a win and nothing for a loss will secure entry to Ron's Lounge on match-day. Furthermore, if last year's ten victories aren't improved upon, the sponsor pays nothing, with his or her pledge written off. Win eleven games, the bill will be £55, and so on. The target membership is 250. Further benefits include a draw with a cash prize every home game, and before kick-off Ron's Lounge is to be the exclusive preserve of War Chest members, where every pint is 50p cheaper, the stadium bars providing a principal source of income.

The club will again not field a reserve team – it can't afford the £25,000–£30,000 it would take to run it. Kev hopes people are optimistic; he certainly is, but it's time to stop talking now, because 'a few of you old folk are falling asleep and you need to get some drinks in'.

After a wet and windy weekend, many of the same faces return for a shareholders' AGM on Monday night, when the chairman sits in the middle of the room, accounts up to 31 October 2014 laid before him. The club had as expected made a loss, though 'that isn't always something to worry about,' Kev says. In 2011, the figure was £14,000, in 2012, £33,000. In 2013, the loss was £25,000 and in the financial year under discussion, £31,000. However, with depreciation of the ground, capital gains tax, grants, cash flow and such, a more realistic figure would be £15,000, he thinks. Despite its careful husbandry, the club is on the losing side of the balance sheet annually and things are not getting any better, with dwindling attendances that contribute only about £60,000–70,000 to the business in any case a further concern.

Looking ahead to the accounts for the year just gone, the chairman expects that turnover will have risen given the income from the RFL, a big gate for the derby with Bradford and an unexpected electricity rebate from the company that supplies the energy- and cash-generating turbine and panels on this very roof; a mix-up meant Batley had been footing their bill. That one-off influx meant that the £15,000 debt could be paid off and for 2015 there had been less winning pay to find too. 'We are not in any financial difficulty as we speak.'

There are two bank accounts – one for the bar and a main one for the club. The bar account currently contains £2,500. There is £8,500 in the main one. 'We are keeping our head above water without being rich,' Kev says. 'As a company we are in a reasonable position – that's why we are pushing the boat out a little. Without that payment, we wouldn't have been able to afford it. Now we feel we can take a couple of risks without putting the club in jeopardy.'

When questions are invited, they revolve around recruitment. Not a single shareholder is investing for financial profit. Nicholas says they are double-checking Ulugia's medical issue. They wish to be sure on doctor's advice that the treatment has worked and his shoulder won't pop out. 'If the doc says there is a 90 per cent chance of it being successful, then it's a risk worth taking. He's a quality centre.'

Catch Kevin Nicholas on a match-day and you might think him brusque. Chats are most likely deflected with a smile or metaphorical hand-off; he is rarely on the same spot for more than an instant. Hail-fellow-well-met, he doesn't intend to be dismissive. Conversations take time, and time like money is a commodity in short supply. 'I don't mind mucking in. I just want to see something done.'

No, to speak to Kev properly, your best bet is to call him in his car on the M62 as he is either driving from or being driven to his offices in Manchester. From 8.30 to 10 a.m., he is on the phone 'via the old Bluetooth' to Iro, often for an hour at a time, or RFL boss Nigel Wood. 'Then at lunchtime I'll ring and on my way home I'll ring. It takes over your life. My wife gets fed up; she says I'm obsessed.'

Kev was born in Carlinghow, in the house in which an aunt now resides, and his schooling began at St Mary's Catholic Primary, 'not far from Batley cemetery'. From there he went to Cardinal Hinsley Grammar in Tong, Bradford, before studying law at Manchester University, the first in his family to enter higher education. Having worked as a solicitor in that city and Leeds, he set up his own business in January 1989. The long-suffering spouse is Beverley and they still live locally in Morley, 'which we have done since 1992. Same house.'

Kev has always followed Batley. 'My granddad and dad used to bring me, though as a child I wasn't that interested in rugby league. I came because they did.' In those days, he would rather have watched football at Huddersfield Town, before falling in with rugby-loving schoolmates and thereafter travelling with his hometown club, home and away.

Though his profession might suggest otherwise, the Nicholas family, in which he was an only child, were working class. Mum was a housewife and dinner lady at St Mary's; dad worked in engineering in Heckmondwike until made redundant in his fifties, when after a spell of unemployment he got a job as a council scheme supervisor. 'He stopped watching rugby for a spell, then came back. He'd come to games with a mate from around the corner. I'm brought up on it.'

By his own admission not good enough to play professionally, Kev did pull on the boots as an amateur with Batley Victoria and an Under-18 Supporters' Club side, while turning out at university on occasion too. Prop or second row. No pace. He took over as chairman in November 1997, having already been on the board alongside Andy Winner and his predecessor Stephen Ball in the mid 1990s. 'If you're not good enough, the next best thing you can do is this, isn't it?'

For a small club, he reckons, Batley have done all right. 'No one in the league does it on a tighter budget than us; we spend less than anybody because we've got volunteers, we are pulling favours.' Bev, for all her misgivings, manages the Bulldog Bar. 'All our wives and children do something. John Miller's lad has been a photographer here. Paul Hull's wife looks after a bar behind the Glen Tomlinson Stand. Andy Winner's wife works in the kitchen; Iro's wife runs the lottery and other things – everyone gets roped in.' That raises the personal stakes: 'Forgetting anything from supporters, I don't want to fail and if we get relegated that's a failure. We've never been relegated since we started and that's a record I want keeping. We can't get to the Grand Final every year, get into Super League or whatever, but we can stay in the Championship.' Every so often they are capable of more than that, though not consistently because the income isn't there. 'I end up doing work for people and asking them to do such and such for the club in lieu of payment. I might have a client who's a plumber, or a builder. It's done on a total shoestring.'

And being criticized by supporters, does that get him down? 'Occasionally. Bev says I should stay off the online forums. She gets annoyed about that. I don't get much hassle face to face; I can face anybody up. I'm used to talking. If anyone has a genuine complaint, I can usually explain. It's when stuff is said behind your back; it's like referees, isn't it? You play hell with them for a decision, but when you see them afterwards it puts them in a different light. I don't know,' he says, weary suddenly. 'I'm hoping to semi-retire next year.'

Tuesday, 1 December marks John Kear's return to the coalface at the Princess Mary Stadium, municipal home to Spenborough & District Athletics Club. It is only 6.30 p.m. but the darkness is absolute, punctured only by pointillist floodlights. It is mild for the time of year but heavy rain has swept the nation for much of the past week and a bright-orange running track shimmers wickedly underfoot.

The players have been hard at it for a month. Since six weeks after the Hunslet match in fact, when they reported back for duty on

Monday, 2 November. A routine tailored specifically to their needs by conditioner John Heaton is gruelling. This part-time squad of twenty-five is on a 'seven-in-fourteen' – Tuesday, Thursday, Saturday, Monday, Wednesday, Friday, Saturday – each session lasting an hour at least. There are eating and personal training plans to follow, all of it squeezed in with family life plus daily and often physical work.

According to Heaton, a former world champion bodybuilder who aims to add 'a yard or two of pace' and 'greater explosiveness', the new boys have freshened things up nicely, though: 'The full-time teams have major advantages in terms of physical preparation. I only see the guys two or three times a week.' A Leonard Cohen lookalike in a woolly bobble hat, he strokes his neatly trimmed beard and blinks one wary eagle eye, phlegmatic in the face of grumbles and wisecracks about throbbing limbs and the like. He's had them doing a lot of leg volume weights this off-season, aches and pains a natural side effect of training hard as he sees it. 'But once the season starts and we are recovering from games, we just do heavy and explosive stuff.' He likes this time of year. It's when the schedule is arranged to suit his needs rather than the coach's, a reversal of the campaign proper.

Tonight, Kear is on a watching brief and likes what he sees. In particular, hooker Luke Blake and skipper Keegan Hirst are in great shape and the rest, though perhaps a little overweight, normal at this stage, aren't far behind. When the season begins in February, track work no longer features. Midwinter, it is an essential weapon in a conditioner's armoury, as is running up those monstrous Heavy Woollen hills to rebuild and strengthen stamina.

Having last week struggled to keep their feet, some lads wear spikes. After a few stretching exercises, those in rubber soles again find it hard to get a grip on a series of lung-busting shuttles, Heaton explaining each task beforehand. Though jokey, all are workmanlike and committed; the new signings do appear to have slotted in well. There are back pats. *Come on, lads; suck it in.* Ten steady metres then twenty at full pace ... *slow, turn around ... again, again.* Do it again.

One player is on trial. John Tinker is the wiry-legged and super-quick son of former Batley winger and Bradford groundsman Roger Simpson. The club has nothing to lose and everything to gain, since payment only kicks in once he has played five games. And if he also has his father's pitch-tending abilities, well, 'They'll like that up at Batley,' chuckles Kear, whom everyone calls JK. 'Special two-for-one offer.'

As one group strings out across five lanes, an approaching group races through in alternate lanes, full pelt. Thus rugby league's defensive line is mimicked. The line holds, every man moves forward, a component in the machine. The backs tend to finish first, as might be expected, though the forwards are hardly slouches.

Drawn broadly, rugby league is built on honest endeavour. In training as in a match, there is nowhere to hide. Though a team sport, individual contributions are laid bare, the ultimate sporting example perhaps of a chain being as strong as its weakest link. At their best, league teams operate like schools of fish or flocks of starlings. They sway this way then that, plugging gaps and anticipating oppositional movement, as if in telepathic harmony, guided by a shared code or language that few but those in the know instinctively comprehend.

Two nights later, up at Mount Pleasant, JK's fingers are doing the boogie-woogie. As rested and relaxed as he is ever likely to be after a well-earned break in the Lakes, it's a sure sign he is itching to get going again, having already achieved one minor miracle since driving away from the Fox's Biscuits Stadium in September.

Namely, taking Wales from bottom place in the 2014 European Championship to first in the one not long finished: an astonishing turnaround ahead of qualification for the 2017 World Cup. It was an achievement that went all but unreported by the press, but then that's how it is with international rugby league. 'It's about making memories and playing for the pride of your country, not about what goes in your bank balance,' he says, all the more altruistic because Kear has not a drop of Welsh blood in his veins – at least none of which he is aware.

A product of the West Yorkshire town of Castleford, this 61-year-old ex-schoolteacher – a stocky 5 ft 7 in. with a distinctive bald dome, fired with enthusiasm and energy, in essence a human bullet – has done more in a twenty-four-year career than most coaches ever manage, the vast majority of it with a smile. And it is this engaging charm coupled with an infatuation with the game that makes him such an attractive go-to pundit for broadcasters. The public loves JK. They pester him for the modern autograph – a selfie – at every turn, their requests unfailingly granted. Like all proper Yorkshiremen, Kear espouses common sense, speaking as he finds. Less typically, what he most often finds is a reason to be cheerful – no weeping prophet he.

Yet as his longevity and list of achievements suggest – coach of England in 2000; two-times Challenge Cup winner; numerous teams saved by the skin of their teeth, et al. – there is a side to Kear's character the public rarely gets to see. A nuggety physique hides a competitive streak as tough and resistant as Sheffield steel, that South Yorkshire city a major part of what, in 1998, was arguably his finest achievement of all. There is ambition too, equally durable, not only for himself but the people under his care and command.

'I coach because I like winning. But I also coach because I like to see group dynamics. I like seeing how people play off each other, how they fit like a jigsaw. When you get your jigsaw right, it's a great, great feeling. But if you make errors, the jigsaw is destroyed. That's what really gets me going. I love the competitiveness, but I love how you've got to fit all these personalities and abilities together into one group that's hopefully singing from the same hymn sheet and striving for the same goals.' He is also a man seldom lost for words.

Kear's involvement with rugby league began as a youngster. He helped operate the scoreboard at Wheldon Road, colloquially 'down the lane'. It was here that the 'Classy Cas' of legend played and where, in November 1954, he was born at number 41. When later the family moved, it was to number 33, even closer to the blessed plot, an end-terrace house four doors up from the Early Bath pub.

JK would not just watch the game in a childhood when every player was part-time, he would play it too, with his mates, on a patch of gravel and ash next to the training pitch, getting in his heroes' way. In time, he would emulate them in Castleford's back line, the shiny pate of today lurking under an unruly mop of blond. His dad, Herbert, a coalman in a pit town, had played six times for Cas himself, after the war, establishing a mini-dynasty that was and remains a source of great pride. Yet JK's path into rugby league was almost blocked.

In his 2012 autobiography *Coaching is Chaos*, written with Peter Smith, Kear describes how upon leaving grammar school with seven O Levels and three A levels, he went to Leicester College of Education, where he studied to be a teacher. It was here, he writes, that a lecturer from Wakefield, Will Sharp, instilled the 'old-fashioned Yorkshire values' of working hard and being honest with yourself and others around you, a philosophy Kear soaked up. In the East Midlands, of course, the favoured code is rugby union, so that was the version Kear played, Wednesday afternoons anyway. At the weekend, he would be back in Castleford playing for the Under-19s and, age twenty, the club tried to sign him. Herbert, though, said no. He had a degree to finish first. To their credit, Cas agreed to wait for the youngster to complete his studies and, when home for the holidays, he played for the reserves in an era when going anywhere near the 'northern code' could mean a life ban in rugby's then supposedly amateur version. But when push came to shove, there could only ever be one winner.

Although Kear can be self-deprecating about his love of money, his CV suggests personal challenge as a greater source of motivation. It was an open secret back then that the top union players were paid and paid handsomely. It was just that any cash earned came stuffed in brown leather boots, rather than anything so taxable as a pay packet, and boot money wasn't enough to live on, 'certainly not for a player of my lowly standard'. It would, though, have supplemented his income as a teacher and been a better fit with his chosen career in the 1970s. 'Things have changed, but in those days teaching wasn't the sort of career professional rugby league players went into, and vice versa.'

His initial reserve-team game was at full-back, a 10–0 win over Batley as it happens. But after a first-team debut away to St Helens – in

which he broke a collarbone and wound up in Pontefract Infirmary
– he spent the subsequent eleven years in Castleford's three-quarter
line, before graduating to the backroom staff as a conditioner and
assistant team boss in the mid eighties. In 1989, he took on a joint
head coach's job at lower-league Bramley with a pal, Barry Johnson.
'I loved playing and was honoured to turn out for Castleford,' he
says, 'but I wasn't any great shakes, a journeyman. I wouldn't have
got into any of my own teams.' As a teacher in an environment where
just about every one of his teammates toiled down the pit or in some
other form of manual labour, he learned what it is to be the source of
amusement in a changing room, though sensed little or no inverted
snobbery: 'I think they were pleased for me . . .'

At Bramley, part-time coaching let Kear continue teaching, a
parallel career that would eventually span fourteen years, initially as
a primary school teacher from 1977–78 in Leicester, then five years
as a class teacher at Sherburn-in-Elmet before, finally, seven years at
South Milford school in Leeds, where he was appointed deputy head.
He also had time to attend coach-education courses run by the Rugby
Football League, where he met director of coaching Phil Larder, who
offered JK a full-time job as his assistant. He said goodbye to the
classroom, though would forever carry the lessons learned there.

Preparation counts. The devil (or maybe a choir of angels) is in
the detail. Be conscientious. You can tell, you can show and you can
get people to do. Getting them to do is best. A manner of communication that is appropriate for one group or individual may not work
for others; adapt your presentation to suit your audience.

At Bramley – no longer in existence as a professional entity, the
ground now a housing estate – he learned pragmatism. If players
are part-time and earn relatively little from the sport, being overly
authoritarian, even when it's in their best interests, may be a mistake.
Thus was a man with a degree in physical education forced to watch
his squad stuff their faces with bacon, chips, egg and beans en route
to Cumbria – the directors' treat. Or put up with a star player sinking
pre-match pints and smoking forty Capstans a day.

Then, in 1996, came Super League and suddenly every top-flight club in the land could afford to go full-time. Such old-school antics, like the Bramley club itself, went the way of oblivion.

By then, though, Kear had been gone from McLaren Field for five years, initially establishing an academy system at the RFL, before taking over the head job itself when Larder took charge of England's rugby league side. And just as Larder was embarking on a code-change that led to two tours with the British and Irish Lions and a victorious 2003 Rugby Union World Cup as defence coach under Clive Woodward, Kear was co-opted back into the club game at Paris St Germain, one of the great hopes of the Super League project, who with London Broncos were parachuted in to provide a European presence that a global ambition demanded. It mattered not that rugby league – or *rugby à XIII* as it is known across the Channel – is at its strongest in the South of France, where a history of *treiziste* struggle has been every bit as intense as that in the north of England. PSG was a great international brand, the equivalent of having Manchester United, Real Madrid or San Francisco 49ers in the set-up. *Mon dieu!* They would have a club shop on the Champs-Élysées.

Despite a wow of a start against Sheffield in Super League's very first match – a night on which the video referee also debuted – the cynics were eventually proved correct. Paris lasted two seasons. When the plug was pulled, that initial crowd of 18,000 had dwindled to a few hundred and league's latest big-city dream was over.

For Kear, though, the experiment had been successful enough. If nothing else, it had given him his first shot at the coaching big-time. He'd arrived at Charlety Stadium during a first season that, after its bright start, took a sharp turn for the worse. Coach Michel Mazare felt he needed help and JK was sent by the RFL on a rescue mission. He was only there fourteen weeks, but performances improved and the club got only its third win of the season – against London – two points that kept PSG above ultimately relegated Workington. It left him wanting more.

That Paris spell also earned him a reputation for success in the face of adversity. Absurdly given what was at stake, many of the PSG players were still turning out for clubs in the domestic competition down south, in places like Perpignan, Carcassonne and Avignon. So they were based there too, training in Toulouse and flying up to the French capital or over to England the night before the match for what, in most cases, was their second game in a week. That he could stitch it all together out of a suitcase and with only a smattering of schoolboy French had not gone unnoticed. He was offered the head coach's job for 1997 but turned it down, realizing that the club was unsustainable. Paris again finished second-bottom in year two, but the RFL's appetite for adventure was gone. The club was given a one-year 'sabbatical' that, at the last count, has lasted twenty-one.

Kear's immediate task at the end of 1996 was to take the Great Britain academy side to New Zealand, just as the full England tourists under Larder were visiting Papua New Guinea, Fiji and New Zealand. While there, Larder bought him a coffee and said he was moving from Keighley to Sheffield. Did he fancy joining him as assistant coach?

Founded in 1984 by Gary Hetherington, nowadays boss of dual-code Leeds Rugby, the Eagles were pioneers too. Pretty much Hetherington's last act before selling the Steel City club was to sign Larder and Kear, a splendid parting gift. Unlike Paris, Sheffield was no stranger to rugby league development work, though crowds were stubbornly reluctant to flock to the Don Valley Stadium. The Eagles were also the first – and thus far only – Super League club to float on the Stock Exchange, a resounding flop. Larder's tenure was short-lived. His hastily assembled side won four of its first twelve games, in which time he 'lost' the dressing room, at one point calling his players 'one of the thickest teams ever'. When he got the boot in mid May, Kear was asked if he'd like the head coach's job. Of course he would.

Performances picked up, though the club still finished eighth from twelve in 1997. To outsiders at least, there was no hint of what was to come – namely, one of the greatest sporting upsets of all time.

After having been involved in an end-of-season Premiership knockout competition that, bizarrely, featured all twelve teams

– another 'innovation' – the Sheffield players and their coach grew in self-belief. They'd thrashed London 58–16 – 'an eighty-minute orgasm,' according to JK – and then ran Wigan close in the semi-finals. That was the spark that, in 1998, fired the Wembley dream that became a reality. On what remains the most memorable day in the history of the Challenge Cup, mammoth odds and kings of the grand old competition Wigan were beaten, 17–8, a victory on sacred turf inspired by coaching unequalled since Henry V did his bit on St Crispin's Day – *We few, we happy few, we band of brothers . . .*

A national TV audience of millions gloried in the triumph of an underdog. Hopes soared that crowds appropriate to a city the size of Sheffield, keen to be associated with success, would now materialize. The actor Mark Addy even wore an Eagles shirt in *The Full Monty*, and JK and his squad posed naked for a promotional photoshoot, with rugby balls covering their particulars. A clue it wouldn't be that way came when Sheffield met Wigan again, at home in the league, a week later. Some 7,356 turned up, the Eagles lost 36–6 and attendances dropped to less than half of that thereafter. On the traditional open-top bus tour, 'four men and a dog turned up – and I think the dog went home early'. So keen had JK been to see the Eagles succeed that he'd turned down an offer to coach St Helens. 'I wasn't ruthless enough, I showed loyalty to the club and it didn't work out.'

And so as Ellery Hanley guided Saints to a Super League title in 1999, Kear led a Sheffield side leaking money to tenth in a league of fourteen. Worse, come the end of the year the club had 'merged' with and relocated to Huddersfield – Gateshead doing likewise with Hull – in reality a couple of takeovers. Before long, both 'moved' sides went out of business and re-formed in the divisions below, the Eagles beaten by amateur side Thornhill Trojans in the Challenge Cup less than two years after that famous triumph at Wembley.

Kear left 'Shuddersfield' in July 2000, euphemistically describing his nineteen games there as a learning experience – the best experiences of all. By then, he had coached France at home to Russia, when asked to do so by his Paris friend and colleague Michel Mazare, and assisted

Andy Goodway with Great Britain before taking charge of England in an ultimately disappointing 2000 World Cup campaign, when the hosts were beaten 49–6 by New Zealand in the semi-finals.

Two spells as an assistant in the domestic game followed, at Wigan and Hull, before the opportunity to return to head coaching came in Hull in 2005. In a city where rugby league is front-page news, he won a second Challenge Cup – Hull's first in twenty-three years – in a rousing 25–24 victory over Leeds at the Millennium Stadium.

When that role ended in acrimony the following year, he took charge of Wakefield Trinity Wildcats, his five-and-a-half-year spell at that pugnacious West Yorkshire club a period of controversy, over-achievement and tragedy. A place in Super League was secured for a cash-strapped set-up that might have folded otherwise, via a one-off relegation dogfight with Castleford. In 2008, they reached the semi-finals of the Challenge Cup and in 2009 came fifth to net a play-off place. He restored Wakefield's club culture, nursing his traumatized players through the deaths of two teammates, so a mutually agreed contract termination in July 2011 left Kear feeling hollow. Having agreed he could speak to Catalan Dragons in Perpignan, the Wildcats asked for £20,000 compensation, scuppering the deal. It had been anticipated that bankruptcy would see Wakefield drop into the Championship for three years at least, the current licensing cycle at an end. Yet in an eleventh-hour twist, live on *Sky Sports News*, it was Welsh expansion club Crusaders who instead got the bullet.

Everyone at the oldest venue in rugby league was delighted, but it was time for a change, the directors said. Kear, nattered by a task unfinished, reluctantly concurred. He could indeed do with a fresh challenge, and applied at Castleford – the role he was surely born for – and Hull KR, but both jobs went to Australians. Super League was now a closed door. But then, as he prepared to travel to Wembley as part of the BBC's Challenge Cup team, the telephone rang. It was Kevin Nicholas.

'Hello, John,' Kev said. 'Do you fancy coaching Batley?'

2

DECEMBER IS JUST three days old, the season still a couple of months away, when the coaching staff and players hold the first team meeting of a new campaign. Leigh will be here for the opening league fixture on 7 February, followed twenty-two games later – Challenge Cup ties notwithstanding – by Super 8s in August and the Championship Shield final and Million Pound Game in October. Another long and demanding prospect on the mountain road ahead.

John Kear arrives a good two hours before anyone else, having planned his schedule meticulously. Iro is here too. He helps kit-man Jonathan Hooley pile training clobber and bobble hats on boardroom tabletops. Hooley, by his own estimation, has been at Batley for ever. He was an A team second-rower in the mid 1980s, he says, and his parents lived behind and ran the Taverners' bar. 'Backbone of the club,' Iro quips of a man more commonly known as Jonny Potts.

No one knows why. Just as no one knows why Iro is Iro. And it is Pottsy, with his cheery grin, that any visitor will likely bump into first, his boot room as cosy as a hobbit's hole alongside the front door downstairs. A bit of a mod on the quiet, from time to time he will turn up with a Paul Weller hairdo, though tonight he looks like a windswept heavy-metal roadie. Then again, everyone is bedraggled this evening. Rain lashes at right angles in the teeth of a raging gale.

He became kit-man, he says, when Batley's then coach David Ward suggested he do better when he complained that his shirt was damp.

'You notice things like that when you start to get old, don't you?' It is a position he has continued to fill for the past thirty years.

Up in Ron's Lounge, JK is deep in conversation with the club physiotherapist Carl Chapman, who is handing in his notice. Family issues. An important part of the group, he appears emotional when he walks through the boardroom, passing players who await the call to ascend. Back-rower Adam Gledhill says Tuesday's sprinting was so tough he could taste blood in the back of this throat. Normally laid-back Gleds is employed at the head office of Asda in Leeds, called upon to pacify disgruntled customers. Like Shaun 'Ainy' Ainscough, he knows what it is to be full-time, having been briefly on the books at Wakefield before winding up here three years ago.

Of all the players, though, 26-year-old Ainy has most full-time experience. He was a first-teamer in Super League from 2009 to 2012, first with hometown Wigan then Bradford Bulls, with loan-spells at Widnes and Castleford in between. Nowadays he helps his dad as a joiner, a lifestyle change that took some getting used to. He drives over from Wigan, one of the few to travel any distance. Smiley by default, he has three young children, so the clock ticks louder in his ears than it might in those of his younger teammates. 'You don't realize how good you have it at the time,' he says. 'Coming here after a full day's work is a lot tougher. You never know, do you? One injury and it can all be over like . . . that.' He sighs and snaps his fingers.

When the meeting begins, it does so without Keegan. A crew from ITV's *Calendar* is in town and has borrowed the headline act, plus Alex Rowe and Joe Chandler, for filming. In Ron's Lounge, the captain's sexuality is just another excuse for banter, betraying vicarious pleasure, maybe even pride, in his growing profile and the attention upon the club that it is generating.

Where's Keegs? . . . Know what he was doing last weekend? . . . Bumming? [laughter] . . . No, out with her out of Atomic Kitten . . . Kerry Katona? . . . No, what's her name, Kym Marsh . . . She's not Atomic Kitten. She's Hear'Say . . . Yeah, and Coronation Street . . . Well, whoever it is, Keegan's gay celebrity lifestyle should not interfere with our schedule . . . How come Rowey and Chandler are being interviewed and not me?

JK gets going anyway, his manner to the point but at this stage of the squad's development verging on kindly. Through the windows, all is dark and filthy, but the players seated before him are keen to be out there anyway. Knees dance. Shoulders twitch. Necks strain like thorough-breds at a starting gate. When the three latecomers arrive, a collective focus descends. JK offers Keegan the captaincy again if he wants it. He very much does want it, receives a round of applause and that's that.

More detail is attached to the preseason schedule. Training is three times a week until Christmas, when there will be the annual Boxing Day 'friendly' with Dewsbury. Return to training on 5 January for a fortnight, then matches with a Heavy Woollen Select amateur side and League 1 team North Wales Crusaders, before two weeks' full-on training and the season-start in February.

The festive derby will feature squads of twenty-one; more than the usual seventeen – thirteen start, four on the bench – but fewer than friendlies usually allow. 'There will be a big crowd and it has to be a meaningful game.' But JK guarantees everyone will have at least two matches in which to 'put down a marker for that opener with Leigh'.

There is also to be a leadership group this year containing 'six good role models'. Keegs, as skipper, will obviously be in it and the coaching staff will select two others, the rest democratically elected by ballot, for which voting slips are passed around. There will be a shirt launch for the supporters a week tomorrow that the squad is expected to attend. Then comes the first potentially tricky revelation of the campaign – squad numbers. JK spins around a white board on which names are written in marker pen, one to twenty-five. Number 1 is full-back James 'Cravo' Craven; last-named is Zack McComb.

Everyone hopes to be in the first thirteen, seventeen certainly, since that implies first choice, though no one seems ruffled by the list. Collecting their kit, they head off in two groups, one to the club gym at the end of Heritage Road, the other to an all-weather training pitch near the bowling green. The usual training ground is waterlogged.

*

The TV crew wants to interview JK in the boardroom but will need Keegan for 'five more minutes' as he is to pose the questions. So back he jogs from the gym, 'I want to do some training' muttered under his breath. Having bounded upstairs, he leans over the back of a chair and interprets the director's prompts in his own words, though not before Kevin Nicholas sails through on his way to a board meeting. 'Hello,' Kev says, doing a double take. 'Have we got two gays now?'

Keegan clears his throat. 'So,' he begins, his coach now under lights. 'I was a bit nervous when I rang you to speak about it. What do you remember from that phone conversation?'

'First of all, when your name came up on my phone, I wondered if there was a problem with regard to training or whatever,' JK says, an old hand at this caper. 'There had been the odd rumour, from both inside and outside the club. It surprised me because of your personal circumstances and because of how you are but, basically, it didn't make any difference. I was more concerned about Keegan Hirst the rugby league player. As long as you played and captained the team as well as you had beforehand, all I was going to do was support you.'

'You've been in rugby for forty years. Do you think times are changing and, if so, how?'

'If you are a rugby league historian, you can see rule changes as well as attitudinal changes, yes. But society's changed. That's the big thing. Instances such as yours are in line with how society has evolved and developed and thankfully become more open.'

'Would the reaction have been different, say, twenty years ago?'

'Without doubt, I couldn't see it happening forty years ago, thirty or twenty. People such as Gareth Thomas and yourself are very brave to be trailblazers, rightly showing how you should be honest with yourself and honest with those around you, because that's the only way you are going to be happy.'

There follows a discussion about league's macho image that has no chance of being broadcast, since these packages tend to be on screen for a minute at most and the theme is complex. How come this supposed province of Neanderthals has led the way so often, while other sports, like soccer, can give an impression of social regression?

'Culturally,' JK responds, 'we've always been a little different. We've led the way in rule changes and acceptance of ladies in our game. We've led the way in the first black coach of a UK national team and are leading the way in this. It's because we've got family values.'

'What message would you give to any player, coach or supporter who is wrestling with their sexuality?'

'It's not just sexuality. Whether it's gambling, drink, mental-health problems or whatever, first of all you've to be true to yourself and identify it. Then you need to seek support from others within the club and community and you will get that. All of a sudden it becomes easier to cope. You can get on with your life in a positive way.'

In a tight-packed room in the tunnel downstairs, next to the even smaller match officials' quarters and opposite the away team door, physiotherapist Carl Chapman peers at his laptop, glassy-eyed. He is teasing at an online advert he has written for his own position. Having spoken with JK, he will work another month, finish on Boxing Day and then help any incoming physiotherapist transition into the role.

A fresh-faced fellow of sandy hair and sunny complexion, tonight he is disconsolate. Four months ago, his wife gave birth to the couple's first child, a boy. Along with the time spent treating referrals as an advanced practitioner in Kirklees, he is here so often, evenings and weekends, that his home life is under strain. His wife needs support, he knows that, but he feels loyalty to Batley too. Before he came here, his wife landed a new job herself. Three weeks later, the company was bought out and redundancy followed, which, as the couple had just acquired a mortgage, was not good news. Fortunately, the calamity coincided with the call that offered him this position. It's not so much that he feels beholden to the place, more that he has come to love it.

'It's everyone's favourite second club, isn't it? No one has a bad word to say about us. Well, apart from Sheffield . . .' He talks fondly of 2013, when Batley and the Eagles reached the Championship

Grand Final, the Bulldogs denied only by 'Ben Black being tripped by a fingernail. That's sport for you.' That was in his first year at the Bulldogs, who made the Grand Final by winning twice en route at Leigh and Featherstone in golden-point extra-time by a drop-goal. Like everyone here, he revelled in that against-the-odds story.

And by which time he had gone well and truly native. In the NHS, you treat individual injuries. Here you might be called upon to be a psychologist, counsellor, assistant coach even, collecting cones, delivering on-field orders or switching on the floodlights. 'It's not a well-funded sport, so you end up mucking in and doing all sorts of things that aren't technically part of your job. But you are happy to do it to improve the club and work as a unit.'

A physio's role, Chapman says, has changed significantly during his time in rugby league. To begin with, it was about getting players fit after injury. Increasingly, strength and conditioning coaches like John Heaton have grown in importance. The two coordinate closely, particularly at this time of year, screening movement – how do they move, how do they lift, how do they stretch – identifying weaknesses. 'The job is now as much about injury prevention.' All of which chews up time: 'Treating injuries, coming up with rehabilitation strategies, doing admin; we've had twenty ECG scans come back from heart screening today that the doctor and I have had to go through.' Plus there are the traditional massages – aka 'rubs' – post-surgery rehab and such.

Chapman's experience as an extended-scope physiotherapist has made him an acute detector of physical trouble; he frequently diagnoses orthopaedic conditions and sends patients for scans in his day job. Suitable replacement candidates are thin on the ground.

'We've had one girl interested who has recently started working in rugby league,' he says. 'But that's with a local amateur team, so she's not quite ready to make the step up to a semi-professional level yet.' Sports therapists have enquired, but the RFL mandate says only chartered physiotherapists will do. Fine in theory.

'There are kudos attached to being the physio of a full-time club, not to mention full-time pay. Here, it's secondary income, an extra job. So you've got to have someone who is willing to give up evenings and weekends. They must do exactly what the players and other coaching staff do. The people who are here are here because they are rugby league fans and want to be involved in the game.'

And as with his colleagues, Chapman likes to think he makes a difference. 'When they need surgery, or tests, I make sure they get them. When they maybe need a bit of a kick up the arse, I'll make sure they get on the pitch properly motivated. I try to be fair to both sides.'

But now it seems the end is nigh. Who counsels the counsellor? Not every injury is muscle and bone. His own league licence is up in January and he has not applied to do the examination again. 'My wife and I struggled to have children. Fortunately, we had treatment and a baby boy came along. As much as I love rugby league, I don't want to miss him growing up. There would have been no point going through that emotional struggle ourselves – deciding that maybe we weren't ever going to be able to have children and then having a child – the heart's got to rule the head sometimes . . .'

And if, when his son grows up, he wants to play rugby league? 'His mother is quite adamant he is not going to do any contact sport. She doesn't want him to spoil his face. Hopefully, he can twist her arm. I grew up without a dad – he left when I was eight – so I didn't have that male influence. It's sort of why I ended up a physio; never excelled at sport myself. I didn't have the confidence to do it because no one was cheering me on. I'd like to give my son that opportunity.'

The all-weather pitch is sodden, its approach treacherous with mud and puddles. Three groups squeeze on to a high open plateau, a billion floodlit diamonds cascading out of infinite blackness. The first pack of Bulldogs trains at one end, Batley Boys Under-14s the other. In the middle are the Under-16s of local amateur club Shaw Cross Sharks, whose usual venue is ankle-deep in water. 'To tell you the truth, we aren't supposed to be here,' their coach concedes. 'But Batley are very good about it and don't seem to mind.'

The coach also points out a couple of youngsters currently on scholarships with Wakefield and Huddersfield, a route into the pro game taken by several Batley players too. In such circumstances, a hopeful might train every night of the week, Saturday morning as well for the lad at Huddersfield. A new season is due to start in February but Shaw Cross have done well in the BARLA Yorkshire Cup so are still at it in December, essentially a twelve-month-long campaign.

This then is how rugby league treats its talented kids, flogging them without end on wintry northern hillsides before offering those who don't get sick of it a professional academy spot perhaps. Then, given the lack of money for reserve grade, in a couple of years' time they will probably be dropped like hot potatoes with nowhere but the amateur game to go. The Bulldogs' class of 2016 are the lucky ones. As are coach Kear and his co-assistants Craig 'Linners' Lingard and Mark 'Mokko' Moxon, ex-players whose careers pre-dated such calamity.

It's Friday, 11 December, the night of the shirt launch, and the board-room reeks of gas. 'The boiler,' explains Jonny Potts, a couple of hours before. A new kitchen is being fitted, which might have something to do with it, though right now it is just a shell with freshly plastered walls. Pottsy claims to have been labouring hard on it all week.

Up in Ron's Lounge, the CCTV cameras have been installed in a tiny room next to the bar that overlooks the field, the replacement PA system operational now also. Iro's son Toby gives it a go, his teenage voice booming out into the ebony night and stratosphere beyond.

'Took a couple of days,' John Miller says. The bloke who did the cameras did the speakers, which saved time and money. The CCTV will record twenty-four hours a day in thirty-day chunks, the screens in here showing just about every part of the ground. 'There's an app for it. I'll be able to sit in bed with my cocoa, seeing what's going on.' The new PA means relocation for John, who, with Derek Ventress, the club chaplain, does the match-day announcements. Previously, he sat in the Glen Tomlinson Stand between a couple of 400-watt speakers, microphone in hand. And before that, he had 'one of them old klaxons. I'll be like a hermit in here.'

The Christmas tree is up, strung with coloured lights, crackers and a large bag of biscuits donated by the stadium sponsor. Most of the squad is present, although a handful of players are not. It's party season and some have other commitments, with work perhaps. The new boys are here, though, whom most fans have come to see.

Keegan is among those absent. He is in London with *Coronation Street* actor Antony Cotton and pals, a friendship struck up since his coming out. Tonight, they are at the Royal Albert Hall watching Kylie Minogue in what the tabloids call a 'sexy Santa outfit'. The other players have arrived straight from the T3 gym on Bradford Road, a link-up arranged by Danny Maun, last seen hanging up his boots with Hunslet. He has just been appointed Batley's part-time sales manager.

Like most rugby league players Maun began young. His first brush with glory came at Wembley in 1992, where he played a curtain-raiser with Dewsbury and Batley Schoolboys in the latter team's kit and thus began to dream of wearing it professionally. Yet upon leaving school, Batley wasn't his first port of call. The Gallant Youths wanted him but so did Wigan, one of the biggest names in the game. He went to Lancashire as a budding stand-off but was back at Mount Pleasant in two years. Ask why and this popular figure with friends in league's every nook and cranny will tell you straight: not good enough. 'Wigan are a massive club. I was seventeen and didn't know how to look after myself.' He had digs next to legendary Central Park and was in at the deep end, but he maintains the experience served him well. Being around Gary Connolly, Jason Robinson, Andy Farrell, 'it was amazing how hard they trained. I trained as hard as I could, but there was a gulf in class. I thought, "I need to get better at what these do every day." People think they get it given, but they don't.'

The ambition now of a man who is up at six every morning to work on the bins with Kirklees council is coaching. It will take some juggling, but he aims to do his badges this coming season while he is out and about looking for business partners, as that is what the club needs. He will help out in training as a way of getting a foot on the ladder and hopes some of John Kear's fabled influence will rub off. 'We've got the best squad since the Northern Rail Cup team. The lads have got to set their standards high and reach the top four or six.'

Although the first off-season game on Boxing Day is still a fortnight away, the players have already passed one little milestone. Their gruelling Saturday-morning hill-running sessions in one of the wettest Novembers on record are now complete. Tomorrow is a rest day, so they relax into an enjoyable evening.

In Cumbria, Storm Desmond has brought devastating floods, more than a month's rainfall in a day. West Yorkshire, too, remains soggy, rivers full to overflowing. But that can't prevent a decent turnout, car tyres spraying as they jostle for position outside. *Should have charged £1 for the car park.* Another missed opportunity.

Items of kit are laid out on the boardroom tables, available for sale – £20 for one of last season's polyester shirts, kids' size £15, hats a tenner; £40 adults and £30 children for the latest design. Guarding the cash float is Mick Turner, chairman of Shaw Cross Sharks, the British Amateur Rugby League Association (BARLA) and owner of Ravensport, a local firm that produces the attire. He expects Batley will sell about a hundred and fifty home shirts over the season, in white, cerise and fawn, and about seventy-five away tops, in a less traditional black and snot green. His company also services Oldham, Hunslet and Keighley, though the bulk of sales are to amateur clubs, his contacts made through BARLA obviously coming in handy.

Batley centre Shaun Squires, a product of Shaw Cross, wanders over for a chat, just as Sean 'Paddy' Hesketh, a bearded giant of a prop, hobbles up the stairs on crutches, breathing heavily. August last year he did it, against Dewsbury. Heavy impact. Left knee. Swelled up. Rested for a week, swelling went down, a cartilage problem it looked like. Told it was fine to play on until he had it taken out, so that's what he did, getting by on painkillers and heavy strapping. Played with Ireland in the Euros but had to pull out in agony. Had a scan. Not the cartilage; that was fine. But his thighbone was bruised and fluid had entered the bone marrow. He needed keyhole surgery. 'They drill small holes to make it bleed, to try and reproduce everything that had smashed and broken away.'

The operation took place four weeks ago, with an order to stay on crutches for six weeks, to keep pressure off the wound. So he has a fortnight to go. The surgeon, whom he sees again on Thursday, says it's like a scab. If he keeps putting weight on it, it will keep falling off and fail to heal properly. Yes, it is still a bit sore. Paddy expects to be out for twelve to sixteen weeks, depending on the speed of his recovery. But in a way it has been good to have a rest. He has not had a proper off-season for five or six years now, what with Ireland and everything. 'I was looking forward to getting down here training and pushing on for next season, but it might also be a bit of a freshen-up. Help get rid of the some of the other bumps I've been playing with.'

Though for part-time players, the on-field business isn't the half of it. The 29-year-old has a wife and young son to support, 'so it's obviously not great at the minute'. A manual labourer, he is on statutory sick pay alone, 'which is next to nowt'. He is the only car driver in the house and what with Christmas coming it's hard. 'But you get through it, I suppose.' So why play a brute of a sport where you are expected to risk everything, whatever the impact on mind, body and kin, without substantial financial reward? Doesn't he ever wonder what the hell he is doing? 'You do sometimes, yes. Especially when you are off work for a long period. But you play for love of the sport, don't you? And being lucky enough to be semi-professional means extra pocket money, really. You are getting paid for something you enjoy doing, although it does take up a lot of your time.'

At this time of year, there would be no match terms available anyway, no winning pay to lose. Currently, his only cash loss is from normal employment. From February, that will change. Out of season, he and any other injured player get the same twelfth of their annual contract salary – on average £8,000 or so – that they receive from

December to November. Players are advised to take out policies for loss of earnings, as insurance against the worst. Not all of them do so and the club makes no contribution towards those. But it does chip in for personal policies to cover medical treatment, which are cheaper if taken out individually. A 'club policy' would be more expensive.

As Kevin Nicholas later admits, in such matters a player can't be too careful. 'Take Johnny Campbell. He had that bad injury, he's off work so can't make a living. He's [got] a young family. We did a bit of fund-raising to make a few quid to help him out.' Since that ghastly event, Campbell, popular here despite misdemeanours that brought wider notoriety during a six-year stay, has moved to Bradford on a two-year full-time contract, perhaps surprisingly given his age, twenty-eight, and unfortunate physical circumstances.

Paddy meanwhile knows several of the new lads, having either played with or against them. Born in Normanton, not Dublin, since his start at Wakefield academy he has roamed wide if not far – from Castleford to Featherstone to York to Batley to Halifax to Keighley and back to Batley. He trained in early November too, as he'd not had the operation then. Thirty is supposedly the prime age for a rugby league prop. If you aren't sufficiently streetwise and grizzled by then, you never will be. But last year was tough. 'We had such a good pack you had to play well to get picked. It will be harder this time.' There is the faint trace of a bruise on his nose.

'With the signings we've made, we've potentially got the best squad ever,' Kevin Nicholas says to rapturous applause. Ron's Lounge has filled up nicely, the players hovering uncomfortably by the exit. 'And it's cost us an absolute fortune, so put some money behind the bar. It's Friday night and the takings are down.'

He tells them about the new CCTV – 'There'll be a few lads here off *Crimewatch* who'll be used to that, won't there?' – and PA system. 'You will be mightily impressed, I am telling you that now. This is top whack. From now on, you'll be able to hear the try-scorers and we are hoping there will be quite a few of those throughout the season.'

Kear is up next, greeted warmly for his Euro Championship win with Wales. He introduces fifteen-year-old Jordan Catling, a pupil at Spen Valley High, who only took up rugby league in June last year and has already helped Batley Girls to win the league and been on their tour to Australia. Supported by local MP Jo Cox, she has been to the House of Commons, where her part in a 'whirlwind' season earned her the Sport England National Participant of the Year award, presented by women's rugby union World Cup winner Maggie Alphonsi MBE. Chris Ulugia and James Craven are then led on in the new kit – 'all glammed up and ready to parade' – to loud guffaws from their teammates.

Before the squad-number revelation, Kev calls a drinks break, table after table alive with optimism. Over the last two years, Batley have been 'a bit limp'. Even the Championship final season hadn't really come alive until the play-offs. But now: *I'm pleased we've kept our pack and added speed and guile . . . I see us getting in the play-offs – top four . . . I've been a supporter for sixty years and you can see by the number of people here that it's exciting everybody . . . We've got the hardest start ever, but I think we can get in the four.*

Others are more cautious, though upbeat nonetheless: *Anywhere in the top eight I'd be happy with . . . Without a cash injection, Batley in the top four is unrealistic . . . We are always optimistic before the start of the season and sometimes, after about four or five games, we lose a little bit of that . . . But that's the thing here, if we have a bad time, it doesn't really matter . . . We are all in it together but, yes, I think we'll go better this year . . . This is the biggest gathering at one of these dos for quite a while . . . It's good to see James Harrison here, Karl's lad. Keeps it in the family does that sort of thing . . .*

Harrison, a tall and rangy student of sports journalism at Huddersfield University, will have to wait for his introduction. His squad number is twenty-four. With a father and uncle playing rugby league to such a high standard, there was a certain inevitability that he might be so inclined, though it almost didn't happen. He began in the Under-10s at Drighlington but preferred football, truth be told.

He was put on the wing, didn't touch the ball most weeks, 'didn't get muddy, it were awful'. But by Under-12s he was a loose forward at Shaw Cross, earning selection in the Kirklees Service Area team and a two-year scholarship at Huddersfield. Aged fourteen, though, he 'got cut' and went back to Drig before landing a trial at Bradford as an eighteen-year-old. He played five games and won a contract for 2015 but was released at the end of that year. With his family connections, there was only one place to come after that: the club where he had once been a ball boy.

Some players merely have their name and number read out; the more talkative are interviewed briefly by Mauny or JK. Wayne 'Reitts' Reittie is the first of those, here with wife Kelly and daughter Mya, having just got back from Florida where he represented Jamaica against the USA and Canada in qualifiers for the 2017 World Cup. Sadly, the Jamaicans missed out. Re the new signings: 'It's good that Kev has put his hand in his pocket for a change,' says the free-scoring right-winger. On the other wing, Shaun Ainscough has an alarming new hairdo, some achievement given his receding dome. 'I was going to get it all shaved off but thought, "No. There's a Mohawk in it."'

Cain Southernwood – 'Ken' to his pals – is a scrum-half, small in stature, large of heart, the one in the boy band your little sister is smitten by. As with Harrison – or 'Young Iro' – the Southernwoods are very much a league family. Dad Graham played for Castleford, uncle Roy was at Cas and Halifax. Cain began as an eight-year-old, on a field across from their housing estate. His own route into the game came via scholarships at Castleford and Leeds, before JK took him to Wakefield as a sixteen-year-old. He then spent two and a half years at Bradford, making the first team twice. Before arriving at Batley at the start of 2015, he'd gone part-time with Whitehaven, a tough journey when your days are spent as a construction labourer. Like Ainy, he'd found it hard; full-time was all he'd known. 'Full of talent,' says JK. 'Improved as the season went on, but he's got a heck of a challenge this year. I'm sure he's up to it.'

The absent Keegan Hirst is applauded – 'sponsored by Antony

Cotton,' Kear jokes – and second-rower Brad Day too is well received. 'He showed great patience to get a place in 2015, but once he did you couldn't get him out. He just got better and better.' His captain too has gone on record as a fan, considering him to be the best back-rower in the Championship in years.

Had Joe Chandler not picked up a knock six or seven weeks before the season's end, he would have been among the awards, his coach says. Prop Tom Lillycrop is 'a young man in a very difficult position. Playing in that middle channel you get knocked about and have to knock people about; it takes years to really learn your trade. But Tom really blossomed last year with the game time he got.' Off the field, 'Cropper' might well be the brightest one among them; he certainly has an impressive job title – project manager for a specialist engineering services provider. What is it they say about props?

And on JK goes, listing every remaining player still here: Alex Bretherton, Shaun Squires, James Craven, Sam Scott, Luke Blake, Adam Gledhill, Alistair Leak, Alex Rowe, James Brown. 'Our final player from last year is a man who swept the board at the awards night. He played in thirty-one of our thirty-three games, this guy, and contributed in a very positive manner. He's training well this year and I'm really chuffed with what I've seen in the gym.'

Brownie, on the face of it a stereotypical rugby league forward, is in reality far from that. Raised in Hyde Park, one of the toughest areas of inner-city Leeds, he is the joker in the pack, 'daft as a brush' his admiring coach's verdict. Put a microphone under his nose and words shudder to a halt. In the real world, they rattle out like bullets, no teammate safe from the spray. Once, he'd have been called a 'foot-balling forward', his ferocious on-field persona belying skills not given to most. He would kick conversions if they'd let him. The sort of bulldog likely to knock you over when your arms are full, Brownie's voice is the first one heard, even when he isn't yet in the building. His dad, an ex-player with Queens, a Leeds amateur club notorious for grit, first took him training to Milford aged four, as smart an idea as has ever been had. Rugby league and James Brown are made for each other: both are big, brutal and belligerent, with depths that pass unnoticed. The man that waits behind a changing-room door with a fire extinguisher and films his victim's reaction is the same man who battles on courageously with injury and yet complains loudly and comically about absolutely everything else.

Signed by Leeds as a sixteen-year-old, he will later admit that his attitude wasn't right. Immature, headstrong and an anti-social early starter, he resented advice; the Rhinos came too young. 'When I was eighteen or nineteen and had lived a bit, it might have been different.' Not that he regrets those days – they made him who he is after all – and he also denies immaturity. 'If anything I was too old for my age, if you know what I mean. I was drinking and doing stuff that I shouldn't.'

Now twenty-eight, Brownie came to Batley via Swinton, after a stuttering start during which he worked – and is still employed – as a builder. Released at Headingley, thwarted stints at Wigan, Cas and Wakefield followed, peppered with amateur returns, seemingly content to drift. His time at Wakey was curtailed by a 'car crash'. Wigan didn't work out because he damaged his cruciate and, upon regaining fitness, struggled with the travel demands. 'I was only nineteen, finishing work at two, then driving over. Not getting back until ten o'clock after leaving the house at seven.' When a baby daughter came along and Swinton rang asking if he fancied coming over though, a rethink was required. 'The extra money would be good, so I said I'd give it a go.' And following an away game at Mount Pleasant, someone else was on the phone: John Kear. Brownie had agreed to sign for York if they won promotion, but when they didn't, it was to Batley that he came. 'I've learned a lot off John,' the former bad boy says. 'Playing-wise, I'm a different person.' At Batley, they know when to have a laugh and when to be serious, and that's important to him. 'I love playing but the biggest thing is the social side. You train. You play and enjoy it. But it's the lads as well.'

Danny Cowling, a centre, is one of two players brought in from relegated Doncaster. He is in his last year of studying sports science at Leeds University and next September will start teacher training. JK had signed him at Wakefield but then left. Full-time by now, Cowling went out on a dual-reg deal with Doncaster, then joined Halifax for a year, Donny for a year and came here when they were relegated. Batley's offer was too good to turn down. 'With the players we've brought in we should do well.' Were he in black and white, Cowling would have the look of a 1930s matinee idol about him, or a Second World War fighter pilot perhaps; Mauny calls him the 'model of the side'.

The other acquisition from Doncaster is full-back Dave Scott, competing with Southernwood and Leak for the title of smallest man in the team. Somewhat unusually, he was born and raised in Stirling, and sports a stereotypically red bushy beard in avoidance of all doubt.

The signing of poster boy Chris Ulugia is now confirmed. The RFL in fact refused the 23-year-old centre a visa as he played one game fewer than required in an injury-hit 2015. Thankfully, to get him off the wage bill, Bradford agreed a loan deal instead, with no conditions attached. 'Kev used his ingenuity,' JK tells the room, while the apparently placid centre looks on, woolly hatted indoors. 'Rumour is Chris once spoke to someone. We are trying to find out who that was.'

Last up are the trio from Sheffield, at least two of whom are familiar in Batley, given that they tormented them during that Grand Final defeat in 2013. Dom Brambani is a thirty-year-old half-back from Bradford. He has been around the block, a smart operator in one of the most crucial areas – if not *the* most crucial area – of the field. Alongside him, stand-off Patch Walker can also play loose forward and, like Brambani, is a deadly goal-kicker to boot. He grins shyly and strokes his designer stubble. Third, the man many pundits have hailed as the one to watch, is James Davey, a will-o'-the-wisp hooker.

'These three players,' says JK, 'bring that bit extra we need. We won ten out of thirty last season; in ten others we were so close to getting over the line. I believe that with these three and our other additions we've got a great chance of kicking on and looking at the top six, if not frightening one or two in the top four. Patch can play 13 or 6. He can take a team around the park. Dom has been around the division a long time, absolute quality. And Jimmy . . . wait and watch when he gets out on that field. I worked with him at Wakefield. He was good at Sheffield; he will be even better with us.'

These then, adds Danny Maun, are the marquee signings, and he asks each of them a question, like who will do the kicking? 'Not Ainy,' Patch replies deadpan, the supporters warming to him from the off. Five of these players – Brambani, Walker, Squires, Reittie and Chandler – are on two-year contracts. The rest, aside from Ulugia on loan and Tinker on trial, are signed currently for one year. Paddy Hesketh apart, the Bulldogs are in good shape, a luxury seldom afforded in rugby league.

Kear concludes by thanking Kev, Iro and the directors for their backing. 'I know we joke that Kev won't spend money; believe you me, they are looking for success. Areas of improvement we identified have been addressed. It's now up to myself, Danny, Craig Lingard, Mark Moxon and John Heaton to make sure they are integrated into the group. If we do get it right, we will have a very good season. I'm excited, energized and enthusiastic. These fellas are; I hope you are too. Join us at Dewsbury on Boxing Day and let's get started.'

3

WHEN NIKOLAUS PEVSNER visited Batley in the 1950s, he noted that it had no remarkable municipal architecture: 'But the principal buildings are at least grouped facing a square, and such a civic open space is a blessing, where mills, so much taller and bigger than any civic buildings, close in everywhere.'

Malcolm Haigh, a less celebrated architectural wanderer, has spent a good deal more time in Batley, eight decades in fact, and is regarded locally as its walking guidebook. Late one Tuesday morning, he meets his latest day-tripper under the clock in the square that Pevsner admired. First, though, lunch will be served at the Salvation Army Hall down on Bradford Road. Mince, carrots, cabbage and potatoes, jelly and ice cream for pudding – £4. He comes here twice a week on average. 'Four pound! You can't beat it, can you?'

There are plenty in. A table for four is shared with two elderly women. One, immaculately made up, distributes free newspapers from a pile she brought in with her. At a facing table sits a young man with two small children, but mostly it's folk of a certain vintage. The busy cooks, servers and other volunteers circulate with good-natured purpose. 'People come here because they are lonely,' the second lady, sad of eye, says. 'For the company perhaps or, like me, so they don't have to cook a main meal for themselves at home.'

Malcolm, born in Batley in 1936, has been a regular at 'Batley football' since he was eight or nine years old. 'You went in the long stand, where you met the rest of the family – the Crosslands and what have you. It was just what you did when you lived in Batley. You went to Mount Pleasant. That was the team to support.' His dad, a worker in one of the town's many textile mills, used to take him. As a boy, Malcolm delivered papers to Batley legends John and Jim Etty's house and, in 1953, upon turning seventeen, began to write about the Gallant Youths too, as a general reporter on the *Batley News*.

Back then, a journalist named Harry Beevers was top dog in Heavy Woollen sporting circles. On match-days, young Malcolm would help out him and the bloke from the *Batley Reporter* as a 'runner'. In those days, the game was on a Saturday afternoon, with running copy needed for the *Pink* or *Green*, to be delivered to long queues at Batley market half-past-six latest. In the short stand, reporters would rattle out a couple of paragraphs while the game was in progress, give them to Malcolm and he would dash downstairs to one of those candlestick telephones with a mouthpiece at the top and a receiver you took off and held to your ear, and phone it all in to the relevant sports desk. After which he would head back up into the stand to see what was happening and, two minutes later, get another slip of paper and repeat the process.

For two years, National Service intervened. Then, when Harry eventually retired, Malcolm got the job, working freelance on sports reports and for twenty-five years doing news for the *Evening Post*, a Leeds-based paper with offices in Dewsbury and Batley.

Though his days as a newshound are done, he is still not quite finished on the rugby league front. 'I haven't officially retired yet but, thing is, there's young lads coming up now. There was one lad last week, he was doing it for two papers at once. Same script. How they can do it like that and not get mixed up, I don't know.' Another issue: he has always worked on phones, not computers. Except in latter years when filing for Monday's trade papers. 'There's no rush then. I can watch the match, collect coaches' comments, have my tea, go home, write and email it.'

Last year, partly due to illness, he opted to cut back. Take life easier. At one time, he was so keen he used to go up and watch the training sessions, but that was a long time ago. He won't be drawn on which era of the game was best. 'With John Etty at centre, they'd set up tremendous attacks; it seemed more open in the days when he and George Palmer made their mark. It's a bit calibrated now, isn't it? But I still enjoying going. It looks very promising this year, doesn't it?'

The townsfolk do still look for Batley's results, he thinks, though he reckons the interest isn't as strong as it was. It's probably down to the population having changed. 'There's lots of Asian lads now and you don't get many of them supporting the club. I've an Asian fellow coming to see me tonight – he wants to write an Asian history of Batley. That's good, isn't it? In the 1950s, I remember my dad saying, "Eeh, some coloured blokes turned up today, but they'll have to work a damn sight harder than that." Anyway, I'd best shut up for a bit or I'll never eat my dinner.'

The food is good, solid and unfussy. 'You're not only helping yourself, you're helping other people by keeping this café going,' Malcolm continues, through a mouthful. 'Hey, we didn't have a prayer this morning, did we? I didn't hear it. We'll have to bring it all back up and do it again. They usually ring a bell for everybody to join in.'

The Salvation Army is on the site of what was once Skelsey's Mill. The houses around the corner were Skelsey Row. 'Anybody who grew up in Batley knows that was a right rough place,' says Malcolm, getting to his feet. 'We were the next gang further on – Bankfield – always at one another.' As a town, he says, Batley reaches back to the Middle Ages, so far as he is aware. Further back, there was a landowner called Bata, and ley means field, 'So it's Bata's field.' He scotches another theory that Batley is derived from bats: creatures represented on various buildings hereabouts, not least the triple-tiered Gothic arch in York stone that watches over the junction of Bradford Road and Rouse Mill Lane. There are a couple of bats on that, though one of them has lost a wing, unfortunately.

Malcolm is particularly interested in the late 1700s onwards, when the modern industrialized period can be said to have begun. There was a time when he could have rattled off facts and figures by the lorry-load, he says, but his memory is going now. This is not good news ahead of a guided tour, but he has brought along a few notes.

Two years ago, he got a bug. The infection hospitalized him for a week and he lost a stone and a half in weight. Unfortunately, it also left him struggling to recall anything connected with names or faces. 'At one time, I could have done it off the top of my head, but not now. I sweat like hell, sorting out the details. Railways, industry, buildings, health and what have you. I've about twelve talks booked this year, and in June and July will be doing four history walks around Batley and Birstall. Never stop, kid. Last week alone, four people came up to me asking about them. I change the routes every three years. A lot of folk don't realize what they are walking on.'

He has an important ancestor too. No less a figure than the man who devised the method of shoddy manufacture himself: Benjamin Law. Put that in your chimney, Pevsner, and smoke it.

Bradford Road was where most of the mills were lined up, as Batley Beck ran along it, all the way down from Birkenshaw and on, roughly, into Dewsbury. The beck runs largely underground now, though when Malcolm was a boy you could look down into it from the footpaths on both sides. Health issues or not, he can still drive, so dons a jaunty baseball cap and turns the ignition on his old green Mazda before motoring back to the cobbled town hall square. It's just up the road, past a clutch of churches, chapels and other such sites of social philanthropy, built in an age when worship of the great god Mammon wasn't quite so blatant as it is today.

The main civic building adjoins Commercial Street, its stone exterior now devoid of the soot spewed into the air when Batley was a booming textile town. Malcolm opens one of his own books and reads: 'Built in 1853 as a mechanics institute, its original purpose was to help people of all ages get better informed, providing classes in art, science and other subjects. In the 1870s, the lease was sold to Batley Corporation for use as a town hall. A front extension housing the council chamber, mayor's parlour and what have you was added in 1905.' The square on which the town hall sits is actually divided in two: the lower level an occasional marketplace and the upper level, in front of the police station, doubling as a car park and well-tended garden of remembrance, complete with war memorial.

'There's the courthouse,' says Malcolm, 'where I did a lot of my reporting in my younger days. I used to spend many Saturday nights here. My mother thought you must be up to no good if you were out after midnight, so she'd bolt the door, wouldn't let me in. If I wasn't home, that was it. This was the only place I could think of to come to. I knew most of the sergeants from working here, so they used to let me sleep in the cells. That were a good thing – if anything ever happened on a Saturday night, I knew all about it and got the scoops.'

There used to be a market hall here with a clock tower on it, Malcolm says, before heading away up the slope and then down a little hill leading to the Fox's Biscuits factory reception, from where on another day he might commence the climb to Mount Pleasant. Here too are municipal buildings. On the right, what began as the technical school and was later the Batley School of Art and Design; on the left, Batley Baths. 'Funny thing,' says Malcolm, 'there's a mermaid carved on the School of Art and nude women on the swimming pool; you'd think it would be the other way around, wouldn't you?' The old art school is now the Al Hashim Academy. 'Bit by bit, the Asians are taking over buildings once used by Batley folk, though of course they are Batley folk too, born and brought up here. Everything changes.'

Fox's Biscuits employs something like two thousand people. Founded in 1853 to make brandy snaps for fairgrounds, Fox's long ago replaced textiles as the biggest employer in town. 'Oh, and just to mention, this building here, Church of the Nazarene, it used to be the town mission, looked after old people.'

Resuming the circuit back up the cobbled hill leads to the square's finest pile: its Carnegie Library, complete with prominent clock. 'That market hall I was telling you about – it wasn't big enough to take all the stalls in wet weather and when it was nice everyone wanted to be outside. So they pulled it down. For a while the clock and its tower stood alone, where the car park is now. Then when the library was built, the clock was incorporated with all its mechanisms and so on. Andrew Carnegie, you'll have heard of him, he gave more than £6,000 towards its construction. Everyone in Batley calls this the town hall clock, even though the town hall is over there. You can see it for miles around.'

Heading north behind the library is where, once upon a time, the majority of Batley's back-to-back streets stood, its residents in varying degrees of squalor. A health centre named for Sir Alfred Broughton, Batley MP for umpteen years, guards a location that is by comparison nowadays merely tatty. The library, though, is under threat. Blaming government cuts, Kirklees Council was about to close it down until the history group of which Malcolm is chairman gave them a petition of 14,000 names. 'I pleaded with them and eventually they decided to keep it open. Then, a short time later, they came back and said, no, they've decided it might have to go after all. So last year we launched a campaign – Friends of Batley Library – that now provides trained volunteers to help run it. In 2016, the official hours are going to be cut. There's so much lovely material in there.'

Alderman George Hirst – presumably no relation to Keegan – laid the first stone in 1906. And further along is Roberto's Ristorante Italiano, formerly a vital post office, which sports a plaque honouring Benjamin Law (1772–1837). To complete the circle, over the road is the Zion Methodist Chapel, marked by a large white cross and known to locals as t' shoddy chapel. Why? 'Because mill owners went to it; if you were out of work, you'd go to service on a Sunday in the hope of getting a job. It's delightful how all the buildings are in harmony, isn't it? So you get what has become an outstanding conservation area.'

Malcolm strides on, along Upper Commercial Street, where Labour MP Jo Cox has just established offices above the Corner Café, he says, the first Batley MP to be officially based in the town. 'A lot of old shops and pubs were demolished under so-called modernization,' although he acknowledges one survivor, the Irish Democratic League

Club, bedecked with shamrocks on a bustling main road. 'It's popular. You don't have to be Irish to go in and it has nothing to do with rugby league, though you do get a lot of ardent supporters in it.'

Over there is the old people's welfare centre. 'It was an idea of a shopkeeper no one thought they'd complete, but there you are.' It now holds meetings, dances and talks just a shillelagh throw from a central estate that, though scruffy, is at least habitable. Once, this would have been the outer edge of the slum, a hellish insanitary place, rife with disease and poverty. A chemist's, newsagent and fast-food outlet now sit where a Sunday school once did, dispensing lessons to children of families with no affinity for a particular religion. *The Batley Sunday School. In the purest spirit of Christian philanthropy and with the most ardent zeal for the redeemer's cause, this building was erected AD 1814*, reads a plaque on the wall. Malcolm says a lot of the people from the slums came here, feeling too inferior to go to the churches.

The pub next door, the West End, was originally a weaver's cottage, as its three storeys betray. And alongside it was another, the Black Bull. Today, the familiar taproom, tiled floor and wooden bar with which the Shaws pub rugby league team were long associated, coached as they were by landlord and former Batley player David Foster, have fallen silent. It has been replaced by a pharmacy.

Walk on. Walk on. To Blakeridge Mill, one of three held in the town by the Taylor family back in the day. And this was the biggest. 'Four windows down, the fancy stonework running top to bottom? That was once the end of the mill. This near end was where Batley's first girls' school used to be. It was doing well, but the teachers found it increasingly difficult to teach because when the mill grew, the boiler house and machines were put next to it. All the *hissshhhing bossshhh- ing hissshhhing bossshhhing –* people were frightened it would explode and take them all to heaven. It got to a point where the head teacher left; she couldn't stand it.' Which meant most of the girls went too and allowed the mill to take over the building, conveniently.

Today, the workers are gone and it has a new name: Jubilee Mill.

The push for expansion is in living accommodation. There will also be a supermarket, though at the moment it is a building site. 'There are few working mills left in Batley,' Malcolm says. 'None produce cloth. Similar story to the steel industry, I suppose: people abroad doing it cheaper. This land was a reservoir, serving the mill. I'm worried that when they get up there [he points in the direction of Batley cemetery] and start digging, they are going to have some horrible falls. Beneath it are the air-raid shelters created during World War Two, so that when Batley was under attack, the workers could get out of the way.'

Not that the workers in Taylors' mills were taken for granted. 'The beauty of it was that they were profit-sharing,' Malcolm says. 'If you worked at Taylors', every year you got a credit. The firm declared an annual dividend, paid to the workers. My dad used to come home rubbing his hands together: "We're in the brass." I used to get a five-pound note! You what?' So reliable was this payout that banks – five down Hick Lane alone – made special arrangements. 'At one time, they were very strict about opening hours. Ten until three – that was it. When the dividend was paid, they opened until ten and eleven o'clock at night.'

Our guide takes a right turn on to a road adjacent to the mill, on which the municipal cemetery lies. 'Long ago, most folk were buried in church or chapel cemeteries around the parish. But of course as the population grew and more people died, they needed somewhere to put them. So this opened in 1866.' Two chapels sit above a path leading up from the main gate, lined by gravestones and memorials, the town's better-heeled residents getting their own avenues up top where monuments and mausoleums are more the thing. One chapel, on the left, is Church of England; the one on the right is for everyone else. 'Designed by the architect Walter Hanstock,' reads Malcolm, checking his own work. 'Born 29 April 1842, died 6 October 1900. His memorial is at the foot of the chapel steps.'

Hanstock's office, it transpires, still stands, next to the stone arch of the parish church, in a town he seems to have constructed single-handedly. These days it is home to the local paper, *The Press*, owned by Danny Lockwood, proprietor of rugby league trade paper *League Weekly*. The town hall extension, library, Zion Chapel – the entire square virtually – Batley hospital and churches of St Thomas, St Saviours, plus the United Reform Church in Dewsbury: all products of Hanstock's imagination. Talented chap. Yet it is the mill owners, merchants and families who take pride of place in a pecking order of bones and dust. Eminences forgotten, carved names and epitaphs worn away by time and the elements: *Look upon immortality ye entrepreneurs and despair.* Money: the elixir of eternal self-delusion.

Out in the open, the wind whips up, though at least the sun puts in an appearance. Malcolm is involved with a cemetery support group. In Victorian times, children died in appalling numbers, most often buried in unmarked graves. The group persuaded two artists to produce a memorial to serve for them all. 'You rarely come past it when it hasn't got some kind of tribute.' Today, it holds a pair of tiny Christmas trees. These were the same artists, in fact, responsible for an imaginative tribute to George Corner, a former scoutmaster who made a name for himself leaping pillar boxes in the 1960s and '70s. The 'wogglehopper', as he was known, lived in Batley, a keep-fit fanatic despite his advanced years. He toured the country, often appearing on local news programmes. Here, he is depicted in a scout uniform and full leapfrogging mode.

In fact, Malcolm is a member of so many organizations that were he to print a list, he warns, it would run to four pages. Batley Community Support Group, People's Dispensary for Sick Animals – on and on it goes. It's a wonder he has any time left for rugby league.

The return route to town leads around the back of Jubilee Mill. 'This used to be a Methodist chapel and there – can you see? – is its manse. Batley has been a very community-minded place. That shop there? Boarded up? Electrical goods store. Used to be Jack Loughlin's tailors. He was a councillor, into everything going.' Turn a corner and a Wesleyan Sunday School now offers 'professional tutoring', before the mill complex heaves back into view, working traffic lights and all.

'It's a bit like Salts Mill in Bradford, isn't it? And of course they came from this area, the Salts. Titus went to Batley Grammar, you know. On your left is the first purpose-built youth centre in the town, and that brick building is the Parochial Hall, for the Roman Catholics.' Turn another corner and before long the Salvation Army church and community centre are spied, today's dining flock long since scattered. 'One-bedroom furnished apartments, £450 a month,' trumpets a billboard for Blakeridge Mill Village, and Stocks Lane is so known because it is where the stocks used to be. 'If folk misbehaved, they were put here for the night, rather than taken to court. The stocks were last used in 1833, on a reveller who had "imbibed too freely".'

Batley Parish Church is the oldest place of worship in the district, going all the way back to the 1500s. 'It's twinned with St Andrews, Purlwell, opposite Mount Pleasant. Let's go in for a look.' Once again, Malcolm reads his own words. 'Mentioned in Domesday Book, 1086. Main building built thirteenth and fifteenth centuries. Porch 1748.' You don't walk into Batley Parish Church; you step down into it. So many bodies are buried here, as near to the church as possible, that the land had to be raised, literally.

Returning to the road brings a traveller to the recently opened Khyber takeaway, formerly another pub with a rugby league past, the Fleece Inn, or as everyone in the district knew it, the Church Steps. Close to the church, this is where out-of-towners might lodge and freshen their horses, and where important meetings took place, such as those attended by the committee in charge of the Dewsbury and Gomersal turnpike, as Bradford Road was once. Further along, there is a 'memorial garden' – a pair of benches, a few bushes and weeds – before a supermarket car park and the Victoria Function Room, aka Victoria Hall, or Conservative Club, with rooms downstairs, a concert room upstairs and a Motown tribute act advertised for Saturday.

'This is the site of the first Batley Boys Grammar School,' reads Malcolm. 'Later on it became the Vic cinema – or "scratching shed" – then a ballroom and bingo hall.' The same bingo hall, in fact, that was run by a youthful James Corrigan, founder of a better-known venue up the road, the Batley Variety Club.

For a brief window in time in the 1960s and early '70s, that famous nightspot hosted many a global superstar. Louis Armstrong, Neil Sedaka, Tom Jones, Shirley Bassey, Roy Orbison, the Bee Gees, Dusty Springfield – all of those and more played to packed houses for weeks at a time. The town sparkled with showbiz glamour. Although even then a stretch of the A652 as likely to be littered with crisp packets as sequins was no Las Vegas Strip.

4

'Too much winning pay, that's what's worrying me,' said Kevin Nicholas as Ron's Lounge emptied on shirt-launch night. 'That's why we've got the War Chest. But what an atmosphere! I'm buzzing, me.'

Two weeks later, he is a mile and a half away at the Tetley's Stadium for the first preseason game. In the dim and distant past, Batley and Dewsbury not only met on Boxing Day but New Year's Day too, league points at stake. Now there is just one match, alternated annually, a nod at tradition played mainly for cash. The players could do without it, though the public still cares and the shared gate receipts are welcome income.

There is also silverware. The Roy Powell Trophy is named after the Dewsbury-born Batley prop whose memorial terrace is at Mount Pleasant. A workaholic forward, he died, aged thirty-three, on 27 December 1998, the year he helped Batley to beat Oldham in the Trans-Pennine Cup final. Having joined Rochdale, he collapsed while simply walking across a training field. Whoever wins, Batley won't let the trophy out of their clubhouse. Too big for the boardroom cabinet, it rests behind the bar in Ron's Lounge. 'They can't have it,' Kev says. 'Roy is ours.'

This year, Boxing Day falls on a Saturday and the players have trained on Monday and Wednesday in the lead-up. They meet at 10.30 a.m. for a noon kick-off. Apart from Hunslet, it's the only ground they must get to under their own steam. A car sluices through rain that continues to plague the north in biblical proportions and pulls up. There have been devastating floods in Leeds, York, Manchester and beyond. 'They don't dredge rivers or clear the drains any more,' says a woman smoking a fag outside the main entrance. 'They used to do it every year, clear a yard either side. Reeds grow over and where's the water going to go now? Hey, love, you can't park there. That's Dewsbury only.' Two Batley players get out of the vehicle in new tracksuit tops: 'There's a Dewsbury player in the boot,' one quips.

John Kear walks the pitch. The grass is long and soggy; pools of water greet every step. Players wander up the tunnel two by two, some chat with their opponents. JK shakes the hand of Dewsbury coach Glenn Morrison, an Australian clad in a T-shirt despite chalk-grey skies and the heavy showers that rattle the main stand roof.

It's a tidy little ground that, like Mount Pleasant, depends on volunteers to keep it that way, swathes of moorland visible over open terracing to the right, a huge water distribution tower looming to the left. Up the road is the village of Gawthorpe: 'Home to the world coal-carrying championship.' The weather will affect the turnout – crowds of 3,000 are possible normally, as the stir-crazy crave fresh air. Nor does Kear expect to see many shapes being run or chances taken. In these conditions, it will most likely be one-out and a kick. Chris Ulugia isn't here; he's gone back to Australia for Christmas. 'We can either moan or get on with it and we choose the latter.'

In the end, a little over two thousand turn up, a fair proportion from Batley, and the first half is the predicted up-the-middle slog, in which Keegan Hirst stands tall. By the break, it is the Rams who lead 4–0 though, Dewsbury scoring while he and Rowey are rotated at the end of the opening quarter, 7–1 ahead in the penalty-count. No one is panicking. Dom Brambani has gone well and continues to trouble the hosts on the restart. His kicks turn Dewsbury's big pack around in the mud time and again. Batley begin to dominate.

Physio Carl Chapman, in an orange bib, arcs on and off the field, passing instructions in what may be his last game, though the search for a replacement has stalled. Craig Lingard relays JK's radio messages, dictated high in the back of the stand. Familiar favourites nudge the scoreboard in Batley's favour, Ainy collecting Dom's kick and dabbing a speculator in-goal, where Alex 'Breth' Bretherton, the oldest man in the team, scores the Bulldogs' opening try. The new boy adds a touchline conversion and, moments later, Ainy is in from a Cain Southernwood pass. A late penalty from Patch Walker confirms a 12–4 victory, before a half-hearted brawl on the hooter in which not a punch is landed concludes the Yuletide fare.

Just as no one was panicking at the break, no one is too excited now. Though, after all the optimism, it is good to get a win that will keep the bandwagon rolling, with encouraging individual displays galore. Diminutive Dave Scott, given a go at full-back ahead of the incumbent James Craven, has defied expectations, as reflected in an appreciative silent look and nod between Linners and Danny Maun.

Outside the changing rooms, two local pressmen wait for the coaches to emerge. Morrison is gracious in defeat, though points out that his side were missing nine players. Losing is disappointing. This is the fourth Boxing Day match Dewsbury have lost on the bounce; he hasn't won one yet. The Rams do have the edge in league meetings, though, 'which is where it really matters'.

JK is all smiles, hailing togetherness and a will to win. With the completion of this match, he's coached a game in every single month of 2015, through friendlies last January, a domestic season and with Wales in October and November. The guys are now off for 'a pint or two' back at the Mount. In fact, the only Batliensian with anything to complain about is Jonny Potts. He is the one who will have to get the white back into what had been a pristine virgin strip.

Dewsbury's next friendly is with St Helens, giants of Super League. Batley are to face a Heavy Woollen Select amateur XIII, coached by Mauny. At least, that is the plan.

The town hall is still bedecked in Christmas lights when the Bulldogs meet five days ahead of that fixture, the evening dry but bitterly cold. JK checks his register. Where there's little difference performance-wise, this attendance record will sway selection: 'The important thing is to be transparent.'

As usual, the players gather in the changing room on arrival, nip up to the boardroom for coffee or pop in to see Carl with injury niggles. There have been two responses to his advertisement, one from a Syrian refugee, the other a chap in Greece. Both saw landing a job at Batley as the rugby equivalent of joining Manchester United.

Tonight, though, Carl is in the boardroom, compiling head-test results on his laptop, very basic cognitive exercises designed to check mental reflexes by asking players to link pieces of information, follow instructions, select colours and such. Their result is then matched up with a personal ID number at the Rugby Football League. If at any stage of the season a player takes a knock to the head or is concussed, the test is retaken to ensure a similar level is achieved. Unfortunately, three players have already failed the thing and the season hasn't even started yet. They will have to do a re-sit.

The failure to source his replacement is due to over-stringency. The RFL has scrapped its lower-level entry requirements; a would-be physio must now be fully qualified. Problem is, very few of those will be attracted to a club like Batley. Though well intentioned, the move is as in tune with reality as those jobseekers from Athens and Damascus. Nor will the RFL circulate the ad via its database, the excuse a conflict of interest. Hunslet too are struggling and others are bound to follow.

The leadership group is to meet for the first time – Keegan Hirst, Dom Brambani, Luke Blake, Joe Chandler, Alex Rowe, James Brown and Alex Bretherton the chosen few. Otherwise, it's a routine already established: train in the gym, then on the all-weather. John Heaton will supervise the weights, JK then assisted by a combination of Mark Moxon, Craig Lingard and Mauny, dependent on availability dictated largely by the first of that trio's irregular work patterns.

Breth is late, delayed by his job as a buyer for a packaging company in South Leeds, on the same industrial estate as Hunslet, in fact. Aged thirty-three and having retired at the end of last season, he might not be here at all had he not been persuaded otherwise during a game of golf with chairman Kev while, by coincidence, the pair holidayed at the same time in Portugal during the close-season. He isn't in JK's plans, he realizes that, but will give it one last whirl. It would be good to put a more positive full stop on a career begun at Dewsbury over a decade ago. Karl Harrison then brought him to Batley; in domestic rugby he hasn't moved beyond Heavy Woollen boundaries, though was actually born in Wigan, one of only five players to hail from outside West Yorkshire. The Bretherton family moved to Ossett with his dad's job when Breth was three years old.

He enjoyed playing at Dewsbury but is happiest here. 'Although they are similar sizes, the clubs are different in terms of character. We always seem to be underdogs.' A creature of habit, after six years at the Rams he had no desire to move but wasn't offered a new deal: 'Blessing in disguise.' Breth views life with wry amusement. He takes it lightly, his grin set off by dimples you could plant spuds in. In 2016, he will play on match-by-match terms – no contract – backing himself to prove his worth if selected. With a four-year-old son and marriage on the agenda, he reckons he is still fit enough: 'They say you are a long time retired. At this level, it's about enjoying it, not money. The amount of time you give up is totally disproportionate, probably works out at a pound an hour, not even the national minimum wage.'

'Your anti-ageing pills are working,' quips his coach, as Breth, suited and booted like Albert Finney in *Saturday Night and Sunday Morning*, takes a seat in a group intended to be a bridgehead between coaching staff and team. Discontent downstairs clocked before any spirit-destroying virus takes hold. The secret, Breth reckons, is to keep the lads happy. New training kit this year has gone down well. Might home fixtures be changed to Friday nights rather than Sunday afternoons? Last year, training on Monday, Wednesday and Friday and playing Sunday led to complaints, especially from guys with families and even more so when games were lost. JK says he'll ask the directors, though doubts they will change Bradford and Featherstone because that's when they attract the biggest crowds.

Out on the hills, snow is promised. At the end of Heritage Road, meeting done, a gymnasium far too small for so many men is soon steamed up, its mirrors distressed by contorted goggle-eyed glares.

Twenty-four men in fact, moving in pairs, exercise to exercise. It appears random but there is a pattern to prowling John Heaton's domain. Bench presses, squats, grunts and gritted teeth – all of it part of a tailored circuit. Kettle bells dangle and swing between legs, weights clatter as they are tossed casually to the floor or between team-mates. An onlooker can only wince at their proximity to unguarded toes, feet, ankles and other extremities.

JK looks in just as Tinker targets an empty rowing machine for a brief rest. 'Can't do that, Tinker lad,' says the coach. 'There's no time for sitting down.' So back to his feet Tinker gets, thumbs up.

Wandering over to the all-weather, Chris Ulugia has a fit of the shivers and suddenly speaks: 'When does the sun come out?'

The Heavy Woollen Select will contain players from local clubs Mirfield, Dewsbury Moor, Batley Boys, Dewsbury Celtic, Thornhill, Shaw Cross and the like. Given that he is in charge, Mauny isn't on duty tonight. He is putting those lads through their paces instead.

This is to be the second such fixture. Batley won the inaugural one 68–6 last year, a bit of a drubbing, though the amateurs took a surprise third-minute lead. 'Too many older players,' was the general consensus, so a few more up-and-comers will feature this weekend. The Bulldogs, though, prepare for it as they would Melbourne Storm.

When more clement weather arrives, hopefully to reveal an occasional patch of dry land, these outdoor training drills will move on to grass. Already, though, they are growing familiar, even for the new guys. The late BBC radio presenter Brian Redhead, champion of rugby league as an intellectual game, once called it 'chess with muscles'. In fact, it has just as much in common with trigonometry.

Even at a semi-professional level, particularly in its modern incarnation, this is a sport principally about lines, angles and shape. There is a mathematical precision about it that can – and frequently does – pass a casual observer by. Like most crafts and industries it has a jargon of its own, thoroughly bewildering on first hearing and slow to reveal itself thereafter, differing slightly club by club. And for the players, every calculation must be computed at high speed, very often under enormous physical and mental stress.

As in all the other preseason sessions so far, there will be no tackling, just defensive grabs. The hard surface allows for little else. Still, commitment is total, with collisions powerful enough to damage lesser physiques. Passes snap, hand to hand, like bullets from a gun, one group with the ball, the other in defence. A runner might receive a pass or he may not, but in any case he must push, or perhaps trail, depending upon the move in progress – a pairs move, red tiger, right or left, a white lion or wide crash, or play to a point and another ploy, fifties pairs maybe. White lion: pivot receives, man drops under him with a hook ball with a lead and back man. Red tiger: dummy-half play that again has a hook with a lead – the lexicography of league.

In attack (offense) or defence – commonly abbreviated as 'D' – it helps if a player is familiar with individual opposition members, their strengths and weaknesses, or else be astute at reading minds and likely angles of approach without over-reading intentions and reacting too quickly, for that way danger lies.

It is often said that rugby league is a simple game. And it is often said by two different sets of people. Coaches and players are one category. So well versed are they in the sport (and the northern art of self-deprecation) that its complications become second nature to them. If they can understand it, surely everyone else must too. The simplicity line is also useful psychologically in team talks. In the second group are those who, conversely, do not truly understand what is going on, whether through casual ignorance or disdain, even if they have watched and supported the game all their lives. Played well, simple is what rugby league is not, whether the description is taken to mean uncomplicated or easy.

It is true that the core principles are straightforward enough. Just as the playing of soccer can be reduced to 'pass to a teammate and score more goals than the other side', or boxing to 'knock the other fighter out', or tennis to 'keep the ball within the lines of the court', or cricket to 'collect ten wickets and score more runs', so working hard and completing sets tend to pay off in rugby league.

JK is a stickler for positioning, particularly in a defensive line: first defender five metres from the ruck, second four metres and third three. Face forward. Turn even slightly to your right and you lose your hips; your body is at an angle, you will be dragged in and left weak on your left side should they then attack it. Straight on, a defender can adapt, tackling to the right or left, as required.

Other such nuances will be apparent as the season takes flight, but for now they are just warming up, figuratively and literally. As thousands of soap opera lives twinkle orange, dots in the valley below, up here are men determined to be the best they can be. All is disciplined. Yet all is enjoyment. 'Look at them,' says JK, with parental pride. 'Players just love playing, don't they?' There is a worrying moment when Sam Scott – Scully as he is known – turns an ankle, but he soon runs it off. Excepting Alex Rowe and Brad Day, who have minor injuries, and long-term absentee Paddy Hesketh, all will feature on Sunday. It will be another chance to test combinations on grass, an opportunity denied them thus far by the winter deluge, though it's clear that the pivotal players in particular are forging an understanding.

Training done, JK calls his squad together. 'I want to hammer these. I know we'll be all nicey-nicey and mates together afterwards, but I want us to be ruthless. Them: fucking zilch. Us: a lot.' And on the way back to the club, out of earshot, he confides his aim for the season – to finish above Dewsbury: 'That'll be a resounding success, as we'll be in the top six.'

On the radio, meanwhile, it is reported that NFL side St Louis Rams are to relocate to Los Angeles. A 1,800-mile move to the new

$1.86 billion LA Coliseum has angered fans in Missouri and will cost the Rams a $550 million relocation fee. The Bulldogs have problems of their own: the weather forecast is bleak.

Get in at C, get in at B and get tight . . . If we call Leeds 4, we are trying to get four of their players on the short side, six on the big side . . . tight on the scrum line . . . This is not a conditioning exercise, boys. Take your time . . . We don't always have to go around the back . . .

Brownie of course does not miss the innuendo, and frustration at having to wait an extra week gives way to guffaws.

Having woken to a Sunday-morning whiteout, three inches of snow on the Mount Pleasant field, it was clear the first game of the year could not go ahead. So here the Doggies were, straining at the leash. The Heavy Woollen game now scrapped, an extra friendly with Hunslet has been arranged instead.

I'm on B, I'm on B, I'm on B . . . That's good that. Good hard line, good hard line.

JK's fingers too are getting a workout, a nervous tic. He hasn't got a clue why they do that. It's just how it is. 'Ooh, I get excited when I see things like that,' he says. 'I do get fucking excited, I'll tell you. What's the objective at that point there, just inside the scrum-line? It's to get eight on six. If they put the numbering up and put three on the short side, we've got three on the short side. I would suggest the dummy-half jumps and goes. What you are going to have is twenty-two yards of space and a four v four because a jump will engage the marker. Then it's up to the other guys to create something. So be real smart here, Blakey. When we set that point up, they go four short side; we always come big. They go three short side, we have a little look at them.' The coach is immersed. His players are too.

As a rule, he prefers encouragement, though if he needs to come down heavily, he will – it's the schoolmaster in him. The other week, after Brownie was overheard complaining, Kear blew his top. 'Hey! Hey! Listen up!' he roared, after the first dropped ball in eighteen minutes. 'I'm fucking sick of hearing you bickering. If we bicker, we fucking splinter. He made an error but the ball is your responsibility, so you made an error too. We don't bicker, that's not what we are about. We stand together!'

Also at training that night was another Brown, this one a winger. Alex, 28-year-old Jamaica international, is hungry for a new contract. If successful, he will have been here four times since 2010, the trajectory of Brownz, as he prefers to be known, a virtual bagatelle. Beginning at Keighley and Rochdale, at age twenty he was picked up by Huddersfield, leaving there for a three-season stay at the Mount, a time that included a game for Widnes on loan. A spell in union came next at Sale Sharks, prior to a return to league with Hull KR, where he played once on loan at Gateshead. Then he was off to Leigh, a move that didn't work out, before a return to Batley in 2014. 'I should have stayed at Hull KR to be fair, but Leigh seemed a good prospect.' Then he was off to Halifax, who farmed him out first to Coventry and then Batley again, where he finished last year on loan. So here he is once more. Off the field, he teaches PE: 'key stage two, so you do it all – maths, English, science'. He's also been a personal trainer and postman, jobs that fit around his rugby. As he approaches the end of his career, he's now happy to play part-time, just wants to enjoy himself.

If Brownz is signed, he won't play this weekend. North Wales Crusaders are the opposition, weather permitting, although the snow disappeared as swiftly as it came. The players have honed methods of regaining their feet for speedy play-the-balls. The tripod: a tackled player gets on his knees and one elbow before spinning up with a scissor kick and placing the ball on the ground. The bridge: a tackled player jerks upwards when pinned on his back – 'we don't want this to happen but it sometimes does' – and rolls into space. 'Space and time,' JK says. 'All you want is space and time.'

At a full-time club, such shapes, techniques and tactics are gone through again and again, day in day out, digested and reproduced as muscle memory. Here, the coaches work with their team at the most three times a week, for just an hour or so at a time. 'Explosive, guys, very nice. Explosive! We like this.'

*

Snow gives way to pale winter sunshine when Batley do make their first appearance of 2016. But it is the men from North Wales who make an explosive start.

The League 1 side, here via JK's link with the Welsh national team, are handy opposition and actually won this fixture last year, 30–20. When they open the scoring on a pitch that, though wet, is lush and green, it is clear that they will again be no pushovers.

As was planned for the aborted Heavy Woollen game, more players than usual will be used, allowing Tinker his start and the chance to shine on an unseasonably mild Saturday. Groundsman Jim Morley pushes a lawnmower back and forth in horizontal lines, releasing a bizarre aroma for late January of freshly cut grass. Volunteers and directors have been here all morning setting things up, the coach and players arrive at a quarter past noon, ready for a 2 p.m. kick-off. It feels like an awakening, an emergence from hibernation.

Y' all right? . . . All right, yeah, you all right? . . . All right, yeah.

Sam Scott and Tinker are the first players to enter the boardroom. Has anyone seen Carl? Nellie Earnshaw, widow of Ron, after whom the Lounge and terrace are named, inspects and approves the new kitchen before putting out milk, sugar and white china cups next to a percolator with her friend Barbara Crossley. Barbara, Andy Winner's mother-in-law, bakes champion cakes, her confections devoured eagerly on match-days. Busying about, Nellie has a half-hearted go at 'You'll Never Walk Alone' but gives it up as a bad job. 'I hope you haven't made a mess or I'll crack you,' she tells one table of players as they rise and head off to get changed.

In the tunnel, referee Dave Merrick surveys the scene with his touch judges while Kev sorts out their expenses. Dave's come to just short of £15, the other two around a tenner. He coaches a team at Pontefract College through the week and works nights in a glass factory. He's just off a twelve-hour shift: 'Only got to bed at half past six.'

Batley Boys have won this morning's Under-12s Yorkshire Cup final, 20–18, beating Hunslet at Kippax. A lad called Levi Evans scored four length-of-the-field tries. They are to be introduced to a sparse crowd at half-time. Two blokes lean on an optimistic crush barrier. *What d' you make of this new sound system then?* 'Eh?' *This new sound system. What do you make of it?* Elvis, denied the Variety Club, belts out hunka burning love here instead. 'Aye, all right, isn't it?'

'Good luck, Tinker lad,' says JK, as the trialist jogs out to warm up. He is at full-back, custodian-in-chief, last line of defence. It's a vulnerable spot on the field, any error out in the open. His first touch is to field a rolling ball, which he copes with well enough, retaining possession when hammered by a pair of Welsh bruisers. With only two minutes gone, though, his team are 6–0 behind, on the back of a converted try, and Tinker has a couple of loose moments. He lets the ball bounce dangerously from a skied kick and then flirts with interception, floating a looping pass to Dave Scott on the wing. Neither proves fatal and, playing uphill, Danny Cowling and Alistair Leak claw back a 12–6 lead at the break. An understandably scratchy second half, in which Tinker fails to reappear, is more comfortable.

A busload of away supporters singing 'Delilah' on loop get their reward with a pair of tries, one while Sam Scott is sinbinned for a late tackle. This occasions a tactical switch and Brownie is removed – 'Oh, for fuck's sake,' he says as he trudges from the field – before Dave Scott's last-minute try, added to earlier efforts from Squiresy, Cain and the newly nicknamed 'Uce' Ulugia, all goaled, completes the scoring, the game ending 36–18 in Batley's favour.

'It showed why we needed to get on an actual field,' Kear tells another two-man press corps. 'We looked heavy-legged. It was useful, we've progressed, but we are not Leigh-ready yet.'

At training on Monday and Wednesday, a routine had been established that would be stuck to all year, more usually on Tuesdays and Thursdays. After every game, JK cuts video footage into bite-size chunks, the better to illustrate and discuss specific points in a team meeting. Ahead of that, individuals might sit with assistant coaches Mokko and Linners, gaining insight a little more personalized.

Some players pop into the physio room, as Jimmy Davey had on Monday, his spell on one of Carl's two treatment tables watched by a couple of teammates. An electrician who like Dom and Patch had no desire to go full-time, the hooker is typical of the type of locally based player Batley and other semi-professional set-ups prefer. Joining Wakefield's academy and moving through the age groups, he eventually signed a full-time contract there and did three years, a favourite of JK's while he was in charge. In the end, though, JK left and Wakey didn't work out. He ended up in Sheffield on a less glamorous path, if any path in league can be called that.

By 6.15, Jimmy was upstairs in Ron's Lounge with the rest. 'Did well enough first half, began the second with a bang and then got sloppy,' was Keegan's assessment on behalf of the leadership group.

JK had by then studied the tape several times. 'We played uphill how you should play uphill. You look after the ball, kick well, and that is reflected in the score. Going uphill, 12–6 is happy days. The second half, as Keegan pointed out, was a bit patchy, inconsistent.' Missed tackles: 'Twenty-one – too many, guys, too many. We want to be aiming at sixteen or less. That means at least one person has not missed a tackle at all and your aim is to be that man.'

Nor had the off-the-ball stuff been acceptable: 'Things people in the stand don't notice. They notice the great carries and big hits. They don't notice all the other little things that allow you to play well. As Keegan rightly pointed out, our contact in the ruck area wasn't good enough.' They'd absorbed ball-carriers instead of hitting them hard, winning the collision and slowing them down. 'We need to really get our shoulder in with that first-up contact.'

Linners piped up from his seat in the gallery, the balcony overlooking the backs of two rows of chairs dragged there for the players, the string of windows behind the assistant coach offering a panoramic view of the pitch when the shutters are up. JK delivers his seminars from the side of the screen on which the clips are shown. They need to be smarter, Linners interjected, with regard to the point in the game they are at. 'Too often on tackle five we were in a wrestle instead of getting up. That puts pressure on the lads who have to get a pass out or put a good kick away. Sometimes you've just got to hit the deck and play the ball.'

They looked at the first try conceded, a good kick that by general consensus was unlucky, the ball having hit a post. Kear, though, belongs to a school of philosophy where you make your own luck. 'Not having a go, Tinker old cock, but watch Billy Slater in the NRL. What does he do when they put boot to ball? He doesn't jog across; he fucking sprints. Sprint, you've half a chance, even if it hits the post.'

Line speed in defence is vital, since it takes up time and space, denying opponents the chance to use their skills. 'What do you reckon to us line speed here?' JK asked. 'Absorb line speed, isn't it? Not hit line speed. You cannot give a team like Leigh room to play. We need to be urgent and work as a unit.' His desire for inch-perfect positioning came sharply into focus when 'C' defender Brownie was caught ten, not five, metres away from Keegan, and a North Wales player broke clean through, wreaking havoc from which the team did well to scramble back and defend: 'A gap a fucking mile wide.' Such things play out in the blink of an eye, their significance missed by spectators and commentators alike. Sam Scott's sinbinning, however, was forgiven: 'Sam's flattened the half-back there, which isn't always a bad thing . . .'

After half an hour in the gym, they went down to the field for the first time. JK insisted that the squad be permitted to train there, whether it was throwing it down or not. Rain sprayed with every impact, the group finally able to tackle properly. Collisions that would knock lesser mortals into last week were shaken off in an instant.

A similar tack was taken on Wednesday, though with no team meeting. Proximity to the weekend saw the pitch again out of bounds, in use instead the scrap of land next to the match-day car park, a mud bath floodlit on the stadium side only, with ten-watt bulbs on poles by the look of it. Ankle-height grass underfoot, lost in shadows thrown by rows of elm, elder and beech trees, their dry-tapered branches splayed and teasing the darkness like Max Schreck's fingers in *Nosferatu*.

'Arse end of rugby league is this,' said Keegs. And it was. A full-time player with a Super League club might be at a warm-weather training camp in Tenerife right now, La Manga perhaps, or, if he was really lucky, Florida. Given the lack of vision and mud as tenacious as a Whitby limpet, catch a ball in such conditions and you could catch a ball in anything, though again it was their D that JK was keenest to address. Shields out in the warm-up, they were soon again into full contact, working on communication, vital in winning and maintaining control of the speed of play. 'It's an audition for the BAFTAs at the minute, fellas. Can we have a bit of stick in it? Where's the thud?'

The thud was duly heard: muscle colliding with muscle, bone grinding on bone. Then another. And another. 'I can hear that one! Good! And that one! That's it. That's better. Hear the thud! Squeeze him, squeeze him ... squeeze him ... when you've got him. Remember, we don't absorb, we hit!'

From the bottom corner, in lines of three, they worked their way up into squalls of icy rain. One player was thrown a ball; he ran to what must at some point have been a bright yellow cone, his teammates darting back to a cone at the rear. Upon turning, the defensive duo first hit and then brought the ball-carrier to ground with as much dominance as they could muster, most often with a sickening thwack, initially to the chest, before the legs man slid down to halt the runner's stride and his upper-body colleague grappled the victim to the floor. Not too quickly. Not too slowly. But always move forward if you can, the better to press your advantage. The defenders were then told to retreat five extra metres, adding even greater ferocity and impact to the collisions.

As the session ploughed on, the land turned to sludge, a grade-one quagmire. Boots, socks, training kit, black as jet. The gladiators slogged on, under moonlight, unwavering, steadfast. 'I'm taking these to my mam's,' said Blakey when, mercifully, it was time to trudge back to the sheds. 'No way are these going in *my* washing machine.'

*

Players and clobber alike are washed and laundered by Friday night, for a preseason dinner well attended by partners, directors, coaches and sponsors. It's a fun affair, held hours after Super League has revealed its latest blue-chip sponsor: Batchelors' Mushy Peas.

In the Championship, there is much talk of the resignation of Leigh coach Paul Rowley, just ten days before the start of the season. The one-time hooker had been on the backroom staff since 2008, led Leigh to the last two league titles and – helped by controversial owner Derek Beaumont's cash – attracted such luminaries as Rangi Chase, Corey Paterson, Harrison Hansen and even former Australia centre Willie Tonga to the side. Unsurprisingly, this made Leigh odds-on not only to reach the middle eight again but also to top the division and go up this time, instead of flopping horribly as they did in 2015. Had all that hope evaporated?

Bev Nicholas works the bar. A chatty no-nonsense Mancunian, she is from a football family really, as folk tend to be in Manchester. She watched her first rugby league game around 1993; Kev brought her here on a date. She can't remember who Batley were playing but, it being winter rugby back then, her first thoughts were, 'It's bloody cold.' There was a little pie hut where the stand is now and, because the couple were young and in love, Kev asked if she would like some half-time pie and peas. '"Yeah, okay then." So he gets in this queue and I'm sort of looking around and he gets to the front and turns around and says, "Do you want mint sauce?" I says, "On what?" He says, "Your pie and peas. Do you want some or not?" I says, "No, no, I don't. You have mint sauce on lamb." "Oh, well we do here." So I cut the pie open and say, "Kevin, this is a hot pork pie." And he says, "Yeah." And I says, "You never reheat pork pies." And he says, "We do in Batley."'

There is one favourite of Kev's to which she will never get used, mind: mucky fat. 'Yuk. We went to a wedding reception at St Mary's Hall in Batley. In the buffet, there were these plates of what I thought was Marmite on bread. He said, "No, it's mucky fat." I'd never heard of it. He said, "It's the rubbish off the bottom of the roasting tin, what's wrong with that?" We have functions here and people ask if they can have mucky fat. I have to tell them no, it isn't right. It's the most disgusting thing in the world and shouldn't be allowed.'

Since her husband took over in 1997, being the wife of a rugby league chairman has had its ups and downs. 'The first few years were horrendous. Winding up petitions, court cases, no money – that was really difficult. It took eight or ten years before we started to see a turnaround, then it got more enjoyable. I don't like it when we go through a bad time, because everybody seems to take it out on Kevin, when it's not always Kevin's fault. "You should be putting your hand in your pocket . . . instead of a scoreboard why didn't we spend it on players . . ." That sort of thing. I don't think people realize how difficult it is, running a club. I really don't like it when they take it out on him.'

Such a position impacts heavily on family life too. Bev concedes that the buck stops at the top but the amount of work he puts in just to keep Batley afloat is enormous. Along with the full-time business in Manchester, where Bev also works, when not at the club he is usually sat doing the books at night, counting money, managing the accounts, VAT and what have you: 'The loves in Kevin's life are Batley rugby league club, then his daughter; I think I might be third or fourth.'

Bev, however, has her own uses about the place. Along with bar work and making bacon butties in the kitchen as required, she checks the staffing, sorts out functions such as tonight, organizes catering and much else besides. In that latter bracket she makes perhaps her greatest contribution and certainly the one that means most to her, the Pink Weekend, on which Keegan so memorably came out last August.

'In 2008, I was diagnosed with breast cancer. And having gone through all the chemotherapy, radiotherapy, the mastectomy and everything else, I'm still here. A couple of female fans were diagnosed after me and I thought that it was time, as a club, we did something. So in 2014 we had our first Pink Weekend and raised £9,700. Last year we did it again and raised £11,400.' No mean feat with a core fan-base of around 500 to 600 people. 'We are doing it again this year.' It kicks off on Friday with afternoon tea, a sponsored walk on Saturday along with a Batley Girls game and pig racing; players in a pink kit on Sunday which is then auctioned off. 'We have a ducking stool, cake stands, tombola – everybody is so amazing.'

When illness struck, it happened to be when Kev took a turn as RFL President, adding to the avalanche. Disposed to positivity, even Bev has to admit that wasn't the best year, though she buckled down. 'I went to work every day and didn't take time off, except when I had surgery. I'd have my chemotherapy on Tuesday; go to circuit training on Tuesday night. I really did not want it to affect my life or my family's life. I can tell women who have been diagnosed that, at this moment, I know there's nothing worse, but it gets better. Your hair does come back. You are at the lowest point in your life but in twelve months' time you'll look back and think, "Perhaps it wasn't as bad as I thought."'

And through it all, there was rugby league. Would she describe herself as a fan? 'Oh yes, I enjoy watching and being part of it. Comes with the marriage, really.' As it does for the wives, girlfriends and significant others of everyone else, hence tonight's do. 'We'd like to do this sort of thing more often because some lasses, the players' partners, seem a bit fragmented. It would be good to get them sitting together; it's companionship as well, isn't it?'

Mr Nicholas, smartly turned out as ever in pink shirt and shiny shoes, is busying about checking names on tables. Then he starts his address: 'I'll have to get a move on, they're burning the soup.' It raises a laugh, although when the pea and ham does arrive it leaves a smoky aftertaste. Proceedings begin with stand-up bingo, participants asked to sit down if they get a question wrong. At stake, eight free drinks, 'which the winner can share with the rest of the table or not'. First question: who is tallest, Keegan Hirst or Julian Clary? 'If you think Keegan, put your hand up. Clary, put it down.' And so it goes until only two contestants remain standing. Whether it's Shaun Ainscough's breeding skills, the head coach – 'Who is oldest, John Kear or Paul Potts? I was going to ask which has the youngest wife, but that might have been tactless' – Alex Bretherton's advancing years or the grooming habits of Danny 'Rylan' Maun, few escape a roasting. 'If you were judging us on wives and partners, you'd say we were in Super League. Some of our boys are punching seriously above their weight.' A table of single players is dubbed 'The Undateables'. Keegs has come alone.

The kitchen christened with roast beef, Yorkshire pud, vegetables, potatoes and jam roly-poly, assistant coach Linners clears the plates and carts them off to the new serving hatch, helping three young female waiters. Other tables do likewise while Kev thanks the sponsors for their invaluable input. The Nicholas nose is ostentatiously rubbed; it smells success. A huge round of applause erupts when he makes reference to 'our absolutely inspirational captain, Keegan Hirst. Now get to the bar. We've to pay for this food.'

Two days later, a Hunslet side containing just two players from the team that lost here last year is beaten comfortably. In the car park, Tinker leaps from a car containing his mother and sister. The attendant ribs him: is he late? 'Bang on time,' Tinker tells him. 'But JK says that if you are bang on time, you are fifteen minutes late.'

Playing with the slope in heavy conditions, the hosts lead 20–0 at the break, never in trouble, and finish 34–6 victors. It is twenty-two minutes before Hunslet play the ball in Batley's twenty-metre zone and winger Wayne Reittie collects a hat-trick of tries.

The pitch is so boggy, in fact, on a grey and drizzly Sunday, that going ahead is questionable. Though with Leigh's thoroughbred runners in mind, chewing the paddock up a little might not be a bad idea. While doing his stretching exercises, referee Robert Hicks – face of a choirboy, demeanour of a junior middle manager – gets into conversation with a spectator at the front of the Glen Tomlinson Stand. *It's not so bad in the middle, worse on the bottom edge. I'm surprised it's on with all the rain that's fallen.* 'Don't you have a say in it?' *They want to play, don't they? Let them play.* He may regret such philanthropy later, when the shower in the officials' room runs out of hot water.

The final try of the first half goes to Sam Scott, who, along with Gleds, scorer of a seventh-minute opener, is the pick of an impressive pack in which Leaky also contributes a try. Brownie is sinbinned for dissent: 'I swear I didn't say owt,' he pleads, trailing back to a packed dugout wherein Tracey, a masseuse from Wakefield, is loaded down with padded coats. She's been here for four years, she says. Came on work placement and stayed. Enjoys it. She wanted to be a beauty therapist and certainly has the looks, but then decided to go into sport and did a college course. She does the rubs before kick-off and at half-time and played rugby herself for a year at school, 'but then they stopped it because we were too rough'. A week from now she will be gone. The rumour is her boyfriend isn't keen.

Tinker is sent on for the final quarter. He fails to get involved and at the hooter is the only man in a clean shirt; upon such moments do lifetimes turn.

February dawns and with it the Kingstone Press Championship launch at the Worsley Park Marriott Hotel, Manchester, just off the M60 motorway at an appropriate junction 13. It is Monday lunchtime. JK and Keegs, the latter in full kit, are joined by the other Championship and League 1 coaches and captains in plush surroundings geared to a sense of occasion. Buzz-phrase: 'This is our time.'

The aim is to meet the press, and the fourth estate is here in gratifying numbers, though from local outlets on the whole, rather than national organizations. Still, interviews are written and filmed, publicity photographs taken – during which Keegan and company are asked to brandish giant sticks of Blackpool rock. Again, much gossip surrounds Leigh. The Centurions will be coached by Neil Jukes on Sunday, Paul Rowley's former assistant. There are tales of upheaval in the ranks, could there be a better time to face them? It is a question Kear fields several times, as hacks and representatives mingle and a buffet vanishes with indecent haste. Leigh owner Derek Beaumont has not endeared himself with a widely quoted prediction that his big spenders would 'go all year unbeaten'.

The RFL often attracts criticism of its organizational prowess. Last week's Super League launch was a shocker, the press standing around for hours, before a pointless floorshow. An outdoor musical shindig intended for families – 'Rugby League Rocks', at Leeds's Royal Armouries – was staged on a freezing cold and wet day in January. Today, something out of their control thwarts them. Pep Guardiola will be the next manager of Manchester City, scuppering any hopes of leading tonight's North West news bulletins. Nor does a speech by the RFL's chief operating officer inspire confidence. Nominally in charge of the Championship, Ralph Rimmer tries to talk up the divisional format. 'I will be amazed if I stand here in a year's time and tell you the season hasn't produced everything it promised,' Rimmer concludes. Frankly, so will everyone. He says that every year.

Back at Mount Pleasant, weeks don't come much busier. That evening, the squad trains at Total Fitness, off the M1 near Wakefield. At a packed gym that is open to the public, conditioner John Heaton puts the Bulldogs through their paces in a private cycling studio.

The use of such a venue is not without difficulty, especially after work when, given the popularity of the place, there is no sole access to weights, which the lads like throwing around. The facilities, though, are first class. Spread out in two rows, each player pedals at varying speeds as yelled out by Heaton, who also 'spins' the music. Muse. *They will not control us. We will be victorious.*

Looking on are JK, Carl and Mokko; there will be the usual three sessions this week but here exertion will be light. Yesterday, in attritional conditions, the playing squad responded well to its preparation the week before. There will be rubs at the club on Wednesday and they will gather to watch tapes of Leigh on Friday.

In his day – and frequently night – job, diminutive Mokko is a fire fighter at Leeds-Bradford Airport. Making training and even games can be awkward. He works four days on, four days off, seven to seven on the days he is on. 'But John is quite happy with me doing what I can, when I can. And I obviously do as much as I can manage.'

After retiring from playing, his highest profile years coming at Huddersfield, where he first met JK after the 'Shuddersfield' merger, Mokko 'kind of stumbled' into coaching. 'My plan was to do just one job and concentrate on family life, but then I was asked to help the scholarship out at Wakefield one night a week, no more than an hour. One thing led to another and I ended up thoroughly enjoying working with the kids, giving something back and what have you.'

Wakefield's head coach by then was John Kear and when he left to join Batley he took Mokko with him. JK's second assistant coach, Linners, isn't here tonight, but Moxon doesn't mind sharing responsibilities; in fact, it works well. 'It's a good dynamic that has come about because of my shifts, but that's how John wants it. If it ever becomes an issue, I'd be happy to step down and let somebody else do the job alone. But I think the lads quite like that they get two different voices, two different sets of drills and so on. It seems to be working. I guess it's always there in the back of your mind that you could progress to being a full-time coach, but I like what I do for a job as well. It gives me security and is the best of both worlds, I guess. Rugby league is fickle. You can be here one day, gone tomorrow.'

In the cycling studio, Dom Brambani is pedalling away just fine, having suffered nothing more than a dead leg after limping off worryingly against Hunslet. Rowey and Paddy are cycling too, edging back to fitness. The latter will soon be off to League 1 side Oxford, with whom Batley are about to strike a dual-registration deal similar to Hunslet's with Leeds, though, as it will turn out, less disruptive or long-lasting. And with the session complete, they head off as one to the swimming pool for a spot of hydrotherapy.

With Tracey out of the picture, the Wednesday-night rubs are done by two second-year sport rehabilitation students, Ally Briggs and James Peck, here through a connection of Carl's at Bradford University. The arrangement is not unusual since it saves semi-professional clubs money and the students themselves gain hands-on experience. Then it's up to Ron's Lounge, where the players receive individual score sheets and 'playbooks' containing advice about injury procedures, nutrition and such. Danny Maun, stung at being compared to a reality TV star, has shaved his beard off. Tinker sends notice he'll be absent.

Looking back to Sunday, JK reports a completion rate of 84 per cent and only ten missed tackles. 'That's the menu. When the conditions are like that, that's how to play and, obviously, they are going to be like that this week.' The playbook is intended to banish excuses. Along with mobile numbers, everything gone through in preseason is written down for reference: wrestle calls, contact, defensive splits, spacing, positioning for kick D, scrums, kick-offs and more besides. 'What we have practised is in here. If you need refreshing or don't understand something, read it. If you need further explanation, Linners, myself or Mokko will go through it with you.' It outlines their attacking structures too. 'We communicate, play quick, look to move and talk to each other when in support. Go forward. Play upstream. Execute well. They are the things, guys. Do those and end up with a very successful season. Yardage sets, a bit about good ball. Study it. If you need to make notes, write in it.'

Carl stresses the need to self-manage injuries and to follow correct protocols. First, rest the injured area. 'If it's a knee or an ankle, you should be seeing me after a game and we can sort you out with crutches, etc. Give you strapping to protect it and make sure you are looking after it while at work. Ice is really important because you need to control the swelling afterwards.' At home on rest nights, if it's a lower limb, the injury should be elevated above the hip ideally; if an upper limb, above the shoulder. Alcohol after injury is to be avoided, 'harder for some than others, but we want to keep as fit as we can'. Normally, Carl will walk around the changing room after a game to check all is okay. He doesn't want them turning up with an injury on a Tuesday that affects planning for the week. If he has recommended an X-ray, the players are to use the hospitals in Halifax, Huddersfield, Pontefract, Dewsbury or Pinderfields, not Leeds. The club can't get to see X-rays from there. When Brad 'Tuna' Day was injured last year, he went to Leeds and was sent to a fracture unit yet didn't have a fracture. 'We lost a week to ten days of training. If we can see the results and aren't sure, one of the consultants we know will be asked to have a look. It's about being professional and speeding the process up, rather than having to rely on the NHS.'

Do not cancel private health insurance, the physio advises; it will pay off at some point, while indicating the recovery schedule on the last page of the book. 'The goal is 100 points. If you go for a swim or do a cycle or a jog afterwards, you've got 100 points. Massage is fifty points. Book a session through our WhatsApp group. Alcohol takes twenty points off, so if you want a drink after a game you need to add twenty points and try to recover in a different way.'

John Heaton, dealing with nutrition, joins in, advising three proper meals a day and maybe a couple of snacks, 'cutting out shit and fizzy pop while you are at work. If you write out a seven-day food diary, I'll go through it with you. If you can't be bothered to write one, then I can't be bothered writing a diet for you to follow.' At this level, the night before a game they should not be on the piss. And he is not talking about overdoing it. 'Everyone drank on Friday; hopefully that won't happen once the season starts. It was a treat. From Thursday, alcohol should be avoided.' Dehydration is massive in sports injuries; that's when soft-tissue tears are most likely. After games, 'take sports drinks, a lot of water and don't go on the ale in here until you've recovered all your fluids and eaten a suitable post-workout meal'.

Breth asks if, in that case, their food might not be better served in Ron's Lounge rather than at the back of the Glen Tomlinson Stand, since that is a two-minute walk away and some players head straight upstairs to their families and pie and peas instead. 'Yes, that would be more convenient,' says JK, rankled. 'But it's really just an excuse, isn't it? You are playing now against four full-time teams. They will be on supplements. They will get information like this, all day, every day of the week. It is a real test of you as part-time players. Professionalism isn't about what you are paid; it's about attitude. About being as good as you can possibly be in your lifestyle, preparation and application to training and game-day. You can be a professional playing for Shaw Cross as much as you can for Cronulla fucking Sharks, believe you me. That's what we are aiming for. To get the absolute maximum out of every bit of our ability.' And then they are off for a short workout in the gym followed by a light run-out on the field with ball in hand.

In the media, JK is circumspect. He tells the press that he expects Batley to have a good season, certainly better than last year, though they'll know better where they stand after Sunday, won't they? No targets have been set. And the media buys it nicely, playing its part by all but writing the Bulldogs off completely. Up against four full-time clubs and what with the wide discrepancy of funding and all, mid-table mediocrity is their best hope. A Championship preview in the *Yorkshire Post* fails to mention Batley at all, positing four Broad Acres teams who might capitalize on Leigh's sudden vulnerability. Bradford Bulls are the main threats to Lancashire dominance, though Sheffield, Halifax and Featherstone are also in with a shout.

On Friday at training, it is clear that JK is entirely comfortable with being ignored like this; in fact, he intends to use it to the team's advantage. As the rest of rugby league bickers about the appointment of an Australian, Wayne Bennett, to the England coach's job, while prodding at the implications of treble champions Leeds losing the first match of the Super League season last night to Warrington, all thoughts at Mount Pleasant are geared towards an upset.

For the first but not last time this year, JK breaks the task down into a manageable narrative, in this case over four matches. The start could not be tougher. Leigh, a team few give them a hope of beating. Then Featherstone away, full-time Sheffield at home and Halifax – who thanks to an impressive middle-eight campaign last year could have afforded to go full-time but haven't – at the Shay. Realistically, all of those will be pushing for the top four. So it would surprise no one if Batley were still chasing their first points of the season in round five. The challenge is there. They must not let that happen.

First up, though, Leigh, and after speaking to the players he hasn't picked, the coach reveals his starting seventeen. An unhappy-looking Breth and Leaky are 18th and 19th men, there in case of late with-drawals. Cowling, Cravo and Rowey must wait at least a week, while Young Iro and Zack will likely join Paddy at Oxford. There is no place for Tinker, again absent, or Alex Brown, who has indeed just been re-signed by the club. His chance, at least, will come.

'This is what we are running with,' says JK tenderly. 'Two areas were difficult. Blakey got the shout over Leaky because he's a bigger kid and covers loose forward. Tuna is in for Breth as he had a great year and earned his start now. I know the lads are disappointed; this is the game we've been working towards since November. But I'll say this. When you get your chance, make it even harder for me, as that will mean we've got a really competitive squad. And support the lads in the shirts. We need to stick together in order to achieve. I could give you the reasoning behind every selection, but if you are picked you don't give a fuck, do you? You just want to get out there and rip in.' Had JK been asked at the first preseason training session who he expected his half-backs to be, he would have said Patch and Dom: 'But this fucker [Cain Southernwood] has trained his bollocks off, so I've had to rejig my thinking. That's what I want everybody to do. Challenge me. Make me uncomfortable, so I've got to select the right seventeen. And then it's up to that team to get out and do it.'

Room darkened, clips are shown of Leigh's Challenge Cup game with Warrington last year, their faults, tactics and flamboyant plays – the Leythers love to run from deep. 'Warrington put a template down for how we can beat them. Look at their defensive line. Are they hang-ing back? Are they letting a good side play? Are they fuck! They are up there questioning their skill. They took their space. They went and got them.' He shares the info that mercurial Rangi Chase will start at full-back, not half-back, and rubs his hands. The weather forecast for tonight and tomorrow is terrible, just as he likes it. Both are factors that can work in the Bulldogs' favour. 'Let's have a look at when they receive a kick. What are they doing? They are shaping up to try and fill the field and shift the ball. So how do we counter it? A full line-chase, guys. We can't have anybody being lazy when we are chasing our kicks.' There must be no gaps. Even if you miss a tackle, by being up there you force an attacker back inside to your defence. 'We need a mad dog hunt.' But there will be attacking opportunities too. 'Keep an eye on this gentleman here. It's that Fui Fui Moi Moi. What do we reckon to that for a retreat? Terrible, isn't it? You've ten yards of space when he's as slow as that, so let's fucking take it.'

Watching the rest of Leigh's middles jog back equally slowly, he tells them this is twenty-five minutes in, 10–4 to Warrington. 'Look at them here and you can tell who is going to break, can't you? They are used to having their own way, being twenty points up and strutting about, nice and relaxed. They don't like it when it's an arm-wrestle.'

When Carl switches the lights on, the film show has lasted under fifteen minutes. Short. Memorable. To the point. He hands out sheets of paper, numbered so that he can tell who, if anyone, has left them in the changing room. 'Before we go to the gym, skip through this. Don't think you've to do something out of the ordinary because you are playing Leigh. Keep it simple and you'll keep it effective.'

Threats: aggressive carries. Be aggressive back in contact. Wrestle. Talk in the tackle. We pin, we reset, we line speed and we don't let the fuckers bully us. Kick-receive and leg plays? Kickers, find the grass. Full line-chase. That will solve that. Yardage shifts? Ruck control, then off the line to take space and do not back off. Put skills under pressure. Dummy-half after a quick play-the-ball? Again, ruck control, tight defence, one-man marker, big guns outside, line comes up. 'If Higham offloads, just fucking tackle him anyway, we'll play twelve on twelve. Fuck 'em. We're not bothered about that.'

Leigh's shapes will be a threat, especially with Chase at full-back. 'How do we handle that? We take space from the inside, we shut the gate, we map out and we stay square. Again, put them under pressure. On line attack, crash balls, how to solve that? We front up. We are physical. We put them to the ground, to slow them. We reset. We space out. We make sure we look after the ball.'

What they must be, defensively, is committed, hard working and urgent. 'Get in their fucking face. Make it uncomfortable for the bastards. And when we've got the ball, go forward; get to the end of sets. Complete. Complete. Don't get bored with it. Carry aggressively. Push. Look to play quick and if Jimmy or Blakey or one of the three-quarters goes, get with him. Flood through so we are ready to play. Okay? Do we know what we are doing? Do we know what to expect? Good, good. Be tough, guys. Be confrontational and don't back down. It's time to ambush these fuckers. Let's get ready to do it.'

First Half – Uphill

The sun was shining and the day was as crisp as a good biscuit.
– *English Journey*, J.B. Priestley

5

1. CORINTHIANS 16:13. *Be on your guard. Stand firm in the faith. Be men of courage. Be strong. Forward. Together. As one* – words pinned above the door in an empty changing room.

Batley Bulldogs begin every season top of the table, by virtue of alphabetical order and a general clean slate. It can only get worse.

On breezeblock walls painted cream with claret wooden rails, laundered shirts hang from pegs, numbers and names visible, strung out around a space some twenty feet square; little piles of boots, shorts, socks and training kit on benches underneath.

Entering, they read, to the left: 7 Brambani; 4 Squires; 22 D Scott; 9 Blake; 17 Chandler. Turn the corner: 19 Bretherton; 2 Reittie and 21 Brown. On the wall opposite: 5, 6, 18 – Ainscough, Southernwood, Lillycrop. Around another corner, tucked in by the showers: 8, 13, 11, 3, 12 – Hirst, Walker, Day, Ulugia, S Scott. And squaring the circle opposite that, beyond a surgical couch piled with towels in front of a dividing wall between showers and toilet block: 15, 20, 14 – Gledhill, Leak, Davey.

It's noon ahead of a 3 p.m. kick-off and all is silent, waiting. Outside this pocket of tranquillity it's another story. Jonny Potts has been in since 7 a.m., he says, 'Sit Down', the James tune, crackling from his boot-room transistor radio. *If I hadn't seen such riches, I could live with being poor.* Outside, down at the Craig Lingard end, Iro and son Toby attend to a malfunctioning electronic scoreboard, next to which sits a shed of standard garden variety. Reeking of creosote and intended to store lawn feed not power points and scoreboard operators, it nevertheless fulfils its function, especially as it is now bolted to a crush barrier, the better to withstand the high winds that did for Linners' sign. Yesterday's deluge has ceased, but the ground is heavy, the day dry and gusty, with periodic bursts of sunshine.

Up in the boardroom, Nellie and Barbara busy about, today's patisserie a lemon drizzle affair. As does Sam Haigh, 79-year-old assistant kit-man, an amiable chap with the hangdog demeanour of a Borscht Belt comic, a regular at the Mount since the age of six. Nellie tells the tale of a winter's day in years gone by when a game looked like being frozen off, only for the referee to declare the pitch playable. So in go a hundred pies and goodness knows how many gallons of mushy peas. Next news, the visiting team bus is pulling away outside. So out Nellie storms. 'Hey!' she yells, standing firm in a Tiananmen Square-like protest. 'You owe us for a hundred lots of pie and peas!'

In his programme notes, Kevin Nicholas writes that he regards the first game of the season as the Million Pound Game: 'Leigh have a million pounds and we haven't.' Unwritten are the words spoken at the shirt launch before Christmas: 'I know we've got a difficult start, but I think we are going to catch these people cold. They are going to come here, these Rangi Chases, these Leigh directors . . . and think that they will run riot over us. Well, they will get a shock these big-time Charlies. Our lads aren't big-time Charlies; they are good players and more, and they are going to do our club proud this year.'

The silence of the home changing room is broken. Beyond the door, a trickle that began with the arrival of the Leigh team bus is now a babbling brook, folk at one end negotiating entry with black-clad doorman Steve, an ex-Batley Variety Club bouncer in charge of comps tickets, and at the other piling out into an awakening stadium or ascending the stairs to the boardroom and Ron's Lounge beyond.

Removed from it all by a width of four centimetres, the players commence to prowl. Under an hour to go, all are at least half-changed.

Some, like prop Brownie, pace back and forth, bare-chested, his short sharp bursts of advice intended to gee himself up as much as anyone. Pack colleague Gleds sits, eyes closed, listening to music, while Dom, Jimmy Davey and Sam Scott withdraw, without aid, into headspace of their own. Scully Scott is one of several Wakefield academy products here, though with a background less ordinary. Studying sports and leisure at Loughborough University when spotted by Sheffield coach Mark Aston, he was raised in a household that watched, played and enjoyed both rugby union and league out near Holmfirth, *Last of the Summer Wine* country. Well spoken, he has an air of educated intelligence and calmness about him, though on the field is as ferocious as anyone. At the Eagles, he featured in a 2012 Grand Final win over Featherstone before moving to York and then being brought here by JK when the Minster city club was relegated. Whatever he is contemplating, it will be in determination. His was one of the better individual seasons last year and he's keen to improve upon it in 2016.

JK and assistants leave them to it, communicating in glances, hearing the talk and gauging the mood. Studs clatter. Aromas are pungent, sharp and, as kick-off approaches, increasingly less pleasant.

The hands on a small plastic clock on the wall reach half past two, and the tension in the room solidifies. Chairman Kev makes a rare appearance in this, the players' domain. In his opinion, giving Leigh a game would be something. 'We need to get the season off to a good start,' he says, faint but detectable irritation rippling over a number of players' blank faces, their muscles twitching, nerves taut. 'But,' he continues, 'I really feel you can win this one.' He really does. And to put his and the other directors' money where their mouths are, there is £100 cash for every man in the nineteen should they prove him right. Irritation is replaced by gratitude and, as the chairman departs, captain Keegan takes centre stage ahead of the on-field warm-up – 'Work for each other – everybody on it.'

Twenty minutes later, with five minutes to go, the door clatters open and they barge back in, the first arrivals throwing training tops aside and pulling on the white shirts in which they will play. It is real now. The abstract actual, the moment at hand, and sweat, adrenaline, blood, power, focus, skill, mental and physical strength, belief – all will be required. Especially belief.

'Good that, boys, shake it out a bit,' their skipper tells them. Batley will be playing uphill, so need plenty of push, plenty of support, 'Right, boys? Everything we do is fucking controlled, yeah? Stay composed, yeah? Listen to the calls and stick with them.' *Yeah! Let's do this, boys.* This is when they stand together: a moment to live for.

At the back, looking on, are JK, Linners, Mokko, John Heaton, kit-man Pottsy and Carl, the most popular man in the room, what with his witch-doctor strappings, smelling salts and other magical potions carted around in an Australian-style portable Esky. Soon, though, silence again falls as each individual is asked to sit and rehearse his own thoughts, to play out inwardly what is expected of him, the feats he will be expected to perform. And then, exactly one minute before the *thump-thump-thump* on the door that heralds a final two-minute warning, JK speaks up, fingers going ten to the dozen but voice calm, steady, confident and measured.

'Right, guys, we've spoke a lot about them and what they are going to do. I am happy we know what to expect. I am also happy that we know what we've got to do. It's a marvellous opportunity this, fellas. It really is. But you've already called it. Bang on. We look after the fucking ball. We turn it over on our terms. We are confident in all that we do. We challenge them with the ball, in the tackle, wherever we chase the fucking thing, whatever the situation.' The tempo rises. 'We are excited about what we can achieve. We are anxious as well, but that will drive you on to better things. The thing we need to be is fucking aggressive; we don't stand down from them fuckers. And we need to work harder than them.' No one is lost in his own world now, all eyes and ears trained on the top dog. 'Let's get out there and put a marker down. Let's show these fuckers how good we are. Let's go!'

The roar is elemental and when the final knock comes, Keegan calls the team into a huddle. Every man is in thrall to the alpha male, the leader of the pack. 'We are all here for each other and we are dogs, ruthless fucking dogs,' he barks, before fists are thrust into the air and clasped, as one, high above the circle: *One . . . two . . . three . . . Bulldogs!* Somehow, the hinges stay attached to the door.

The electronic scoreboard, though, is knackered. So student physio James is periodically sent from the dugout by JK to ask the official timekeeper in the back of the stand how long is left to play. In rugby league, timing is essential. Still, the Doggies are immediately in the muddy battle, their ambition exemplified by Chris Ulugia's bone-jarring smash on Rangi Chase early on, just to say hello, like.

'Shithouses,' spits one spectator. Leigh are cast as pantomime villains – not that the massed 'Leythers' behind the posts or cash-strapped hosts are inclined to worry about that. Villains oil turnstiles.

On his full home debut, linchpin Dom Brambani fluffs a couple of first-half kicks, but he and the team otherwise settle to the task against their celebrated full-time opponents. The hits are fierce and before long Joe Chandler is led from the field, blood pumping from a smashed nose. Carl wraps a bandage around Chandler's face above the upper lip, where it supports the offending protuberance, a make-shift measure to ensure he can return to the fray as and when required. When the opening try comes, though, it is scored by Leigh and has lasting implications for one of the Bulldogs seeking to prevent it.

Second-rower Scully spots a Leigh half-break on the outside. Defending his line, he instinctively sticks out a leg attempting to get close to the ball, but the limb gives way and down he goes, the weight of the attacker upon him. A twist. A loud pop and his season is over, less than twenty minutes in. Prognosis: cruciate ligament injury to the right knee. In shock rather than pain, he tries in vain to crawl out of the scene, a wounded soldier dragging himself clear of no man's land, before being removed in a twin-substitution. Scully and Keegan, nursing a bruised rib, for Brownie and Chandler, the latter's hooter propped up by sticking plaster.

The opening stages have been brutal, with no reward to show for it on what ought to be a scoreboard, until Brownie lifts home spirits by diving through a pile of bodies for Batley's first try of the campaign. Patch Walker's conversion draws the sides level, 6–6.

Toe-to-toe they go, all the work Batley have done on defence during the close season paying off. They repel raid after downhill raid. The performance is far from error-free; there is too much at stake for that. Feelings run high. One too many errors gifts Leigh a second try on the half hour, before Ulugia, who moments before had been limping badly, powers in from centre just before the break, allowing a goal by Dom this time to level the scores, 12–12. Batley deserve to go in level and while the second half will be just as testing as the first, they will at least have the slope in their favour. The home fans bubble with excitement, anxiety too. The visitors noisily philosophical, still certain of victory. A little local difficulty is all.

The Bulldogs stomp into the changing room, the door slamming behind the final man. Uce's late try could not have been better timed. They are up for this. Recharged. 'You could tell, right,' says Brownie, breathless with effort, 'while they warmed up . . . they don't want to be here. They don't want to be getting knocked about by blokes who get paid fuck all. We are dominating the life out of them.' Psyched. Talk. Buzzing on adrenaline and testosterone; gladiatorial. Warriors all. But expending energy they will need out on the field.

'Have a minute, guys,' says JK, with all the calm he can muster. The interlude calls for management of time and resources. 'So let's have a look at what we've done well. It's a lot. But the biggest one is how controlled we are. Twenty sets completed out of twenty-four. If you look after the fucking pill, fellas, you'll trouble anybody. My challenge to you is replicate that downhill. And just because we are downhill, it doesn't mean we do anything any differently, does it? We buy pressure. We buy field position and points will come, believe you me. We've been up there four or five times and scored twice. If it's the same ratio second half, I'll be fucking happy and I think we'll be smiling in here.' Leigh's tries were on the back of penalties, 'so let's be squeaky-clean. Let's be physical, aggressive, hard-working.' One was caused when the right-edge didn't move up quickly enough. 'That's where their centre went through, isn't it? I'm happy, though, because it won't happen again. We'll come up together, take the space and put their skill under pressure. That's what we are going to do all the fucking time.'

As for the slope, when they are down there, he wants them to be happy about it, build a bit of pressure and, on the last tackle 'put a fucking contest up and let's see if we come away with something. If not, just tackle them. Challenge the fuckers to come out of the bog, down in that 20. Then Dave will catch it on the full, or Ainy, and we'll start again. We've to keep that control. We've to keep that work ethic. We've to keep that fucking belief and we've to keep doing what we've done. Are we happy with that? It's in your hands, guys.'

And with the knock on the door, out they go again, chattering, on pins. *No fucking piggy backs!*

Things, though, start badly. On a pitch getting heavier by the minute, Jimmy Davey is forced off with a pulled hamstring. Batley suddenly lack impetus and the tide turns noticeably in Leigh's favour.

Visiting hooker Micky Higham starts to dictate play, the tempo drops and he scores the try that makes it 16–12. The goal is missed, but that is temporary respite surely as a team of full-timers kick on against part-time opponents depleted in numbers – Gleds too now leaving the field injured – and low on energy after an admirable first-half stint. Stand-off Ryan Brierley is next in, diving swallow-like between the posts from a pass from Higham, who steps brilliantly out of dummy-half after a rampaging run from Tongan behemoth Fui Fui Moi Moi, mild of manner, wild of hair, the goal stretching it to 22–12.

Perhaps JK's pre-match words to the media weren't head games after all. 'In all honesty,' he'd told them, 'nobody is expecting Batley to get anywhere near Leigh. It takes the pressure right off, but it will allow us to look at how we compare against a star-studded team with a wealth of talent.' As the game moves into its final phase, the home supporters pray only that there will be no late blowout; a competitive marker needs to be put down for the season to come.

At least one man, though, has other ideas. Dom Brambani, who successfully executes a 40/20 – wherein a kick from one side's forty-metre zone finds touch within twenty metres of their opponents' line, thereby gaining possession at the scrum. And spirits lift further when the field position precedes Ulugia's second try of the game. Patch fluffs the goal, but once again there is only a converted score in it.

Higham has led Leigh brilliantly, but even a man destined to be the Championship Player of the Year needs a breather. While he looks on from the dugout, the spilling of a bomb by full-back Chase is greeted by a roar fit to shower rust from a grandstand roof. Dom kicks ahead and Ainy is only inches away from scoring, before he crosses the line for real with only five minutes to go. The roar that time might be heard, if not in space, then at least in Birstall, and the volume lifts another notch when Patch coolly converts the leveller from the touchline.

Having fought back when they could perhaps have been forgiven for fading, not once but three times, a draw would be just reward, but for Batley the best is still to come. When Chase drops another spiralling kick with only a minute left on the clock, he compounds the crime by pulling at Tom Lillycrop and concedes a penalty in front of the sticks that Walker dispatches with ease. Unbelievably, it is 24–22. Nerves flutter when Dom then fumbles the restart, but the line speed is turned up to eleven and all is well.

The Leigh contingent is stunned; their owner's boasts of an unbeaten season already in tatters. Batley are in ecstasy. Battered and jubilant players milk the glory for all they are worth and why not, when that worth, in purely monetary terms, totals that of Rangi Chase's salary alone – some £150,000 – in a wage bill of £1.3 million.

'Tremendous. No doubt about that.' JK is beaming fit to burst when his squad finally fights its way through to the sanctity of the changing room. 'In the third quarter, we were under the fucking pump, giving penalties away; we couldn't look after the ball. But when we played to what we practised, we fucking cleaned them up, I'll tell you. There have been outstanding efforts. We've been busted, tired, had players playing long minutes, but sometimes you've got to deal with it and you fucking dealt with it. So, well done, guys. It's only two points, but enjoy it and remember, next week we've to get over to fucking Featherstone . . .'

'Yeah! We owe them bastards!' yells Brownie. And with one mighty cheer, led by Keegan, they sing the song.

Doggies . . . Doggies . . . Doggies . . . Doggies . . .

A jungle beat; call and response. The hammering of walls, doors, plastic bins, chests – whatever is closest to hand.

Never is a changing room more alive with camaraderie and brotherhood than when the victory song is sung. And nowhere are conventional ideas of masculinity more orthodox and exposed.

Victory songs are by definition hubristic. Doubtless, they would be judged misogynistic by some and at least a couple of other 'istics' too. Batley's is catchy, has an irresistible rhythm and expresses sentiments you'd hope no one would seriously act upon, bringing to mind a war-dance around a tribal campfire. Prior to the invention of smartphone video, they seldom travelled beyond the triumphant few.

Shirts off, torsos scratched and bloodied, hands clapping, the Bulldogs gather in a circle, their captain pink and sweaty, back like weathered marble, at its heart.

> *Doggies . . . Doggies . . . Doggies . . . Doggies . . .*
> We're Bulldogs, we're bastards, we do it doggy style
> *– We're Bulldogs, we're bastards, we do it doggy style*
> If you see a Batley Bulldog then you'd better run a mile
> *– If you see a Batley Bulldog then you'd better run a mile*
> We're rough; we're nasty; we're powerful and lean
> *– We're rough; we're nasty; we're powerful and lean*
> We come from Mount Pleasant and we're real fucking mean
> *– We come from Mount Pleasant and we're real fucking mean*

We're schmoozers, we're boozers, we've got the Midas touch
– We're schmoozers, we're boozers, we've got the Midas touch
We shag too many women and we drink too fucking much
– We shag too many women and we drink too fucking much
We're skilful, we're classy; we're Yorkshire's premier team
– We're skilful, we're classy; we're Yorkshire's premier team
Believe what you see because we're not a fucking dream
– Believe what you see because we're not a fucking dream
– Woof, woof, woof, woof . . . hooowl!

Previously, in sweet consideration of their friend and leader, the line about shagging had briefly been un-gendered, 'but it didn't sound right,' Keegan concedes. *We shag too many people and we drink too fucking much.* So women it remains, though when the line arrives, Rowey obliges his pal by spraying a couple of bottles of chocolate milkshake over him, a workaround as imaginative as it is outrageous.

The skipper claims not to mind such mischief. He seems as amused by it as anyone, giving as good as he gets, such piss-taking being a sign of acceptance not ignorance, he reasons. Rugby league is a down-to-earth environment he is used to by now, although, truth to tell, he was a late developer on the macho front. Young Keegan was a tubby bookworm who didn't start playing until he was twelve. His mother knew a youth coach who turned up outside their council house one day in a minibus. 'Your mam said you've to come training,' he said. So off Batley's future captain toddled. 'It took me about four games to get dirty. I was shite.'

As he grew, though, the weight dropped off and he began to impose himself. When his first club folded, so enamoured with the sport had he become that he played for Drighlington and Dewsbury Moor, two local amateur sides, before a scholarship at Huddersfield, joining Bradford's academy and ending up at Dewsbury Rams. All of which was quite a turnaround for a kid who hadn't liked sport. 'At fourteen or fifteen years old, I got a bit more athletic. Puberty's a wonderful thing, isn't it? My mam never wanted us hanging about around the estate. She brought us up on her own, didn't want any trouble coming to the door, so tried to keep us in as much as she could.'

With a sister and brother four and six years younger than himself, Keegan was effectively 'man of the house', though one who would rather read or play computer games than ride a bike. But when rugby came along, the thought struck him: some people play games for a living. So when, aged sixteen, Bradford offered him a contract with a promise to put him through college, he 'binned off' his biology, English and history A Levels and gave it a go. 'And they did put us through college, but what they didn't say was that it would be a shitty sports thing that wasn't worth the paper it was written on.'

The Bulls began to struggle, a future he'd set his heart on didn't work out, 'so I kind of fell into the part-time Championship thing'. He made his first-team debut with Dewsbury as a seventeen-year-old in 2007 and then went to Hunslet in the division below, where his first full season in 2008 was almost his last. 'I fell out of love with rugby league. I wasn't sure it was for me, what with having to go to work now too. And then the guy I was working for, Warren Jowitt, got a job coaching Dewsbury and said come and have a go. So I did. I'd been ready for packing in.'

Dewsbury went unbeaten in Championship 1, as it was then known, in 2009. In the next year, they won every match, only the second team in rugby league history to do so, and gained promotion back to the Championship in 2010. Keegan missed only one game, stayed for three years and signed for Batley, his hometown team, in 2012, timing his arrival with that of John Kear. 'It was up the road. I knew a few lads and no one had a bad word to say about it. Everyone spoke highly of Kev and Iro, the club and fans, so I thought, "Yeah, go there."' Also appealing was the club's reputation: namely that, unlike at Dewsbury, the discipline wasn't so stringent. 'At the end of the day, everyone wants to have a beer and a good time, don't they?' Kear was more laid-back, his players encouraged to express themselves. 'I kind of got back to playing how I had as a kid. A lot of stuff I know now technically, I know because of John. My career kicked on; John helped me. The year after that, we got to the Grand Final.'

After such an achievement, the team also got raided. Early in 2014, Keegan went to Featherstone. He reached a Grand Final there too, but, 'it was really cliquey. There were groups of players who didn't want to . . . they were arseholes, to be frank. I hated it. Hated going there, hated the place, hated everything about it.' The coach who signed him, John Bastian, was sacked midway through the year, so in 2015 he came back to Mount Pleasant and its idiosyncratic brand of sanity. 'I'd been on a two-year deal at Fev and took a pay cut to end it. I didn't care. When you've to come here three or four times a week, you need to enjoy yourself otherwise you just play shit. You can't put a price on enjoyment.'

Yet a struggle lay in store. Missing the start of the campaign with an ankle reconstruction, his first serious injury, Keegs came into a team with high targets but which perpetually fell short, leading to a second nerve-wracking climax in as many years, before the relief of that season-ending roast of Hunslet. The craic, though, was back. He likes 'having your mates around you, knowing they'll do whatever they can for you and you'll do whatever it takes for them. But then you can have a laugh.'

Not that the money and competitive element aren't important too. 'Would I play amateur? No. At least here you are getting a wage. You might not get win-or-lose money if you get crocked, but you'll get a bit of something. There's prestige. It's nice to say you play or played professional rugby league. You get players who are laid-back and others who are uptight. Some are competitive about every-thing and some let things go. But out on a training park, if someone goes in a bit harder than maybe they should, watch how quickly it ramps up. No one wants to look a dick. No one wants to be a loser.'

Keegs might be your mate, but he will tell you the truth. If he considers a teammate out of order, they get to know about it. It's a remnant, perhaps, of a firm but loving upbringing wherein his 'old-school' mam, who 'always had the tea on the table, always a proper meal', ensured her kids did as they were told. 'I had the belt when I was younger. Only once, but I'll never forget it. For lying.' His mother instilled the same morals and principles he now tries to instil in his own children, 'though not in the same way, like. She did a good job.' And captaincy, like parenthood, has responsibilities, if you are going to be any good at it anyway. Along with discipline, concentration and having fun, there is a need to inspire people in common cause. Which must surely have been an added pressure when he took the decision to come out. 'Yeah. It was a worry,' he says, elaborating on the paper talk. 'The lads look after you and you look after the lads. I didn't want to put a big elephant in the room. You know, you've to get showered together. You go out on the piss together. There's all that. I've been in situations where if one group of players doesn't like a person, they get segregated quickly. Playground stuff. And if people don't want to get on with you, that can affect how they treat you in a game – will they pass you the ball?'

As soon as he'd had a few beers and told Chandler and Rowey, though, he knew he shouldn't have been worried at all. 'It was just as if one of the lads was in a spot of bother. There are jokes about it; I get ribbed at training and stuff. But when we go out on to the field or are having a drink uptown, if someone from outside the group was to do that, I know without a doubt that every one of them would stand up for me, as we would for someone else with a different problem. They were just gutted I hadn't told them sooner, that I'd carried it around with me on my own. They made it all about me, rather than them being really surprised.'

Had he known he was gay, growing up? 'It's easy to look back now and say "that was attraction rather than admiration", but any lad can look at another and think, "oh, he's good looking" or "he's got a good body" or whatever, can't they? I didn't know for sure until early last year, because I didn't know anybody like me. All the gays were like Elton John or George Michael or whoever, who are ringing me up now. So I was thinking, "I can't be gay. That's gay and I'm not like them." I had no one to relate to. I just thought I might be a bit fruity or that everyone had these thoughts, but just didn't talk about it.'

He pauses, collecting his thoughts. 'I didn't know growing up. Certain things happened.' He met Sara, working in a local pub. They got married four years later in November 2011. They had children. 'I honestly thought I was going to be with her for ever and that was it. And then . . . it wasn't like there was a Eureka moment or epiphany or anything, it was just that my marriage waned and I began to wonder, "Is it because of me?" It was a gradual thing. I could never say, "I'm gay" because that would make it real. I couldn't even think it. "I'm not gay. How can I be?" It was inconceivable. I couldn't be further from a gay stereotype, so I thought, "I can't be gay."'

Keegan says his mind back then was like one of those cartoons, devil on one shoulder, angel the other, arguing about right or wrong. 'I got down about it. There was no one I could talk to whatsoever.' So it drifted and progressed until the marriage ended, 'probably because I was feeling more confident about who I was. We'd been together for eight years and had grown apart. I was nineteen when we met. We separated for a bit after my daughter was born, then got back together. It just petered out, a culmination of things.'

In many ways, his wife is the overlooked party in all of this. The two do their best to stay civil, for their children's sake if nothing else. But occasionally the fracture lines show, with Sara too going public in the papers and on social media. 'Even after realizing Keegan was gay at fifteen, he went on to marry and have two kids,' she shared on social media, after her ex-husband's appearance on *Calendar*. 'While he's now out and proud and rightly so, he's lifted that weight from his shoulders on to his family's and it will take them years as it did him to come to terms with it.' Keegan coming out hadn't just affected him, she was quoted as saying:

Brave, yes for saying 'this is who I am', but brave also are the kids dealing with the comments and the looks, battling with their own feel-ings, and the mum carrying on as best she can for those kids! While I want to support the LGBT community because no one should feel like they have to conform and society's attitudes need to change in order for people not to feel this way, I also think the LGBT community can support EVERYONE affected by someone's sexuality.

After the marriage was officially dissolved for 'unreasonable behaviour' in January, she was again on social media: 'Divorce is through which means I'm legally free to re-marry . . . Erm no I'll pass thanks,' a message illustrated with sad-face and pistol emojis. Later, Sara will object to the 'unreasonable behaviour' thing. Her preferred grounds for divorce were adultery, of which she told the press she continued to suspect Keegan despite his denials, and which the law dictated could only occur between a woman and man. 'The law now accepts same-sex marriage,' read an interview in the *Mirror*. 'Divorce needs to adjust for same-sex affairs. If I'd fought and lost, then fine.' Neither she nor Keegan, she said, wanted unreasonable behaviour. 'It's like saying it's unreasonable to be gay, when what I object to isn't his sexuality. The law is out of sync with 21st century life – I believe he cheated and wanted my chance to say so in court . . . It's about the betrayal, not the gender.'

By then, Sara had appeared on *Calendar* herself, on a campaign to make support for 'straight spouses' more accessible, attempting to remain positive. In September 2015, she had told the *Sunday Mirror*: 'I wanted to rip his head off and kill him.' The couple were recently separated when Keegan walked into the kitchen, 'a pile of washing under his arm', ahead of his confession. She had heard a rumour but laughed it off. Ridiculous idea. As he stood 'umming and aahing', she feared he'd got another woman pregnant. At the truth, both were in tears. 'I was just like "right, it is what it is" and I said to him "we'll get through it. I'll support you".'

Over the hours and days to come, though, hurt it seems turned to anger; then anger became rage. 'I was never angry because he was gay,' Sara told the paper. 'I've got gay friends. I was thinking, "Was it all a lie? Why have you strung me along? Was our marriage a sham? Have you been with a man? Have you cheated on me?" It all just chipped away at me.' Keegan then went public, after he had promised her that he wouldn't, she claimed.

Which is when the rows really began.

Something snapped and the ranting started on the phone. We'd split once years ago after our daughter was born, so I was like 'Why didn't you just leave me then? Why did you come back to me and propose and have another child?' I still loved him and wanted to support him but needed answers.

Once, she said, after he accused her of being schizophrenic, she stormed into his house, shouting, 'This is what you've made me. Are you happy? You've had years to get your head round this. I haven't.' And then she threw his wallet at him, followed by a kitchen utensil pot, something that would hurt. 'But he's so big it bounced off him.'

Her estranged husband, meanwhile, was a 'gay hero' on TV, as seen by his kids: 'Why's Daddy on the telly?' She could have lied, she said, he was a rugby player after all, but no. 'It's not a big dirty secret and I don't want my kids to grow up thinking it is.' She sat the two of them down, along with her eleven-year-old son by an earlier marriage, to explain: 'Mummy and Daddy are getting divorced. Daddy might meet somebody new and it might be a boy or a girl.' As children so often do, they accepted that, matter of fact. And as time went by, helped by their acceptance and resilience, so has she, up to a point.

'I can see now I've got two beautiful kids from our relationship and they will grow up to know I don't regret them and I wouldn't change them for the world.' She had been in 'a dark horrible place' but was coming through the other side. Some seven months on, she told *Calendar*: 'When somebody questions their sexuality, there are quite a lot of charities and helplines. In my situation, nothing or very little.' (A contact address: support@straightpartnersanonymous.com)

As for her now ex-husband, as sympathetic as he is able to be, Keegan is pleased that people, more widely, are no longer 'rambling on' so much about his personal reality. As the news cycle turns, so he hopes it will become a non-issue. 'When I first came out, I didn't think there'd be a big reaction. I mean, I play second-tier rugby league, a northern sport, don't I? But obviously there was. It kind of struck a chord.' He was glad too that the RFL hadn't made a song and dance of it, 'because it doesn't change me as a player. I suppose we'll know how people outside the club will react now the season's started.'

And this week will be something of an acid test: Featherstone, hardly his favourite place at the best of times. What's more, he's back in the papers, a Monday-morning story in the *Mirror* revealing that in his own darkest hours he'd contemplated suicide.

> I had a lot of things going on in my head. Was I gay, wasn't I gay? Was it a phase? There were one or two occasions when I did think about taking my own life. I even got as far as thinking about how I'd do it, where I'd do it. But then you start to think about who'd find you, what effect would it have on your family and friends and things like that. That always kind of brought me back.

He concedes that it can't have been easy for family and friends, most of whom took it well, he says, though his mum struggled for a while. 'I suppose I've had twenty-seven years to get my head around it, but when you tell someone and they're not expecting it, you're kind of dumping it on their feet. I suppose they have to come out with you.'

But anyway, here he is now. The season is underway, off to a flier, rugby league's long and proud idea of itself as a flag-bearer for inclusivity set to be thoroughly tested. This is a sport that gave the home nations their first black representative, George Bennett of Wales, as long ago as 1935. Britain's first professional black team boss, Roy Francis, arrived in the 1950s. And rugby league can also boast the first black man to captain a Great Britain side, Clive Sullivan, in 1972. Ellery Hanley was the first black Great Britain coach in 1994. The first black professional rugby league player signed for Hunslet in 1912. Their colour of skin didn't matter, though it would be wrong to infer that they didn't suffer verbal abuse. Rugby league has traditionally been nothing if not pragmatic; if your talent was such that it brought spectators through the gates, then you were picked, even if that didn't always translate to attitudes on the terraces, pitch and boardroom.

For race, now read sexuality. Again, off the field, wider public support for Keegan and the RFL's reaction were hopeful signs. Such enlightenment had led, in 2010, to recognition as the first governing body to appear in the Stonewall Index, prompting that organization to praise league for leading the way in combating homophobia. In 2012, the RFL won the Stonewall Sports Award. Oldham, Sheffield, Leeds and London Broncos had all staged games dedicated to LGBT inclusion. Manchester now has a gay amateur rugby league club – the Canalsiders, pun intended. But how would it be in the white-hot heat of battle? When temperatures off the field rose with the action on it? Fans can be cruel, immature and one-eyed, no matter what their age. The insult they throw will be the one perceived as most unsettling, especially when their target is a player as dangerous to their team's chances as Keegan Hirst. And in Fev's little patch of West Yorkshire, up the road in neighbouring Castleford, the sport had previous.

Homosexual involvement in rugby league was simply never acknowledged before prop forward Ian Roberts came out in Australia in the mid 1990s, while playing with Manly. To be 'a puff' was to be soft, play posh 'rugger' maybe, where forwards lifted each other in lineouts and backs had pockets in their shorts to keep their hands warm. League was, as the notes on Eddie Waring's 1969 book *The Great Ones* put it: 'a man's game if ever there was one. Gentlemen have played rugby league. Gentlemen still do. But the hard core of rugby league players, with their cauliflower ears, their broken noses, their busted and bruised bones, would far rather be called . . . MEN.'

Roberts had challenged perceptions. A giant of a man with a reputation for needle and a frame of purest Aussie granite, he was no namby-pamby. Only a fool would say otherwise. Upon retirement, he turned to acting, playing Lex Luthor's henchman in *Superman Returns*. A decade later, he would sell a Bourke Street apartment and its wrap-around balcony with sprawling views for 1.41 million Aussie dollars. In the interim, no one had followed in his footsteps although, also in 2016, league did become the first sporting code to have a float in Sydney's LGBT Mardi Gras, banner: 'Gayme On'. Via Twitter, New South Wales Rugby League declared: 'We support and stand by our mates, no matter what their sexual orientation is.'

In the Aussie press meanwhile, State of Origin star, Canterbury-Bankstown favourite and 1985 Grand Final winner Steve Mortimer celebrated the marriage of his son, Matt, to an American doctor, Jason. Matt's three uncles, Peter, Chris and Glenn, also league heroes in the supposedly backward 1970s and '80s, were in attendance. 'For anyone wanting to know what it is like to have been a supposedly tough foot-baller who has a gay son, my answer is simple,' said Mortimer senior. 'I love him. I hope any father who is having trouble accepting their son is gay will read about our relationship and realize you need to allow for your child to be who they really are, and just as importantly to respect them for who they are.'

Still, the fact remained that no player had followed Roberts' lead, referee Matt Cecchin the only other known gay NRL participant to date. And in Britain, until Gareth Thomas signed for Welsh rugby league club Crusaders from Cardiff Blues during their three-year stint in Super League, open homosexuality had been even more rare.

That the former captain of Wales and the British and Irish Lions was gay was old news when he ran out at Castleford in only his second league appearance after switching codes in March 2010. His story – similar to Hirst's in that he had been living a life of denial – was, since December 2009, widely known. The league authorities and no doubt the 35-year-old player himself held their breath. Thus far, the welcome had been positive, if guarded. Many expected him to struggle, but that was more about advancing years and the fact that he'd played a supposedly less physical code than sexuality, or so it was claimed. His debut – in a 14–6 victory over Catalan Dragons at Wrexham's Racecourse Ground – added grist to that mill. Thomas took a clout within a few seconds of kick-off, then a knee to the head some twenty minutes later, and was led staggering from the field after only half an hour. A week later, though, he was back, resilient as ever. But how would fans in traditionally macho northern areas react to this exotic presence? The answer to begin with, alas, was badly.

The chanting and comments came from only pockets of a crowd numbering just over five thousand, but chants there were. In his 2014 autobiography, *Proud*, Thomas called them a manifestation of his worst nightmare. 'This wasn't "banter". It wasn't the ranting of an isolated homophobe,' he wrote. 'It was an abusive chant taken up by a couple of hundred people . . . who stood on the steeply banked terraces and had decided to belittle me and everything I stood for.'

Three months later, the Tigers were fined £40,000 by the RFL, half of it suspended, though not without complaint. 'We totally refute the outcome of the hearing,' said Castleford's then CEO, Richard Wright, 'shocked' at the severity. Legal advisor Rod Findlay said:

The club condemns any person who makes or chants obscene remarks towards players or officials. But the charges . . . are that the club failed to take its best endeavours to prevent or stop [it]. This the club refutes totally. The club has a well-established system for dealing with chanting and could not have done any more on the day.

To which, in his book, Thomas responded:

It didn't happen once, but three times. Castleford officials would later claim two of the chants were drowned out by public address announcements. They weren't – they were replayed on a tape loop in my brain for the rest of the match, and for months afterwards. Even today, I need only close my eyes to recall the braying ignorance of those cowards, who sought refuge in anonymity and sheer weight of numbers. It was a form of mass bullying which made bile rise to my throat.

*

Happily, it did get better for the man known as 'Alfie'. There were no further such incidents and in October 2010 his game had improved to the extent that he became a cross-code international, scoring a try on his debut against Italy in the first of four eventual Welsh rugby league caps. Settled at centre, in June 2011 he extended an eighteen-month contract for a further year, although by October, shortly before he was due to face England in that year's Four Nations tournament, he changed his mind and retired from rugby completely, aside from an ambassadorial role in league's 2013 World Cup. That dark experience in Castleford, though, left an indelible stain.

And in June 2014, Leeds full-back, future Man of Steel and Featherstone academy product Zak Hardaker was fined £300 and given a five-match ban for homophobic abuse, after a TV camera caught him calling referee James Child 'a fucking fag' during a match with Warrington. He later apologized and did 'community service' with the Canalsiders in Manchester, but once again the character of this particular stretch of the M62 corridor was besmirched.

Keegan won't be drawn on it but had his coming out been at Featherstone, well, who knows how the reaction might have differed. At Dewsbury, he suspects, he would have been fine. Batley, though, was the ideal place for the real Keegan Hirst to emerge. 'It's just so tight-knit. It's everyone's favourite second club, is Batley. I mean, they might hate playing against us, but they don't mind coming here, even with the hill. It's a nice atmosphere, good crowd – a nice place to be. There are no airs and graces. Whoever you are, people will take you at face value. You get shit off the lads, even the coaching staff, but it's all between us. A siege mentality, I think. What we say to each other is all right, but we won't accept it from anyone else.'

6

WALKING INTO THE visitors' changing room, physio Carl goes arse over tit on an old and ragged black rubber mat, an indication that all may not go to plan. He is lucky. Calamitous injury is avoided only by a reflex extension of his left hand that slows the descent of his head on to a heavy wooden bench, itself on iron footings. It's a horrifying moment and he still smacks his jaw, along with injuring a leg, hip and ribs, and gashing an elbow. For a moment, he doesn't know where he is, though is soon reminded by relentless mockery.

Shaken and in pain – ice pack strapped to thigh – he takes it all in good part, though is drained of colour. Nor can he run, so Mokko dons the orange bib instead and takes over his on-field duties, such as delivering messages from the bench. Otherwise, he struggles on. A second table is dragged in, upon which he straps ankles, chests and shoulders and carries out the rest of a physiotherapist's pre-match duties until every player feels fit and ready to go.

A shirtless Uce climbs on to the table for a jab in the sternum. *You've got an inverted nipple*, someone helpfully points out. 'Is this gonna hurt?' he asks, having found his voice a little – but only a little – in recent weeks. Paddy Hesketh, with fellow non-players Jimmy, Tuna and Brownz here in support, rubs the centre's shoulders. *Relax.* Ulugia grimaces as the needle goes in but it's over in a split-second. 'That's where the joint is,' says Carl as the area numbs immediately. 'Same stuff as they use at the dentist. Codeine.' In a corner of the shower is a little red bag containing kit-man Pottsy's toiletries and on which is written: *Northern Soul. Keep the Faith.*

Batley's first away match comes at the end of a week in which the Bulldogs were a hot topic, the game abuzz with Leigh's humbling. JK had praised his side's commitment and desire. They used their last available interchange with ten minutes to go but 'hung in there and found a way to win'. In a dominant third quarter, the Centurions had ten sets to Batley's five and three consecutive penalties. Dom's 40/20 was the turning point. 'It lifted us. Even though we were down on numbers, you felt there was only going to be one winner after that.'

The result was translating into success off the field too, with Kev's War Chest having now passed a hundred members. In Ron's Lounge on Tuesday, JK finished preparations for the evening's team meeting, while in the boardroom Mokko studied Sunday's video clips and Leigh's first couple of tries in particular.

There are two basic systems of defence. Slide side to side, trawling the field, or move up quickly as a line and 'jam' your opponent, which is Batley's preference. Get in an attacker's face and he has less time to think, his skill-set pressured. It is disruptive. In the first score, Batley's right centre Shaun Squires hesitated momentarily, so when the ball-carrier reached him he was slightly off balance and the player was able to crash through, wreaking the havoc that ended Scully's season. The footage of the aftermath is chilling. And Leigh's second try was similar. Unused to the system perhaps, Dom mapped out, named the ball-carrier as his and left the two outside attackers to Squiresy and Reitts. Expecting to jam, the former again hesitated and in the end did neither. Winger Reitts went with Dom, and the scorer sailed through the gap. Slowed down and analysed by Mokko, this was crystal clear. Live, it was over in a split-second. 'You will always get mistakes,' the assistant coach said. With perfection, every game would end 0–0. 'But you work on these things until they come naturally.' Practise. Repeat. Practise. Repeat. Practise. Repeat.

JK had already watched the tape three times. After a match, he comes home, pours a glass of stout and views the game again with his wife, Dawn, online. Next morning, he will get up, take out his notepad and dissect the performance, making notes and compiling the clips that best exemplify the points he wishes to get across. To ensure there would be no hangover against Featherstone, rather than tell the lads, as he had done with Leigh, that this lot weren't as good as everyone was saying, he took the opposite tack. Featherstone were a good team who would belt them if they weren't on tip-top form. Individual score sheets were distributed and the leadership group was asked for its view. Chandler reckoned they'd have lost that game last year. Breth noted how the full-timers hadn't looked any bigger or stronger than them. JK wrote their thoughts on the whiteboard and spun it around to reveal his own.

'Positives. Our contact was good, which gave us line speed. Our edge defence, I was really pleased with. Get up and you put people under pressure. Our kicking was exceptional, as was our kick D. With a set completion of twenty-one from twenty-four – that's 94 per cent uphill – you'll compete with anyone. You outsmarted them.

'The negatives. We get too near at marker and it stops us from working. We need to give ourselves a good arm's length so our markers can be more effective. There were soft errors. Dom kicked out; Patch's pass from the scrum; Blakey, you knocked on at dummy-half – they're not forced errors, so we can get better at that. You cut them soft errors out and, fuck me, are we going to take some beating.'

A good review then but, 'I'll tell you, fellas, you can play better. Don't be getting sore patting yourselves on the back, because we need to do it again this weekend, the weekend after and weekend after that. If we are really going to do something this season, you can't do a one-off and then fall in love with yourselves and let your standards drop. It's got to be a one-off, two-off, three-off, four-off. Our standards have got to be high. Would you agree with that?' Yes, they nodded, they would.

Then came the clips. Squiresy admitted he wasn't square on. 'Yeah. You've to square up and whack him. Either say "Fuck it, I'm gonna wallop you" and clean him out, or stay in your system.'

By Thursday, the focus was on Rovers, though comments by Neil Jukes in that day's *Leigh Journal* hadn't gone unnoticed: 'I saw some good semi-pro guys, some plumbers and bricklayers, who did the simple things better than our guys.' A reasonable point, if couched in terms guaranteed to raise hackles. Jukes said that the first clip he'd shown his squad was of after the final hooter when 'it looked like every single person from inside Batley had won the EuroMillions'.

Prior to training, JK and Iro had a lively debate sparked by the latter's assertion that past players were far more skilful than 'you lot', a playful jibe at Tom Lillycrop, also at the table. Cropper laughed but JK was having none of it. 'No one coached defence,' he said. 'You'd get one person coming up to tackle and one hanging back in case he missed. It's far tougher to carve a well-drilled side open nowadays.' Moving the defensive line back to ten metres rather than five – as was the case from the 1960s to the early 1990s [three metres in the fifties and no metres at all prior to that] – had been intended to open up play, but players just got fitter and faster, so it hadn't done so. League had consequently gone from contact sport to collision sport.

Iro thought they ought to be allowed to ship the ball about, express themselves, kick on the first tackle if they like, concepts that left JK incredulous. 'Are you saying Peter Sterling and Garry Schofield weren't more skilful than what we've got today?' Iro asked. JK was, yes. Look at Queensland and Australia half-back Johnathan Thurston, who can do everything they did and under far greater pressure. 'Ah,' said Iro. 'But he's a freak.' He noticed Craig Lingard busying about in the background. 'Isn't it all right to run it from anywhere, Linners?'

'Well, yes, but if you are going to run it off your own line, it's got to be well executed,' said the assistant coach, who otherwise stayed well out of it. Iro pointed to Leigh as an example of how it was still possible to play fast and loose and do well. 'You are all fucking robots,' he chuckled, getting up to head off home, working day done.

Outside, the temperature was just above freezing as Linners put the pads, balls and cones out. Yes, Sunday had been enjoyable but, no, he hadn't yearned to be out there. Doesn't miss playing at all, though that was what he was brought up to do, raised in Sharlston, the only pit village in the world to boast three Lance Todd Trophy winners, the award for man of the match in the Challenge Cup final. His father played with Batley and Dewsbury, his paternal granddad was at Featherstone. As was another relative, Ivor Lingard, his dad's cousin or uncle or something, in Australia now. Linners' own cousin played at Scarborough; the Lingards are a rugby league family. He too followed Fev as a kid and by then, his dad was on the board. 'I remember sitting on his shoulders at Wembley in 1983, when Rovers beat the famous Hull team with all the Kiwis.' After captaining Sheffield's academy, he graduated to the reserves with future stars like Keith Senior and Mark Aston; it was good schooling, the Eagles a pioneering club at the time.

Sheffield, though, when persuaded to offer him a contract of any sort, came up with one that barely covered his travel expenses. He refused it, so they failed to pick him and he spent six months in the amateur game with Sharlston until his dad rang Batley's then coach, David Ward, an old mate at Featherstone, asking if his lad could trial for the sort of reserve or alliance team that doesn't exist any more. He did and thus a romance began, though the blossoming was daunting.

'Back then, they had a first-team changing room and an alliance-team changing room, you'd got that separation. If you got in the first team, you could move your bag in, got a peg, which was a massive, massive thing.' But it must be a spare peg. 'If you went to the toilet, when you came back your bag would be in the middle of the room. It was a bit of an old-school club really, which I liked. It had a real good family feeling, still does. Not many players come here and leave with a sour taste. Players who have left come back and watch. That says a lot.'

It took a man who now has twelve stone steps at the bottom of the ground named after him ten games to score his first try here – the longest drought of his career as it turned out: 'But once I got the first, you get hungry and want a bit more. The best advice I ever had was from Wardy. Going into my second season, he said, "You're only a surprise package once." I didn't know what he was on about but he was right. I couldn't just do the stuff that went okay last year when no one knew who I was, run certain lines or pick certain holes, because people knew now what I was going to do, so the holes weren't there. I had to change my game a little bit, which develops you as a player.'

A prison officer in his day job and a self-confessed 'miserable get', he will, though, talk to anybody, available always for a chat. That's handy when you remain the club's leading try scorer (142) and explains why he is such a popular figure on the Mount still. He recalls conversations as a ten-year-old, asking for autographs or trying to squeeze a word out of the players. 'That was a big factor in enjoying the sport. These people pay your wages, your match fees. So what right have I got to say, "I haven't got time"?'

By 2008, Linners was struggling with injury and form. 'I didn't play as well as I wanted.' The roll call of pain – four shoulder reconstructions, full knee reconstruction, broken thumb (several times), broken ankle, trapped nerve in his neck – is a major clue why. His body wasn't recovering as quickly as it used to. 'I could have carried on, dropped down a division, but always wanted to play at a certain level and not be that person who stayed just a couple of seasons too long for a couple of quid.' Happy with his contribution, he retired, aged thirty, in his testimonial year, a decade after he began.

As for coaching, to begin with he stayed at Batley, helping out, and was meant to take over the reserve team the following year, until it was scrapped at the end of the season. With no position to fill, he left the club completely and, as a new father, took nearly two years out of the game before being offered the head coach's job at Bramley. Then, in 2012, Iro rang. Mark Moxon, Batley's assistant coach, had just got a job as a part-time fireman at Leeds-Bradford airport, situation semi-vacant. The job-share was struck.

Would he fancy the role of full-time coach one day? Yes, he would. 'I've always had aspirations to coach as high as I can. I'm happy here at the minute, learning off JK. Not many people have won the Challenge Cup twice, coached national teams, been in Super League for fifteen-plus years . . .' Linners is thirty-eight now, fairly young in terms of coaching, but aware that he's not a big name as such. 'You've got all these players, Kevin Sinfield and the like, all these that have won things, done things I've not – easy appointments to Championship or even Super League clubs – so I know I've got to make a name for myself.' Whether that's at Batley or elsewhere, who knows?

On the pitch – where training will take place now the campaign is underway – two groups were formed, bibs and no bibs, twenty steaming kettles. Sunday's injuries meant numbers were disrupted already, Patch looking on in an ankle-length coat as they practised offloads. Nothing serious. Just a knock. No point risking him. Brad Day was absent too, with headaches caused by concussion.

As the session progressed, Keegan limped off to Carl's room, where he lay on the treatment couch, an ice pack on his dodgy ankle, having rolled it slightly. A cortisone injection had worn off; he'd have to put up with it. Earlier, he'd been at a Stonewall event, got himself a new agent in Manchester and was mulling an offer to appear on a TV dating show.

JK sensed concentration levels had dropped. Left-to-right passes drifted forward or missed their target completely. Sets went uncompleted. 'We need to maintain high intensity, fellas,' Kear told his squad as they departed for the changing room. 'We can't afford ten-minute spells here and there when minds begin to wander.'

Saturday morning had dawned bright and frosty, though blue skies soon turned leaden with sleet and, higher up, snow that the lorries on Bradford Road had already turned to slush. The sort of day, in fact, when grim is less cliché than reality. Stone piled on stone. Burnt-out speed cameras. Deserted parks. Dreary forecourts and boarded-up mills punctuated by forlorn little patches of scrubland; empty-eyed folk at bus stops, en route to dispiriting destinations. Or perhaps it was just that their bus was late.

Up on the Mount, on this his twenty-eighth birthday, it was Keegan's turn to mind the kids, so they were at training too. His daughter had a doll; his little boy raced around with a Spiderman action figure. 'Is that you, Daddy?' he asked, pointing to a picture on the wall.

'No, I'm in this,' Keegan replied, redirecting his son's gaze to one where he leaps high above a pack of teammates celebrating a try.

They looked out of the boardroom window at the lads doing extras below. 'How can you practise when no one is trying to get you?' his daughter asked, just as Wayne Reittie wandered in.

'Haven't you brought them any sweets?'

'He can lick the window.'

'Haven't you anything for them to do? Any crayons or paper? You can't just tell them to watch Dom goal-kicking, can you?'

The little girl read the lettering on the K2 Stand seats. 'B . . . A . . . T . . .' she read aloud. 'What's it going to spell?' asked her dad and she smiled.

Then Shaun Ainscough arrived with Mrs Ainy and their three kids. Playmates, though the youngest was in a carry seat and wailed until comforted by mum. The place had begun to look and sound like a crèche, though no one minded, least of all coach JK, who wandered by with a grin. Part-time players, family obligations – at Batley this was just how it is. Carl said he'd find something for them to watch on his laptop; the Disney Channel they hoped, not clips of grisly injuries.

The trade papers lay open. 'Who writes this report?' asked Ainy. 'He hates me. I can have my best game ever and he still gives me five,' though in 'Wiganese' the rating is pronounced 'farve'.

'They used to hate me,' said Keegan, 'but they can't now. It doesn't matter how I play, I get eight.'

Extras done, the rest of the squad piled up the stairs and it was in to Ron's Lounge for the tip sheets and JK's clips of Featherstone's game with Bradford last week.

Rovers' challenge would be stiff. Impressive in defeat and top-four favourites themselves, like Hunslet they had now partnered with Super League champions Leeds. The Rhinos' top twenty-five players would be dual-registered at the Big Fellas stadium and three were in the squad.

The opponents were assessed, individually and as a team. Samoan hard-man Misi Taulapapa: 'Loves carrying the ball. Annoy him. Piss him off by getting him on his back. He's a handful, but if you get into his ribs, he can drop the ball and work for us.' Centre Michael Channing, whom Batley had hoped to sign until he was tempted by an extra £20,000: 'Good player, the kid, wicked late left-foot step.' Anthony Thackeray: 'Real good half-back, very quick. Keep him quiet and we win. Get up, namedrop, but tag his runners. Inside tackle, tag runner. Outside tackle, lead runners. Broken field, takes advantage. It's red-alert time when he's got the ball and he's a fucker for a steal.'

The door opened and Keegan's lad poked his head in. 'I need the toilet, Daddy.' So out his dad went, while JK pressed on. Family club. 'Defence is an attitude of mind. Last week we were brilliant but you're playing the team ranked five on their own midden now. We are underdogs again but we love that. You've set that standard.'

As the team bus pulled into Big Fellas stadium, formerly Post Office Road, in what you hoped for the locals' sake is the tatty end of town, chairman Kevin Nicholas was in paroxysms of mirth.

Batley to Featherstone isn't a long journey – a short stretch up Soothill Lane (not a speck of soot in sight these days) and a handful of miles further along the M62. Time enough to tell the story of an aged pensioner and bully fifty years younger. 'Next time I get chance, I'm gonna have him,' the eighty-year-old had warned, before the irritant in question, a plague on the community, one day blocked his drive. 'If you don't move your car, I'm going to drop you,' he told the pest and then proceeded to drop him anyway. With the thirty-year-old decked, a few more jabs went in for good measure, until he pleaded: 'Stop, stop, I've had enough.'

'I'll tell you when you've had e-fucking-nough,' replied the indomitable OAP, who belted him again.

And then Kev remembered a joke. 'There's this bloke, right. His numbers come up on the lottery and he goes to a fancy car show-room to buy himself a brand-new top-of-the-range Jag. So, he says to the salesman, "I'd like one of them, please," and the salesman says, "Have you ever driven a Jag before?" The bloke says, "No, I've never actually driven a car before. I've never passed my test. I can't drive." So the salesman says, "Well, look, you don't want to be buying one of these then. Go get yourself a motorbike, to get a bit of road sense like." So off the bloke toddles and . . . *pschwaugh . . . knarfff . . . wheeze* . . . tries to buy a beautiful souped-up motorbike. But the . . . *wheeze* . . . salesman . . . *wheeze* . . . in the bike showroom asks him the . . . *cough . . . choke* . . . exact same question: "Have you ever driven one of these before?" "No," says the bloke, "I've never driven a motor-bike." "Well, you don't want to be riding one of these," says the . . . *cackle* . . . salesman. "You'll kill yourself on it, they're very powerful. Get yourself a . . . *gasp* . . . pushbike instead." [Kev takes a second to calm himself.] So off the bloke goes to the bike shop . . . *pschwaugh . . . knarfff* . . . and asks for one of them top racing jobs you see in the Tour de France. "I'd like one of them please," he says. Salesman says . . . *choke . . . wheeze . . . fnaskekker* . . . "Have you ever ridden a pushbike before?" And the bloke says, "No, I haven't actually," and the salesman says, "Well, here, why don't you have a go with this instead" and hands him a hoop and a stick.'

The coach parked up and the players moved down the bus, passing their chairman in what looked like the midst of an asthmatic attack. *What's up, Kev?* 'He's telling a joke.' *Oh, right.*

"'A hoop and a stick? How much?" says the bloke . . . *hsssk . . . hsssk . . . hsssk* . . . "Only a quid," says the shopkeeper, so he takes one, like. That night . . . *wheeze* . . . he's out on the piss and messing about with it in the street when a police car pulls up by the roadside. "Have you been drinking?" the officer asks him and when he says that, yes, he has, they give him a warning and confiscate the hoop and a stick. "You . . . can't . . . do . . . that," says the bloke . . . *pschwaugh . . . knarfff . . . howl . . . hsssk* . . . "How am I gonna get home?"'

*

In the changing-room huddle, Keegan doesn't go so far as to accuse Rovers of attempting to murder Batley's physio but he does bring up one or two other insults. 'They only give us nineteen tickets,' he growls, 'stick us in the academy dressing room, warming up on a cabbage patch. Let's stick it to 'em.' *One . . . two . . . three . . . Bulldogs!* And out they go, around a corner and down a pathway on to the field of play.

Though the slope here isn't quite as pronounced as that at Mount Pleasant, there still is one and the Bulldogs kick off up it. It is a matter of seconds before someone in the stand yells, *C'mon, ref, open your eyes!* Happily, that is as strong as the off-field abuse gets at a ground that, with the help of volunteers, has scrubbed up nicely. In the black and white days of BBC2's Tuesday night *Floodlit Trophy* – second half broadcast only – the television picture wasn't the only thing in perpetual monochrome; grounds like Post Office Road were synonymous with an image of rugby league as dour and downbeat, never entirely fair, though you can see how it arose. These days the Big Fellas (a sponsorship thing) is considerably tidier though still pleasingly down home, as attested by the row of dormer-windowed houses overlooking the bottom terrace, in which it is easy to imagine wirelesses tuned to *Two-Way Family Favourites* and *Waggoners Walk.*

Batley's increasingly impressive and confident full-back Dave Scott opens the scoring, on the end of a pairs shape practised again and again in training. Patch adds the goal: 6–0. Along with clockwork willingness to take the ball up, Stirling-born Scotty seldom spills a high kick and has an impressive cover-tackling technique to boot. In terms of ability, the Bulldogs have found a gem. The 22-year-old won the Dave Valentine Award for Scotland's player of the year in 2015, the first home-grown Scot ever to do so. The only factor against him is his size; potential was there from the start. He grew up with rugby union, which he played in Glasgow. It was there where a scout from Hull KR spotted him trialling with Scotland Rugby League. Subsequently, he spent a year in the Rovers' academy, then played in the reserves. 'I was told I would get a full-time contract, a first-team squad number and towards the back end of the following season have a little shot at Super League. But then the reserves were scrapped, so that was that.'

He managed to get a gig at Featherstone, played on this very pitch for a season with the reserves, made a couple of first-team appearances, then went on loan to Doncaster after Fev scrapped their reserves too. He'd been there a couple of seasons before coming to Batley. With thirteen full international caps and a memorable campaign with the Bravehearts in the 2013 World Cup behind him, he has already made his mark on a game he immersed himself in on Humberside. Yet as with everyone else at the Bulldogs, he feels he has more to achieve.

'I just love how quick and physically demanding it is,' he'd said earlier. 'It sounds like a strange thing to say but I love it when you are really *really* blowing out your arse but still willing to work. You don't really get that in union. The physicality as well, the level required to play the game. I absolutely love it.' Not that his arrival had been entirely straightforward. 'I sent my CV and clips to John and got hold of his phone number to follow it up: "Have you managed to have a look, what did you think?" He said, "I've not received it. Did you send it to my home address or the stadium?" I told him the stadium. "Well, here's my home address, get that DVD to me as quickly as possible. We'll see if we can sort something out." Other clubs were interested but as soon as JK texted me – I was in Manchester at the time – I went straight home, got the disk and drove to his house: "There you go."'

At the start, he'd met with the sort of resistance any lad from a non-traditional rugby league area might. 'They kind of test you, look at you with suspicion – what's he doing here? We've got other players, local ones, why are they not playing? I just got on with it. I knew that was going on, but I was there for myself and determined to be the best I can. I was going to stick it out.' If his form continues in this vein, it is already difficult to see James Craven dislodging him.

Towards the end of the first quarter, though, Featherstone draw level. Leeds man Ash Handley climbs high over Ainy – a verbal piñata for the crowd on his first visit here since you know when – for a try that is followed soon after by one from a threat they were warned about, Taulapapa, both converted. 'Sit down, Keegan. We can't see,' one wag shouts, as the rotated skipper stands on the touchline. And on the half hour, injury strikes again when Squiresy goes down with a twisted leg in a tackle and is stretchered from the field after a lengthy delay.

'The talk's good, fellas,' says JK as they gather in the changing room at the break, having almost tripped over two blokes who had been removing some of the matting, though not the particular bit over which Carl had tumbled, before fleeing the scene. 'What you are saying is right, it really is. We need to look after the ball. There's a wind coming down that hill, so if it's been tough for us, what do we do? Make it tough for them. Exactly right. Keep the fuckers down there, keep the chase up and restrict their yardage. They are shitting themselves, believe you me, they really are. If we get good ball down there, we'll come away with points.' Coach Kear is confident, real confident. 'Just stay with the processes, are we happy with that? Let's get juiced up and have another fucking dig at them, okay?'

Batley, having been warned by JK to be 'squeaky-clean', gift two more penalties in as many opening minutes, the second kicked to put Rovers 14–6 ahead. The key moment, though, comes late in the third quarter. Now trailing 7–2 in the penalty count, a high tackle in front of the posts gives Batley a golden chance to reduce the deficit to one converted try. Their coaches signal to kick but the players opt to run it. 'That's all right,' says JK in the dugout. 'Let them back themselves.' It looks the right call, too, as Leaky burrows through a pile of bodies. But after shaping to award the try and then jogging to a touch judge forty metres away, the referee returns to the spot and disallows it.

On the hour, second-rower Gleds – a convert perhaps to Iro's play-what-you-see philosophy – kicks the ball in-goal, where Reitts touches down, Patch converting from the touchline: 14–12. But in a thrilling last twenty minutes of bone upon bone and flesh upon flesh, every collision that of two heavyweight human missiles from which it's a miracle anyone emerges unscathed, the scoreline will not change. This just isn't Batley's day.

The players are exhausted, having given their all. Disappointed too. JK, though, is far from downhearted. 'The challenge was, guys, to maintain fucking standards, and you've done that. Really committed as individuals, committed as a group. We could have tidied things up better. We'll look at that on Tuesday and regroup for Sheffield. But if we keep playing like that, we'll end up in a really good position. They were shit scared, them, and had every fucking rub of the green. So feel good about yourselves and get ready for next week. Well done.'

Last year, says Keegan, they'd have been happy with a two-point loss like that. Yet this season they are gutted. 'Let's keep that.'

Outside, as most players climb a staircase to the supporters' club for their after-match meal, Shaun Squires cuts a mournful figure at the bottom of it. On crutches, he bemoans not only the pain of the injury just suffered but that he has 'a big day planned tomorrow'.

As the owner and director of a gas and central-heating company, he has four lads on the payroll. His firm has a lot of work on and is getting behind. Struggling into his parents' car – he's not waiting for the bus – he says he will have to go in anyway.

On Tuesday, Squiresy was in a knee brace, the diagnosis a Grade 2 MCL injury. Normally, that means four to six weeks out, but it could have been far worse. JK had been sounding clubs out re loan signings.

Come Friday, the dual-registration deal would be announced with League 1 club Oxford, whose coach, Tim Rumford, Kear taught at school, Iro calling the partnership 'exciting' in the press. Oxford have 'a great plan to develop rugby league away from the M62 corridor and being part of their development can only be good for the game'. After their efforts at Featherstone, the coach promised to look after his players and he was again as good as his word – a team meeting, then off to Total Fitness.

Beforehand, it was Cropper who this time had a one-on-one with Mokko. Every player receives individual clips of their performance, to help them study and improve. Although attending these assessments is voluntary, it is there where the attention to detail lies. How they hit the floor in a tackle. At what speed they snap – or fail to snap – to the knees. Leg position. Running angles. In certain situations, such as a four-man tackle, struggling is futile. Go directly to ground on your own terms, as that makes for a quicker play-the-ball.

Brad Day wouldn't play at the weekend; on a mandatory lay-off. This wasn't his first concussion. He had one last year but hadn't kept his insurance up and, as he'd already had a head knock, the insurers wouldn't pay out this time either. He would have to see a neurologist and that would cost the club around £1,000, a price they are willing to pay, as they want him back on the field. Contact was off-limits but he could still throw the weights around – just as well since he looks like he lives in the gym. He felt a lot better if a bit sick now and then in anticipation of seeing the specialist next week.

In the team meeting, Keegan reckoned that in the last twenty minutes everyone panicked. JK agreed that, after a good start, the standards dropped: 'I'll take some responsibility for that, as we changed our tactics and it didn't work as well. When teams throw numbers in, you need to push, go a bit wider perhaps and make sure there's a bit of shift prior to the tackle. Our shape was fractured.'

A discussion began regarding the wisdom of running that penalty. 'We [the coaching staff] felt it was worth taking two points; you chose to run it. This is about composure. If we'd have taken the two, we had it in us to score one try and then, if it's even-steven, we can try a drop-goal or whatever.' Yes, interjected Blakey, but they'd had them on the back foot. At that moment, they were fucked.

'At the start of the second half, they got penalty, penalty and then took two,' JK pointed out. Looking at the scoreboard, Fev's decision to take two and Batley's not to was the difference. 'It's something, guys, just to think about, because it's easier to chase within one score than two. And . . . well . . . our lass could have kicked that goal. I could understand it if it were thirty-five metres out towards the sideline. Kick it in the corner and keep 'em going. But it's like being a golfer. If it's a gimme, a six-inch putt, just fucking take it and get on with it.'

Patch agreed that they should always come away with points when down that end.

Generally, though, it had been an encouraging performance. 'It's a great learning experience this one for us in many ways. The first lesson is we can't let our standards drop even by that much. Second, we've got to keep working for us mates; we don't send them up in ones. The third is mine; I changed the fucking yardage distance and it was wrong. We'd have been better staying tight, so we'll revert to that against Sheffield. Take the fucking points and let's show that element of composure and belief when we are executing skills.'

Sheffield at home was a chance to take another step forward. 'These first four games are great, I'll tell you. We've done ourselves great credit after rounds one and two. We can do ourselves a hell of a lot more credit in rounds three and four. I've watched the Halifax v Sheffield game. Mokko's watched it. We've got the beating of both. But we've got to bring our A-game, one to seventeen. We can turn them over, believe you me. I'll show you how in the week to come.'

On Thursday, they began that work on the field. Come Saturday morning, after watching clips of their next full-time opponents' last match with Workington, the starting seventeen put the final touches to specific plays. Not only was this a chance to get back on the victory trail, many already writing the Leigh result off as a flash in the pan, but for a variety of reasons any game with the Eagles felt personal.

'Sheffield prefer broken field, a loose game,' JK told them, as through the window Batley Boys Under-13s trooped up Heritage Road on their way to the first friendly of the season. Normanton were the visitors, the pitch the usual one down Victoria Avenue, a piece of open ground overlooked by a row of terrace houses and the Madressa-E-Zinatul Islam mosque. 'They hunt like a pack of hyenas, separating prey from the herd. As soon as the defence is a man down, they flood through.'

After the clips, JK gave out his tip sheets, intended to sum up the game plan. 'Aggressive, good talk in the tackle, quick reset, line speed. High energy. Kick receives, find the grass, they'll take you on, they like the collision. They'll try and trap you. Scoots from dummy-half – keep them on your outside. "A" defenders get tight, get off your line. Even if they offload, take them to ground. The more they go to ground, the more pissed off they'll get. Left-side attack, you are going to have to be tough. Front up. Midfield kicking. Knowles loves that short-side kick. Reitts has got to come up, so, Dave, you move further across and, Ainy, you've got to sweep around the back. Let your centre know you're going. Let's be committed. Let's be tough. Let's be hard working and let's get into their fucking space. Yardage, we are gonna wrap to "C", complete, carry aggressively. We are going to push and we are going to play quick, so we can get the kicks away. Good ball. We practised it on Thursday; we will practise it again this morning. We are going to pepper their right side, but we'll get some joy as well hitting short leads. We can go again and get at their right side on the back of that. We'll have a set, them fuckers will have a set, and it'll just be low risk. Let's have that attitude. Remember, fellas, this is our house. We've already beaten the best team here. There's no reason why we can't turn every team over on our own ground. They don't take anything from our fucking house. We get amongst it.'

On the field, training over, some players went off for breakfast and some hung around a while, passing the ball back and forth and kicking goals. Among them, in pink bobble hat, pink trainers and pink earmuffs, was Reitts's wife, Kelly, who kicked a goal herself. 'Fancied a go,' she said. 'It looks easy, doesn't it? You wonder why they miss.'

7

DOM BRAMBANI'S PREPARATION never wavers. The night before a game, the self-employed thirty-year-old gas fitter from Bradford tries to relax. Other than drinking plenty of water and eating the right things – 'no crappy food' – he tries not to think about the coming game at all. He will stay in, watch Saturday-night TV – 'usual rubbish' – and chill out in the front room, playing with the little 'un.

Past experience has taught Dom that mulling a game over too much is unhelpful. And that would especially be the case with this one. Like Patch and Jimmy, he could have still been at Sheffield and for him, personally, last year was frustrating. Coach Mark Aston's son, Corey, often got the nod on the team-sheet. True, the supporters in South Yorkshire loved him, but to pack in his one-man business and go full-time at the back end of his career would have been crazy.

He does, though, love his rugby league. And has done from the start. It's all he has known since shivering on the windswept heights in Queensbury's Under-8s, having been introduced to the game by his dad. He was an amateur at Wibsey, not much lower in altitude, and came through the academy ranks at Odsal, where his hometown club plays. His first professional contract was signed with Castleford, whom he joined in 2004, aged eighteen. He had three years there as a full-timer before going to Halifax and has been part-time ever since.

If he can, he will blank the match out totally until he arrives at the club, at which point everything changes, including himself, often before anyone else. Up at 9 a.m., after breakfast he will again try to chill, though he might do a bit of stretching maybe, or a bit of foam rolling, to keep the nerves that are seldom far away under control.

With no game to consider, a smile is seldom off his face. But short and stocky with light-brown hair, right arm almost entirely covered in tattoos and with the physique of a man who spends hours in the gym, he takes his duties as a rugby league player seriously.

Once at the ground, he will go out to check the pitch. Have a chat with the lads. If, as today, he has mates on the other side, he'll share a word or two with them. But once in the changing room, the real routine kicks in. He will apply a bit of strapping, stretch a little more, get ready to go out and find his kicking range, rehearse the game plan in his head. He will ask how his teammates are feeling and talk about what he and they are going to do, where on the field they will get to, how they are going to break their opponents down.

His studs first touch turf at least half an hour before kick-off, maybe sooner, a regime he began as a junior. He practises kicking two or three times a week in his own time, perhaps more as it gets lighter. It's a groove he has been in since the age of ten, when he'd go up to Wibsey Park or to the pitch next to where the municipal school swimming pool used to be and boot a rugby ball around for hours.

The captaincy is Keegan's, but given that Dom is a scrum-half – effectively a rugby league quarterback – he has enormous influence too. He gets around the team, forwards, backs and especially Batley's right-side defence, *his* side of defence, checking how they'll combine, which individuals they need to watch, reheating tactics ahead of the warm-up. One such is Danny Cowling, antsy about his seasonal debut.

For Dom, trying not to think about this game was harder; every player hopes to impress against a former club, don't they? He doesn't so much have butterflies as pterodactyls. Jimmy is out injured, but he and Patch talked it through. The Eagles know Dom's kicking game is his strong point, so he expects a lot of kick pressure. Patch agreed to act as a bit of a get-out valve if necessary, and vice versa. If Sheffield defenders do rush up, both now know that the other will be there.

Either way, he is in the firing line. As a half-back, if the coach wants you to get set plays on and they aren't happening, then it's you who gets the rocket, because it is you who is in charge.

In the changing room, anxiety intensifies in the build-up. Focusing on the job in hand, though, he tries hard not to show it, aware that once that first ball is passed or kicked, nerves evaporate like spit on a heated stove. It's a day full of weather, all the seasons at once, though the north of England has avoided the snowfall that has plagued Scotland. Occasional sunshine has given way to an overcast afternoon. A cruel wind tears down the wet and muddy ground, dumping heavy, vicious rain showers as it sweeps through.

Dom runs out of the tunnel and on to the pitch, receiving a slap of the hand from Jimmy Davey, passing seats that are red towards the back of the K2 Stand, cerise at the front, bleached by sunshine or more likely washed out by rain. Keegan won the toss and decided to play into a driving gale. As Dom and teammates await the signal for kick-off, Kear's resounding pre-match team talk still clatters in their ears. A former Sheffield coach, this match very much matters to him too.

'They are expecting a tough forward battle, which we'll give them, and we've got to expect the same. You've chosen to go uphill and I'm happy with that because it shows your faith in how you can defend. And that will win us the game. We've got to work our fucking rocks off, especially on our line. When we've got the ball, play it direct, short passes, in-locked to fucking leads; no need to go long, long, long around the back. Play through the fuckers. In yardage, complete, wrap, wrap, wrap. When it's weather like this, you can get some shitty tries by the ball holding up in the wind. Chase everything because there are no lost causes when they kick to us or we kick to them. Are we fucking ready?' *Yes!* Never more so.

And then Keegan in the huddle: 'We go together, work hard, pagger these cunts, yeah? Stick to the fucking processes and work hard. That's all we do – get to half-time and we'll go again, eh? Bulldogs on three!' *One ... two ... three ... Bulldogs!*

The kick-off is Sheffield's and it is a high and spiralling one that

Reitts drops to give Sheffield an immediate scrum in Batley's danger zone. Somehow, though, they hold on and scramble again on the back of conceding a pair of penalties in succession. A third proves one too many as Cowling, keen to impress, pulls off an impressive tackle but hangs on too long. Moments later, Menzie Yere, a Papua New Guinean cannonball in human form, is in at the corner.

Patch Walker's restart, though, finds touch, giving Batley an uphill scrum in Eagles territory, and energy floods back. So much so that near the end of the first quarter Batley nose ahead. The move is off the cuff. Cult hero James Brown takes the ball up and at first Dom pushes on his outside. But then, noting the Eagles' defence is a little lazy on the inside, the scrum-half spots the gap and instinctively cuts under the prop's run before taking Brownie's lovely flicked pass to score. A fairy-tale start to what, for him, will be a fairy-tale game.

Minutes later, Dom puts in a mammoth relieving kick that, had he been a few more feet downfield, would have resulted in a 40/20. And even when Sheffield take an 8–6 lead on the half hour, after a bare-backed Brambani – torn shirt flapping in the wind like a close-hauled Viking sail – knocks on, there is no doubting the better team. Jersey changed, he drives the Doggies to the break as Reitts twice goes close and Cropper – who, as ordered by his mother, is now clean-shaven and no longer looks like he might be about to open a hipster cereal café in Drighlington – is held up over the line. Each opportunity owes much to Dom's awareness.

Play like this downhill and we've a real chance, says a voice in the K2 Stand, while others bemoan the performance of the referee: *He wants to swallow that chuffin' whistle.* Dom knows the ref is one of those things. A force of nature, like wind and rain. Get together as a team and tell each other you can't give him any reason to pull you. *Be squeaky-clean.* Keegan, though, goes one better and has a little word in the official's ear as they leave the field at half-time.

'C'mon!' Brownie shouts, barging into the changing room. 'Fucking great effort there.' Everyone speaks at once, a point to get across. JK prowls in the background, listening to his muddied troops. Keegan, having had a word, reckons the ref will even the penalties up now. 'Camp down that hill,' says Brownie. 'Mad-dog defence!'

After his early error, Cowling – as with Chandler, his surname passing as a nickname – has settled into a fine game. Face red as a berry, *Boy's Own* comic-book features aglow, he has tactical advice of his own, though no one is listening. 'One voice, boys, one voice,' says Reitts, but there's little chance of that. Dom looks down at the floor, his expression intense, very much still in the zone.

'There is a buzz, guys, and you are excited . . . you *should* be excited,' says JK as all fall silent. 'But the hill does not win us the game. *The hill does not win us the fucking game.* It won't post the points. It won't bring us home. What will bring us home is this, you fuckers working equally as hard. You've got these in contact, I'll tell you. We've got 'em when we are carrying. We've got 'em when we are fucking banging 'em. So be absolutely relentless with your contact. Bend your backs; sit 'em on the arse. Maintain that domination. Let's play it quick as well, guys. When we play it quick, they cannot fucking cope. It doesn't matter if we score the winning points on forty-one minutes or seventy-nine minutes. Know how to build pressure, don't we? We put the thing down there. We challenge them to come out. Mad-dog sets. Hunt. No time or space to kick or anything. This referee won't keep doing us; he's ruined by the crowd. Keegan was really intelligent having a word, so let's get off the line and jam them. We'll get some penalties as well. Stay composed and the game is ours.'

'Mentally and physically, we are tougher,' says Brownie. 'These don't like it. They are looking for ways of getting out of it.' Keegan is mindful of last week. Do not panic. Blakey warns to start this half with intensity, which is exactly what Batley – and Dom – do, sticking to the script. The call was to keep the ball on the ground to Sheffield's back three, not in the air, and the scrum-half threads a kick through the line, always a tough test when an attacking side is chasing hard in such conditions. Under pressure from Cowling, who puts a huge shot on, the ball is spilled, his hard work and push giving Dom the chance to touch down again. Not only that, with Patch off the field, he knocks over a 499th career goal to give Batley a lead they never lose.

And when it comes to goals, there is another long-standing routine to follow. Dom has always been taught that if you swing and kick exactly the same way every time, then you can't go far wrong. He places the ball down, takes the required amount of steps back, the exact amount of steps to the left and then, when boot leather meets ball leather, keeps his head down as long as possible while following through, only lifting his head at the very last moment. There was the wind to consider too. It's an important kick at a pivotal time.

As the half progresses and he continues to boss his new side around, it's clear Brambani – and Patch – have settled in. At first, you have to get your feelers out, learn what everyone's about. But, ultimately, you gain respect through the way you play. And Dom is now comfortable directing everyone around. Respect has been won.

When, on the hour, hooker Leaky goes in for a try the visitors would doubtless call soft – the 5 ft 7 in. Cumbrian tucking the ball in an elbow before being helpfully pulled over the line by a mob of defenders, Patch converting – it is 18–8. Sheffield are visibly sickened by the non-stop ferocity of their opponents in a climatic uphill endurance test fit to blanch a polar bear on a North Sea trawler. There is no such lack of fibre from Batley, however, for whom Joe Chandler, for the third week in succession, jogs back to the bench with blood streaming from his nose.

The final quarter passes without points after Patch's long-range penalty makes it 20–8 on the hour, although there are a few nervous minutes late on when Blakey is sinbinned for throwing the ball away. But Batley hold on and conditioner John Heaton's beaming face tells its own story. Who were the full-time team again?

Back in the sanctuary, Dom tears off his strapping and removes his boots and shirt in silent satisfaction. Two tries and the sort of all-round organizational display any coach worth his salt would value. What's more, he realizes now that this is one of the best packs he has ever played behind, which will surely make it so much easier to plan and launch attacks. The decision to come to Batley was clearly the right one.

'Okay, guys,' says JK. 'Let's sit down for a minute. Real good that. You were controlled. You were smart. You were tough. We've done two full-time teams. In Tuesday's team meeting, I said I'd watched Halifax versus Sheffield and we could not only beat one, we could beat them fucking both. Well, that's the challenge now.' Shirts removed and cast aside, torsos glisten with blood, saliva and sweat. The captain calls his tribe, and the doors and walls are thumped as Heaton drums the familiar beat on an upturned plastic bin.

Doggies . . . Doggies . . . Doggies . . . Doggies . . .

Along the corridor, the visitors' door swings open on a different scene. As song bounces off concrete, the Eagles, shattered physically and mentally, sit, shoulders slumped in gloom. Socks, boots, bandages and other debris lie in a heap, fuel for a fire extinguished. Not that Dom Brambani sees or cares much about any of that. Through the wall, he hollers as loudly and as lustily as anyone. At Mount Pleasant, he is once again enjoying his rugby.

A week later, Batley's 'Battle Bus' pulls into the Shay, home of Halifax RLFC, the last of a quartet of top-four favourites the Bulldogs have faced in as many weeks.

Once again, it hasn't been far to travel – the club won't cross the Yorkshire border until April. Nor is it anything like the fabled 'coma bus' of the 1990s, from which passengers are said to have been carried unconscious. A director once hitched a ride to Workington, giving some miscreant the opportunity to stuff an embarrassing pair of knickers in his pocket. The Battle Bus is a statelier affair unrelated to those organized by the Woodman pub and, before it began to struggle for numbers, the official Supporters' Club. A new initiative, it has been laid on by the Bulldogs, though is nothing like as spacious as that which the players and modern-day directors travel upon.

The original Batley Supporters' Club held its first meeting in November 1928, a reported £138 raised in the year since its launch at the Commercial Inn, Wellington Street, a sum of £100 then passed on to the rugby club. And it was through this organization that the Winner family first got involved, elder statesman John serving on the committee and later being made a life member of Batley RLFC. After which, branches sprang up in Batley, Staincliffe, Birstall, West Ardsley and Carlinghow. From the start, raising money was a primary aim. 'Workshop' knockout competitions were staged on the Mount, with teams representing local collieries, factories and mills. Once, twenty-eight teams took part, raising £162. Along with Christmas parties, galas, donkey derbies and even a Miss Batley Rugby League Queen contest, the supporters had their own team for a while too, its members responsible for laying terracing, painting railings and, in 1952, buying a scoreboard later flattened by gales.

Nowadays, the Supporters' Club's struggles are offset by the contribution of BISSA, a 'squad-builder' organization formed twelve years ago by current chairman John Earnshaw, brother of Ron, and nine others. It is thanks to them that Dom, Patch and Jimmy could be afforded. Members pay monthly. A music festival was set up, Dogfest, at which a dozen bands played – 'although it rained from first minute to last,' says John, 'which was a bit of a downer'. Still, it made money. Annual dinners are held and DVDs of games produced: 'We sold more of the Featherstone match than we did all last season.' The directors might approach BISSA with a potential signing who is after a couple of hundred quid more than the club can afford. Or maybe wants £20 a month beyond budget. Can they help? If the funds are there, yes, they can. Alex Rowe is another who, offered a better deal elsewhere, was retained with BISSA's assistance. Given its troubles due to falling membership, funds raised by the Supporters' Club at the moment, through the sale of replica tops and so on in the 'Doghouse' shop, subsidize that organization alone. They hold dinners, concerts and the like, as do the Bulldogs, which risks undercutting BISSA's efforts – 'we want to raise money for the club, not subsidize a bus,' says John Earnshaw – as the cash-strapped are apt to pick and choose. Nevertheless, the organizations try to work together and largely seem to do so, despite fishing in the same small pool.

Back in 1930, the first ladies section run by a Miss Lily Turner came along, when coffee mornings and whist drives were the thing. The passenger list today, though, is almost exclusively male. The cost of £25 includes a match ticket and portion of pie and peas, consumed in the boardroom prior to departure. It was then that the single female fan bought her ticket from Kevin Nicholas who, like Andy Winner, looked smart in white shirt and club tie. 'You're not a concession, are you?'

'She doesn't know what a concession is,' said her gallant.

'I do!' she replied. 'It means you are old.'

'Not necessarily,' said the chairman. 'You could be a student. Although if you are a student over twenty-one, you are work-shy.' Camel coat on, he gave his daughter, serving pies in the kitchen, a hug and went to join the team bus outside, telling the punters he'd see them there.

The Battle Bus had turned out to be a white twenty-four-seater minibus, soon full and devoid of air-conditioning. And there was, in fact, a second woman on the trip, its driver. Approaching Halifax, the occupants of this 'economy-class' charabanc were grateful it didn't have a tarpaulin roof. Coming over, the thing had rattled along like a tin bucket, its underside scraping on every speed bump or pothole, of which in Batley and its surrounds there is no shortage. On the tops, the landscape opening vast and wide, passengers joked about having to get out and push on upward stretches. Given an average age of around sixty, that might have proved fatal. But on the chara ploughed, expertly guided, trailing more sparks than Sydney Harbour Bridge on New Year's Eve. Until, at length, it dipped, rose, dropped again into Calderdale via Lightcliffe . . . Hipperholme . . . Stump Cross.

It has an unconventional topography, Halifax. The scenery, on a crisp and sunny day teasing the first hint of spring, is as dramatic as it is in places worn and shabby. Expansive yet bleak, its vertiginous hillsides support stone buildings in a semi-rural palette of greens and browns. Under a flyover and over an old painted bridge, Dean Clough Mills complex to the right, home of Barrie Rutter's theatre company

Northern Broadsides, the Shay lies in wait. It has been home to the club since 1998, when a 112-year residence ended at the suitably eccentric Thrum Hall ground at the top end of town, on the site of which there is now a supermarket.

At a glance, the Shay resembles a building site, due to interminable redevelopment. Inside the main stand, though, the facilities are plush and impressive. There are escalators to every floor, a variety of bars – all mod cons. Out the other side, a tidy little venue is revealed, full of blue seats, with two covered terraced ends, an older stand opposite, and this main one with its media area and spacious viewing platform for wheelchairs. Transfers between areas are not allowed, a legacy of sharing with football club Halifax Town, on their way to relegation in National League North. The capacity is 10,061, comfortably enough room for the 2,010 supporters today.

Pitch-side, JK sits in a dugout reading a rugby league paper. On Wednesday, with only one point from three Super League games, Hull Kingston Rovers coach Chris Chester was sacked. A handful of coaches were tipped to replace him, though Kear was not among them.

The pitch is flat – the first level field of the season, in fact – and more importantly dry. Council-owned, matches here can be called off with little warning, a source of frustration. Otherwise, it's easy to see why the club was tempted to go full-time, before deciding it was not quite ready. It is a venue to put some Super League clubs to shame.

Keegan leads the side out in their new black away kit, lime green bands and trims. At training, they'd been told to keep it tight and that is exactly what they do; twenty-six minutes pass before the first score. It goes to Halifax, but Batley scrap on and are level shortly before the break. Dom's jinking run and inside pass send Breth in, the scrum-half adding his 500th career goal and then his 501st, a penalty moments afterwards giving the Bulldogs an 8–6 half-time lead.

Batley have lived dangerously. Fax have had a try disallowed for crossing and, as predicted, tested the Doggies' resolve and enthusiasm. On Thursday, under floodlights ablaze like golden paws, they'd prepared for this eventuality, thwacks on tackle shields echoing in the evening chill. What to do if a man is down; how to plug a defensive hole. Fax love to offload, therefore any impact in collision must be heavy, as 'if they are going backwards, that offload becomes either uncontrolled or less controlled, then the ball can go anywhere'. Like many of JK's coaching tips, it is a metaphor for life.

And so it continues in the second half, at the start of which Halifax again go ahead, 12–8. But Batley, one sub down after an injury to Joe Chandler, scramble magnificently. Scotty, rock steady under the high ball, is equally adept at bringing the final attacker to ground. His teammates, content to trust him to do so, keep their heads and chase back, tagging and disrupting Halifax's support runners instead.

After a show-and-go try from Dom – in good form again – and conversion nudges the Bulldogs back ahead, Patch adds a penalty goal on the hour: 12–16. With a quarter of the game remaining, some scratch their heads at the tactic, a lesson learned from Featherstone. The onus now is on the home team to score but Batley's defensive line simply will not give them time to settle. With the clock ticking down, Keegan is penalized for a high shot and a comedian in the stand yells, 'Where's your lipstick?' On the field, a mini-scuffle ensues and a reference is made to handbags. Halifax tap but are going nowhere.

When Jake Eccleston is brought back for a forward pass after another touchline run with only two minutes to go, a howl of despair fit for Cordelia floods the Shay, though the winger is by no means a certain scorer given that Scotty has again covered across. And their agony is complete when Dom kicks a last-second drop-goal: 17–12.

'I couldn't watch that every week,' gripes one elderly gent, a home fan presumably, 'they didn't play a bit of football,' as Batley's travelling supporters cheer their favourites up the tunnel and clamber back on the Battle Bus with glee. *I can't be doing with these close games . . . That Brambani's made a difference, hasn't he? . . . He's a magician* . . . the latter words belonging to Steve, aka 'Pieman' because he once had a pie stall near Batley station. He likes a wager, but his wallet had taken a hit lately. He'd predicted a 2–0 win for West Ham over

Sunderland, but Andy Carroll's late volley crashed off the underside of the bar. He'd had Adam Swift to score St Helens' first try against Hull KR and that should have happened too, but the daft sod chose to pass. And he had Leeds to lose by six in Perpignan last night, when a late try meant they lost by four. His beloved Batley, on an eight-point start with the bookies, have lifted his spirits no end.

'Maybe now they'll start giving us a bit of credit,' says his mate, and the bandwagon rolls on.

Workington Town are next at Mount Pleasant, on Mothering Sunday, and prove tougher to see off than expected. At the end of a frustrating first half, Batley hold only a 14–12 lead, although they are playing uphill. The mood when they trudge back into the changing room is grim, a sign of rocketing expectations.

'We've talked about standards, well, we've dropped in virtually every fucking area,' JK tells his charges as they flop to the benches, mortified. 'We completed fifteen out of twenty-one sets; one of the worst halves we've had. Yet they've not done anything to put us under pressure.' For the first time this season, Batley are at least ahead in the penalty count, but 'be careful with this referee. At some stage, he's going to give them a run of penalties. And that's when your balls will be really tested, fellas. Believe you me.'

In the team meeting yesterday morning, Kear had warned them about Jarrod Sammut, Workington's mercurial half-back: 'the space cadet who just does what he likes'. He is a wildcard, unpredictable, apt to mess with your head, a jack-in-the-box on legs. But he's a talisman too, as the clips showed. 'Things happen around him. Look. He's gone for an interception and blown it . . . what a plank. Then all of a sudden this . . .' Having gone through the attacking line, the Aussie-born Malta international was able to take advantage when a London player dropped a pass. 'We've to be on red alert.' Spawny, someone reckoned. 'Happens too often to be spawny,' JK said. 'He doesn't know what he's going to do, never mind anyone else.' Time almost up with Workington trailing by four, he'd kicked a one-pointer.

On the day, though, Batley's worst enemy is themselves. Energy levels have fallen alarmingly. When Workington opened the scoring via the sort of right-wing break the Bulldogs dealt with so admirably at Halifax, it was clear the lung-busting heroics of the last four weeks had caught up with them. Keegan lifted his side with a midfield burst that ended with Cain touching down, Patch kicking for 6–6 at the end of the first quarter, but every step was an effort. Even when a conversion and penalty goal were then added to a Chris Ulugia try from Dom's cross-field kick, Town managed to get over the line again minutes before the break. All the more impressive as, at the time, they were down to twelve men due to a sinbin for dissent.

'What we need to do now, guys, is wipe the fucking slate clean and start doing the things we are good at,' says JK. 'This is your little test now. Can you turn an indifferent performance into a good one?'

'Hey, boys,' growls Keegs. 'We've been asked some questions this year and now we are being asked another, eh? Let's answer it.'

The week had begun with beer and pizza. On the first Tuesday afternoon in March, pursued by an empty plastic Coke bottle down Heritage Road, JK knew that a slump might be in the offing.

Rugby league is a physically and mentally demanding sport. Having risen to great heights one week, a team will very often crash to earth the next, especially if their opponents are even marginally more desperate for the two points than they are. So tonight, the wise owl decreed, would be light. The players would train at a local gym on Bradford Road, return to discuss Halifax and then tuck in courtesy of a club sponsor, a team-bonding exercise that was also a reward for hard work and concentration. They must be kept in the zone.

Injury news was mixed. Squiresy, commencing rehab, had a damaged medial ligament on the inside of the knee, not the posterior or anterior one Scully injured that is hardest to fix. The centre was up until 11.45 p.m. last night, he said, doing paperwork, with more to do when he got home. He had quotes to calculate for £60,000–£70,000 jobs that, with material and labour to think about, needed care. 'Stuff it up by £5,000 and that's your profit margin gone,' he told Carl who, with his wife, had now employed a Brazilian cleaner for a couple of hours every other week, to explain partly at least why he was still here.

Uce had twisted an ankle late on at Halifax – nothing serious – while Chandler had been concussed; he would have to go through the protocol and miss Workington. Tuna's position was less clear. The specialist had advised that playing rugby league meant he would always be at risk of concussion, whether he did so or not was up to him – true, no doubt, though not very helpful. MRI scan results that would with luck confirm no bleeding were yet to arrive: £1,000-worth of treatment that for a club like Batley is a significant sum, particularly when a few come along at once. Should Chandler be concussed again any time soon, he too would have to undergo the same routine.

Upstairs, renovations to the bar were coming along nicely and the place smelled of sawn timber. The tables in Ron's Lounge were stacked with bottles and glasses, so, with the gym session done, the team meeting was in the boardroom instead. But not before Mokko had another one-on-one with Tom Lillycrop, who sported a shiner and complained of having damaged nerves in his face. Even his eyeball hurt. 'I was shite,' he said, disconsolate, of his twenty-six-minute spell. The assistant coach did not put it so bluntly. He'd lacked venom – odd for a player who is more usually a rolling ball of angry.

As the year progresses, if anyone will get on the wrong side of offi-cialdom it will be Cropper, which might give the impression that there is not a lot going on upstairs. Not so. This prop-forward-cum-project-manager is clued up politically and currently has the hump about the Conservative government's so-called 'bedroom tax', the implications of which struck close to home. Great-granddad George Lillycrop, a centre forward, had in 1912 helped Barnsley beat West Bromwich Albion in the FA Cup final and then been the subject of a world-record transfer deal when he went to Bolton (with whom he scored thirty-two goals in fifty-two games) the following year. To be able to afford to stay in the family home, George's son, Tom's granddad, had been forced to sell his father's football medals for £16,000 at Sotheby's.

Cropper is built for the oval ball. As a boy he played stand-off but grew and kept growing, not higher just wider. By the time he was good enough to be picked for England Under-16s it was at prop. On a scholarship at Leeds from the age of thirteen, when offered a contract at Headingley or Bradford he chose the latter, which, in hindsight, he admits may have been a mistake. He was at Odsal for three years and then signed at Wakefield immediately before JK departed. 'I was a bit disappointed in that. A new coach came in, Richard Agar, and I don't think he fancied me, so I ended up going to Dewsbury the following year.' After 'a bit of a disagreement' there, he went to Sheffield for a season, another ex-Eagle in the ranks. He enjoyed it, got on well with coach Mark Aston, but travel and work commitments clashed, so when Kear came calling with an offer on the doorstep, it made sense.

Aged twenty-three, he feels comfortable, more relaxed, playing his best rugby, until last Sunday anyway. Five feet eleven inches in his socks, he is short for a prop but makes up for that in heart, strength and weight. Yes, it would be nice to be taller and perhaps that's why he has been overlooked by bigger clubs, but he is 109kg, pushing 17 stone. It's a mental image coaches can have: 'Big kids, 6 ft 4 in., big muscles, but I'm comfortable with my size and it's more of a challenge, coming up against people who are taller. The bigger they are the better.'

The fourth-round draw for the Challenge Cup had been made, a competition for which JK has affection, unsurprisingly. Alphabetically first and so ball number one, Batley would be at home to Whitehaven in a couple of weeks' time. 'But let's put that to bed for now,' said the coach, and proceeded to commence the review of Halifax. Among all the good things, thirty-two missed tackles. 'Too many, to say we did seventeen last week. But they are a good attacking team.' Brownie was targeted at marker. 'They got you there, son. Your mate helped you out, but it's a matter of concentrating.' Standing too wide, he'd given them his inside shoulder. On the whole, though: 'Tremendous. I tell you what, it's a hell of a standard you've set yourselves. If a team busts us, I wouldn't expect the fuckers to score. We can defuse it.'

On Thursday, after another gym session, they were back on the pitch, polishing moves and drills. The temperature had plummeted, bringing frosty mornings and blasts of sleet and snow. The day after, the game looked doubtful for a while, the pitch under a white blanket that once melted left it waterlogged. Fortunately, come Saturday morning, though a little boggy in the 'nine 'oil' it was playable and suitable for training. Pottsy, bizarrely linked with the kit-man's job at Castleford in one trade paper, reminisced about a time when Kev, Iro and an army of helpers had swept the pitch clear of snow ahead of a friendly with Halifax. The damage they did cost brass to put right, so they wouldn't be doing that again. The wooden scoreboard was back, insurance against the electronic one going on the blink. It had since transpired that every club must have a working tannoy, doctor and scoreboard before a game can begin, so it is to be hoped no one noticed against Leigh.

Later, director Andy Winner will confide that the game was never in doubt. There's only three feet of topsoil and then it's natural rock; water runs off to a quarry over the dip at the bottom of the ground. 'The only time it gets really bad is in torrential rain and then it can bubble under your feet.'

Chandler arrived early – 9.30 a.m. – to do a cognitive test with Carl. He felt fine, out weight training last night. But his concussion and Uce's ankle meant the team-sheet wasn't settled yet, so the tip sheets, clips and so on were pushed back to 10.15. The laid-back Samoan was nowhere to be seen. 'A later meeting is supposed to be so we can get these two sorted, not give Chris an extra half hour in bed,' JK said of a lad so easy-going that he might indeed be horizontal.

Chandler remembered a time when he was concussed for three weeks on the trot but went on playing anyway. 'Much better system now,' he said, before pressing 'yes' when he meant to press 'no'. They decided he should retake it. The omens weren't good, though, when he looked around Iro's office door and asked whether he'd got the injury seven days or one-to-two weeks ago, prior to failing again.

'Muscle and bone are one thing,' mused John Heaton sagely. 'You can't mess with the head.' Ainy wondered if Joe now needed his comp ticket, leading the conditioner to recall an ex-teammate who, while being led off with a broken jaw, was asked: 'Can I have your pie?' Uce meanwhile passed his fitness test, or declared himself fit anyway. 'I'm sure he's just limped on his good leg,' said Heaton, watching through the boardroom window. Alex Brown would now be on the bench as insurance, ahead of his latest club debut and in front of the fit-again Jimmy Davey. There was a round of applause too for Young Iro, James Harrison, named as nineteenth man for the first time.

High overhead, the windmill kept turning.

As the players prepare to return for the second half, JK asks Reitts, 'Does that need stitches?' Yeah, probably. 'Well, might as well get it done now, then you can get back out there,' says his coach. The club doctor, Doc Findlay leads the winger off to the treatment room. It happened just before the interval, Reittie leaving the field with blood pumping from his inner lip. Brownz is bustled on for his latest seasonal debut and there he will stay – the cut is simply too deep.

Whoever is out there, they must get back to what they do best. Forget the scoreboard. Grind it out, set after set after set after set. As they trot up the tunnel, Elvis sings of *strong winds of promise that will blow away the doubt and fear*. It's bloody freezing. Oldham v Bradford has been postponed due to snow; Iro asking John Miller to tweet: 'Bulls season-ticket holders in for a fiver.' Former Leigh boss Paul Rowley is here, linked with league's latest expansion adventure Toronto, a Canadian club that will, unlikely as it sounds, be playing alongside Hunslet and co. in League 1 next season. Is he scouting for players?

It is Alex Bretherton who, having missed out on the opening game but since staked his claim, settles nerves by crashing over after only two minutes. And soon after Breth has left to get stitches in a head wound on the hour, the hosts lead 26–12. Brownie is the scorer this time, Patch spotting Workington's 'A' defender lolloping back before dropping the prop a sublime inside pass. He almost undoes his good work by lobbing a wild one out soon after and the lurking Jarrod Sammut, quiet otherwise, pounces but the ball goes astray. Brownie puts his hand up in acknowledgement of the error. 'No point putting your hand up,' mutters JK in the dugout. 'With him around, you'll be putting your hand up under the posts.'

There is no longer any real concern, though. When Dom, playing his opposite number off the park, makes a break, supporting Alistair Leak darts in, Walker's conversion making it 32–12. Batley are having fun now. Their next try is the score of the season so far. Batley switch to the left, Uce breaks clear and feeds Ainy – the ball going through seven pairs of hands in all – scorer Cain on the inside and all of it on the back of the sort of strong aggressive carries JK dreams about.

The coach is in charge off the field but the captain leads on it. Keegan never stops demanding the ball, even when physically shattered. Late on, he drives yard after punishing yard, pushing forward and seldom pushed back, inspiring Batley to turn a stodge of a first half around. And after a bandaged Breth jogs back on with ten minutes remaining, Dom's immaculate kick to the corner is plucked from the air by Brownz to maintain a personal record – he says – of a try on every debut. Patch's final touchline conversion completes a perfect kicking display in a comprehensive 44–12 win.

'When you journey through a season – and I think it's a really fucking exciting season and one we'll enjoy, we'll create a bit of history – you have times when you have to evolve as a team,' JK tells them in a changing room that is now as jubilant as it had been morose. 'Today has been one of those times. First half, it wasn't us. But I tell you what, you are good enough to flip it round. You went back to looking after the ball, playing smart, being tough, working hard and they were absolutely fucked. So let's get that on board, fellas; same recipe for every team. Well done, guys, you are a credit to yourselves.'

Cue the song and yet more good news: Chandler has passed his head test.

8

THERE WERE NO head tests in John Etty's day – nor his brother Jim's, one of several former players and lifelong supporters gathered at the Breakfast Club. As on every Tuesday morning through the season, the boardroom is busy; most of those present having arrived for the 9.30 start, though stragglers appear on and off until around eleven.

Two quid gets you a pot of tea or coffee and a bacon sandwich, prepared by an aproned Jonny Potts and other volunteers in the new kitchen. Barbara and Nellie are here, along with other familiar faces, for a chat about the old days, surprisingly few moans about the new, a quiz and catch-up at a club that everyone thinks of as their own.

On that table: Jim Etty and wife Joan, Gwen and Ken Whiteley (uncle of former Batley coach David Ward, taken in aged six by the couple when Wardy's father died) and Nellie. Gwen does the match-day raffle, and woe betide anyone who won't buy a ticket. Jim and John, it turns out, are second-generation players. Their dad – christened John but widely known as 'Mad Jack' – also turned out for the club either side of the First World War. If the opposing hooker was any good, Jack's tactic was to crack him and then they would both be sent off. In fact, Etty senior played in the first post-war match at Hunslet in 1918.

One table along: Kath, a fundraiser with her greetings cards, and Barry Lee, who used to work in a garage owned by international winger Norman Field. Over there: Bill Winner (son of John, father of Andy) and local author John Roe – not long returned from the funeral of former Batley hard-man George Palmer in Hull. George, who'd had a fine send-off aged ninety-one, had been a publican or run working men's clubs until his retirement. Once, when a fight broke out in one of his premises, the then sixty-five-year-old vaulted the bar and grabbed a culprit in each hand before banging their heads together and slinging them into the car park: 'Don't come here again.'

Over there, behind the ketchup: singing Jim McVeigh, who it is reckoned installed the electrical cables and floodlights that went up in 1980, among much else. Announcing raffle winners and serving sarnies is Stuart Hull, father of director Paul, alongside Sam Haigh and Hazel ('I can't remember her surname, Miss Batley in the 1980s,' quips John Roe) and several more lifelong fans, including Barbara and Fred. Barbara first came to Batley aged fifteen but had to stop when her friend swore at home and her dad said they'd heard it at rugby. 'We'd clap them in, pat them on the back.'

Her dad was a butcher at Batley Co-op. When work finished on Saturday afternoon – which is when they played in those days – he'd go for a drink then come up here, the Sunday joint wrapped in his apron. 'He would watch from the bottom end with it tucked under his arm. It was all cinder banking then.' Fred, who sports a fine handlebar moustache and to whom she has been married for sixty-one years, played football, so for a while she watched him mainly. Then their daughter started going out with Andrew Winner, so back she came. 'That's how it is here. Family. Inter-mingling, everyone related to someone else.'

Barbara and Fred also help with Batley Boys, and Fred picks up litter, helping where he can. On game day, Barbara and Nellie act as hostesses and Barbara bakes. 'When Susan and Andrew got wed – they are married thirty years this year – I thought, "Right, I'm going to do something I want to do now." So I started baking and entering shows.' This year, she won the Centenary prize at Mirfield, her lemon drizzle cake a triumph, though maybe not for much longer. 'I'm saying I'm retiring this year. When I get to eighty, that's it.'

She and Nell will still serve coffee though, until they are sacked anyway. During matches, they can be found seated at the boardroom window, separating half-time draw tickets for Kev: 'We work while we are watching.' As for Nellie Earnshaw, cheery and with a wicked sense of humour, she would like to share a few photographs of Ron.

Everybody knew Ron Earnshaw... well turned out, enthusiastic, devoted to Batley since childhood. From the start, he'd been keen to help out where he could, selling programmes to begin with, before, as an adult, filling just about every role a rugby league club has to offer, short of coaching the team and playing in it. Always running around. Irrepressibly optimistic. 'Mr Batley', that's what they called him.

His wife Nellie, too, began coming here young. Seventy-three years ago, in fact, when her father first brought her in a pushchair. 'I had to sit in that pram and I had to shout out. He kept telling me what to say.' In fact, the only time she didn't watch Batley was as a young woman. Aged twenty-four, she lived and worked for a while in London and New York as a nanny. Even then her widowed mum – her dad having died when she was fourteen – sent letters telling her how they had got on.

It was upon meeting and marrying Ron, though, that the club really got into her blood – how could it not? When Ron became chairman in 1995, it was the biggest moment in his life: 'me and the family came second'. It's a remark with no hint of resentment, since Nellie was and remains steeped in rugby league herself. In earlier years, she worked at the Queens Hotel, Leeds, answering the phone for Eddie Waring. 'Lovely man, was Eddie.' Less happily, she also took calls for 'that other nasty fellow', Jimmy Savile. Between her and Ron, she reckons they've notched up 130-odd years of service.

Graduating from programme seller, Ron went on to become a ball boy, kit-man, ran a daily lottery in numerous town pubs for the club, performed an array of voluntary backroom duties, helping to make

Batley what it is today. And when Stephen Ball took over in 1989, the new man wanted him on board. 'He knocked on the door one Friday night and Ron said, "Look, I've got no money." "I don't want your money," he said, "I want this . . ." and tapped his forehead. Ron knew every telephone number in rugby league; he didn't have to look it up.' He preceded Iro as chief executive: 'They are supposed to be paid for that, but he didn't take anything.'

Club secretary and general manager were other positions filled by a man with enough imagination to stage three fundraising shows at Batley Variety Club, introduce fêtes on the cricket field and more. Those eighties revues were sell-outs, twice hosted by Bernard Manning and once by Jim Bowen, presenter of TV quiz show *Bullseye*. The fêtes were known as the Batley Show, with carousels, horses and such. Over the next seven years, he and Ball as good as pulled Batley back from the brink of extinction. Ron and Nellie put their home up as collateral one year. Any time he was able to share went into his hometown club.

Kevin Nicholas, next in charge from 1996 when Ron stood aside as chairman, first got to know him as a lad in the seventies. Back then, Ron had sat on the Supporters' Club committee, an experience that helped later when he served as a handy and popular link between the board and fans. In the 1980s, the supporters began to stage video nights with commentary regularly provided by Ron Earnshaw.

'Ron would do a favour for anyone,' says Kev. 'If he had a fault, he was too nice. He'd commit to stuff and make it difficult for himself. I don't know anybody who had a bad word to say against him.'

Warm and encouraging, Ron Earnshaw was the man everyone would turn to, especially in defeat. He'd be upbeat, a rare quality in rugby league, always looking ahead. After a loss, everyone would be down, but Ron remained positive. 'We will win next week,' he would say. It was infectious. If a fundraiser went under-supported, he found the bright side. His enthusiasm never waned.

Ron's affability didn't just make life difficult for him; it could give the rest of the board a start when they discovered what he had committed them to. 'You'd be saying, "What's he said we'll do that for?"' Kev laughs. Ron always did his best to accommodate everyone.

In good health, he'd be running around the stadium all game, up to something or other, a hundred miles an hour. But as the years advanced so his health began to fail and – by then honorary president – he took to watching matches from a seat near the end of the balcony in the lounge that now bears his name, with a couple of pals for company. By this stage, he was having mini-strokes from time to time and had lost mobility. Even then, as indomitable as a bashed-up prop forward, he got up to the club every day to do something in the office – admin, ticket sales, just for an hour perhaps. By lunchtime, he'd be shattered and head off home for a nap, driven back and forth by Nellie or his half-brother, John.

In 2009, Ron was inducted on to the Rugby League Roll of Honour in recognition of his contribution not only to Batley but the game more widely, an achievement he cherished. Wigan and Great Britain wing legend Billy Boston helped him down off stage, as he was keen to remind everyone thereafter. Ron loved rugby league and Nellie appreciated that. So much so that when her husband was hospitalized for the first time, she spent three months doing his job, morning and afternoon, 'keeping it going for him'. And in September 2013, his wife launched a daring and successful escape bid.

'He was in Pinderfields then and I was a bit cheeky and asked the sister if I could take him out. I said, "Batley are playing Sheffield at Leigh in the Championship Grand Final." She said, "You can't take him all the way to Leigh!" I said, "I'm not taking him to Leigh; it's on telly at home." So she went to the doctor, who said, "Go on then, but feed him and have him back by seven." So I kidnapped him.' Driving home, the couple went along a dual carriageway. 'I never thought I'd be coming back along here,' he said. Nellie asked if he was excited. 'Ecstatic,' he said.

Having reached the Grand Final from fifth and despite leading the Eagles 12–0 at half-time, Batley in the end lost 19–12. 'I don't care,' was his response to commiserations. 'We've been in a Grand Final, haven't we?' He died the following Saturday.

It may sound trite to say that Ron Earnshaw's death left a hole in the club, yet it is the simple unvarnished truth. Kevin Nicholas and the board wasted no time in establishing a memorial. The Family Stand end in which the changing rooms now sit began to be extended in 1995, part-funded by a 'City Challenge' political initiative in which the track predating Heritage Road, then owned by the club, was redeveloped as a public highway in return for the financial investment. More improvements were made from 2000–02 when what was initially called the Vice President's Lounge – effectively a replacement for the Taverners' – was installed over the Batley Boys' changing rooms. In 2013, that room was renamed Ron's Lounge, confirming his place on the Mount for as long as the club is here too.

As for Nellie, she will carry on regardless. Even now, if she goes into a pub, an arm will come out: *I'm buying that.* 'I love going out; it costs nowt,' she says. She will continue to be feisty, holding a grudge against one former Super League chairman, for example, because 'people like him forget how rugby league started out and that really annoys me', ready to put a flea in the ear of all who need it. 'I love my rugby and I love my lads.' When a new one arrives, she makes a point of meeting them. The other week, one was looking out of the boardroom window. 'Now then, love, what's your name? "Jonathan Tinker," he said. "My dad used to play here."'

Later that night, in Los Angeles, Maria Sharapova weeps tears of mitigation. Having tested positive for meldonium at the Australian Open, she is destined for a two-year ban, reduced to fifteen months on appeal.

Are there drugs in rugby league? How can there not be in a sport whose combatants are so physically impressive and under such week-to-week strain? Every so often a player will be banned, usually though not always in the lower leagues, but routinely enough for it to be a semi-regular occurrence. The RFL reckons that only goes to confirm the effectiveness of existing procedures. Cheats are caught, they say.

At training, John Heaton, former world champion natural

bodybuilder, agrees, though admits that for some players and clubs the temptation will always be there, especially when the majority of spectators don't much seem to care. 'You go to the zoo to see lions and tigers, don't you?' In the global phenomenon that is WWE, for example, the public wants to boo and cheer huge muscly men, not those of average build. As of now, Batley are yet to undergo a drug test this season, though their conditioner reckons it is only a matter of time. 'They aren't as frequent in the Championship, but they'll get around to it.'

The tests are carried out in association with UK Anti-Doping (UKAD) and in compliance with the World Anti-Doping Agency (WADA) code, described on the RFL website as: 'one of the most thorough and effective testing programmes in sport'. Education, too, is seen as key: 'The RFL want to create a generation of players who have confidence in their ability to succeed in rugby league without the misuse of prohibited substances or methods.' For the moment, though, athletes who have got where they are by being 'clean' must surely be greatly annoyed by teammates and opponents who have succeeded otherwise? Rare is the changing room devoid of 'gear'-related banter. 'Some lads work hard, lift weights, eat well and are genetically gifted to be able to build muscle,' says Heaton. 'They will always get teased by others not as physically blessed. But players who have grafted do feel resentment towards those who haven't worked as hard and seem to get more benefits. Sometimes that's when the temptation comes in. They train their balls off and see lads they've known from youth level rocket to Super League.'

At Batley, issues of doping and other forms of drug abuse are taken seriously, Heaton insists. 'Every year, Kev tells us, "We don't want any drug scandals. If in doubt, speak to John [Kear], myself or Carl." And we will say, "Check your banned list, check your labels. If it's on [the website] Informed-Sport, then you are fine."' Though as a part-time club, they cannot of course have full-time eyes. 'I can never be 100 per cent certain about what they are up to, but I am 100 per cent certain that I've never advised anyone to do it, nor has the club, and I trust my players. I would be surprised if they were at it. Drug testing never bothers me. I wish they'd do more of it.'

As the rest of the world talks drugs, rackets and tennis, there is big news in rugby league too. Brian Smith, whose coaching helped to keep Wakefield Trinity Wildcats in Super League last year, has quit. JK is linked with the vacancy – paper talk, most likely – as Smith departs with an ill-judged volley of insults at the board. A far cry from Kear's dignified exit after five-plus seasons of thick and the thinnest of thins.

When the Fox's ovens are on and the wind is in the right direction, this end of town whiffs of custard creams, golden crunch and other twice-baked aromatic delights. So it is tonight as Reitts wanders in with a stitch in his lip. Doc Findlay put in three, but two fell out in bed. Breth is drinking a disgusting green concoction – a liquidized kale, spinach and avocado smoothie – 'it's for the fibre'.

Danny Maun has jogged the four miles here from his home. He browses the weekly score sheets in Ron's Lounge, the renovation now complete and looking smart. These evaluate aspects of individual performance match by match, allowing players to measure their efforts against those in the same position. Ainy is scoring more than Reitts, the latter's place in danger given Alex Brown's impressive return against Workington. Gleds and Cropper have dipped in form, while JK fears Dave Scott's small frame can't take such punishment forever. He will most likely rest him for the Challenge Cup game, an opportunity for James Craven perhaps?

Keegan, meanwhile, has 101 points. It's a mighty score but no surprise after his weekend display. He'd shared the captaincy with Johnny Campbell before 'Mr Enthusiasm' broke his leg; responsibility suits him. After Breth, he and Rowey have been here longest. He feels part of the club, has played at this level for ages; he understands how players work, gets their mentality. With JK, a working partnership has developed and he often re-emphasizes the coach's points in meetings. 'JK was here when I first came and wasn't getting in the team,' Keegs says. 'It was the right decision because I wasn't playing well. At

Featherstone, that opportunity to take a penalty, if I'd been on the field we'd have taken the two. Nine times out of ten he's right.'

Keegan reckons we all like to think of ourselves as leaders. We'd all like to imagine we have the ability to inspire others and tell them what to do, but the fact is those are skills not given to everyone. When some people talk, you listen, in any walk of life. They have that air of authority. 'Though you have to be careful and pick your battles,' he says. 'A lad might be playing shit, but it's not my place to single people out. That's John's job. My job is to lead by example.'

On Sunday, some of the younger lads thought they had a God-given right just to turn up and Workington would roll over and die. No rugby league team does that. 'Don't ask someone to do something you are not willing to do yourself. If I'm putting my bollocks on the line, I can tell the lads that they need to be doing that too.'

As a starting prop, he is well positioned to judge. 'All I said was what everyone on the bench could see. When you've been in it, you know what the talk's like, and then you are out of it, so you get the whole picture.' A captain is in some ways a bridge between coaching staff and team – fine when things are going well but what about when they are not? 'Sometimes it's hard to tell your mate, "Look, you need to wind it in." Brownie and Rowey both like to fuck about, but it has to be done. Not often. They're both experienced and know normally how far to push it.' Anyway, he has always seen the assistants as the link between coach and players. 'I'm a filter. If JK says something to the boys, I'll try and make it more palatable.'

Studied in the team meeting, the Workington performance is revealed for the cliché it was: a game of two halves. First half, loose. Four uncompleted sets in the first twenty minutes, people waiting for others to do something. Second half, exceptional. Completion: 83 per cent. Points from yardage: around the 1,400m mark. 'That's fucking phenomenal that, fellas.' JK shows Cain's try again, 'one of the best I've ever seen here,' which owes everything to Ainy's work off the ball. First, in his own half, he brings it clear. Then, when other wingers might have stood there, hands on hips, soaking in the acclaim, he loops another fifty metres before coming into the line again in support of the try-scorer. 'An absolute cracker, though he doesn't know he's done it.' The watching Ainy does look surprised by his contribution. Most encouraging was how they changed gear within the game. 'We went from sloppy to tight. But let's make sure we start better against Bradford. Treat it like a Grand Final. Big game, big crowd – we should be absolutely barred up to fuck and ready to play. We really should.'

By Thursday, the mood is calm but focused. As ever, both clubs' coaches, JK and James Lowes, say the right things in public, playing their own team's chances down while privately scenting blood. The night is tranquil, dark and quiet, bitterly cold. Even the sail on the windmill lies dormant, as if having unilaterally decided it's not worth the effort.

For half an hour, the squad is divided between Mokko and Linners. They go through tackle combinations: who is on top gripping the ball-carrying arm; who is beneath, taking the legs; communication between the two. Squeeze. Push off, back to the marker position. He who controls the ruck, controls the dance.

Later, they'll go through it from the opposite angle, *with* the ball. 'Your head is too high,' Rowey will be told. 'Get your eye right down on the ball.' Microscopically close. Close enough to see pimples. 'If you are up there, knees tucked in, he can wriggle and the ref sees a struggle. Get low, legs back and squeeze and he can't move, can he? The ref sees you are dominant; we buy a little more time in defence.'

'Don't get bored with practising the right things,' says Mokko. 'Don't get bored with keeping high standards.'

Brad 'Tuna' Day is still not right – unable to participate in anything other than gym work. As mellow a soul off the field as he is fiery on it, with a winning smile, were he to have haystack hair and a straggly beard he could pass as a perma-chilled piccolo player on the *Old Grey Whistle Test*. In reality, built like a tank and twenty-one years of age, playing rugby league is his life and immediate future. The idea that he might be forced into retirement is too awful to contemplate.

The nickname is satirical. Its roots lie in an unnamed player in Oldham who, after a single close season, came back pumped up like Bluto. His teammates sensed steroids, though the lad himself claimed only to have trained hard. Oh, and eaten loads of tins of tuna, a fish that subsequently became shorthand for 'gear'. In Brad's case, it is meant ironically. He is the type of player John Heaton spoke about – naturally stacked, athletically gifted, seldom out of the gym. His diet is meticulous; he takes care of himself, as anyone with ambition must. He tries hard to hide it, but these concussions are getting him down.

Like most of the others here, he began young, as a nine-year-old. 'I used to play football but I was a bit rough for it, so decided to play rugby instead.' His mum knew a bloke at work who coached and helped out at East Leeds. He told her to bring him down and he loved the game from the start. His step-granddad used to play 'when it was Bradford Northern, or something like that', but otherwise league had not been in the family. As big as an outside bog even then, he started at prop, then played a bit of centre and is now in the back row where he regularly wreaks havoc, when he can get on the field anyway.

After Leeds Service Area, a scholarship and academy spells at Wakefield and Castleford, where he spent a year full-time, Tuna arrived at Batley in 2015 with a desire to play week in, week out. Away from here, he fits windows and doors, a job landed through Reitts, whose neighbour needed a lad. His dream is Super League. 'That's what I'm trying to push towards. Hopefully it will happen sooner or later. If not, I'll just have to continue working.'

Nor it seems are physio Carl's issues resolved, the Brazilian cleaner presumably not cutting the salsa. A prospective new physio from Beverley is shadowing him. The 24-year-old has finished his masters and been at Huddersfield for about a year, part-time. 'It's an exciting time for Batley and it would be a very good opportunity for me,' he says. He looks promising but is never seen on the Mount again.

An MRI scan has now revealed that Squiresy has a fractured leg. It's not serious and should only add a couple of weeks to his recovery, but it's as well it was spotted. He was about to resume training.

Saturday morning kicks off with an address by Kevin Nicholas. 'The position we are in, I just want to say I am absolutely delighted. It's near perfect. One of the best situations I've been in as chairman.' If they beat Bradford Bulls – a third full-time team in six weeks – their league position is indisputably correct. 'But whatever happens I'm happy with where you as a group of players have got us. But if we can win – and I can smell it [rubs nose] – you'll each have a £100 cash bonus.' Reittie, who has been dropped for Brownz, asks if the non-playing eighteenth and nineteenth men are included. They are. 'I didn't want your bottom lip coming out. So you've got that little bit extra incentive, though I don't think you need it. You are up there anyway.'

The chairman gone, JK takes them through the clips, pointing to second-rower Dale Ferguson, hooker Adam O'Brien and half-back Lee Gaskell as danger men. Patch offers considered analysis and Brownie also puts in his tactical two penn'orth: 'We don't fucking back off!'

'Bradford like a loose game,' concludes JK. 'When the ball pops out of people's arses or it's dropped on the floor, they love that cause they can step in and play. We like structure. Set for set. Arm-wrestles. And last thing, guys, it's gonna be big. These are the ones you should be itching to play and do your best in. And that's all I can ask of you.'

'It was one of those March days when the sun shines hot and the wind blows cold: when it is summer in the light, and winter in the shade.' Dickens's line from *Great Expectations* could have been composed with the Fox's Biscuits Stadium in mind. Morning mists have cleared and hazy afternoon sunshine encourages a carnival atmosphere.

Both sides have players making a 100th career appearance, Luke Blake and Bradford's O'Brien hoping to mark the anniversary with important contributions. Three hours before kick-off, a man in an orange bib hauls a car-park sign two thirds of the way up Heritage Road. It will most likely be the biggest crowd of the season.

In the boardroom, five tables are laid out smartly with fawn table-cloths, cerise serviettes and a central flower arrangement of white hyacinths from Barbara's garden. Prior to the season, Batley were expected to have won only one match by now if they were lucky – last week's home game with Workington. Yet as it stands, they have won four out of five and should offer a real test for a once-mighty club that most still consider a top-two certainty.

It feels like the morning of a cup final, expectant but anxious. Kev strides in, tense, though soon perks up as he busies about. 'I can smell it,' he says, with the now familiar rub. 'I can smell it.'

A specially brought in burger van occupies the derelict area between the electronic scoreboard and two portable green toilets, next to the K2 Stand. John Miller says the club will cater for 250 sponsors as opposed to the usual hundred or so, with two boardroom sittings. Fox's have let them use three car parks at the factory, to cope with any overflow.

Director Paul Hull is responsible for operations in and around the Glen Tomlinson Stand, walkie-talkie in hand. Sunshine is bringing the place to life, beer-garden benches filling up nicely. Prior to joining the board, the 47-year-old lifelong supporter helped out with BISSA 'for a couple or three years' before Andy Winner, a mate from cricket days, put his oar in. That was eight years ago now. Like the rest of them he is Batley born and bred and works here entirely voluntarily, taking out nothing but satisfaction at having put a shift in.

For Paul Hull, the main goal this season is top six: 'The amount of money we have invested is more than we've ever spent at the club. The quality we have brought in around the ruck area is phenomenal.' They've always had ambition, but never the financial clout. 'We hate losing but we've got a fantastic hard core of fans who, I feel, are the best in the league. They support us whatever happens. It is a struggle sometimes but you pick yourself up and carry on the best you can.'

Nor is the discrepancy in funding helpful. The four full-time clubs should top the table, 'so if you want to win something there's not much on offer. One of our best days was winning the Northern Rail Cup and then they scrapped it. After £800,000 in third or fourth place, suddenly it drops. And even £800,000 isn't a lot of money for a full-time club, is it? What will happen, for example, if Sheffield don't get that funding again? Financially, they may have a problem in 2017. Unless you've got a sugar daddy, it could be boom or bust.'

At 12.45, Keegan is out on the pitch, kicking goals and playing ball with his children. Inside, the promising start and fine weather have brought out the great and good. Among them youth coach Brian Foley, Batley-born, who nurtured, among players too numerous to count, Shaun 'Ainy' Ainscough at Wigan. He has an explanation for 'nine 'oil' that has nothing to do with golf. As nine lines traverse the field, not including try-lines, the last bit of the pitch before the in-goal area – the red zone in today's parlance – lay behind the ninth line, looking down. Kickers, duelling back and forth with the boot in the old days, were therefore told to land the ball in the 'nine 'oil', i.e. the furthest point in play, to pin a team back, preferably in the corner. At Mount Pleasant, the field descends steeply in that direction. In the right – or wrong – conditions, it is a defensive hellhole.

From a window on the other side of Ron's Lounge, Brian points across to the cricket pavilion, where the rugby changing rooms used to be. Once upon a time, players would loop across the wicket from there, brave an avenue of supporters either side and enter the field by the back of what is now the Glen Tomlinson Stand. Clashes with cricket were rare, rugby league being a winter sport back then, but if it happened in late spring, say, play paused for this procession, or maybe they took an early tea. Once, when Batley met York, a brawl between two opposing players scared nine-year-old Foley silly.

It's busy outside today, though not as vibrant as it was back then, when rivers of people heeded the call to the Mount. The Bulls squad arrives by luxury coach, its twenty-minute journey complete.

Down in the corridor, Steve the doorman is in place, handing out comps and giving directions, while Jonny Potts guards the boot room and Tony, the 51-year-old inside Batley's mascot, Battler the bulldog, looks hot and sweaty without his head on. He's watched Batley 'thirty-odd year', sixteen of them incognito through eyeholes. Ron Earnshaw got him into it. 'He came out the Taverners' and said,

"Tony, will you do us mascot today at Sheffield? Other lad's rung in."
I says, "Go on then." It was only supposed to be for a couple of games.'
The costume seems clean and fresh considering. 'Aye, though it's got
a bit of mange.' Some sporting mascots do somersaults, not Battler.
'I'm getting a bit old for that; I'd never get back up.' He's only been
sent off once, at Hull KR in 2004. 'Apparently, I made a rude gesture
towards Colin Morris, the referee. He was on the halfway line and saw
me. He blew his whistle and pointed at me. I looked behind, but there
was no one there. Front page of the *Yorkshire Evening Post*.'

At the other end of the corridor, Batley's non-players chat. Paddy
Hesketh and James Harrison played for Oxford yesterday in a 26–16
loss in Tottenham, home of London Skolars. Young Iro played the
full eighty but Paddy hurt his shoulder in the last minute. Not serious,
he says. Otherwise, his leg went fine. Tuna too, having just been in the
gym, reports no more headaches and hopes to be available next week.

Robbie Hunter Paul struts in, Bradford totem since the dawn of
Super League and nowadays the club's CEO, impeccably attired as
ever. He is met by a waft of liniment as the Bulldogs trot out for
the warm-up. Someone welcomes him to Mount Pleasant. 'There's
never anything pleasant about coming here,' he retorts, an echo of
one former Great Britain centre's 'what a shithole' comment during
Sheffield's visit three weeks ago. Pottsy looks hurt.

Another arrival is 'Grit' Barlow, brother of Batley hero Peter, a
hooker here himself in the 1950s and '60s. Elderly now, he walks with
the aid of crutches, his progress slow and painful. But on he pushes
towards the light, before shuffling out into the arena beyond, reborn
in a rectangular blast of colour. Bruises and breaks shrugged off by
healthy young men can carry a lifetime of repercussions.

'Wow!' says Dewsbury coach Glenn Morrison, another observer
surveying a lively scene. The final attendance will be 2,742, among
whom, in his Bradford tracksuit, is local favourite Johnny Campbell,
recovered from his horrifying injury last August but yet to make his
debut for the Bulls. The soft-spoken 28-year-old is still a favourite
here despite that two-year deal. Given his age and circumstances, no

one begrudges him that. Passers-by pat him on the back, welcome him home. He's had a haircut. Gone is the funky 'fro in photos on the boardroom wall; today he is close-cropped. He tells well-wishers that he'd rather be playing. *We wish you were too . . . for us.* The hair? It had been doing his head in. 'New year, new me and all that . . .'

He is back in training now, in rehab, strengthening everything up, good to go. But with the team the Bulls have got, 'it's a big squad, isn't it? Hard to get in. I'll just have to keep plugging away.' Leaving for Bradford hadn't been easy but he doesn't know how many years he has left. And when you've got a young 'un seventeen months old, well, full-time helps with job security. 'If you get injured, you can't work, and there's only winning and losing pay on offer at Batley.'

His six seasons and 125 appearances at the Bulldogs didn't pass without controversy. In 2014, Campbell was given a twelve-month ban reduced to nine on appeal for betting on the 2013 Grand Final against Sheffield, in which he played. And even more seriously, that followed an incident on a night out in Dewsbury in November 2009, when former soldier Brett Garside was left brain damaged and Campbell received a twelve-month suspended prison sentence, a year's supervision order and 100 hours' community service.

If it is any comfort to his victim, he is now determined, he says, to make good. 'I've done some stupid stuff and I want my young 'un to be proud of me, not go to school with people saying, "your dad's done this" and "your dad's done that". I want the good things about me to outshine the bad. I'm at a big club, following so many great players: people like Lesley Vainikolo, who I looked up to myself. I want to be part of that history, know what I mean? I've always been all right at Championship level,' he goes on, with understatement, 'but wouldn't mind taking my chance in Super League. If I don't, I hope I can always come back here. If I'm good enough or not, well, at least I'll know.'

Batley's progress has pleased him. 'Last season, we weren't a million miles away, just a couple of players who weren't quite up to the mark, or who went missing in big games. This year, they've turned close games into wins. The team spirit is back. I saw the Sheffield game here and everyone is hunting like dogs. It's good to see Danny Maun back too. He took me under his wing while he was here.'

He went into 'a dark patch' after his injury but was flooded with messages of support. It all happened in a split-second. 'Leaky broke through. I remember screaming at him to give me the ball, and to be honest I ought to have scored. I got half-tackled and the ref shouted, "Play on". As I got up to carry on, my studs stuck in the ground, I got clattered from the side and my ankle span all the way around.' He is sure he'll get over it. 'When we've been doing drills in training, where you've to step off to one side, if I have ten seconds to think about it, I think, "Right, this is my bad foot." When it's attack and D, full on, you just get in game mode. It's flee or fight, isn't it?'

Beer bottles totter precariously on crush barriers. Fans, players and officials of both sides mingle noisily but happily. On the tannoy, Chaplain Derek Ventress asks spectators to stay where they are at half-time. The crowd is too large for the usual routine of swapping ends.

In the changing room, tension is high. Mauny stands guard. Anyone outside now is staying there. Three thumps on the door. *Thud. Thud. Thud.* One-minute warning. JK's voice is unruffled, though perhaps his fingers tell another story. 'Let's have a sit down, please,' he says. 'Look at their team, a compliment to you middle men. They are putting a guy on so they can rotate, as they know they are in for a challenge. But if they know they're in for a challenge, they'll be ready for one. Great out there, isn't it? Well, let it fucking inspire you. Let it drag out every ounce of energy, so you give a performance that justifies us being in a game like this.' *Thud. Thud. Thud.* More urgent now. The audience awaits. 'Let's get out there, let's rip in, let's give it fucking everything. Leave it all out on the field.'

The players roar. Keegan draws his brothers together, one player nudging in at the last moment having clipped a nervous shit. *Thud! Thud! Thud!* 'The last time we played these here we knocked on the door, didn't we? Well, this time let's kick the fucking door in! Bulldogs on three . . .' *One . . . two . . . three . . . Bulldogs!*

The opening is torrid. Both Ulugia and Breth are held up over the line, but Bradford open the scoring with a try and a goal. When Brownie's rash offload then goes awry, the visitors storm through in midfield and are thwarted only by some desperate scrambling D and a last-ditch Scotty tackle. JK, in the dugout, yells at water-carrier Mauny, 'Get on there and tell him!' But soon Batley draw level.

Alex Brown – who, like Ainy on the other wing, makes good yards throughout – starts the move, bringing the ball to the right of the posts. From there it is worked left, where his front-row namesake – back in the good books – cuts inside and is felled on tackle two. The ball is again niftily moved left, where Cain steps around a stranded Bulls winger and feeds Uce in the corner; a sweet try against the club that didn't want him. Patch converts out wide.

Just before the half hour, Scotty is up in support to finish off a sweeping move that, echoing Ainy the week before, he began himself at the other end of the field, four tackles ago. Ulugia this time tears away, finding Cain on a parallel inside run, deliverer of the scoring pass. The full-back does a jig of delight. Patch's goal makes it 12–6.

The lead, though, lasts just three minutes. When Bradford field the ball in the 'nine 'oil', they seem unlikely to get upfield in a single set. But when the ball is hacked inside after a right-wing surge, Dom fails to clear and Dale Ferguson touches down, the conversion doing the rest. Although still in the game on the scoreboard, Batley appear physically and mentally exhausted. Firmer ground? Nervous energy? Full-time opponents? Pressure and high expectations have begun to get to them and the Bulls soak up all they have to offer in attack. Two penalties are conceded as the half moves to a close, a Bradford try inevitable. A first effort is denied for crossing, but the one that counts comes via a switch in direction and a couple of missed tackles. As the goal sails over, Batley, trailing 12–18, will be glad to hear the hooter. Yet it almost gets worse when big Alex Rowe offloads with less than a minute to go. Batley haven't had the ball in fifteen minutes, the dugout response close to apoplectic. Fortunately, the Bulls knock on.

Bradford are by far the toughest opponents faced to date. Their quality is impressive. The Bulldogs are being made to work harder than ever before and what's more they have been playing downhill. 'They are testing us down the middle,' says Keegan, to a forest of haunted eyes. 'Dropped balls. Silly offloads. Errors we don't need; we need to go set to set, play the long game.' JK listens, lets the players vent. 'Play them at our speed.'

When the coach speaks, his advice is not to play the scoreboard. 'Play the fucking game. We've been us own worst enemies, guys. I'll tell you, we were fucking controlling the game, 12–6 up, knocking sets out, putting them down there. Then they had eleven sets to our five and of those five we ain't completed two. We haven't had the ball for ten minutes and then, Alex, you come up with that . . .' His bad, the prop admits, lungs refilling slowly. 'The other one, you've picked it, inside defence. They are testing you, big men, to see if you are working. Let's make sure they don't catch us with those fucking inside plays. The markers need to work and communicate, and we need to maintain this defensive line when we pin 'em in a corner.'

But there are plus points: 'Playing our game we looked every bit as good as them, so we need to get back to that. Play and complete. Field position. Keep those attacking kicks coming and something will come of them, believe you me. But you've a fuck-ing challenge, I'll tell you, because they feel as if they are fucking barred up and have got us. Well, it's up to us now to tell them they haven't.'

The chat returns, urgings on. From having looked beaten, every player is now straining to return. 'Hey, let's not be apprehensive,' says Keegan. 'They've asked us a fucking question. Let's all step up individually and answer them as a team. Winners on three . . .'

And, at first, they do put up a fight. After another Bradford score is thwarted only by a forward pass, they continue to scramble gallantly in the face of mounting odds, holding on by cracked and bloody fingertips. But the scavenging hordes cannot be repulsed forever and soon the Bulls are in again as the midfield struggles for gas. With the goal, it's 12–24 and Bradford have not only pooped the party, they have stamped on the balloons. 'It's all gone quiet over there,' their fans sing, overlooked by the Ron's Lounge windows.

So it has, for a while, until Keegan Hirst returns to the fray with a quarter of the game to go. He staggers forward, yard after yard, swatting tackler after would-be tackler off his back with all the imperiousness of King Kong swiping biplanes. When Cain puts up a bomb that is a risk to aircraft itself, the Bulls defence goes AWOL and his captain plucks the bouncing ball from the air and touches it down, Patch's conversion reducing the gap to six points. Bradford's restart then goes out on the full and Mount Pleasant rubs its nose.

The breakthrough arrives with just three minutes to go. Cain is again involved heavily, the Bulls' desperate attempts to add to their tally continually repulsed. The half-back first shimmies to wrong-foot an on-rushing defender, then sends up another high kick that falls in the unlikely arms of Alex Rowe. On its way to earth, the ball touches enemy hands, the tackle count is reset, though the Bulldogs move it wide anyway with Dom Brambani's final pass sending Brownz in at the corner. Joy is unconfined but the levelling kick is far from easy. Not only will Patch have to hammer it uphill at the end of a gruelling personal stint of his own, he will be forced to do so from far out on the touchline. With all eyes upon him, it couldn't be any tougher.

Patrick 'Patch' Walker has been here before. During his ten years as a professional rugby league player and goal-kicker, such moments have been common, to begin with at stand-off but now, aged 30, at loose forward, where he says he is better suited: 'The older you get, the slower you get.' Married for two years to Amy, the couple had their first child, a boy, in October. Another life change that will ground a man, well, some men, though he is stable enough anyway.

Like Dom and Jimmy, he has slotted in well, having already known a few of the lads. He played alongside Keegan, for example, at hometown Dewsbury, where he launched his career. From there he did three years at Sheffield. He is enjoying Batley. It is a friendly club, which made it easy for his wife and him to integrate. He has a couple of lines of script tattooed along the back of his upper arms, done while on honeymoon in Thailand. The one on the left translates: *I'll either find a way or make one.* And on the right: *Every man is the architect of his own future.* He likes that one, he says, as he is a builder.

Patch was self-employed until about three months ago when a local company came out of the blue and offered him a managerial role. If any member of JK's squad is destined to be a coach one day, it is surely he. Although Keegs in the forwards and Dom in the backs get most attention, Patch is also a major influence, a calming conduit through which good work flows. The conveyor belt of goals from his right boot comes in handy too. No one ever won anything in rugby league without a dependable goal-kicker, though like the drop-goal, worth only a point in the thirteen-a-side code, it is a skill undervalued.

A good-looking man with a toothy smile and aura of serenity rare in such a confrontational sport, it is easy to picture him puffing at a pipe in his elder years, sat by some hearth in sober reflection. But for now there are those memories to write and the stillness at the heart of him will help no end if he is to rescue a precious draw.

In hush broken only by the jeers of the visiting fans, he steadies himself and rubs his stubbled chin. A stiff wind is behind him, a fact he accommodates as he steps up and lets fly. He has judged that the ball will curl in the breeze and, for a moment, it looks a sound idea. But as it heads towards the crossbar it then comes back the other way and semaphore flags are lowered. The Bulls' jeers turn to cheers, more in relief than exultation.

With two minutes and thirty seconds left, it has in the end been a close-run thing, but Batley, courageous in defeat, will have to forego the cigars on this occasion. Still, they were far from disgraced in a game from which an experienced coach like JK will find positives. As the hooter sounds, the home crowd rises to applaud a praiseworthy effort, not realizing a touch judge on the Long Stand side has rushed on with flag raised to indicate foul play; how and where is a mystery. Crafty Rowey, having got up half-heartedly to play the ball, drops back to his haunches before referee Ben Thaler, on the young official's advice, awards a penalty, thirty-five metres out and to the right of the posts. The position is marginally better than for the conversion attempt a moment earlier, though by no means straight-forward, and if the penalty itself is controversial, that is as nothing to what comes next.

Patch lines up the kick and goes through his usual routine, solid and phlegmatic. Under such pressure, a few doubts could be forgiven, though if he has any he does a good job of hiding them. 'I tend not to be nervous. It's just my job as a kicker. It's your chance to shine.' Nor does he visualize it going over, just clears his brain and tries not to think about anything at all. And up he steps again, this man with the metronome boot. Up . . . up . . . up the oval ball goes again on its arcing route toward the posts. The angle is tight, so he skies it deliber-ately high, calculating that if there is an ounce of doubt it will have a better chance of going his way. The attempt is indeed perilously close to the near upright, so close that the convulsing Bradford contingent behind the sticks leaps high in celebration, convinced in that moment and for months afterwards that the ball has gone wide. Gazing skyward, the two officials decide otherwise. It's 24–24, a finale for the ages.

Once they have extricated themselves from the field, another far from easy task, the scale of achievement begins to sink in. They haven't won, so there's no victory song, but these weary battered few have underlined an already remarkable statement of intent.

'Sometimes, fellas, you can play good football – and we scored two great tries in that first half – and sometimes you've got to batten down the hatches and scrap your knackers away. You worked your rocks off in that second half, guys; I've got to compliment you there. We are just getting better and better and better and, I'll tell you what, we can play better than that. Believe you me. We can play better than that. But at the minute, enjoy this because you were magnificent.'

As the sun begins to set, youngsters flock on to the pitch, each in his or her own little world . . . *I'm Patch Walker . . . I'm Dom Brambani* . . . while mum and dad sink a nerve-settling snifter and a lone press man taps at his match report behind glass at the back of the main stand. Yet in cars tuned to local radio on the way home, there is one more surprise to digest. As usual, JK is asked for his thoughts on BBC Leeds. He reveals that the penalty was given for a choke tackle and praises Walker's nerve, pointing out how Batley have only missed three kicks this season; then comes the real revelation. *Your name has been linked with Wakefield Trinity Wildcats. Are you preparing to leave Batley?* Wrong-footed, he resorts to cliché, his response tellingly noncommittal. 'I've no thoughts on that at all. I'm really enjoying being part of this group. What's in the future is in the future. You turn up for work, you enjoy your work, and I'm certainly doing that at this moment in time.'

Monday morning, 9 a.m., JK confirms the story is true. He is in a quandary. Something special is happening at Batley, but Wakefield would be full-time, more beneficial career-wise. It's a difficult one.

'I don't know what I'm thinking yet. I've spoken to my wife about it in great detail but we don't know yet. We don't know.' The papers report that he is on a shortlist but he knows nothing about that and keeps schtum on that evening's BBC *Super League Show* also. By Tuesday night, he walks around as if a weight has been lifted. The papers now have Willie Poching, Chris Chester and Glenn Morrison as favourites, caretaker coach Stuart Dickens out of the running. In Ron's Lounge, Kear confides that, yes, he will be going to Wakefield, but as their director of rugby rather than coach. And next season, not this. He hasn't slept for four nights. He's been in turmoil about it, torn both ways. They wanted him now but conscience dictated otherwise: 'I just couldn't do it. I couldn't look these lads in the face.'

Wakefield do, though, mean a lot to him. He would love the chance to have a Super League swansong, walk out with them at Wembley maybe, but not yet. His promises about an historic year weren't just changing-room rhetoric. 'This is a special group. I want to lead them to something special as intended.' Nor is the job set in stone yet. He will meet Kevin and Iro tonight to confirm details, but it does look a done deal. Chester will be named coach this week and JK will take on his role at the end of this season, if Batley agree – and he doesn't see why they wouldn't.

The boardroom smells of baking. Representatives of a three-year project, Creative People and Places, are in the kitchen conjuring various loaves, one of which is pink. It's an Arts Council scheme to enthuse the areas in the UK with the lowest arts engagement, North Kirklees being one. The aim is to break down barriers and appeal to multicultural audiences. Aptly, given that Batley don't have any, this trio's piece will be called 'Dough'. 'So what we are looking for is food memories,' says Olivia, a postgrad from London. 'The food people eat in those communities and the kinds that come from dough: bread, pasta, chapatti, naan, doughnuts . . .'

Downstairs, Carl says his wife enjoyed her visit on Sunday. It had been a good idea to bring her and the baby. Less optimistically, Paddy Hesketh has in fact torn a shoulder joint. Across the corridor, in the away-team changing room, Chris Ulugia waits for a rub from Ally or James, the former driving her elbow into Rowey's back, Dom face down on a bed alongside. 'He just put his arm around my neck and started choking me,' the prop says of the key incident. 'Their stupidity, our gain. Happy days.' The others don't bother to suppress a chuckle.

Uce sits in quiet satisfaction, with the watchful grace of a jungle cat. He enjoyed Sunday. He played well, was a threat throughout and felt he'd made a point that even a disallowed try couldn't ruin: 'I got it down, no one else saw it,' he says, voice barely above a whisper. The 24-year-old former Parramatta Eels junior signed at Odsal on a two-year deal from Queensland side Mackay Cutters, but in 2015 hadn't much figured. The family background is Samoan but Uce was born in New Zealand, his parents moving to Australia when he was three. Hence he grew up in Sydney, where he too began young, aged eight at Fairfield United, a junior club that only last year was saved from financial collapse by sponsorship from local businesses. It's not only in the northern hemisphere that clubs capable of producing grass-roots talent for the elite leagues struggle. At Fairfield, the trajectory for promising youth is Parramatta. That was Uce's story too, initially via the Cabramatta feeder club in Sydney's south-western suburbs, then into the Eels' junior set-up, aged sixteen.

He went to a sports high school, classmates including such future superstars as Kangaroos and New South Wales State of Origin winger Jarryd Hayne, destined for an aborted punt as a running back with NFL side San Francisco 49ers. Everything revolved around rugby league. 'It set up my schooling, paid for my fees, took a lot of pressure off my parents. Parramatta paid for all that.' At the Cutters, he heard one of the boys had signed in England. Having been at Mackay for two years without going anywhere, he got an email contact and sent his highlights and CV. The Bulls were initially impressed but even prior to that health issues had brought frustration. In Parramatta's Under-20s, he'd been forced to stop playing for a while after surgery to remove his thyroid – hence a telltale scar on his throat. They told him to take the rest of the year off, but then it all fell quiet, so to the Queensland Cup he went, a very good standard of rugby league but, after the Eels, a sizeable backward career step – in Australia anyway. Maybe Bradford could be a stepping stone back to a full-time future and, who knew, one day the NRL. Stranger things have happened.

West Yorkshire wasn't what he was expecting, that's for sure. Preseason training was tough; he hadn't realized how dark it was going to be, early. He arrived in October just as winter was setting in, the weather cold, the evenings gloomy: 'I guess I found it a little depressing.' His girlfriend, awaiting a visa, came over six months later, everything in that line since resolved. And with the season underway, to begin with it went fine. He played in a couple of friendlies, scored a try against Leeds, picked one week, out the next. Not bad. But after the first injury, he couldn't get back into the side. 'I struggled and just wanted to play. It's hard training every week and not being selected.'

Ten miles away up the A652, meanwhile, JK sniffed his chance and negotiations to bring Ulugia to the Mount began. Though it was hardly Bondi Beach, he liked the place immediately; for a start he felt wanted. 'The boys at Bradford were pretty quiet, but here everyone is loud, their attitude is good. I like that.' Tending towards introversion, it's nice to be around people who bring him out of himself. Still, from a playing point of view, this year is mainly about having a good year and gaining another full-time contract, wherever it may be. He wants to further his career and take any opportunities he can. If that means staying in England a few more years, so be it. 'But whatever happens I'll not be too bummed. I just want to enjoy my rugby and do what I can.' Maybe the Bradford game was the start of that? 'I try to prepare for every game the same, but, yeah, it felt different, which I wasn't expecting. I didn't think it was going to get to me as much as it did.' He is glad now that the Bulls let him go.

9

If Ikram Butt gets sick of debunking the myth that rugby isn't for Asians he doesn't let it show. In February 1995 – the centenary of the Northern Union – he ran out against Wales, in Cardiff, to become England's first Muslim rugby international, either code. Twenty-one years later, he is still putting himself about tirelessly with trademark charm and good humour.

Born in St Mary's, Leeds, in 1968, this enthusiastic child of first-generation Pakistani immigrants had a playing career as solid as it was wholehearted. Growing up in Headingley, rugby league got him young. Brother Khurshid, known as Tony, turned professional first, a prop forward with Featherstone. Soon Ikram, a powerful and stocky winger with an appetite for defence, was joining him there via the junior ranks at Leeds. It was at Rovers that he made his name before moving on to London, Huddersfield and Hunslet. Upon retirement in 1998, he became a development officer in Bradford and formed BARA – the British Asian Rugby Association – answering a calling. These days he has political connections and promotes organizations like White Ribbon, a campaign to tackle male violence against women and girls, and Connecting Communities, a regular at the House of Commons. His kitchen at home must be immaculate since, if social media is anything to go by, he mostly eats out while promoting myriad good causes and both codes of rugby across the UK, Europe and South Asia. No great surprise then that when he arranges a get-together to discuss why more members of the Asian community aren't attracted to Batley Bulldogs, he chooses to meet in an ice-cream parlour.

Though a globetrotter these days, West Yorkshire is where Ikram's heart is; rugby league is his game. And while he never played for Batley, he played against them many times. Due to the town's large South Asian population he has visited often and knows it well. Gelato's is on Commercial Street, at the end of a drag filled with bookies and charity shops opposite Batley Shopping Centre, whose 'modernity' has in turn been overtaken by the superstore behind it. The grand old Cooperative Society Central Stores that the Shopping Centre replaced, now long gone, once stretched along here also, an architectural delight in its day, topped with minarets. Around the corner, en route to the stadium, is the Job Centre and a boarded-up Batley Working Men's Club, second in pull and popularity only to the Variety Club once upon a time but which, come summer, will be a pile of rubble.

Four of tonight's guests are of Pakistani extraction, a fifth, solicitor Mohammed Sadiq Patel, will share an Indian perspective. He is delayed with a broken-down car in Blackburn. Nadeem Iqbal, a gas engineer, kicks us off with a bit of local history. The reason there are so many Muslims around Mount Pleasant, he says, is because the first 'proper' mosque was built there, so it's where everyone congregated. Prior to that, there was a room on Bradford Road, down among the mills where the first Asian arrivals in the 1950s and '60s worked. Not many of the newcomers spoke English. If one did, he could translate, fill in forms and so on, the better to help with the settling-in process.

Nadeem has lived in Batley for eighteen years, two streets away from Mount Pleasant in fact, but admits the only way he knows a game's on is when cars park outside his house. Hasn't the roar of a crowd inspired him to nip over and see what all the fuss is about? 'No.'

Shahzad Sadiq, an advice worker for charities Age UK and Macmillan Cancer Support, is also present, as is Abdul Ghaffar, a prospective independent candidate in May's council elections, a likeably eccentric chap in a woolly hat, beard and green Macmillan sweatshirt. A natural comedian with a Yorkshire-Pakistani accent, Gaff's speech is peppered with local colloquialisms. He is a familiar figure in these parts and every bit as obsessed with sport as Ikram. He arrived in Batley with his parents, apparently destined for the textile industry. Making up the quartet is Professor Tariq Malik, professor in business and management at Dongbei University of Finance and Economics, China, who has just bought a holiday home in the town.

Shahzad, softly spoken, nibbles at a common theme. Rugby wasn't much played at school: 'Our communities are more involved with football and cricket.' The FA is trying to get Asian schoolchildren more involved in football, but he hasn't heard of anything like it being done by the rugby league authorities. 'Maybe there's a lack of interest and that's why the rugby league doesn't bother, but there won't be any interest if they don't get involved, will there?' It's a vicious circle.

Were they here to defend themselves, the RFL, like the Batley club, might point to a shortfall in financial and human resources that has impacted upon the number of development officers Red Hall feels able to employ nationally and locally recently. But it doesn't change the bigger picture. Schools must be engaged somehow. 'You've got your Messis, your Ronaldos; you need a few big-name rugby league players. I met Ikram when he was at a cricket do.'

Gaff arrived in Batley aged seven, in 1967. 'I'm coming from a village background, about 50km away from Rawalpindi, don't know what western society is, what England is . . . land at Heathrow and cry all the way here for five hours.' Three days later, he is in a Catholic school, the same one as Kevin Nicholas in fact, though neither man is aware of it. 'Don't know a word of English; parents say, "Whatever you do, don't eat any meat as it won't be halal." The teacher took out a box of crayons. I thought, "Is it lunchtime? Am I meant to eat these, or what?"' Watching the other kids, he figured it out. 'That's how you learn, isn't it? I cried every day in the playground, got moved to an Asian school and off it went from there. Went to junior school, started picking up English. First words I learned were Bobby Charlton and Georgie Best, I'm still a Man United supporter because of that.'

Though he loved sport, he played only one game of rugby at secondary school and hadn't liked it because they all jumped on top of him. Upon leaving, though, he did watch a bit of Dewsbury at their old ground when a schoolmate turned pro there. He launched a business in Leeds, becoming, like Ikram, a regular at Headingley. After uprooting it to Knottingley, he followed Castleford to Wembley, mainly because, as a sponsor, the club supported him. 'But for some reason, despite living in this town – if I ever moved, it was only from Batley to Dewsbury or vice versa – and even though it's just at the top of the hill where I go to play cricket, I have never been to watch rugby league at Batley Bulldogs. Never. No idea why.'

Is it a myth, as Ikram says, that Asians don't like tough sports? Kabaddi, after all, is one of the toughest on the planet. 'Personally? I didn't want to play anything in the cold. Indoor games preferably. I was a top table-tennis player and, even though I didn't have the height, joined the gymnastics and basketball clubs.'

Ikram interjects. 'I've done a fair bit of work in Batley and Dewsbury with the club and they have gone into schools. To me, it works both ways. If you are familiar with a sport and there is that engagement, a sense of belonging, then you want to be part of it. I think rugby has found it difficult, particularly in areas like Batley, Dewsbury, Keighley and elsewhere, because a large percentage of Asian communities haven't been reached out to. School is great and that's your first taste of rugby – it was certainly mine – but it needs to go further. Not necessarily up at the club, as people might be wary of going there because there are still barriers to be broken down, but maybe doing something within the locality. But that takes the club to come to the locality and we don't really see them there, do we?'

Professor Malik listens intently in a corner. He knows nothing about rugby of either code but is happy to contribute an outsider view. 'There seems to be barriers, intended or unintended, but it *is* possible to promote music, rugby or whatever, it is just a matter of conditions. In our business, we call it attention structure. We have twenty-four hours in a day when our attention is on whatever it is we are doing. If you bring forward rugby players, you put attention on them for fifteen or thirty minutes. It's not that people are Muslims and Muslims are not interested; it's just a barrier, and awareness is the only way to break it down.'

One reason Professor Malik has bought a home in Batley is that having seen an old building, built in 1881, he became interested in its history. But might not that same history be a reason why, perhaps, so many at the club are so jealously possessive of it? The chairman sees himself not so much as its owner but protector, the club a legacy to be passed down to descendants when he in turn is called to the great kennel in the sky. The so-called 'greatest game' is also known as 'our game'. Furthermore, might 'the Muslim issue' not be a red herring? After all, not only do Batley fail to attract Asian audiences, they find it hard to attract anyone, from the town's younger population especially.

The professor elaborates: 'Bradford University made Imran Khan, the Pakistani Test match cricketer, Chancellor in 2005. Why? Because he was well qualified academically? No! It's because he was idealized by so many in the city as one of them. Ikram here has to do a similar job for rugby league.'

Shahzad sees that. 'Someone might like the sport but just shy away from it. With somebody to look up to, they are more likely to think, "Yeah, why not?" If that person can do it, they can too.'

Gaff, having sponsored teams, knows the economic imperative is important. 'Kids grow up playing rugby, that's how it starts. In Batley and Dewsbury, Asian kids start playing cricket from the age of ten. Rugby? No. I've got a nephew, really big for his age. I said to my brother, "Get him into rugby." Some parents don't back them up, take them to training or say, "Try this." Then again, you can't push anybody into it. Rugby is a tough contact sport. I mean, Dewsbury have Asian sponsors, or did last time I looked; Fox's Biscuits is now owned by Asians. But for some reason the clubs haven't been pushing it.'

Shahzad points out that some Asians do compete in and watch contact sport. 'Look at boxing. You've got Amir Khan and his brother, Haroon, a few boxers of Pakistani heritage, Qais Ashfaq of Leeds . . .'

To which Gaff responds: 'You still need to be backed by your family, that's what I'm trying to say. The mentality in Asian families is often: "Rugby? Why do you want to play that?"'

Ikram's father, obsessed by sport, passed away when his son was eleven. 'Fortunately, before then, he was very supportive. So, yes, family is very important. But when I lost my dad, it was more down to myself. You need that interest. In terms of physicality, I would argue that kabaddi is just rugby without a ball. That would be a challenge . . . maybe we should offer to play Batley at kabaddi and vice versa?'

Older and wiser nowadays, Ikram concedes that mindsets are slow to change, though he would never say it is impossible. 'Attitudes are passed down. It happens, though. Look at the Mount Cricket Club playing at the Vatican. Nobody thought they could achieve something like that, but they did. Everything is possible. Gaff, tell them about what we are doing with Bill Beaumont in rugby union.'

'Yeah, well, I don't even know the rules of rugby union [no one does, he is assured, not even the players], but we went to a match at Fylde, Bill Beaumont's club. That led to us trying to arrange a match for deaf people against a Knottingley RU amateur team; if it comes off, brilliant. They were so surprised. Four Asian guys from Batley.'

It's not just about playing either, is it? Not everybody is barmy or tough enough to cope with open-age rugby league. It is about audiences too, enjoying the spectacle. Seeing a rugby league match as a viable entertainment option, an event to tell your friends about.

Professor Malik stresses the importance of prestige and respectability in a community where parents very often dream of their children becoming professionals in another sense – doctors, perhaps, or lawyers. 'Prestige is indirectly related to the ability to earn money. It's a commercial thing. There has to be some link with sponsors and promotion, very important. Once you attract attention in that way, people get involved and it becomes reality. But it isn't a short-term fix; you have to be persistent. Persistent people survive.'

Ikram asks the professor a question. 'Our parents have been here fifty or sixty years now and there hasn't been great change in terms of integration. What would you say to that?'

'One reason is we ended up in ghettoes. You must communicate in the local language, not only in terms of speaking but culturally too.'

With that, Gaff fully concurs. 'Although I live in Batley, I've had businesses all over. I played cricket at Knottingley Town for twenty-five years; I can't now because of my eyesight, but I am president of the club. Go into a town with only one or two Asian businesses, the newsagent or whatever, and they welcome you. It's important to mix. Ikram played in what is a predominantly white sport. I used to say I knew him, even though I didn't. Good for business [*laughter*]. Once the white community gets to know you, they welcome you. But if they don't know you and get told on television that we are all terrorists, it's another matter.'

Are circumstances better now than in Ikram's playing days? An era when he received little understanding from coaches, particularly during Ramadan. Wouldn't the atmosphere be far less intimidating if they could be persuaded to give the sport a try? 'Yes,' he says. 'You've got coaches like John Kear who have greater knowledge, experience and understanding of the communities they serve. An individual just needs to do his job right. No one is asking for special treatment, just to be treated like everyone else. People respond to different techniques. You might have to shout at Gaff to get him going but put your arm around Nadeem. "Let's have a chat, this is what I want you to do . . ."'

And back the discussion turns to role models, of whom league in northern England has too few. Players like dual-code international Sonny Bill Williams, a New Zealand Maori converted to Islam, formerly with Batley's NRL namesakes Canterbury Bulldogs, a club with huge Muslim support from Sydney's large and vocal Lebanese community. Asian cricketers like Moeen Ali, Samit Patel and Yorkshire pair Adil Rashid and Azeem Rafiq. The bottom-end stuff is worthy, but perhaps as the professor suggests, money, prestige and a higher profile will ultimately talk more, especially to Millennials obsessed by glamour and social cachet. Maybe the RFL simply does not have the resources or connections or energy or intelligence or vision to make it happen?

Still, they must do what they can and having worked with nationally acclaimed Leeds Rhinos for three years trying to stimulate engagement with the city's black and minority ethnic (BME) communities, Ikram knows how even in that big-city environment, South Asians have been notoriously tricky – if not impossible – to engage regularly in club affairs. But still, he insists, it can be done. 'Batley, for example, have had years and years to develop partnerships with the local community and, until recently, never showed interest. That's changing now, better late than never.' Then again, maybe the problem doesn't so much lie with individual clubs as with the structure of rugby league as a whole.

'You've got to get people at ten, eleven or twelve,' says Gaff. 'That's when it starts. Do you like it? Do you not like it? They get into the system; you build bonds. There might be fights on the field but afterwards you are mates. I go to pubs and drink tonic water. That's fine. No harm done. Great banter. Asians have banter. English people have banter. It is communication. They call me names; I call them names. It starts at grass-roots level and families have to be involved.'

'Compare Batley's Asian population in relation to white and it is quite a lot,' says Shahzad. 'Yet do the same sum in relation to the amount of people watching Batley and it is extremely small. If that continues and Batley's Asian population continues to rise, who knows what will become of Batley rugby league in future?'

As Mohammed Sadiq Patel is keen to remind everyone, when he rushes in just as everyone is getting up to leave, Batley's largest Asian population is not Pakistani Muslim, it is Gujarati, also Muslim, rather than Hindu or Sikh. 'There are sub-sects within religions too. In Islam, you have Iranian Sunni, Saudi Arabian Shi'ite; everyone wants to be part of a gang, tribe, club, family – call it what you will.'

A third cup of tea – and perhaps another plateful of chocolate fudge cake or jam coconut sponge – will be required.

Unaware he is a legal eagle you might nevertheless guess it. Dapper, well spoken, confident and prone to a confrontational style of discourse – *I put it to you* – his conversation is that of a man with a brief. He could be grilling a character witness in a courtroom drama.

'The Barrister', as his friends call him, played union at school, 'because Mr Foster played for Rotherham and Terry Simpson, head of PE – nice gentleman, I once played cricket with his son at Hanging Heaton – was a union man. Weird that, isn't it? Batley High – very working class, rough and tough, playing rugby union, remarkable.'

Of all Ikram's guests, rugby references trip most readily from his lips. He grew up watching union internationals like Rob Andrew and Jonathan Webb – 'a surgeon, wasn't he?' – and has memories of Kurt Sorensen's Widnes 'when there was a lot more rugby league on terrestrial television than now. Martin Offiah, Andy Gregory – we knew all the icons and watched it at home.' He has vivid recall of the Hull–Wigan Challenge Cup final of 1985 – 'The great Peter Sterling, Brett Kenny' – but knows nothing at all about Batley. 'To use a football analogy, you might live in Barnet but you follow Arsenal, don't you?'

Slightly more recently, he attended the 2002 Super League Grand Final between Bradford and St Helens, won by Saints with a late drop-goal at Old Trafford. 'But let's be blunt. It's never been a sport for Asians, has it? Aside from Ikram. I'll tell you why. It's predominantly white working class. And for some reason they don't think Asian men can play rugby. Well, what I don't understand is that an Asian man can work in a factory under very difficult circumstances for fourteen, fifteen, sixteen hours, yet can't play rugby league? Nonsense. I'll tell you what, if we had Asian lads playing rugby they'd be really good at it, because they don't want to get a smack, do they?'

The best policy with the Barrister is to toss him a line and let him get on with it. 'You tell me where it says in your rulebook that you've got to be of a certain weight or height to play. The best players have been under 5 ft 8 in., have they not? Jonathan Davies isn't the biggest bloke in the world, is he? Bobbie Goulding, Joe Lydon.'

Given his knowledge of rugby league players, he clearly takes a passing interest at least. Yet here is another local lad who has never so much as seen inside the ground on his doorstep. 'Well, give me one reason why I should? When I went to the Grand Final, it was the first time I'd been to a live rugby league match. I enjoyed it. The humour, how both sets of fans were so well behaved and amiable. Completely different to football, so I don't think it's about intimidation or the wrong kind of people. It ticks all the boxes for family entertainment. But let's be frank, and please don't take this the wrong way, you've got to look at social demographics, don't you? Great men, leaders of men, run important organizations. Who is the chief executive of the rugby league? Is he a captain of industry? Is he a learned man? What exactly is his background?' The chap in question is Nigel Wood and an explanation of his credentials, such as they are, is embarked upon, though nowhere near swiftly enough. 'He can't be much of a CEO if he can't open up such a great game to a wide audience, can he? I don't believe in this ethnic/non-ethnic nonsense. It's an entertaining sport that people can enjoy, children can get fit playing to get rid of this nasty thing obesity, so clearly the administrators are not doing their jobs, are they?'

Why, Mohammed Sadiq Patel wonders, has Yorkshire County Cricket Club's CEO gone out of his way to visit India, learn about the Indian Premier League, and then specifically earmarked an area of Headingley where there will be no consumption of alcohol after an unfortunate incident when Muslim families had it thrown at them? 'There will be a prayer room in the stadium, because when a Test match is on, or a one-day international, they want lots of people of faith or no faith to go to the cricket. If people wish to pray, they can.' In August, that multi-faith facility will indeed be opened.

Batley may well counter that Mount Pleasant isn't Headingley; space is at a premium. And as for an alcohol ban, what of Kevin's precious bar takings, such a vital source of income? 'What do you mean, no money? One second, let's get this right. One thing I love about the English, they only do business when there is money. If led to believe there is no money, the English stop doing business. Think of the famous Irish Catholic priest who went to run an orphanage in Kenya. How many gold medallists has he produced? Who won the 800m final in the London Olympics? David Rudisha. Lord Coe called it the most exhilarating athletic performance he had seen in his life; smashed the world record, such artistry, elegance, pure aesthetic beauty. Are you telling me he had Loughborough University Centre for Sport and Excellence backing, rehab baths, nutritionists, sports scientists and everything else that goes with it when he was learning how to run in the hills of Kenya? And you are telling me that Batley can't engage with the community because they don't have any cash?'

Well, no, not exactly but . . .

'How much would it cost for Batley Bulldogs to open their doors at noon on a Sunday? So the chairman . . . Kevin? . . . he writes a letter, doesn't even have to post it these days, the English are skint after all; he can email it and can save 28p on the stamp – we assume they have internet – email every school in the area asking if they can send five boys and five girls to walk out with the team as mascots. Are you telling me that will cost money? For that child there in line, it would be the proudest moment in his or her life so far, to walk out with a rugby player holding their hand. Let me explain to you the difficulty with the English, right . . . [he looks around for a conceptual tool] This is milk. And you put the milk in the tea. Then you put the milk down. Then you get the spoon, you lift it up and you put it in the tea and you mix it – that's the English. Everything must be a process. If anything else can affect that process, they are not open to ideas or thoughts. But can anyone put a price on social capital, as a famous Harvard professor put it? How much value do you put on that? Parents might think, maybe I should take my boy to this game because they made us feel welcome. They made him feel very proud and he's inquisitive about it. That's the problem, you see. Your solicitor, who you have defended, can't think outside the box.'

Ikram recalls being at a Breakfast Club once when Kev, in comic mode presumably, called this 'a Christian country' when he was the only Muslim in the room. The memory of it still rankles. 'Well, if he's a Christian,' says the Barrister, 'he should follow the example of a very famous Olympian who didn't run on a Sunday. *Chariots of Fire* – that guy. Why is he making money on the Lord's Day? Let's not beat about the bush, my friend. What is the general IQ level in rugby league? When they sat in that famous hotel in Huddersfield, what was their main bone of contention?' How ironic, he says, that a sport founded on the principle of financial independence should find itself so much poorer than the organization it left or was engineered into leaving.

'Certain sports, colonialists used in order to export the values of empires, namely rugby union and cricket. League didn't fit in with that and as soon as it wasn't exported to the Commonwealth it was never going to be internationally popular or powerful or wealthy.' Similarly, football couldn't be exported 'because it has no structure that expresses colonial values'. English unrest at the mishandling of FIFA by Sepp Blatter and chums, not to mention the awarding of World Cups to Russia and the Middle East, owes more to a need for revenge on a world that 'stole' the game from them, he reckons. 'Why do Welsh rugby fans sing? It's cultural, my friend, because the Welsh sang on their way to the coalmines and on their way home.' Hang on, what about the coalminers of Featherstone, Leigh and Whitehaven? Why don't they sing? Too late. 'Because the Welsh worked underground they've got higher lung capacities to belt out a tune, yeah? So it's also physical, isn't it?'

This is debate JK style. Get on the front foot. Be relentless, in their face; don't give an inch; challenge. Take space. 'What's Batley's DNA? What do they represent? I know what Fox's represent. What is the brand of the Bulldogs? Is it Churchillian? Is it military? Why focus on bulldogs?' Doubtful anyone gave it much thought, to be honest; alliteration most likely. 'A-ha! That then proves the point. If these people can't even understand their own identity, what chance have they got to engage the grass-roots community, my friend?'

His own firm of solicitors is in Keighley, around twenty miles away, en route to Skipton in the Aire Valley, home to the Cougars, who are currently trying to win promotion from League 1. 'They are becoming aware. In order to succeed, you've got to have partnerships, work with the local authorities. Why are you there? What is your purpose?' He met former Great Britain coach Brian Noble at a dinner and found him impressive. 'If Mr Noble ran the game, it would be in a much healthier position.'

It is pointed out that, historically, rugby league has been a far more inclusive sport than most, albeit for pragmatic reasons rather than any intrinsic passion for human rights. Those pioneering black players and coaches are brought up, there's Ikram himself, Keegan Hirst: '... but no, no, no, my friend, it's political. I'll tell you why it's political, yeah ...' and the Barrister is off again, tongue at least partly in cheek, with a rant worthy of any barroom philosopher.

'I put it to you that the north is predominantly Labour and there is definitely an affinity between rugby league and the British Labour Party. The Labour Party doesn't want people to educate themselves. The Labour Party wants people to go to the working men's club and drink. Then go and watch the local rugby league team, right? Not have intelligent, fiery, visionary people saying, "We can aspire to go the next mile." It's a vicious circle, isn't it? The point I am making, my friend, is that you've got the working class going to Batley High School, destined to become painters, decorators and bricklayers; apprenticeships at best. Then go blow your money at the local pub or working men's club because your dad and grand-dad did it, right? If you're good enough, go and play rugby league, because you don't have to give articulate interviews. There's no aspiration. The Establishment has kept down the masses and I'll tell you who is at fault – the Labour Party. When was the last time you had a Tory Prime Minister present the Challenge Cup?' Goodness knows, though a pre-ascension Margaret Thatcher once went in the 1970s and Her Majesty the Queen is patron of the RFL. 'Well, yes, but she's got to keep her subjects happy, doesn't she, my friend, because those loyal working-class subjects are more patriotic, right? It's the Labour Party that wants this apartheid. Give money to Asian clubs so they can remain Asian. Give money to the white working class so they can remain white working class.' And never the twain shall meet.

'Batley. One of the oldest clubs, right, first to win the Challenge Cup? So basically the Notts County of rugby league, great for history, nothing else. It's a shame. If you took away the politics, cut away all the history and culture, we Asians as a community share the same lives. We weren't born with silver spoons. Our parents grafted just as hard as their parents grafted. We've more in common with rugby league players, rugby league families, with rugby league stadiums than with the snobs in rugby union and cricket. And it's a tragedy that our community has not aligned itself to rugby league or that rugby league has not aligned itself with the ethnic community because, let's be honest, our parents when they first came here worked in the factories. They were in the unions. Extended families. Very tight-knit communities. That's the rugby league family, isn't it?'

10

IF JOHN KEAR is linked with any competition it is the one he won with Sheffield and Hull, whose final has been contested at Wembley since 1929, some twenty-nine years after Batley last won it in Leeds. Why is no mystery; his brand of coaching lends itself well to lifting a side for a one-off game, however unlikely the odds. But there is far more to it than inspirational words. Few coaches read or predict a game better, or better equip their players to rise above the ordinary.

For JK, this year's Challenge Cup campaign began six weeks ago in February, when he and his Eagles skipper, the club's current coach Mark Aston, conducted the second-round draw at RAF Coningsby, Lincolnshire. No professional teams were featured then; just eighteen surviving amateur set-ups from round one. League 1 clubs would enter later that month, with Championship clubs coming in from round four and Super League clubs from round five onwards.

Why RAF Coningsby? An acknowledgement of a relationship between the Armed Forces and the Challenge Cup dating back to the early 1990s, the game having prior to that been banned in all three Services. By 1999, with help from Parliament, that blatant injustice was overturned and several Army, Navy and RAF teams were up and running. Nowadays, servicemen and women take league far and wide. In the Challenge Cup, there have been memorable wins, most notably for the British Army, who beat Featherstone Lions in round two in 2009, before being beaten by Featherstone Rovers. A forward-thinker,

JK was all for doing his bit, even if that meant a long Tuesday-night drive, car-sharing with his old skipper, through the Fens.

Aston pulled the home teams from a plastic bowl, Kear the away sides, before the former shared his thoughts on the latter in a hangar whose operational, if nowadays purely ceremonial, Second World War fighter planes put sporting heroism into proper perspective. 'Everybody there in 1998 is indebted to John: what he did for us, how he prepared us, the detail of his preparation, how he made us believe. Rugby league isn't only his passion, he watches and thinks about little else. It's a compulsion.' 'Tubby', as Ashton is known, called the night before Wembley 'emotional'. 'People were crying over what they were going to do for each other, how we were going to win the Cup. For anybody to beat us, they'd have had to be special. At the captain's run, he had us walking up to the royal box, pretending to lift the Cup: "Get used to it, because tomorrow you're going to do that." When people ask what the game was like, I say, "Watching a recording of what we were going to do before it happened." The preparation was so precise.'

In March, ahead of Batley's entry into the Challenge Cup and the fourth-round clash with Whitehaven, confirmation of the coach's delayed departure tossed a pebble into still waters. How would the players react? Were all those fine words just that, words? He had called them a band of brothers, a special group destined for special things, and every single one of them had bought into it. *One . . . two . . . three . . . Bulldogs!* But players are practical too. They move on, coaches move on – or are moved on; it's the nature of professional sport, isn't it?

Yet sport, like life, hangs upon illusion. It is a distraction from the sheer vast pointlessness of time, space, existence – an attempt, heroic in its way, to impose order, even temporarily, on chaos. Every man and woman needs a code. Concepts like loyalty and betrayal in such circumstances may be delusional, but the shirt, the cause – in the moment, they matter. And if they don't, well, why bother?

There are practical issues too, potential conflicts of interest. What if Batley were to make the top four and Wakefield, currently eleventh in a twelve-team Super League, finish in the bottom four and the two are in the Qualifiers together? Where then are JK's loyalties? What if Batley meet Wakefield with not just relegation at stake but his full-time job in 2017? And what if he takes Batley's best players with him? How will the fans react, the directors too, though for the moment they seem to be giving the plan their support? JK knows more than anyone that if results do now suddenly dip, in many eyes the blame for sinking a happy ship will be his.

By Thursday, the coach has phoned every player personally to explain the situation. At training, bobble-hatted Ainy is first to shake his hand, congratulates him, bets he's looking forward to it. He is, but he's looking forward to the rest of this season too. More handshakes with Keegs, Dom and Chandler, who is getting wed in the autumn and thinks it will be okay to miss training on the morning of the wedding, though with a new coach – whoever it is – you can't be certain, can you? When the team meeting begins, JK addresses them as a group. 'As far as I am concerned, it's irrelevant until November. All we do, we carry on how we are. There is nothing I would love more than for our last match to be a middle-eight game with Wakefield. That would be my driving force – it really would – to see if we could turn them over. Then I can ask for an extra few grand.' When laughter subsides, he puts on Whitehaven's clips against Sheffield. He warns against underestimating them – they will be tough opponents. Lose and the grapevine whispers, the doubts, will take hold. Win and he and his team will be on their way to putting the issue to bed.

His warnings are justified. The game lacks intensity. We score. You score. By the end of the first half, Batley, playing uphill, are 24–18 in front. Substitute Jimmy Davey, hamstring healed, scoots through with his first touch, though Haven had led 18–6 at one point after Brownz opened the scoring. Rowey and Reitts also cross and Patch kicks the goals to save Batley's blushes but it hasn't been convinc-ing. 'I'll have that substitution,' quips JK, leaving the dugout, before a less jovial 'If we've got our foot on their throat, let's choke the bastards by being professional, okay, guys?' in the changing room.

The Bulldogs make an effective start to the second half, Rowey barrelling in again. The Cumbrians' reply, though, is soon forthcoming and even when Chandler's first try of the season pushes the margin back out to twelve, the visitors still claw it back to 36–36 with fifteen minutes to go. Surprisingly, tries dry up, extra-time a possibility until Dom slots a drop-goal five minutes from the end to send Batley through, 37–36. In the boardroom, the visiting directors sit around a table bearing daffodils, sombre as a Victorian family portrait.

'Lose on Saturday,' Kear had told his charges, 'and we'll be sat with us feet up watching *Grandstand*.' Instead, after the draw on Tuesday, they would be on the box themselves a fortnight later, at home to Featherstone Rovers in what unexpectedly becomes the first of two televised matches, albeit on Sky Sports rather than the BBC, the Cup's primary broadcaster. Since Sky took rights to the Championship from subscription channel Premier Sports two years ago, the division has lacked exposure, so the cameras are welcome.

It's Keegan's 100th game for the club, so he leads the team out on to the field holding the hands of his children, also in Batley kit. With the big screen up and TV trucks here since dawn, the contrast in atmosphere with round four is stark. Bustling about the boardroom, Nellie and Barbara – armed with a raspberry sponge cake – clocked on at 8 a.m. for a 5 p.m. start. With television here, the *Songs of Praise* effect kicks in. A good crowd rocks up, along with notables like RFL chairman Brian Barwick and the Challenge Cup itself. One of the most attractive prizes in sport, the Northern Rugby Football Union Challenge Cup, to give the silverware its proper name, is placed directly below the trophy cabinet, behind a red VIP rope, Batley etched upon it three times. Children smaller than the Cup itself pose for photos.

The stadium too has had a spring clean. A new Fox's Biscuits sign takes pride of place outside and other such hoardings are strung around the perimeter of the pitch. Less welcome were the eggs and flour bombs thrown at a turnstile wall during the week. A regular occurrence, according to Dan Winner, son of Andy. The vandalism took place in a camera blind spot and was a sod to clear up.

Roughly speaking, the clubs will share today's proceeds fifty-fifty. The £20,000 received from Sky is to be split two ways, though Batley will keep bar receipts, as they had to pay two to three grand for TV scaffolding. Gate receipts too will be divided, once VAT has been paid. According to a Dewsbury Celtic Under-15s player here for the curtain raiser, the tunnel smells of 'Deep Heat and farts'. An anxious match commissioner enquires about the whereabouts of official RFL time-keeper Colin Morris, who rushes in late.

Going by the formbook, the game is too close to predict, although according to the statisticians Featherstone have not won at Mount Pleasant since April 2004 and they last beat Batley in the Cup, 9–6, in 1933. At half time, it looks as if Rovers might redress that, Oldham having already delivered a bigger upset, beating Super League side Hull KR, 22–36, away. Roared on by fans wearing ironic flat caps, the visitors go in at the break 6–4 ahead but, having won the toss, Batley were playing uphill and are content with that. A first try of the season for Squiresy, on his return, had nudged the Bulldogs ahead but when Fev hit back it took something special. Defending fifteen metres out from his own line after Patch's sensational 40/20 kick, giant Samoan Misi Taulapapa caught Scotty high in the chest, legally dislodged the ball and raced away, yellow boots pumping, over the other eighty-five. That score went unconverted but Featherstone took the lead just before the break when Luke Blake was pinged for ball-stripping.

Returning to the field through cheerleaders dancing to 'Jai Ho' – 'let victory prevail' – the Bulldogs' patient approach continues in the third quarter. They are tested but hold firm until a message goes on to give the ball air, up the pace, Featherstone are beginning to look tired and pedestrian. That they do and with Alistair Leak – small, strong, terrier like – at the heart of things, four tries in a dazzling six-minute burst follow.

Few sports if any suffer a dearth of play-by-play analysis quite like rugby league, whether in commentary, newspaper reports or on the terraces. No one is likely to discuss or even notice a second tackle play in which no try is scored or penalty given. Who pushed? Who trailed? Short side or open side? What play was selected and to what point on the field was it intended to reach? A situation designed to encourage the calumny that this is a simple game for simple people. Why is it so? Perhaps because too few observers truly understand what it is they are looking at. Or, more charitably, because the game moves along so rapidly that such moments pass in the blink of an eye, tough to register in the instant. The pace is so fast that the skill and speed of thought required of the participants can be lost in the rush, almost impossible to process, making rugby league players among the most criminally underappreciated athletes in world sport.

Who, in the maelstrom, would either recognize or have time to comment upon a side wrapping to C, before arcing and putting on an inside move to get behind poor positioning? Or a net out the back; the trailer in a push play; a sinker play; a cut back inside dummy-half to aim behind the marker, a spot teams rarely if ever defend?

Try one is scored in fifty-one seconds. Dave Scott picks up the ball when Ainy traps a clearing kick on Batley's ten-metre line. *First tackle.* Ainy, Patch, Tuna, back inside to Patch, Breth. *Second tackle.* Forty-metre line. Leak to Tuna, short side. *Third tackle.* Leak to Cain to Keegs on the big side. Leak to Patch to Cain. A pairs move to Dom behind James Harrison, now promoted to the first team, on the thirty-metre line. Dom puts on gas, races twenty metres, passes to Young Iro. His diagonal inside run through two defenders and a right-foot step around the last man brings him a debut try for the club. He removes his gumshield and punches the air as the cameras linger on dad Karl in the stand. Featherstone pivot Danny Craven is knocked cold. Rovers have declined to spend £250 on a doctor of their own and, coming round, Craven tells Batley club physician Doc Findlay – acting for both sides – that he can't remember what happened and so must leave the field.

Try two. Also fifty-one seconds. Dom collects the restart safely and passes to James Brown. He takes *tackle one*, fifteen metres out. Leak to Hirst, grounded fifteen metres further downfield, *tackle two*. Leak to Brown, offload back to Leak in midfield, halted on halfway. *Tackle three*. Brownie steps in at dummy-half, passes to Hirst, more midfield yardage made to Fev's forty-metre line. *Tackle four*. Leak scoots, finds Brown on the short side, he is working hard, the big man. He fends one defender and breaks a ragged line, before getting a pass away to Breth. He tempts the last two defenders towards the corner flag and pops a deft little inside pass to Ainy, who falls over the line.

Try three. Longer in preparation – sixty-four seconds. Restart again taken by Dom, who passes to Brownie. Takes the tackle on the twenty-metre line. Leak to Harrison, who reaches the thirty-metre line. *Tackle two*. Leak goes it alone to the forty-metre line. *Tackle three*. Patch to Keegs. *Tackle four*. Leak, Brown, Scott, Leak again. Offload to Hirst on Fev's forty-metre line, who rampages another ten metres downfield. *Tackle five*. Scotty in at dummy-half. Passes right to Patch, who shapes to kick but, instead, passes around the back of Harrison to Dom, who, this time, receives the ball on his opponents' twenty-metre line and opts to go himself. He slices back infield, sidesteps Jamie Cording and Taulapapa and reaches out to score. Physically and metaphorically Rovers are on their knees.

Try four – sixteen seconds. Fev kick the restart directly into touch. Penalty halfway, Dom finds the thirty-metre line. Leak taps, Harrison charges in, tackled just shy of twenty metres out. *Tackle one*. Leak to Brownie. He passes around the back of Patch to Dom – props aren't just for heavy lifting. The half-back puts Hirst into a gap. Batley's skipper goes on a charge to the posts before selflessly offloading one-handed to Cain, only the full-back to beat. *Coup de grâce*.

Walker kicks three conversions and though there is still some defending to do, much of it frantic, at 26–6 the game is up. Fev sound a note of defiance with a try but Patch's late penalty goal completes a 28–10 victory and the champagne cork on the bottle awarded to Dom as man of the match confirms Batley's place in the last sixteen.

With the big guns having entered, there are hopes of a money-spinning crowd-puller. Wakefield would be interesting, wouldn't it? Leeds? Wigan perhaps? In fact, Thursday's draw pairs them with Catalans Dragons, going well in Super League but with virtually no travelling support at all. Any disappointment evaporates when Sky – having been given permission to attach a microphone to JK in the dugout and at half time – opt to televise Batley's sixth-round tie too.

No one seriously anticipates a home victory, although if the Dragons do have an off day then JK ensures his side is in a position to capitalize on it. The precedent, however, isn't good. In the sides' one and only previous meeting, a quarter-final clash in 2010, the Bulldogs were thrashed 74–12. This time it is nothing like as bad. The full-time Catalan players are strong, physical and talented, not least the former NRL forward Dave Taylor whose backside is as big as Antarctica. His fellow Aussie, the controversial Willie Mason, is also in their ranks, as is Richie Myler, one-time England half-back and husband of BBC TV presenter Helen Skelton. As a seventeen-year-old with Widnes, Myler made his professional debut on this very ground. But while *le sang et or*, the blood and gold, run up a 12–0 half-time lead, on an otherwise serene Friday night more Pyrénées-Orientales than Spen Valley, Batley perform admirably.

Midway through the first half, Sky's Terry O'Connor, in the commentary box, enquires about the coach's last message. 'I can't remember,' says JK helpfully, immersed as ever in the action from the bench. In his half-time talk, broadcast on delay to be on the safe side, he praises his team's defensive effort: 'Absolutely outstanding.' The second half is more one-sided, Catalans' superior fitness, skill, strength and pace delivering four further tries in a 40–4 victory, but Batley do at least score a deserved try of their own, Alex Brown the hero from a sweet Uce Ulugia pass. 'Baaaattttllllleeeeyyyy!' roars Bulldogs fan and resident air-raid siren Tracey Grundell, seated next to the dugout in the Glen Tomlinson Stand as usual. Her mum and dad first brought her as a girl in the early 1970s and she's been a regular at Mount Pleasant since. Her dad is no longer with us but her mum still comes and is on the row in front of her daughter. The Batley players and other supporters are used to her explosive contributions by now, but the Catalans bench alongside jumps as if under sudden attack.

'When you get beat by a better team, you get beat by a better team,' JK says, his players exhausted but equally philosophical in the sheds. Tomorrow they will enjoy a barbecue here with their families. Gallant Youths or not, a Wembley visit in this day and age is a dream too far.

Back in the league, the Bulldogs had their most testing spell of the year, beginning with two games in four days on Easter weekend.

At Dewsbury on Good Friday, Tuna had finally passed his head test. In fact, he'd done so before the cup tie with Whitehaven, though was given a further week to recuperate. At Tuesday-night training, he had been presented with a 'due diligence' letter. The decision to sign or not was entirely his, though no signature meant no selection. After a cursory scan, he put his name to it without fuss.

Rugby league was founded on disagreement and one issue that stirs more debate than concussion is the annual Easter hullaballoo, the most demanding spell in a sport that is exacting enough anyway. It is usually Australian coaches unused to such treatment who complain loudest and longest. Coaches like Warrington boss Tony Smith, who ought to be used to it by now, having been in the UK long enough to hold a British passport. This year, he is at it again, calling the period 'madness' and telling the media: 'It's not just those two games, it's the two or three weeks afterwards which can catch you and make you pay the price. As science has told us, fatigue is the greatest cause of injury – not even the pundits can argue that one. One day we'll get some sense.' Club owners, though, are steadfast in their refusal to change, Easter a cash cow to be milked. A week from now, no fewer than forty Super League players will be added to the injury list, with Hull Kingston Rovers losing seven players in total and Widnes six.

Before training on Thursday, the topic had been discussed. By and large, Batley's players agreed that too much was being asked of them, though noted wryly how Easter's even heavier impact on part-timers was ignored. All the attention was on the top flight, where no one had to cart house bricks up and down ladders all day, or engage in some other form of manual labour. Financially, taking Monday off can mean losing a day's pay or holiday, especially for those in retail.

No one could accuse Batley of taking it easy when they rolled up at Dewsbury's Tetley's Stadium. The leadership group had asked for more physical contact in training which, with the squad physically and mentally drained having over-achieved in many eyes, verged on masochism. On the tip sheet was Glenn Morrison's quote from Christmas: *They win on Boxing Day, but we win when it matters.*

Dewsbury came into it having beaten Bradford 31–30 in the Cup, so were on a high. Batley had Breth out with muscle spasms in his neck and Chris Ulugia with a broken hand. The official line was that the latter injury had come against Whitehaven. In fact, it was the result of an altercation on a night out, Uce released without charge when the police accepted he had acted in self-defence. With Squiresy still in rehab and Zack McComb presumably not ready, Batley's only specialized centre was Danny Cowling, so a dual-registration deal with Castleford was on the cards, young Greg Minikin, struggling there for game time, the target. He would not be available until after the holiday weekend, though, so for now they must muddle through.

With no Uce to call upon, Ainy moved inside, Reitts and Brownz on the wings. Patch replaced Cain, who was resting a hurt shoulder, at stand-off. Brownie was dropped to the bench – 'to sharpen his ideas up a bit' – from where Young Iro made his debut after impressing in training. Alistair Leak began at hooker and Luke Blake moved to loose forward as Kear rotated his squad, no doubt mindful of the busy schedule ahead. In the tunnel, Pottsy was glassy-eyed, the loss of JK bothering him. 'I've not been the same since it came out. This always happens here when we are on the up . . .'

Lessening his pain, perhaps, Batley sped into a 20–0 lead in as many minutes, their best quarter of rugby so far. Keegs and Rowey were unstoppable, Chandler won every ruck and Leaky scored twice in the first six minutes, the Rams shell-shocked. It was a start summed up by Leaky's second. Given his diminutive size, swamped by defenders he had no right to ground the ball yet did so anyway. 'He's a strong little bugger,' said Mauny. 'It must come from wrestling cows.'

Of farming stock in Cumbria, Leaky first picked up a ball as a kid at Egremont Rangers and played union too before his education took him to Leeds University. While there, he represented England in the 2013 Student Rugby League World Cup, was spotted by JK and invited to train at Batley, which he did impressively enough to earn a contract. The year after, a knee reconstruction kept him out all season, 2015 his first full campaign. If anyone symbolizes Batley's David v Goliath complex it is Alistair Leak, regularly felling men twice his size, no need of a catapult. Work-wise, he is in recruitment in Huddersfield, he says, though as the season progresses he will start to turn up in a pest-control van, the 'rat-catcher' of tabloid shorthand alongside the squad's builders, joiners and plumbers. He likes the culture: 'With not a lot of money around, everyone's got to muck in.'

Aged twenty-three now, he grew up in Corney Fell, where the dairy farm bought by his granddad was located. The farm is winding down these days but at its height his dad and uncle milked a hundred cows, twice a day. Then milk prices began to fall. 'At the moment, they'll just kind of let a cow calve and then sell it on. Last year, they sold thirty cows alone.' It's the sort of life that will build a work ethic. 'Up at half-five and what have you, growing up I had to help out. We had sheep back then as well.'

As Leaky got older, he developed other interests, though still mucked in at weekends or when his uncle had time off. His parents travel down to watch him when they can, his dad milking in the morning, his uncle taking over in the afternoon. 'With fewer cows they can have more holidays, but they still work hard like. It's tough, especially if milk is your only income. In the larger farms now, with upwards of a thousand cows, you've got parlours where they milk themselves. For ones that are family run, it's difficult to make a living. It's got to be run as big business, rather than a family concern, and that's taken something away. Ours milked sixteen, eight on each side. You've got some now that'll do sixty at a time, thirty down each row, all automatic. You used to put them on yourself, but it's all machine done with businessmen at the back.' He laughs at the suggestion that he'll ever take over, doubts his dad would want it. 'It's all right being interested as a kid, but as soon as you get an idea of what's outside, it's a big world, isn't it?' He and his brother aren't interested, nor are his cousins. 'This will be the last generation.'

Olé, Olé, Olé, sang the portion of a 2,020 crowd in Dewsbury's South Stand. Non-regulars maybe, high on the bank holiday and the season's first night match? Floodlit shadows lengthened across the rough surface, the aroma one of hot dogs, burgers and fried onions.

Leaky's brace was added to by a couple from Reitts – one a thrilling seventy-five-metre breakaway – but Dewsbury soon clawed their way back to 20–12, though Patch's kicked penalty and Alex Brown's try with fifteen seconds to go still gave Batley a 26–12 advantage at the break. The home side, having had three players sinbinned, were losing players with abandon, their bench used up alarmingly. Surely they would tire. No, Keegan warned in the half-time huddle. 'They are going to come out with a hard-on. It's a fucking derby. Meet fire with fire. We keep it intense. We keep it simple and we get a win.'

'They'll be getting a fucking next door,' said their coach, 'so expect them to respond.' When Ainy almost immediately touched down Dom's superb kick to the corner – one of many – to re-establish a twenty-point lead, those warnings seemed unnecessary. Especially when Patch added another penalty goal to make it 34–12 at the start of a half in which Batley won the penalty count 14–1.

On social media, Andy Hunt, senior sports reporter of the local paper, the *Dewsbury Reporter*, called that 'ridiculous' and was soon bemoaning being called a 'C u next Tuesday,' as he put it, amid other 'vile comments'. And the mood had darkened in the South Stand too. Violence suddenly flared, stewards flocking to a scene that spilled over on to the pitch. Some said Dewsbury fans were fighting among themselves, others that visiting fans reacted to plastic bottles being thrown at non-player Squiresy, walking past in a Batley top. Either way, alcohol seemed to be at the heart of it.

Amid the chaos, it almost went unnoticed that Dewsbury had

scored again in a half described by the *Yorkshire Post* as 'the craziest Heavy Woollen derby ever'. Tuna, red of face and utterly shattered on his return, had knocked on at the restart. *Tick . . . tick . . . boom!* went the Hives on the stadium PA. Cue James Harrison's entry and when Patch kicked another penalty with the disintegrating Rams on a team warning, a twenty-point advantage had once again been restored: 36–16.

Some still questioned that tactic, but given the mayhem that followed it would be more than a handy cushion. Dewsbury scored again, forced a goal-line dropout (GLDO) and added another: 36–24, they would not go away. The latter conversion was ruled wide but, in a mirror image of Batley's draw with Bradford a fortnight before, all in Rams colours were convinced it went over. And with eight minutes to go, Dewsbury romped in again, Batley's once wide margin cut to six points. Without Patch's trio of penalties, it would be all square.

The hosts now had the bulk of possession; Batley desperately needed the ball. In the dugout, JK turned to Tuna, who had sat much of the second half out, the colour of a red-hot chilli pepper. Was he fit to go back? 'Don't tell me yes if you can't.' Tuna nodded and moments later went in for what was surely the match-winning try, Dewsbury's defence shaping to defend a drop-goal under a tangerine moon. Patch's penalty on the hooter confirmed a final score of 30–44.

Singing the song, Rowey gave the adjoining changing-room door a hearty couple of thumps. Otherwise, celebration time was limited. Tomorrow, at 9.30 a.m., Ally and James would be at Mount Pleasant bright and early. Team meeting 10.30, stretch session from John Heaton, then half a dozen sets: 'just to get a bit of stiffness out and be ready for Monday', a second home game in a fortnight against their Cup opponents Whitehaven. 'Easter can make us this year, guys,' JK said. 'We've got two points tonight, we pick up another two on Monday and, I'll tell you, we've got real momentum. Then we can get excited. Believe you me.'

Groundsman Jim Morley fertilizes the pitch, pushing a little green dispenser of blue pellets back and forth. He has the weather-beaten complexion of a man whose time is spent outdoors by choice.

A Batley fan since 1963, the club is his passion. He was at Dewsbury last night, chuffed to see Batley still at the top end of the league. Asked to fill the role by Ron Earnshaw, he has been tending to the ground for fifteen years now, having initially been reluctant. 'I thought it might be too time-consuming, but I agreed and am glad I did. I feel like I've improved it in the time I've been here.'

A volunteer like everyone else, Jim's weekly routine depends on the time of year. He laughs at 'summer rugby'; the game is played over ten and a half months. End-of-season renovation work starts in September/October, the lads back in training in November. This last winter was wet and mild, so the grass has been growing all year. He would like to fertilize every month if he could, but it depends on the 'budget'; in reality it's a cap-in-hand job. Realistically, he'll do it two or three times a year. 'At our level, it's beg, steal and borrow.'

The weather dictates how often Jim is here. 'Sometimes you can kill a pitch with kindness. A winter such as we've had makes my job harder because I can't bring in big machinery.' He makes do with little wheeled dispensers like this one and lawn mowers, more time consuming. But hey ho, spring is coming and it's drying up a bit. A big factor then, though, is lack of moisture or any irrigation system. 'In summer, the ground can be harder than in winter.'

The groundsman confirms Andy Winner's earlier observation that the Mount is a pitch unlike any other. 'We've eight to nine inches of topsoil then sandstone. Without rain it dries out quickly, like being on a patio. We rely on Mother Nature.' You might imagine that would raise issues of player safety, though for the moment at least, rain is forecast, 'so I thought I'd put this on and it will get watered in'. When it does arrive, the deluge is of biblical proportions, complete with bank-holiday-appropriate high winds.

Indoors, Pottsy reveals that he kipped on the boardroom floor: 'I had to wash the kits; we need them Monday.' And sure enough, wet towels hang from the Family Stand crush barriers. Ainy is first in, not having had time for breakfast yet. On the schedule are ice baths, though naturally no such facilities exist here, plastic bins filled instead with water and ice. Plunging in might not be so bad, but getting back out could be tricky. If it goes wrong, says Breth, we could be left with a single player in there, frozen blue with hypothermia.

Young Iro Harrison is still buzzing about his debut. Having spent the first half on the bench, he must have been worried he wouldn't get on. 'When we went twenty points up, I thought if this carries on I might get some decent game time. But when they scored twice before half-time, I thought, "Is he going to risk me?" Then with half an hour to go he said, "Right, you're on." I knew that as soon as I made my first tackle I'd be all right and that was how it was.'

He stood his ground well, going toe to toe with veteran forward Tony Tonks. 'Patch passed me the ball and I got wiped out. Then we got a play on their line, Reitts gave it me and I nearly got over. I knew Tony Tonks when he was at Halifax under my dad; he's massive. He ran straight at me and Jimmy Davey got him on his back. Then he sent me flying. I tackled him four times in two minutes and he kept picking me, calling me out – "Get at him, the tall one, get at him . . ." – but the lads looked after me.' He has a bruise from Tonks's elbow on his bicep. The news is less good for Danny Cowling, who may have torn a pectoral muscle. His arm was forced behind his shoulder, the injury occurring as he tried to push back. The centre shortage is a concern, though Breth can cover if necessary and Squiresy will be fit soon. In the team meeting, JK lays it on the line: 'I've always felt that Easter tells you loads about your players. It tells you who's fucking soft cocks and who's mentally tough. It really does. Who can back up? Who can push themselves through the pain and fatigue?'

In the wider world, the week before Easter began with atrocity in Brussels. The bombing of that city's airport and Metro system pushed radical Islam back into the headlines, heightening tensions across Europe and worldwide. Closer to home, Batley's self-styled 'Intelligent Weekly', *The Press*, reflected that anxiety. As usual, copies were scattered about the boardroom by Saturday morning. In this week's paper, the abduction and attempted sexual assault of a seventeen-year-old Dewsbury woman was reported. The victim escaped though was said to be 'very distressed'. An artist's impression of an 'Asian male in his twenties with dark brown eyes, dark curly hair and a beard' drew one wry comment: 'That narrows the field, doesn't it?'

Easter Sunday marks the start of 'Communities United', an initiative mentioned by Ikram Butt and friends at Gelato's. As per Jim's prediction, the weather is unkind, the Fox's Biscuits factory windsock blown rigid. On the cricket field, around fifty children – some white though mainly Asian – run about regardless. Some play cricket. The two Craigs – Lingard and Taylor – show one group how to pass and kick a rugby ball, helped by Dan Winner.

Down Heritage Road, Gaff wanders out of the rugby club. Ikram and the Barrister were here but have now left, the event almost halfway through. The wicket should be resplendent with stalls but a sign indicates those are now in Ron's Lounge; the high winds perhaps a blessing in disguise. 'She's enjoyed it, you can tell,' reports a young Asian mum, woolly-hatted babe in one arm, cell phone in the other.

In the cricket pavilion, more families with children sit drawing, drinking pop and watching a televised football match. Outside, a woman dressed like a carrot greets Ahmed Daud, Batley Cricket Club chairman, and Kirklees council official Nisar Mayet. Having assumed chairmanship three months ago, a committee member prior to that, Ahmed wants to improve community relations through closer ties with the Bulldogs. 'For years, rugby and cricket haven't worked together. This is the first time we've made a real effort. It's small scale, as you can see, but hopefully the first of many.' The low turnout is due to the rain, plus there are seven weddings in the area today.

The cricket season begins in a couple of weeks. In 2016, a club with a rich heritage will participate in the Bradford League – a traditionally strong feeder for the county game – after coming sixth in the Central Yorkshire League last term, their highest position in a decade. Ahmed used to sponsor the Bulldogs, he says, although he's a Wigan fan, really. This is a great year to partner up, as they are doing so very well. He has suggested a charity Twenty20 game between the two neighbours later in the season should the Bulldogs be interested. Has the rugby side been amenable? 'Oh yes, the willingness is there, I think, but it's never been taken forward.'

Nisar Mayet is Kirklees's 'engagement development officer' and this is one of a number of similar projects. 'We want to use sport as an asset and in particular these two grounds, side by side for over one hundred years. We have tried to give it a heritage theme. W. G. Grace once played here, you know.' Nisar met Craig Lingard about a year ago and found he couldn't do enough to help. 'This hasn't cost much money, about £200. The clubs have provided the venues and we've got tag rugby, quick cricket, football, stalls, health messages, coaching, arts and crafts. Look at all these kids. They'd have been stuck inside, in front of a games console, wouldn't they? It's lovely to see so many people enjoying themselves and having a laugh. Batley is a diverse community; this just needs to be the start.' Down at the rugby club, through an adjoining gate that Nisar says they couldn't open at first, so badly was it rusted, the boardroom and Ron's Lounge are alive with multicultural activity, the weather a happy accident. 'You'd have just had people on the cricket field, now they are going in both directions. It's great to walk around inside a stadium they've never been in before. They know what it looks like now. Fantastic.'

As Linners and Dan officiate a game of rugby golf, in which a ball is kicked from distance and has to land between set cones, Craig Taylor too reflects on the benefits of a joint approach. Aside from this, the club now runs a Monday-night fitness club in the gym. A twelve-week programme has been extended, such is its popularity. The policy, he says, is to aim for young and old. They get a lot of granddads to the gym and that's important, since they have influence. He tells the story of a young Asian lad who turned up for training one day with a youth team of his. He had talent, so the club looked after him, made sure he had the right food available and so on. But after his first and only match at Normanton, his parents wouldn't let him come back once they'd heard he'd been in a working men's club. While Taylor, a practical man intent on getting as many involved in the sport as possible – whatever their gender, religion or anything else – sees that merely as one more social hurdle to be overcome, there are others who present such accounts as evidence for why Asians and rugby league are simply not meant for one another.

In an online review of *The Islamic Republic of Dewsbury*, a book by Danny Lockwood, owner-publisher of *The Press* and rugby league trade paper *League Weekly*, the BBC World Service presenter Owen Bennett-Jones reheats the supposed experience of one particular amateur club in a neighbourhood densely populated with British Pakistanis found within its pages.

> The players – all white – found that, each week, bucket loads of broken glass were strewn across the turf so that when they dived to the ground they cut their flesh – sometimes with wounds so deep they required stitches. Then, after the games, they would find their cars, which they had parked in streets with almost entirely British Muslim residents, vandalized. Out of sheer obstinacy they kept on playing for some years, but eventually gave up. Local officials, wondering what to do with the now disused pitch, then decided to hand it over to the only local community organization they could find – the Tablighi mosque, which was given a 999-year lease for the sum of £1.

It is common in the pubs, shops and streets of Batley to hear Mount Pleasant referred to as 'Pakiland', sometimes in a pejorative sense, often by people who think it merely descriptive if they think about it all, and on occasion by members of the Asian community itself, with knowing irony. Pakistan after all translates to just that. In the rugby club, such utterances are commendably – and, given the white working-class nature of the place, perhaps surprisingly – rare. The young Asian men who sit for hours in parked cars on Heritage Road every night of the week are tolerated. The Mount is a place to meet, perhaps before street soccer, to smoke, chat and drink, if the empty vodka bottles, fag ends and other detritus that lie scattered on the tarmac until some volunteer takes them to the trash are anything to go by.

If anyone cares about the lack of Asian involvement with the club, they tend to keep it to themselves, in public anyway, mindful of the sensitivities. Most, like BISSA's John Earnshaw, take a pragmatic view. When he began watching the Gallant Youths in the 1960s, the club was far bigger in the town. There used to be hundreds walking to the ground but 'now everybody comes in cars. I wouldn't want to go down the trail of "the Asians aren't interested", though. They are to an extent, just not enough to come regularly. They'll dip their toes in. Mick who does the car park once saw some lads playing football and said, "Do you want to come and watch a rugby match?" About a dozen said yes, so he brought them in, free of charge. In five minutes, they were back outside, playing football. Can't force people, can you?'

That there are no Batley players here today is not surprising on such a busy weekend, that no directors are present a little more so. It's not about racism, Craig Taylor says, but old-fashioned attitudes. Mount Pleasant is a bit of a white working-class island, though he points out that attitudes can change, even among old-timers. Look at the success of Batley's Girls teams, he says. Initially mocked but now a source of great pride for the club with their successes.

Mid afternoon, a gigantic cloud the colour of volcanic ash deposits its ice-cold load like some vengeful despotic deity and the cricket field is instantly soaked and deserted. At the back of the Glen Tomlinson Stand, a bouncy castle drips empty and forlorn, though the Bryan Cooney Suite and Bulldog Bar are packed with women, girls and Asian elders, eating, chattering and having a high old time.

Later that evening, when news breaks of a bombing at Gulshan-e-Iqbal Park in Lahore, the Taliban claims responsibility. Reports say the terrorists were targeting Christians enjoying the Easter holiday, though many Muslims perish too. Over seventy people were killed in the attack, including seventeen children, with more than three hundred wounded. As people of every faith and race rush to donate life-saving blood, online blogger Anthony Permal reflects that every drop will: 'mix with the blood of the injured. Muslims and Christians will share their bodies tonight. You have lost.'

Down south, Storm Katie had wreaked havoc; up north on Easter Monday is blowy too. The fence around the cricket field is in tatters, with even the reporter from BBC Cumbria impressed: 'Wind's a bit raw, isn't it?!' In the boardroom, Nellie and Barbara munch pork scratchings and discuss a love of mucky fat. John Miller is no fan. 'Rare is a funeral in Batley with no mucky-fat sandwiches on,' he concedes. 'They say the best way to have it is spread on thick with extra salt. Death upon death; it's as if the undertakers are lining up repeat business.' Sam Haigh wanders in, unusually tardy. 'Where've you been?' chorus Barbara and Nellie. 'We tried to phone; thought you were dead.' The clocks have gone forward but the one on the wall still lags by an hour.

A late team change. Cowling's torn pec means Breth is moved to centre, Gleds coming into the second row with Jimmy Davey on the bench. Haven take an unlikely 6–0 lead uphill, but no one panics and by the end of the first quarter tries from Scotty and Gledhill and two goals from Dom have put the hosts 12–6 in front. The anticipated roll-on, though, never materializes, the next score, a close-range job by a fired-up Brownie, only coming four minutes before the break.

'Every fucker's trying to be man of the match,' the try-scorer says as he comes barging through the changing room door, his side ahead 16–6 but with an uphill half ahead of them. 'This isn't us, boys,' says Ainy. Patch chips in: 'Where we are coming a bit loose is, we are winning the ruck, and when they are looking to play wide, "A" and "B" are coming up, then "C" and "D" are sitting in instead of swinging off. That's when there's panic on the edges and everyone's jamming in. We need to dominate and talk from inside . . .'

JK is calm and reflective. The usual tale, he reckons. 'Their try came after five sets, all on the back of penalties. With this wind, if you give away loads of penalties, you are defending deep in your own half. Would you agree with that?' They must play through the line, make it lower risk, be sure to push and trail, but play quick. 'We'll have loads of yardage sets now, guys, and we are good at those. They will have time on our line, so our goal-line D has to be the best it's been. It's all about energy this, guys. We are in a great position.'

As the wind howls and swirls down the ground, the crossbar and goalposts rattle like skeleton's teeth, behind which Haven get in first, eight minutes after the restart. Brownie drops the ball, the visitors break and Reitts is lucky not to be sinbinned after tearing across the field and belting the man in possession. Two minutes later, Whitehaven are level, with an unconverted four-pointer this time.

With half an hour remaining, the omens aren't good, and they worsen when Carl and the Doc lead Jimmy away to the treatment room, injured again. The wind has grown ferocious. Playing into it, against the slope, is a mammoth challenge that few now seriously expect Batley to be up to, so when Whitehaven take advantage of a Reittie fumble to take a 22–16 lead, there is a mood of inevitability. With a gale at their back and confidence soaring, Haven threaten to carve the Doggies open with every play. Batley, by contrast, look knackered, pure and simple. The next score is but a matter of time, the only surprise being it goes to Batley. Ainy is helpfully clattered about the head; the resulting penalty tapped and moved left to Alex Brown, who squeezes over just short of the hour. There is still a touchline conversion to be attempted that, even with Patch on duty, in such extreme conditions seems unlikely. The connection of boot on ball, though, is sweet. The ball rises high, is buffeted this way and that, before dipping between the posts: 22–22.

There are still twenty-three minutes to go and what torrid minutes they turn out to be, though Batley's ranks are given a boost when Jimmy trots back on to the field, having passed his statutory fifteen-minute head-knock assessment. The visitors still have the advantage of weather and slope, the home resistance remarkable as it thwarts raid after raid; only a superb one-on-one tackle by last man Scotty saves one such certain try. Even so, when Haven half-back Grant Gore hammers a drop-goal to make it 23–22 moments later, it seems to be the final nail in beleaguered Batley's coffin. Order the mucky fat.

Yet they try a short restart and miraculously gain possession. Haven coach James Coyle – a candidate to replace JK it later emerges – is unhappy. The ball hadn't gone ten metres, he insists, but his objections are waved aside and when his team then concede a penalty it is some forty metres out from their posts.

Cometh the seventy-third minute, cometh the man. Up steps Patch Walker, eyes narrowed into the wind and rain. Clint Eastwood in *A Fistful of Dollars* but without poncho and desert and cheroot. And over it duly goes: 24–23 to Batley.

When the hooter blares and the referee's arm points to the heavens five metres from the home line, the relief is palpable. Another narrow loss refashioned as narrow victory. In the changing room, JK asks them to sit a while. 'We said Easter was about will, not skill. The effort, work ethic, your desire to stand by your mates . . . but I was wrong, because there was skill in that as well. That goal was tremendous, Patch, well done. But Easter to me includes the weekend after. We've to enjoy this win, it were dug out of granite, but the Easter period finishes when we play Oldham. That will make sure all this work has been worthwhile.'

In the boardroom, the Whitehaven directors are once again seated funereally, chairman Kev milling around in a state of shock. 'I couldn't smell it,' he says. 'I lost my sense of smell.'

11

BOWER FOLD IS a soccer ground, but then Oldham are used to that. And nor is it in Oldham, but then Oldham are used to that too.

Since relegation from Super League in 1997, a club that was one of rugby league's founding members, finishing fourth in the very first Northern Union season and boasting its leading try-scorer, Jack Hurst, has led a nomadic existence. Historically a conveyor belt of talent – more recently having produced Kevin Sinfield MBE among others – their town hasn't known quite what to do with them. After avoiding a merger with Salford and a proposed renaming as Manchester, the first two seasons of summer rugby had, in fact, turned out to be a series of wet weekends. Upon relegation, a £2 million debt was uncovered that nearly wiped what by then was Oldham Bears off the map. Their famous old Watersheddings ground – at 770 feet above sea level the highest professional rugby league ground in the country – was closed. The then-chairman also departed under the mother of all storm clouds before, in the nick of time, a saviour stepped in to rescue a club he'd supported as a boy.

The saviour's name was Christopher Hamilton and, along with another three directors, he immediately re-adopted the splendid old nickname 'Roughyeds'. Though to call this a happy ending would be pushing it. Nowadays run within their means, every year since has been a scrap for survival, promotion in 2015 a long overdue ray of sunshine. Yet even that wasn't without a twist. The ground they were by then at – Whitebank – was deemed to be not up to scratch for the Championship. If they were to go up, a new venue was needed. When a deal could not be reached with Oldham Athletic for Boundary Park – another ex-home – Stalybridge Celtic emerged as welcome hosts for the Roughyeds, their seventh new ground in nineteen years.

Few enjoyed a visit to Watersheddings. As its name suggests, the ground was most often cold, wet and inhospitable, particularly in its terminal years. But while there, at least Oldham belonged. An object lesson perhaps for Batley, the club with whom they have so much in common; a Lancashire Theia to Mount Pleasant's Yorkshire Earth. And somewhat appropriately, in a season of surprises, today was set to deliver a watershed moment.

When the visitors' bus pulls up, Hamilton is beavering away sorting out this and that at the end of a corridor lined with cabinets of soccer paraphernalia, a celebration of achievements and times past denied to the rugby tenants. Being three and a half miles out of town isn't ideal, the bespectacled chairman admits, although the fans have responded well. As ever, it's preferable to the alternative. The club would not be here without his tireless and often thankless efforts, plus those of a mini-army of volunteers trying to make the best of it.

Batley arrive confident. Unbeaten in seven matches – having won six and drawn one – the first trip out of Yorkshire was pleasant and relaxed. True, it had been a week of distraction. The grapevine suggested that a trio of coaching candidates had been interviewed, ex-Leeds players all – Francis Cummins, Andy Hay and Matt Diskin. Keegan Hirst was linked with Wakefield, as was Chris Ulugia. Would others follow? Yet the atmosphere was unruffled. Before heading for a holiday on the Algarve, Kevin Nicholas confirmed that while the players were hesitant because they didn't know who was coming in next year, they were happy for JK to see out the season. He'd asked what would happen if, for whatever reason, a new man came in at some point, to which they replied that as long as nobody was shafting anybody or falling out, it would be with the squad's blessing. In any case, JK was involved in the interviewing process, part and parcel of finding his own replacement. Kev referenced cheerful images of the previous five Batley coaches on the boardroom wall, to emphasize the club's desire for structured transition. 'We've had five coaches since 1997, all of them left without being sacked.'

Craig Lingard, it turned out, was among those interviewees, though he didn't hold out much hope. JK told him he came across well but still he wasn't confident, surmising that as Batley have in the last twenty years valued continuity, should he not land the role then he would probably have to wait four or five years for another go. Ambitious to get on the head coach's ladder, he would have no choice but to re-evaluate. And what if he wasn't wanted or the new coach brought assistants of his own? These were uncertain times for every member of the backroom staff, it seemed.

In training, though, all had remained calm. In fact, the midweek talking point was the away game after Oldham against a full-time London Broncos, where it was agreed they would have an overnight stay. The vote on whether or not to do so was passed by a 100 per cent raising of hands, despite a potential cost to the players of their match fee, as Keegan explained. 'The last couple of times we've gone down there we've lost and started like a sack of shit; the club basically wants us to back ourselves to win.' Usually they get £50 for defeat by more than twelve, £100 for less than twelve and £250 for a win. 'If we get beat by more than twelve, we'll get nowt; if we get beat by less than twelve, they'll give us fifty sheets, and if we win we'll still get the full £250.' He warned it wouldn't be a jolly, though.

By Saturday morning, JK was shifting tables in Ron's Lounge – 'ah wain't miss this' – as *The Press* predicted the new name would be announced in the next three weeks, once Kev was back from holiday. In the team meeting, the whiteboard had a nice surprise for Cravo, still unable to get a look-in ahead of Scotty but named as nineteenth man, so he would at least earn match fees, a reward for having not taken his bat home. Uce Ulugia had hacked the pot off his arm, it was getting a bit sweaty and itchy, and there was a new face in former Hunslet and Halifax centre Callum Casey, who arrived in the gym on Wednesday sporting a 'fuel your ambition' T-shirt, here on trial. 'Don't be waking up tomorrow thinking we've got a comfortable afternoon,' JK warned. 'Everybody's got to contribute or else we'll get our backsides bitten.'

The sun puts in an appearance and as the players get the feel of a heavily sanded pitch, there is no hint of a shock. Oldham coach Scott Naylor looks thoroughly cheesed off, no doubt mulling over last week's defeat at fellow relegation favourites Swinton, a display he called their worst of his time in charge. Yet when Oldham, pleasingly in traditional red and white hoops, force two GLDOs in the opening minutes, a few Bulldogs shift uncomfortably in their seats.

Try as they might, Batley cannot get into the game. The first half ends 12–2 in Oldham's favour, a solitary Patch penalty all the Bulldogs have to show in a shift that has turned into a full-on wriggle.

In fact, they are being out-Batley-ed. Oldham's defence is up too quickly, in their playmakers' faces, forcing errors, frustration and bad decision-making from a team whose success has been built likewise. Scoring chances are squandered. Scotty drops his first high ball of the season as Alex Brown crosses his field of vision. It's all going wrong.

'They are flat as farts,' says JK, early in an equally poor second half. He sends Mokko on to generate enthusiasm, but instantly it is 16–2, the trip back across the Pennines destined to be less cheerful than the ride over. Nothing will come off. The anxiety in the dugout shows itself on the pitch and players start to bicker behind the posts. The penalty count is against them too, some looking to the official for help, never a good sign. When Oldham's scrum-half throws the sort of short-side dummy sports reporters are contractually obliged to call 'outrageous', it's 22–2, then 28–2. At least the Roughyeds in a crowd of 814 enjoy it. *Easy, easy, easy . . .* they chant. Defeat is one thing, but the manner of this one is deflating, a perfect Easter spoiled. Late tries from Cropper and Reitts in an eventual 28–12 loss can't remedy that.

But if that reality check is grisly, it is as nothing to an injury sustained by Alex Rowe, who, having been held up over the line for a second time, is led off clutching his hand. 'His thumb's hanging off,' says Pottsy, and indeed it is, the bone having broken the big prop's skin. Batley director John Miller is called down from the stands. With the game finished, he is asked to drive Rowey – waiting for the car park to empty a little in muddied kit, his blood-spattered bald dome registering nonchalance – off to hospital. No softy southerner this.

A cockney by trade, as he puts it, Rowey grew up playing union, a riser through the ranks at Blackheath. Big and powerful, his league journey began when scouted by London Broncos, who asked him to come down to training. There, he joined a youthful conveyor belt of future exports like the Worrincy brothers, Rob and Mike, and St Helens prop Louie McCarthy-Scarsbrook. At sixteen, he turned pro, trained with the Broncos' first team, played a few friendlies and signed for Castleford in 2005.

From there he went to South Yorkshire, at Doncaster to begin with then Sheffield, where he spent 2008–12, a time that included a prison sentence for GBH. The assault on 23-year-old Sudanese man Haroon Khater could not have been more out of character. Pleading guilty, Rowe called the takeaway incident 'ten seconds of stupidness'. In his defence, the court heard he'd been called 'a mixed breed' and had since received 'glowing testimonials' from officials and a retired policeman. It's hard to square all of that with the archetypal gentle giant he is now, but on his release in 2009 he made a fresh start to a career that began again in Sheffield and included a spell at Gateshead before he came to Batley in 2013.

Given how there is no Shaw Cross or East Leeds nursery in the capital, the ease with which this relative late starter took to the game is impressive. And it in turn has changed his life. Though his wife was also born in London, the couple met in the north and she was raised a Yorkshire lass. They have two boys with another on the way and live in a nice area of Leeds, Temple Newsam. He's thirty-one now, older and wiser, and doesn't expect his career will go on too much longer but still enjoys the game: 'It's what I do.' Nor can he see himself going back south. 'I've lived as many years here now as I did down there, though I've still got my accent.' His parents, based in London, also love league. 'They come up, not as often as they'd like, but a bit.' When Batley play London, the lads usually travel on Sunday but he goes down Friday for the weekend. Alas, he won't be there next week.

'How long will he be out for?' JK asks Carl, who, assisted by a distinctly queasy-looking Oldham medic, has wrapped the wound in polythene to keep the ligaments moist. Eight weeks, he reckons. It will depend on whether or not there is an infection. Given that he has fallen on mud and grass, that's possible, so he doesn't think they will operate tonight. They'll want to leave the wound open to check that no pus 'or other crap' develops. Carl arranges by phone for Rowey to see a hand specialist tomorrow and Oldham's doc asks to be updated by text, so concerned is he at the extent of the injury. You'd hazard a guess that he doesn't attend rugby league games often.

In a subdued changing room, Keegan calls it a result that has been coming. 'We've been thinking we are world-beaters. What got us here was doing what we were told, not what we wanted. We started noticing we were top of the league,' he says.

'Fuck me, boys,' adds Wayne Reittie, mindful of the fall-outs behind the try-line. 'Let's stick together, eh?'

'We disrespected them, fellas,' concludes JK, in measured tones, tinged with sorrow. 'We were walking about with our fingers up our arses, thinking we were ten-bob Tommies. They belted you and you couldn't fucking handle it, simple as that. There's a humility pill, a hard-work pill and a togetherness pill that want taking pretty fucking quickly. Listen to that . . .' Next door, Oldham's victory song is in full flow. Walls are thumped. Doors clattered. Conquering warriors howl. *Easy-beats are we, Batley? Cop for this.* And on this side of the tiles, total silence as strapping is unwound and tossed on a filthy floor.

Up next: London, the season's other surprise package, also near the top of the table. A team whose away game in Whitehaven last night was called off just forty minutes before kick-off, after a six-hour and 350-mile trip north. So they'll be in a good mood.

*

A week of soul-searching and brutal training climaxed with that overnight stay in London at Wembley's Holiday Inn. JK and his staff were pleased with the squad's response. With the Broncos going well, a competitive game would silence the doubters who predicted that Batley would fail to stay the course. They'd be back in the saddle after a stumble.

Tuesday-night training had been sombre, the gloom lifted only by new two-year deals for Cain Southernwood and Tom Lillycrop, the first of the current squad to commit signature to paper for 2017. JK had made twenty minutes of clips from the Oldham debacle before deciding not to show them, as, 'We'd be here all night.' Confidence had slipped into arrogance, their response against opponents they were not expected to beat vital. Even Keegs, after a day 'on the tools', failed to spark banter upon spotting a plate of fairy cakes. He ached badly. Yesterday, after mixing plaster he couldn't stand up. 'I spent three hours in the bath last night. We got knocked about a bit.'

Carl shared good news of a sort. Rowey's injury meant a four-to-six-week absence, the thumb dislocated not fractured. 'The tendon had wrapped around the bone, so they couldn't pull it back in. They had to take him to theatre to extend the hole where it's come out, to unwrap the tendon, put the bone back in place, fix the ligament and stitch him up. They tried to do it Sunday night but couldn't, because of the tendon.' As the wound had broken the skin, he is on antibiotics. He will be in pot for a week and a splint for four weeks after that.

Re Sunday, Patch reckoned some of them got too excited, those who haven't been in this position before: 'It's about experience and professionalism.' Teams watch the tapes and might also be wising up to their tactics. 'They see the ball coming out the back, are learning to expect it and are defending against it.' Down on the field, though, the system that got them here was rammed home. *Get up quickly. Knock them back. Challenge skills. Come with a fend, chop them down!*

'Body's ageing tonight,' said Breth, trudging off the paddock while Ainy, unthinkably, was forced to withdraw from the drills, troubled by a knee he took a blow to at Stalybridge. 'Should I strap it up,' he'd asked Carl, 'or go balls deep?' *Balls deep.* JK stuck his head in to check all was well. *Okay?* 'Yeah, unless I move it.' Injury equates to weakness, both of body and spirit. 'I don't tell 'em,' he later admitted. 'It gives them an excuse to drop you, doesn't it? When you're my age, with a wife and three kids to support, you can't afford not to play.'

JK had set the tone, bringing the players down to earth with a bump before departure. Having listened to their 'school-trip' chatter for a while, he suddenly broke in: 'Are we preparing for a rugby league game or a mothers' meeting?' Awkward silence. 'Let's get us fucking heads on.'

On Thursday, under twilight clouds of burnt marshmallow, he'd seen the game as a puzzle with a simple solution: 'Don't try to solve it on your own, solve it as a group. Let's get our mojo back in defence; middles get aggressive, wrestle and talk. Ball in hand, major on completions. I admire you for backing yourselves but let's make sure we go down there and do it.' And afterwards under leaden skies, raindrops applauding on the K2 roof, it had, he said, 'been the best week's prep since Leigh'.

The intent was back. Bibs attacking downhill, non-bibs defending up it. Movement. Everywhere movement. Get in line, come forward. *Nice! Good hunting. Put 'em down!* Paddy, having returned to training this past two weeks, trod on Brownie's foot. *Gerr'od of 'im! Gerr'od of 'im! 'Elp 'im! 'Elp 'im! Line speed! Moooove! Hellllld! Nice boys. Nice!*

Saturday was Grand National day, so the bus was awash with wagers. Carl put the big race on his laptop. Linners had 33/1 winner Rule the World in the £2-a-head sweepstake, a hollow victory since he also had £50 at 8/1 on Last Samurai, which came second. Others fared better. Carl, a keen student of arbitrage, all possible outcomes, made £275 thanks to Sergio Agüero's penalty for Manchester City. At Toddington, Alex Brown scored a double jackpot, shorts bulging as he climbed back aboard with £400-worth of coins from a slot machine. The driver's luck ran out on a choked-up North Circular. 'Who'd live down here?' he said, crawling through traffic at 7.30 p.m., the Wembley arch looming to the right. 'Horrible place is London. Ought to put a big wall around it.'

Parked up and checked-in, true to their word the squad had a quiet night broken only by sirens at half past three in the morning, the police heading off to some other rumpus. Assembling early, Patch was first to breakfast, followed by Linners, Cropper and Gleds. One group strolled off to see the rugby league statue at the top of Wembley Way, upon which the name 'John Kear' is etched. Batley never appeared at the old Empire Stadium, their Cup glories coming before the event was controversially moved south in 1929. In the venue's first days, though, there used to be a biscuit factory around here too, albeit the rather more upmarket Huntley & Palmers.

That Tuna was asked for his autograph in the hotel foyer was a surprise, until his admirer said she was from Batley. Sunday sports supplements were leafed through that told of teenage jockey David Mullins's romp home at Aintree; Danny Willett's soon-to-be historic display in the Masters at Augusta; Anthony Joshua's two-round win at the O2 Arena; and contrasting fortunes for Arsenal and Leicester in the Premier League title race – without so much as a fixture listing for the rugby league game in Ealing. Why would it be otherwise?

A rugby union venue tucked into a West London residential area, Trailfinders Sports Club is not your usual rugby league ground. Entry is via a single gate at the end of a suburban street, where cars, pedestrians and the team bus are waved through. A place where a kid might easily creep through a gap in a fence around the back, if the kids around here had the need or interest to get up to such mischief.

The pitch is artificial, 3G, soft and springy underfoot, of rugby union dimensions, shorter it seems and wider. The league markings are in blue – not helpful when getting to a point – though the place is a pleasant one for spectators, with its beer tents, barbecues and ease of movement, particularly when the sun shines. Today's attendance numbers around five hundred and it's hard to see where many more could be accommodated.

In one very important respect, though, London's story is rugby league through and through. Like Oldham, Swinton and many another northern outfit, the Broncos have constantly moved around, living hand to mouth, day to day, week to week, year to year, like sporting refugees. Having kicked off as Fulham some thirty-seven years ago, and spending four years as London Crusaders, roots have steadfastly refused to be planted. There have been good times. After beating Wigan, watched by 10,000 people at Craven Cottage on that opening night, they won the Second Division Championship in 1983 in front of far fewer. Much later, they were runners-up to St Helens in the second year of Super League, 1997, a key part in the revolution. Also in 1997, around 8,000 and 10,000 saw them meet and in the first case beat Canberra and Brisbane in the World Club Championship at the Twickenham Stoop, a ground they called home twice. In 1999, London reached the Challenge Cup final, led out at Wembley by then chairman Richard Branson, but lost heavily to Leeds. Most often, it has been a struggle to get by, a painfully compiled fan-base allowed time and again to drift away as the club zigzagged from Chiswick to Brentford to Barnet to Charlton and other such places besides. Ealing seems just to be the latest of these. Although the move from Barnet's Hive last year brought an upturn in form (and facilities ideal for the full-time set-up they remain), it is difficult to see how they can build here if they ever do regain a place in Super League lost in 2014.

Batley's Battle Bus rolls in at about the same time as Mokko, the assistant coach, direct from a night shift after about half an hour's sleep. With less than an hour to kick-off, Dom and Cain practise kicks for position, every ball landing with a plume of black rubber crumb. JK had been warned that the changing rooms were tiny, but it turns out they are fine. What they do lack is toilets, thus Patch Walker is forced to queue at a public urinal moments before he is due on the field. Nor is there much relief out there, Batley almost immediately 8–0 down. Brownz is at least partly to blame for both tries – too far infield – and admits later to a 'bad day at the office'. Batley's dugout – a spacious double-decker affair in which Linners sits upstairs compiling his stats behind glass – is tense. JK and Mokko prowl the touchline.

There is a lot at stake here, that's clear, and as at Oldham the visible anxiety, their coach incandescent at times, transmits itself to the pitch, though all calm down a little when Batley's first sustained spell of possession ends with Scotty darting in for a try; Patch's goal makes it 8–6. And when London's restart goes out on the full, a competitive encounter looks set to break out, but it's a false omen.

Scooter! Line speed! No piggybacks! The orders come thick and fast as Cropper fires a jet of water through his teeth, calmly awaiting his call to the fray. Jimmy Davey paces eagerly; it's a ground made for him – fast hands, quick feet. 'Slow it down,' says John Heaton, vainly. *White lion! Get with him! Push! Push! Work Brownie . . . work, Brownie!*

When Keegan and Gleds jog off after their first stint, they do so gulping like grounded fish, no air left in their lungs, as Batley win a penalty that lets Patch level the scores on the half hour. 'Take two,' said the bench, so he did, Luke Blake's face failing to hide his opinion: a chance to put London under the cosh for a bit had been squandered.

And that was the signal for London to regain the initiative: GLDO forced, a penalty run, Broncos 14–8 up. 'C'mon, Jimmy, give us a lift,' says the substituted Blakey, dripping with sweat and taking slugs from a bottle of glucose drink. Yet there is little the replacement hooker can do when Brownz drops a bomb fifteen metres out and London spin the ball this way and that before scoring their fourth try and second conversion. Starved of the ball, Batley are 20–8 behind at half-time and the match already feels like it's beyond them.

In fact, only one man has a grin on his face. Tuna, as usual, who Carl confirms has taken another blow to the head. As the second half gets underway, Brownz fluffs a glorious scoring chance, failing to take Cain's kick to the corner – *his confidence is shot to shit* – before the frantic pace resumes, though almost entirely one way. Soon after William Barthau stretches the lead to 24–8, Cropper receives Batley's first red card of the year, sent off for flattening the French scrum-half. A couple of ambulance men dash on like the vultures in *Bedknobs and Broomsticks*, almost beating the touch judge to the incident, before skulking off dejectedly, their presence unrequired. As Barthau regains his feet, bloody-mouthed having bitten his tongue, Cropper's walk to the sheds meets with a ripple of polite applause for the victim and a chant of *You dirty Yorkshire bastard* for his assailant, the RFL disciplinary panel later deeming it sending-off sufficient. At least his record of one sending-off a year in each of his four Championship seasons was maintained. Last year he'd gone at Leigh, for fighting.

With twelve men on the field, Batley let in two more tries, both unconverted despite the PA announcer's attempt to regain decorum by shushing everyone before the kicks. 'We're feeling sorry for us fucking selves,' says Brownie, elbows on reddened knees. In a 32–8 win, the Broncos have scored seven tries to one.

'I don't understand why we've lost us buzz,' says Keegan, the dugout now in silence as more late consolation chances go begging. The skipper will stay in the capital tonight to film a contribution to the Channel 4 show *Celebrity First Dates*, to be broadcast in July, and a limo is sent to collect him. For the rest, it would be a long trip home.

A day after the London reverse, Kear appeared on the BBC *Super League Show*'s online *SLS2*, where the subject, perhaps not coincidentally, was confidence. 'You need to win games to have confidence, but you also need to have confidence to win games,' said his fellow guest, Luke Robinson, formerly of Huddersfield Giants.

'As a coach,' said presenter Tanya Arnold, 'and you get in a run like this, do you try to change things? Do you reinforce? Or do you get to the point where you've got to throw the whole thing out?'

'Well, what you've got to do,' said JK, 'is remind the players of exactly how good they are. Sometimes they forget and that's when confidence is eroded. It's not only players; it's the group. You've got to first of all point out what they've achieved. Secondly, you've to set little targets that rebuild that confidence within that. It's a really difficult job to get self-belief, but it's a really easy job to lose it.'

By training on Tuesday, JK had watched the tape three times, as had the other coaches. The consensus was that the right-side D had been chief culprit, too much indecision. Some jammed, some held and turned in, there had been too little talk – they had moved away from basic principles. Mauny was asked to bring the relevant players upstairs, where they all gathered around Mokko's laptop, the assistant as calm and methodical as ever: 'Come on, fellas, let's have a chat about this.' There were no histrionics and no finger pointing, just a collective determination to put a problem right.

In the team meeting, Cropper reckoned they'd panicked, his suggestion shrugged off. Rowey, although he hadn't been there, was back, thumb held together in a question mark of stitches, as angry and swollen as a fried plump sausage. He doubted it was panic, a view shared. Better to see the fault in a rational, even mathematical light. Positioning, numbering and decision-making were the processes to be addressed. Emotion, like chance, is a hydra. Keep it fixable, in control. Hindsight is your friend.

JK: 'Where he passed that ball, that's where you jam. Breth needs to get up and everybody needs to follow him; that's the key is that fucking pass. If he hits the lead, you've got to hold there and if he hits the back man, we go get him. What we are doing is going lateral, backing off and giving them time and space to play.'

Mokko: 'It depends on their shapes going forward, but then if one goes, everyone has to. He got the ball out the back and had time to pick a pass and came up with the right play, didn't he?'

JK: 'As an edge defender, if they play away from the line, you can map out. If they play at the line, you get them. But within that, you've got to talk to your fucking mate. And if he goes, three-in goes, two-in's got to go, and outside's got to go. You've to mirror the inside men, you really do. The only time you don't is if there's a lead and a back man, that's the decision, but once that decision is made, the rest have to react with the man who made it.' Nor did a whopping forty-three missed tackles help.

Mokko: 'It's easily fixed, fellas. We've just got to work together.'

JK ended his team talk by noting that they'd gone away from the acronym at the foot of the tip sheet: *K.I.S.S.* 'It stands for what? Keep It Fucking Simple Stupid . . .'

By Thursday, as off-field events began to clear up, so did the bumps and bruises, cuts, scrapes and burns from London's artificial pitch. Cowling who, like Squiresy, had returned to the side, had come off worst, his leg weeping so much on Monday he was 'wiping brown stuff off it all morning'. Squires too had another ailment with which to contend: a cracked toenail. 'Oh fuck,' said Chandler, tossing the centre some 'special padding', a box of sanitary towels from Carl's cupboard. 'He'll be out for ten years.'

On the coaching front, a shortlist of five was narrowed down to one, Batley confirming the appointment of their new head coach for the 2017 season. Matt Diskin, thirty-four years old and a classy hooker with Leeds from 2001–2010 before his retirement in 2014 after a further four-season stint at Bradford, was 'a very determined character'. At the Bulls, he had gone on to coach Bradford's Under-19s and assisted head coach James Lowes with the first team. He would arrive at the Fox's Biscuits Stadium in October on a three-year deal.

'For Matt to come to us in a part-time capacity shows a big commitment from him, with the support of his wife and family,' Kev Nicholas wrote on the club website. The three-year commitment had been the new man's suggestion, shaken on without hesitation: 'If he can improve us in that time, then he will leave us at some point and no doubt progress to full-time. His clear ambition is to be England coach and we want him to achieve that goal after he has shown the rugby league world what he can achieve at Batley.'

Diskin said he saw taking charge of Batley as a great opportunity. 'Batley is a very well-run club and it suits where I am with my life at the moment,' he told the *Yorkshire Post*. 'I hope Batley finish fantastic-ally and I can build on that next year.' On BBC Radio Leeds, a man who also had his own business to run spoke of how he had always been confident in his abilities as a player or a coach; he'd done the latter since the age of sixteen with amateurs Dewsbury Moor and Dewsbury Celtic, local schools and such. Batley made enquiries regarding his availability, the chance came for an interview and he didn't think he could turn it down. There will be restrictions like a smaller budget, lesser facilities than at other clubs, but 'getting the best out of that group of players is the exciting part'. And though going part-time wasn't the immediate appeal, 'In retrospect, yeah, it does fit well. My wife will be pleased, as she'll see me a couple more hours a week, which will make life easier at home.'

Will having so long to plan be helpful? 'I wouldn't say it's a help or a hindrance. It allows me to get Batley at the end of what will hopefully be a very successful season for them. John Kear has done a fantastic job and it gives me good foundations to build and improve upon and make my own mark on the team. So the build-up allows me to do a lot of preparation, review the current playing staff, coaching staff and everything else, and make sure I'm ready to go in October.' And Kev's line about England? 'That's a long way off and probably a bit of a blasé comment from Kevin, but [international recognition] is an area where I underachieved a little bit as a player, so I still have a burning ambition to achieve something at that level. Longer term – in five, ten, fifteen, twenty years maybe.'

By and large, the squad took the development in its stride. JK wasn't going anywhere yet, 'though if we lose the next three games, that might change,' he said. Earlier, like Cain and Cropper, Ainy put his name to a two-year deal. He'd been putting up the new Fox's Biscuits signs with Complete Services Ltd, his new employer, a job that took in a college course funded by the RFL and the joinery, plumbing and electrical firm, also a club sponsor, in tandem. 'I only came in for a brew. Iro took me into his room and asked if I wanted to stay.'

In fact, the only unhappiness belonged to Linners, who, having missed out on the job would nevertheless later that night successfully pass his final level-three coaching appraisal. There are four to aim at. Levels one and two are needed to coach children and amateurs, level three to take charge of professional sides and level four is a diploma of sorts. Only three people in professional rugby league have one of those: Denis Betts, the coach of Widnes; Richard Agar, nowadays assistant to Tony Smith at Warrington; and John Kear.

Linners told some of the lads he now expected to be leaving at season's end and Cropper asked him why. 'Personal progression,' he replied, a satisfactory answer, though Cropper saw beyond it. On the field, he might be full of testosterone-fuelled belligerence but off it his is a watchful and perceptive eye and he looked genuinely saddened by the club legend's predicament. Professional sport can be cruel.

Yet there were more rumblings. First, the *Daily Express* 'exclusively revealed' that Keegan was 'set to become the only openly gay player in the Super League next season', a revelation that at Batley was no secret; no one begrudged him his ambition. Of more immediate concern was Brad Day's pinned thumb, broken in the Challenge Cup victory against Featherstone the Saturday after their defeat in London, and likely to keep him out for five to six weeks. Shaun Squires had a dead leg, though was hopeful of a speedy recovery.

Having come in with an eggshell-blue foam sling on his arm bigger than the grin on his face, Tuna took the teasing with good grace. The injury had occurred in only his second carry; he'd played almost the entire game with it before telling Carl afterwards that it was throbbing a bit. The physio told him to get it X-rayed at Leeds General Infirmary. 'At least it's not my head,' he'd said.

But news had also broken that James Lowes had left Bradford for 'personal reasons'. Matt Diskin would take 'interim charge' and if the Bulls began to do well, what then? His agreement to coach Batley was likely to have been sealed the usual way here, without anything so formal as a written contract.

Even without the shadowy presence of a waiting coach, April is an uncertain time. Clubs must make offers by an end-of the-month deadline to be sure of retaining players out of contract in November. Agents agitate. The squad morale, however, appeared to be undented. Dom and Chandler had agreed to commit to the club until the end of

2018 and there was another new hopeful on trial – Dave Petersen, a 24-year-old back-rower from Hull, currently out of favour at Odsal.

JK, canny as ever and determined to complete his own stay, sought to play events down. For a while at least he would be a more relaxed presence, let jokes on the training field ride a little. After showing the Featherstone Cup clips, the coach asked the leadership group for a word apiece to sum up a performance that they all hoped had put the London defeat to bed. *Desperate. Patient. Unbreakable. Determined. Disciplined. Willing. Organized.* 'Coherent,' said Breth, to laughter. *Attitude. Our defence were awesome.* 'Spot on that,' said JK. 'We were all those things. That's the standard, guys, would we agree with that? Well, this game on Sunday is as important if not even more so. If somebody had said, "Beat Swinton in round eleven and you're in the top four", we'd have said, "Fucking hell." It's the stuff dreams are made of, is that. Well, it's in your hands. Don't come with a soft-cock attitude, come with the attitude we had in the Cup. Let's nail them.'

On Saturday morning, JK warned again that Swinton were dangerous. They had won three games on the bounce, including an away victory at Halifax in their last outing. They score points but concede a lot and love broken-up games, anathema to Batley's set-by-set mentality. 'When we get loose, we are in a bit of bother,' he said.

And on game day, a comparison in atmosphere with the previous week's cup tie was stark. In the boardroom, Toby Harrison, son of Iro, sold tickets for the Blackpool Bash, a Championship round played on the spring bank-holiday weekend at the end of May, when Batley would face Dewsbury by the seaside. Business was slow.

A cloudy nondescript day on which Batley CC were out in their whites ahead of their first game of the season and Zack McComb was named nineteenth man for the first time was brightened only by Swinton's canary-yellow shirts. And by the end of the opening quarter the Lions, the rugby league equivalent of Brazil, were 18–0 ahead playing uphill. From Brownie's penalty conceded in the opening minute to the end of a set count 'won' by the visitors 15–6, in which Batley made more errors in six than Swinton did in fifteen, the Bulldogs couldn't get into the game. Patch Walker limped off with a torn calf after nine minutes. *C'mon, Batley! Waken up!* yelled a voice in the stand.

Playing with pace and panache, the Lions were mauling their hosts, so it was a relief when Adam Gledhill came off the bench on the half hour to score a try that Dom converted. But when a dazed Reitts was led from the battlefield, concussed, blood gushing from a now susceptible bottom lip that had collided with an opposing shoulder, Batley held up over the line three times in the last set of the half, it was clear that here were more opponents who had been underestimated.

'Listen, fellas,' said JK. 'They caught us. I'll tell you, they fucking caught us. That first set, we were flat as fuck. We kicked off. They won two rucks. We get too wide, lazy fucking tackle; they kick it up here, get a repeat set and score before we've touched the ball. These fuckers can play, so we need to keep them away from our line. Okay? Little efforts mean a lot from all of us, so let's make sure we do them.' What's more, they had got a bit too anxious now, trying to win the game on their own. 'We will win it as a group. We've got to play the fucking shapes. When we get to the last tackle, contest it. And we don't want any fucker arguing; let the pivots decide the play.' At 18–6 behind, and now playing uphill themselves: 'This is a real test of us. Have we got the balls to come out and say, right, you've done us for forty, we will do you for forty? Let's turn this game around.'

They almost did so too, though the likelihood of that fell further away when Swinton added to their total on the restart. With only fifteen fit players and now coming up the slope, 24–6 really ought to have been that. Yet as mutters on the terraces intensified regarding the reason for this decline . . . *he should have gone straight away . . . we want Diskin now . . . too much uncertainty is what it is . . .* the team spirit that had carried them this far suddenly came flooding back.

First, Gleds, who had scored only one try last year in that final game with Hunslet, doubled his tally in a single game. Then, after

Leaky made a sparkling break only to throw an inside pass forward, Scotty burrowed in too. With Dom kicking both goals, the score was suddenly 18–24, a margin of one converted try, the comeback on. Two minutes later, though, came what in retrospect was the defining moment. Brownie, playing well with ball in hand, attempted to move it right on another foray but it hit Blakey on the shoulder and went to ground in Swinton's half. On the free play, it was hoofed down-hill and hacked on again, possession regained in the corner. Rivelino could not have done it better. The goal attempt hit a post, but it was now 18–28.

With a quarter of the game to go, there was still time and after Dom kicked a superb 40/20, Ainy was only denied a try when Breth, at centre in a rejigged backline, passed too soon and the winger was gang-tackled into touch. No matter. Scotty soon added his second via a scything inside run from Brownie's clever pass – a move six of them had stayed behind to practise the previous morning. A Brambani conversion made it 24–28 – four points in it. Could they?

Well, when James Harrison was spear-tackled on Batley's thirty-metre line with nine minutes left, earning a penalty that again helped Batley upfield, it seemed that they might. But the move stalled and a minute later Swinton were in again before converting for a final score of 24–32, to inflict Batley's first home defeat of the season. Leaky's torn shirt collar flapped at half-mast. If only the Bulldogs could have unleashed all that confidence and brio in the first half.

Delighted Swinton whooped, hollered and high-fived as the home players and coaching staff trudged to a disconsolate changing room. They were halfway through the regular season now, extra Summer Bash fixture aside, and had played everyone. Would Batley, plucky part-time underdogs, slip back to mid table just as the experts had predicted they would? After all, in modern-day sport, money talks, doesn't it? Even in the Championship. Not old-fashioned ideas of heart, desire and a willingness to pull together in common cause.

Had the naysayers been right all along?

Regular season halfway Championship table – 24 April 2016

1	Leigh	11	9	1	1	400	224	19
2	London	11	9	0	2	291	179	18
3	Bradford	10	6	2	2	342	208	14
4	Batley	11	6	1	4	253	237	13
5	Featherstone	10	6	0	4	232	162	12
6	Halifax	11	6	0	5	264	213	12
7	Sheffield	11	4	0	7	298	293	8
8	Dewsbury	11	4	0	7	252	300	8
9	Swinton	11	4	0	7	242	349	8
10	Whitehaven	10	4	0	6	143	276	8
11	Oldham	10	3	0	7	175	245	6
12	Workington	11	1	0	10	160	366	2

Half-time Entertainment

THE STICKY CARPETS, blackened walls and fabric ceiling-sashes are much the same as they ever were, brightened only by neon strip-lights and spinning mirror balls in otherwise total darkness.

More unusually, the queue outdoors stretches right up Bradford Road. Welcome to Batley Variety Club – the Frontier in this day and age, as testified by the three coloured bands, flashing blue, red and orange, of vertical bulbs that give an impression of light dancing around the building, Blackpool Illuminations style.

In 2016, the place is more used to visits from stag and hen parties and a younger clientele apt to turn up after midnight. Posters say someone called DJ Jules is coming soon, as are 2015's *X Factor* runners-up, Reggie 'n' Bollie, on May Bank Holiday Monday. Doors open tonight, though, at a more age-appropriate 6.30 p.m., or at least are supposed to, risking the wrath of a perma-tanned line that last saw youth in the 1970s and '80s, here for an evening of nostalgia.

Though the Variety Club from which it sprang was nationally – nay, internationally – admired in its heyday, the Frontier's reputation in Batley is at an all-time low. In fact, it's a standing joke, though if rumours are correct it may not be standing for very much longer. All very sad given the attention it brought to the town once upon a time. At least this Saturday night the old place will show that, with acts folk want to see, it can still get close to the pulling power of its glory days. The audience may be of more antique vintage, many a suspect hairdo and shirt opened a button too far. Queues like this are an oddity now. But as signs tied to railings and roadsides for miles around have been predicting for months – and will continue to do so once he has been and gone – 1980s soul singer Alexander O'Neal is in the house.

Julie from Tingley squeezes behind her and her partner's half of a four-seater table, as Joe waits for drinks at one of the two bars running along either side of the club, backed by mirrors for depth. It is from there that enough chickens-in-baskets were served to oil the wheels of England's poultry and wickerwork industries for, as it seemed back then, eternity. Toe-tapping Motown tunes blast from speakers, stage empty, front and centre, before an equally deserted dance floor. The bench-style seats sit sideways on, so those facing away from it risk a crick in the neck and must sit, arms on their other half's shoulders, with elbows draped over the back. On the walls are posters for Shalamar, soon to perform in Liverpool and Manchester, who presumably share a promoter with the star turn tonight.

'Is there a support act?' asks Julie, the fluorescent lights turning tonic water a radioactive blue. As the clock turns nine it appears not, the only 'entertainer' a bloke waving his arms to eighties hits, trying gamely to fill the floor. Until on they come, the backing band, and the first strains of 'Hearsay' break the air, joined by the artist himself.

Alexander O'Neal, live in Batley, but only just by the look of it, a portly version of the man whose image has been slowing traffic. He could be someone's grandparent, though the same is true for most of the audience. Nor is much of the music familiar. The majority seem vaguely aware of three tunes, possibly two, and definitely the most famous one. And for the latter, not unreasonably, he will keep them waiting. The band is tight, the singer taking a rest to mop his brow and get his breath back now and then. After one break, he shares his accumulated wisdom of the years: 'As I got more of this [pats stomach] and less of this [pats head], I came to realize you are where you are because that's where you're supposed to be. Enjoy your life.' If that's not worth a cheer, what is? 'Hello England,' he says, reaching for precise geographical reference without finding it. 'I love you guys.' And then off he goes into the dimly remembered 'Saturday Love', recorded in 1985 with fellow R&B star Cherrelle, before finishing with 'Criticize', as big a showstopper now as it was in 1987.

On the whole, though, Julie isn't impressed. 'I knew one song,' she says, as she and Joe head off back to Tingley, the evening in her estimation a bit of a damp squib. Oh, for another James Corrigan.

Some songwriters would have bought an English Tudor retreat in Laurel Canyon, but not Sammy King. A lad whose life was transformed by Batley Variety Club prefers a cul-de-sac in Heckmondwike.

Ten minutes from the centre of Batley, the town in which he was born, Sammy and wife Linda share a neat suburban home with panoramic views of Bradford, Huddersfield and the hills beyond. He can still knock out a tune as circumstances demand, but life is more tranquil these days, he admits over coffee in the couple's kitchen. Certainly quieter than in the 1960s when the Variety Club's influence was at its height. Back then, friendships with Roy Orbison and others took this Batley boy from wannabe to musical first team, with one particular ditty written for the 'Big O' as popular today as it ever was. But Sammy King's story began long before Louis Armstrong told him, 'With a name like yours, you ought to be black', much of it already in his autobiography *Penny Arcade*, its title the song in question.

The book is a rollicking read with a foreword by Roy Orbison Jr, who explains how, in the sixties, 'Yorkshire became an Orbison stronghold', with Sammy part of the extended family. It details his upbringing in the Heavy Woollen District with potted accounts of post-war Batley long before Alan Twohig, son of an Irish father and piano-playing Liverpudlian mother, adopted the stage name by which he has since been known. A childhood mostly spent in Batley Carr – 'Carr' the old Nordic word for 'wasteland' or 'bog'; home to refugees, the destitute and gypsies – back then one among many close-knit communities.

'At the turn of the [nineteenth] century,' he writes, 'Batley Carr boasted thirteen pubs, over a hundred shops, a large social club, two churches, umpteen chapels, three schools, a library, park, cinema and half a dozen large mills, all squeezed into an area less than a mile long and half a mile wide.' By 1941, the year of Sammy's birth, the after-effects were still felt: cramped living conditions and regular outbreaks of illness, the nearest toilet fifty yards away and frozen up in winter. Many relied on Victorian gas mantles for light. Along with 'the obligatory whooping cough, measles and chickenpox', Sammy twice suffered double pneumonia, a worry for his parents, as a doctor cost sixpence. No National Health Service then. But adversity brought out the best in folk, neighbours donating buckets of coal for families struggling with sick children, husbands fed with hot meals after work when their wives were ill. In other words, just the sort of community in which rugby league might plant roots and flourish.

As befits a songwriter, Sammy has a nice turn of phrase. The neighbourhood chapel might organize a picnic to Shipley Glen, near Bradford, or a day at Wilton Park, or Howley Hall – 'conveniently flattened for us by Cromwell during the Civil War'. Some summer Sundays it felt as if the whole world was in Batley Park, enjoying the floral gardens, manicured bowling and putting greens, tennis courts, boating lakes, bandstands, swings, slides, roundabouts. What chance such an amenity today with no consumers and financial gain? Less healthy and virtuous but just as popular were Saturday-afternoon matinees at the local fleapits that stank of 'piss and stale biscuits'.

As a pupil of St Bede's Grammar in Bradford, though – alma mater of 'angry young man' John Braine, author of *Room at the Top* – disaster struck. Injured while playing soccer, Sammy's hip became infected. It took two inches off one leg to give an already diminutive fellow the pronounced limp he would carry thereafter. He spent two years in Pinderfields Hospital, his life saved only by penicillin.

Asked by his dad what he wanted to be when he grew up, this 5 ft 3 in. dynamo replied, 'Big'. And so he would be, though never in height. At Batley Art College, he drummed in a band whose trombonist, Derek Wadsworth, later wrote the theme tune to *Space 1999*, played in the brass section on Dusty Springfield's 'I Only Want to Be with You', and on the Rolling Stones album *Their Satanic Majesties Request*. In awe of Lonnie Donegan, he joined a skiffle group and taught himself guitar. When rock 'n' roll came along, he and his brother formed a duo that with a lass named Betty Gledhill became a trio, 'The Three Lloyds', as 'that was the bank we intended to keep all our money in', their tour bus a Morris Minor Traveller.

After that, he joined an R&B band, the Dingos, part of a then thriving Bradford music scene, and the Voltaires, with whom he had a top-ten hit – in Dewsbury anyway. Their cover of the Platters' song 'Only You' reached number seven in a chart compiled by Thornes' radio and record shop, Westgate, with the Righteous Brothers at number one and the Kinks, Moody Blues, Cilla Black, Sandie Shaw and Gerry and the Pacemakers also featured. He shared billing with the Beatles at the Queens Hall, Leeds, screamed at by a couple of thousand teenage girls. Or at least that's what he thought, until he noticed Paul McCartney's head poking through the curtains.

In the summer of 1963, he toured with Gene Vincent, among other legends. On opening night at the Southport Odeon, he was surprised to discover that Vincent had a caliper on one leg, publicity shots giving no clue of this disability. 'Oh God,' Sammy thought, as they limped towards one another. 'I hope he doesn't think I'm taking the piss.' Also on the tour were Cliff Richard and the Shadows.

With the Voltaires, the original idea had been to dress up like the French philosopher, something in the manner of Johnny Kidd & the Pirates, though that never eventuated. It was then, though, that the band's manager, Bernard Fenton, suggested 'Sammy King', and it was then that the songwriting took off too. Wally Ridley, much-respected head of HMV Records, liked their demo and asked to hear something original. But on *Juke Box Jury*, Cilla voted that debut disc recorded at Abbey Road a 'miss' and so it turned out. The recording career fizzled out, Sammy and a new Voltaires line-up turned to cabaret in the dancehalls, working men's clubs, casinos and nightclubs, before a nervous breakdown put an end to all that, temporarily at least.

Discharged from hospital, Sammy gravitated back to the stage and went along to Batley Variety Club, a part of town he knew well since prior to its development the land had housed Batley sewage works and a wall he used to walk the length of to catch the train to school. Now, as he walked towards the entrance, Batley Variety Club's founder and owner, James Corrigan, came out. The two had 'a little natter' in the car park, the upshot being a fortnight's residency if he wanted it. Sammy, on his uppers, very much did want it and so began a time, from 1966 to 1977, of working with a roll call of sixties showbiz royalty: Shirley Bassey, P. J. Proby, Johnny Mathis, Gene Pitney . . .

Along with performing, he began to write songs again too, Wally Ridley's advice that it might provide him with a pension one day proving prescient. The one that really lifted his fortunes came to him as he looked out across the bay one night in Anglesey. Just as darkness set in, a series of tiny coloured lights twinkled on the headland opposite. The first two lines arriving in a flash of inspiration:

A light shone in the night, some way ahead.
Blue, turned into green – then it was red . . .

To begin with, a jaunty little number, one-part Eurovision Song Contest, one part marching band, sat on a tape recorder unloved, one of several tunes he dreamed of selling. Since his breakdown, Sammy had lost contact with London recording studios and therefore had no way of getting his music under the right nose. Until, that is, Variety Club compere Jerry Brooke took Sammy and his friend, former band member Bill Clarke, backstage to meet Roy Orbison. There the Big O was, head to toe in black, standing tall behind famous dark glasses, smiling and impeccably well mannered.

'Jimmy Corrigan always liked to be called James, you know,' Sammy says now, just as Linda comes in with the shopping. 'Jimmy Corrigan was his uncle in Scarborough. He was a great guy, but in a small town like Batley you usually find envy.' He shares an instance from his youth. 'Where we lived, in the close confines of a yard with about six houses there, so long as you were all the same you were okay. Once, my mother and father gave up smoking so they could buy a new suite. Eventually they had it delivered. Two neighbours came in. "You never told us you were buying a new suite," and didn't speak to us for a week. Don't get me wrong, wonderful people in times of hardship, but go that little bit above and you aren't one of us.'

As Malcolm Haigh pointed out on his tour, Corrigan embarked on his entrepreneurial course from what had then been a bingo hall. 'He had this idea that all the famous people worked in London, so he would bring London to Batley. They thought he was mad, but he did it. Batley owes him a lot. I got to meet people I could flog my stuff to.'

His first song, Sammy admits, was terrible. 'Like most people, the first time I wrote music was when a love affair broke up, full of emotion, in the early sixties. The first song I got anywhere with was "What's The Secret", the one written for Wally Ridley. It wasn't a big hit but it got heard in America and I got my first fan mail. A girl I used to go out with was working as an au pair in New York, heard it and rang me up to tell me at 3 a.m. I'd just got back from a gig.'

The first time the Voltaires – 'Note the "e", the posters always left that off' – played Batley Variety Club, they were booked to appear with Guy Mitchell, a huge star in his day: 'What a fantastic experience. Batley had atmosphere. You can spend a million pound on a club, but if it hasn't got atmosphere you've lost. The big turns would be booked for a week, maybe two, and it was always full to begin with and for a long time after. The rot set in when agents started to ask silly money for the big names. Neil Sedaka was on "x" pounds when he first came, then demanded the same for a night that he'd previously been getting for a week. They got greedy.' A friend, Yvonne, married Maurice Gibb of the Bee Gees. 'I tell you who was great. Jimmy Ruffin. He was about 6 ft 5 in. Talking to him I got neck ache. In fact, I played him a couple of songs he thought were lovely, but he said, "Have you got any soul?"'

And what did the stars think of Batley? 'Well, Louis Armstrong, they took him to a building site in the middle of nowhere and he said, "Where's the club?" They told him it wasn't finished yet. Big smile on his face; he was smashing. The big stars didn't show any superiority; the ones who thought they were big stars did.'

Elvis Presley never played Batley; it's said Colonel Tom Parker wanted £100,000 for himself before negotiations could start, though the manager not having a passport as a Dutch-born illegal immigrant had more to do with it. So Sammy never met 'the King' but nearly got a song to him. Whenever Orbison played Batley, he rented a private cottage at the back of the Black Horse pub in Clifton. It's easy to see why. A twenty-minute drive up into the moorlands, it's a place with an otherworldly feel, about a mile from Brighouse and a stone's throw from Hartshead, whose main claim to fame aside from Patrick *Brontë* once being assistant curate there lies in giving its name to Hartshead Moor, last service station on the westbound M62 as it starts its climb up and over the Pennines via Windy Hill and on into Lancashire.

'By that time, if I'd got owt new, he'd listen to it. I took him an up-tempo song, "Mississippi Fireball". "Hmm," he said. "Good song, Sam. I don't think it's me, but Elvis could do that." Orbison was always Elvis's favourite singer; they were very good friends. "Can I take the tape and play it to him?" I never knew whether he did or not.'

'Penny Arcade' was for Roy though, eventually. Sammy took a clutch of his songs down to the Variety Club, arriving just as he was about to go on. 'I tell you what,' says the Big O, 'we are going to the Beefeater afterwards [they kept it open late for him], do you want to come up there when we're through?' So there's Sammy, at two in the morning, sat with his mate's tape recorder and surrounded by the superstar and his entourage. 'Okay, what you got Sam?'

'I played him "After Tonight". When it finished, Barbara, his wife, said, "Do you know, I don't think that's Roy. Have you anything else?" So I put "Say No More" on. He was listening; everyone else was talking. When that finished, I hit stop and waited. "Are those the only songs you've got?" I told him, "No, there's a few more." I'd been told never take more than two, because they'll forget. He said to just leave it running. I was talking to Bill when Roy comes over and asks if I had a copy of the tape. I said, "No, it's the only one I've got", but that he could take it. He said he was going back to Nashville next week and would like to play it to Wesley Rose, his producer. We left at 4.15 a.m. on 11 May 1969; he could have pinched the songs or anything. About a month later, a package comes through the door. "Penny Arcade, Roy Orbison's next single, released 20 August." I thought, "Bloody hell."'

A three-year deal was signed, a hefty advance royalty cheque received, shared with Bill. When the song made the Top 20 for three weeks during a three-month period in the Top 50, he became a local celebrity, signing autographs in the street and opening garden fêtes. The record might have gone bigger in the UK had Orbison been here to promote it. In Australia and New Zealand, where a tour coincided with its release, it went straight to number one and won a gold disc. Its shelf life since, however, is impressive. A favourite in gay bars and working men's clubs and pubs on the Spanish costas, it has more recently become the semi-official anthem of Glasgow Rangers. The ideal song to play as Batley take the field, you'd think, but no. In some it inspires cultural cringe, a shame given its composer's fondness for the place.

As a youngster living at the bottom of Victoria Street, Sammy would climb up through the rhubarb fields to Mount Pleasant. 'When Batley were at Dewsbury, you couldn't see for the masses of people. Where I lived, you could hear the cheering.' He supported Dewsbury at first, 'because at that time you couldn't get white wool. My mother only had red and amber and black, and I wanted her to knit me a scarf. But as I got older I'd walk up through the allotments and climb over the wall.' One of his proudest memories is fielding the ball for one of his heroes, John Etty – he looked massive. Though a Huddersfield Town season-ticket holder now, back then he watched rugby because it was cheaper and more accessible than football: 'Threepence, although half the time we used to sneak in. They got big crowds then. There was only one league and you used to get Wigan and St Helens coming. It was a big part of the town's identity. People identified with it.'

After which, being hospitalized, he didn't watch much of anything and while on crutches didn't feel safe in crowds: 'They didn't take any prisoners.' Later, he performed at player reunions and such – 'always on the cheap because they'd no money and I always loved the club' – and was made an honorary member. 'They were lovely folk, friendly and all that. I got to know all my heroes on first-name terms, what an honour.' Nowadays he watches rugby league on telly.

As for the Roy Orbison connection, it still pays dividends. 'After Tonight' is on the Big O's latest posthumous album: 'His youngest son, Alex, got in touch to say his mam was wrong, he should have done this as a single. The third song on the tape, "I Got Nothing", is on it as well. "Penny Arcade" is on the box set, as is "Say No More".' So Roy did four of the six in the end and never stopped playing 'Penny Arcade', a favourite in his live act ever afterwards that audiences insisted on.

A few years back now, Sammy, the old band and Roy Jr had a reunion at the Black Horse. The latter told Sammy his dad had seen something in the song that no one else could. They said he was silly to record it, but time has proven him right. 'Penny Arcade' could be said to have revived a flagging career. 'I'm proud I helped get him on his feet again.' Not bad for a kid from Batley Carr.

Second Half – Downhill

Was the sound of distant drumming just the fingers of your hand?
– 'The Windmills of Your Mind', Michel Legrand, Alan and
Marilyn Bergman, 1968

12

'CAN WE SHUT the fucking door, please,' said John Kear, fingers twitch-ing, as non-playing squad members trailed in after the home defeat to Swinton. 'Real disappointing was that.' They had lacked composure, played as individuals, not as a team. At least three of their tries they hadn't had to work for. Tuesday: meeting at 6.15, Total Fitness at 7.00, 'then we'll try and pick ourselves up for Leigh, because there needs to be a massive improvement in performance'.

If players and coaches need narratives, supporters and media do too. Though Batley remained in the top four, just about, in the aftermath of this latest defeat, terrace pundits' attitudes hardened. The slump was down to JK's situation. And given that Bradford had beaten Workington in James Lowes's last match, the agreement with Matt Diskin could not be relied upon, so the theory went. The players were discontented; it was obvious. Kear should leave straight away, not hang around souring the joint. Two and two made five.

The truth was that while there was a degree of uncertainty with regard to the futures of individual players and coaching staff, every-one was as determined as ever to achieve something remarkable. Looked at in isolation, every defeat was explicable. Poor starts. Indecision. Human error. And though no one in rugby league would ever be likely to admit it, rank bad luck at times, just as earlier in the season good fortune had turned games. Expectations had clearly risen; small-town Batley were in a relegation battle last year.

Some supporters, though, continued to wonder whether getting the new coach in now might inject fresh enthusiasm, replenish belief. This weekend's trip to Leigh, unbeaten in the league since day one at the Mount, was a home banker. Then came the visit of Halifax, level on points with fifth-placed Featherstone in sixth. Make or break time? Win that and the dream was alive. To lose might mean a parting of the ways.

At Leigh Sports Village, the contrast in resources could not have been more pronounced. On the first day in May, a wet and grey Sunday, the M60 rammed with traffic heading for Old Trafford, where Leicester City were to face Manchester United in a title decider, Leigh's pre-match Premier Club lunch was impressive.

Guests of honour were Karl Harrison, ex-Batley coach and father of James, and Karl Morris, a sports psychologist currently with Huddersfield but with a background in cricket, football and especially golf. In 2013, he'd helped the Giants to the League Leaders Shield, the club's first major trophy in eighty years. Golf, of course, is an individual sport. As a former professional, he did what he needed to do. But coming into a team game he learned that coaching a group is tough. 'You've to keep a lot of people happy,' he said, and not just players and directors. 'It's interesting to hear golfers talk about fear of the first tee or putting or whatever. When I came to rugby league, where your head genuinely is on the line, I saw fearless individuals, day in, day out. So many other sports could learn an awful lot from it.'

Having mind-coached Rory McIlroy, Graeme McDowell, Darren Clarke and similar, Morris shared title-winning secrets: 'Most of the time it's about getting them to reduce the amount of thinking they do. It takes a really smart coach to keep things simple. There's too much information flying around now. We over-complicate.' As a Manchester United fan himself, Morris joked that manager Louis van Gaal had been hired by Liverpool as a special agent, mission almost complete. 'I see them making all these notes and read some of the plays – it's so, so complicated. When a football team has two shots on target in an entire game, what on earth are you doing in training? I remember a story about Matt Busby, what he used to tell players before they went on the pitch: "Lads, just make sure you pass to a red shirt." As ridiculously simple as that is, if you think about it, you keep passing to the blokes in your team and you can't go far wrong.'

Morris also worked with Michael Vaughan, England cricket captain, ahead of the Ashes. What kind of things did he tell Vaughan before he faced Glenn McGrath and Brett Lee? And what does he say to Huddersfield prop Eorl Crabtree before he goes into battle? 'When it comes to Eorl, not much, other than just get on with it. With Vaughan, you've got guys sending missiles down at ninety miles an hour, moving around, so you don't get him too involved in what may or may not happen. We worked on little routines he did on every ball he got. That's the theme. With most players it's about reducing that thought process, making it simple and getting them back to things they've done as kids, naturally on the pitch. You take the importance of the situation away if you can. Play it as you see it. Just react.'

Leigh Sports Village, which Leigh have called home since 2008 when their creaky old ground of sixty years Hilton Park was destined for demolition, is an impressive 12,500-capacity venue whose ambitions are realistically pitched. Shared with United and Blackburn Rovers' reserves teams, its facilities are regularly farmed out for big events. Keegan Hirst fan Sir Elton John appeared here in June 2014, telling a 17,000 audience that, 'As a kid I used to watch rugby league with Eddie Waring on TV but never dreamed I'd play the Leigh team's stadium. I'd rather play here than Manchester Arena.' Four weeks ago, Bayern Munich had hired it ahead of a Champions League game and insisted that all advertising hoardings be removed, merely at training. No one knew why. In fact, the only downside to the place from a league perspective is that with the stadium being council-owned, Leigh are not allowed to brand it. With no photos of former players or the like, it can feel a little impersonal. That said, a shining example to clubs in both the Championship and Super League, this founder member of the Northern Union is imposing its identity by stealth.

Whether through Premier Club lunches or other marketing efforts, the Centurions have found a way to interest both the public of the town and its corporate community.

Could Batley Bulldogs be like this one day? In a modern yet compact stadium on a brown-field site alongside the M62 perhaps, or a revamped Mount Pleasant – a community hub in a wider sense? Leigh's Premier Club, after all, began in a boardroom with twenty or thirty people, each shown a video of the previous game and fed a pre-match meal. Nowadays, 120 diners are catered for at a minimum in a sizeable banqueting suite. For around half the games it is filled to capacity with 220. Club legends like John Woods are brought in to speak, sports figures from further afield invited too. A Leigh lad like Nottinghamshire cricketer Steven Mullaney, or Durham's Gary Pratt, who ran Australia skipper Ricky Ponting out as a substitute fielder in 2005's Ashes. Peter Reid. Joe Royle. Fran Cotton. Members hear the team-sheet first from the coach's own mouth, receive 'executive' seating, complimentary half-time tea or coffee and access to VIP post-match player presentations, dress code smart but casual. And all at a cost of £750 a season, for up to fourteen league games plus play-offs.

Then again, they don't have Barbara's baking, though she, the Batley board and their families were installed in a directors' box of their own, complete with coffee facilities and wall-mounted flat-screen TV. Further along the carpeted West Stand corridor, Manchester City icon Francis 'Franny' Lee watched the game as a guest in another such box, having just had a titanium knee fitted.

With Karl Morris interviewed, it was the turn of the other Karl, Harrison, to take the stage. He was asked about James, a late call-up to the Batley bench, Adam Gledhill having unexpectedly withdrawn. Does 'Rhino' get as nervous about his son playing as he did himself?

'His mother does,' he said, pointing out that 'kids like James need a reserve set-up in which to earn their spurs. He was released and only taken on somewhere because his uncle ran a club.' Mrs Harrison – also in the room with Young Iro's grandparents – must be especially nervous, it was suggested. Her boy was up against the infamous

Gareth Hock, one of the most menacing forwards around. What had he told James? 'Just to go out there and twat him.'

Well, Karl Morris did advise keeping it simple.

The first surprise was on the team-sheet. Despite doubts about his fitness, Paddy Hesketh began in the front row. A fortnight ago, the scales went missing just as the big prop was due to be weighed. Last season he'd come in at 121 kilos, around 19 stone in old money. After Christmas, that had risen to 124 kilos, though no one was concerned. There was the leg injury to consider and weight gain is not unusual at that time of year, the gruelling off-season intended to shift it. Lately, though, the extra timber was alarming. Paddy blamed the niggling shoulder injury picked up at Oxford, though to the coaching team that was an excuse. He was given a four-week weight-loss programme and an ultimatum: get back down to 121 kilos or that's that. To begin with, he lost about 1.5 kilos in seven days, an excellent effort. But when a battery was found, he'd put half a kilo back on. His reddened face said it all.

On the bench, Dave Petersen took a place alongside James Harrison, and there were a couple of debutants at centre; Greg Minikin came in from Castleford and Callum Casey got his chance. The team therefore had a patched-up look about it, although the opportunities stretched only so far. Although Tinker was named in the squad on the back of the match-day programme, he hadn't been seen at the club for weeks.

It had been an eventful seven days. After a flying visit to Cardiff on Monday for the inaugural Wales Rugby League Hall of Fame Dinner for coach Kear, Tuesday saw hailstones the size of golf balls and talk of a worsening injury situation, the boardroom atmosphere glum. The leadership group met for what felt like a crisis meeting, the balloon re-inflated by the Featherstone Cup win again blowing raspberries. Keegan thought their incredible start might have caught up with a few, Rowey that they'd gone a bit soft. JK casually dropped dual-registration and loans into the mix. 'Against Leigh and Bradford, the atmosphere in the changing room – you could cut it with a knife.

It's not there now. Is it tiredness? I've got to solve it somehow.' As in any walk of life, tired people make bad decisions. Breth thought he should bring men in to freshen them up.

'We are doing it tough, aren't we?' said Brownie, who knew that of which he spoke, having been playing with a torn meniscal cartilage in his knee – 'I can't get out of my van, it keeps giving way.' He, like Gleds, would miss the Leigh game, but thereafter battle on. Danny Cowling's knee tear was severe, concern about an ACL graft thrown in for good measure. Brad Day and Alex Rowe: thumbs down. Patch Walker out for two to three weeks. And that was without long-term absentee Sam Scott and the other 'minor' rips and strains being ignored or jabbed or not admitted to.

More encouragingly, Chris Ulugia was fit to resume non-contact training and the dual-reg arrangement with Castleford had already been concluded, which, on Thursday, brought Minikin into the stable. Casey and Petersen were announced as signings. Salford's on-loan second-rower Matt Sarsfield too had been due to come but rumour was that by the time Iro got around to phoning him he'd thought Batley were no longer interested and went to Halifax instead. Another Cas man, Ryan Boyle, was pencilled in at prop but failed a fitness test on a calf.

'They'll have a shock, will Leigh,' JK chuckled, darkly. 'Fuck me, they'll say, where've they got that team from?'

In the circumstances, that Batley should begin by holding the favourites at bay for twenty minutes was testament to the quality of a week's training in unseasonably cold conditions ahead of the year's first bank holiday weekend. Under finger-numbing frozen skies, Mokko had had them passing tennis balls along the line, before hit after full-on hit in the teeth of an icy rainstorm. 'Absolutely first class,' JK yelled. 'That's the standard.' Preparation done, wet and bedraggled, they walked to the showers with purpose, their coach grinning his approval.

On Saturday morning, he'd given them another of his pep talks before re-showing clips from their opening-day victory. 'Hungry as fuck, weren't we? Confident, confrontational . . .' He didn't buy into this 'scratching around' stuff, 'although if we can play that for the press, all well and good. We can feel sorry for us-selves, with a pet lip, or we can stick us fucking chests out, look people in the eye, stick us chins out and say, "Are you going to take us on?" I prefer the latter.'

Next day, Paddy Hesketh did just that. Huffing and puffing some-what, he made tackles, doubled up in defence and lasted longer than expected. His teammates too scrambled well, the defensive line once again crowding Leigh's playmakers, disrupting their skills, just as it had done twelve weeks ago. Then Breth had a brainstorm and kicked directly into blindside touch – a handover to Leigh on the thirty-metre line, penalty tapped by Micky Higham. Moments later, winger Liam Kay had gone in for a try out wide before Martyn Ridyard added the first of his six-out-of-six conversions.

When Batley were awarded a penalty in front of the Leigh posts, the dugout this time signalled to keep playing and nothing came of it. On the half hour, though, the squandering of two easy points was, for the moment, shrugged off when Dom Brambani forced a first GLDO before Ainy darted in from dummy-half, number 7 tagging on the goal. All square. The contest was scrappy, but in the Bulldogs' eyes the fact it was a contest at all was encouraging. So all the more disappointing then that Leigh should barge over three minutes before the break for what looked like a 12–6 half-time lead before a drop-goal was added to the conversion: 13–6 on the hooter. Still, the visiting side was in it, disgruntling a near 3,500 crowd that expected more. As marquee signing Rangi Chase limped off having only just got back from injury, *What a waste of money* was heard.

If Batley scored first in the second half, anything might happen. In defence, they had scrapped away, defied the odds, just as they had at Halifax in game four. But when Cain slipped on the wet turf – part grass, part 3G – taking a pass in yardage on the last tackle of the very first set, a second handover culminated in another home try and goal, the signal surely for Leigh to cut loose. Batley's defence was indeed soon stretched and by then Paddy was leaving the field clutching his shoulder, though Petersen and in particular Minikin had settled in well; Casey, after a nervy start, was busy too. It was he who harried Leigh into a second GLDO; not long after, Leaky broke the line and Dom's conversion made it 19–12.

Young Iro's first contribution was a knock-on at the play-the-ball as the game once again got scrappy, most Batley errors unforced and Leigh's on the whole not. And when Liam Hood span out of a weak tackle and over the line on the hour, a 25–12 score suggested that gallantry would not be enough. But then came an astonishing ten-minute spell in which a trio of Batley tries looked to have stolen the game. First, Breth won the race to a Brambani kick. Then, with the Bulldogs hunting like the pack of old and forcing another mistake, Dom conjured space on the right in which to sidestep and go: 25–24.

A late arrival in the Leigh directors' box was benefactor-in-chief Derek Beaumont, timing his return from a trip abroad to coincide perfectly with Batley's revival. 'Bollocks!' he cried when they were awarded a line-clearing penalty. 'He's taking the piss!' He was even less thrilled when Young Iro then took a pass off Dom's inside shoulder that with a third successful conversion made it 30–25 to the visitors. After a troubling few weeks, a morale-boosting victory looked in the bag.

There was, though, still three minutes to go, pressure and field position crucial. The very last thing Batley needed to do was concede the penalty in Leigh territory that gifted easy yardage. Aware of the ticking clock, Higham got on with it, tapping and passing to Jake Emmett, who made it to the thirty-metre line. Higham to Hock as Leigh packed three men on the short side. Batley's right-side defence held steady, though, and he was brought down twenty metres out. Tackle two, stadium bouncing, Higham infield to Ridyard. Offload to Sam Hopkins. The big man straightened up the angle of attack and was hauled down with ten metres to go. Tackle three – Higham back infield to Dayne Weston. Roared on by fans behind the posts, the prop tried to continue the forward momentum but lead-runner

Harrison Hansen was supposed to be the dummy, Ridyard trailing to take the pass. Under pressure from Luke Blake, Weston got his wires crossed and the ball went to ground. Barred-up and desperate Batley had the chance to regain possession and close the game down. As Breth collided with Hansen, the ball bounced behind Cain and out to Callum Casey. *Fall on the ball, Callum! Fall on the ball!* A textbook re-gather was required. But in a febrile atmosphere and with opposing centre Richard Whiting closing in fast, the debutant, on his knees by now, could only watch in horror as it squirted from his grasp. Cain nearby stretched to get a foot to it but couldn't; the ball was picked up one-handed by Lee Smith, who chipped it over a frantic Batley rearguard, just getting his hand on the ball in front of Scotty and Cropper before it could go dead. With sixty seconds remaining, Ridyard's simple conversion ensured that Leigh had pulled it from the fire, 31–30. But there was still time for a further converted Hopkins try and flattering 37–30 final score.

It had been a courageous effort, cruelly denied, but the fact was that Batley had now lost four league games in a row. They had again lacked composure when what was needed was 'heart in the oven, head in the fridge', as Karl Morris had earlier put it.

In *This Sporting Life*, Lindsay Anderson's 1963 film of David Storey's novel, rugby league is the realm not of men but beasts. A game then at the heart of Yorkshire and Lancastrian culture is less a harmless escape valve, more a symbol for corrupted humanity. Here are the effects of unbridled capitalism, it says – perverted values and brutalized masculinity. Oh, where is Rousseau's noble savage?

Among the last of the great northern kitchen-sinkers, even the chairman of makers Rank called it 'squalid', the film's anti-hero Frank Machin (Arthur in the book) begins as a rugby league wannabe in a West Yorkshire mining town. As portrayed by Richard Harris, he is part Rottweiler, part tethered goat, chewing the cud – or gum – as if awaiting sacrifice. To Frank, players are 'frogs', the opening sequence pinning its subjects prior to dissection. According to his landlady

Mrs Hammond (Rachel Roberts), Machin is 'a great ape on a football field'.

The film is set at a time when rugby league is still 'football' in these parts, the Victorian vernacular not yet passed from memory. And football is an arena in which money gets one over on morality every time, the enjoyment factor ignored since that would muddy the metaphor. Anderson and Storey – who unlike the director had played rugby league himself when younger, at Leeds – present a view of the working-class male, and by extension female, as caged victim; their world some mad circus in which only the hungriest or craziest thrive, and maybe not even then. The characters in this anthropomorphic wasteland are there to be stared at, pitied and feared, if admired then at the level of a wild bear in chains; in any case dehumanized.

Yet *This Sporting Life* is undeniably enthralling, thanks to its exceptional leads, a fine ensemble cast and a representation of the north that, though very much of its day, mines truth in a cinematic seam between social realism and expressionism.

The Wakefield Trinity club played a big part in the production. Action and crowd sequences were filmed at Belle Vue, with complete co-operation. Players and officials appear, mostly as extras. Upon its release, though, many in the town and sport felt betrayed, not caring for the slant *This Sporting Life* had put on such an important aspect of their personality. And maybe, though they would not have admitted to it, a little shocked and possibly embarrassed by their own reflection.

After Roberto Gerhard's ominous opening score – xylophone tinkling like loose teeth, it will become apparent why – the game is afoot. A player falls on the ball, choreographically, before it is kicked from his grasp. Machin – one letter away from machine – bursts into shot, handing a frog off, taking a tackle. A scrum is formed, filmed upwards, front rows locked. 'C'mon lads, put some weight into it,' someone says as Frank packs down at loose forward. 'Get stuck in.'

The ball is hooked – a sure sign of the film's vintage – and Machin takes a smack in the gob from his opposite number, with whom he has just been butting chests. Blood trickles down his jaw. Cut to black. A coalmine. Machin drills, still chewing ferociously, before light returns and he is carried off, arms wrapped around his trainers' shoulders, the mob's baying loud within his skull.

Much of *This Sporting Life*'s narrative is shared in flashback – the dazed player's recollections in the changing room, in the back of a car, under gas at a hastily arranged dental visit, on a bed in a spare room at a Christmas party wherein it all comes back to the present . . .

'Bloody 'ell, he's broke his front teeth,' says a trainer as Frank is hit with a mucky sponge. 'You won't want to see no tarts for a week.' In a world ruled by money, tarts are what women are. Machin is a brooding urban Heathcliff captured amid dark mill chimneys, cooling towers and crags of ragged moorland. Like his romantic interest – the painfully repressed and grieving Mrs Hammond, very slowly referred to as Margaret – he is quite unable to articulate his emotions except, in his case, through rage and the violence afforded by rugby league.

That and the sort of communal bath that with the advent of HIV would be replaced by showers, where there are scenes of horseplay. Thus does *This Sporting Life* suggest the homoerotic implications of the game for spectators and players alike, a daring angle for its time no doubt, though not so far removed – if at all – from the hackneyed view that heterosexual women only like football because it allows them to ogle men's legs. Teammates towel one another's backs, replicating miners when emerging from the pit. *How do I look?* 'I've seen worse. Go on, you're dry . . .'

Johnson, an elderly flat-capped hanger-on played by the future *Doctor Who* William Hartnell, is deemed suspect by Mrs Hammond: 'He looks at you like a girl.' *Now don't come that, he's interested that's all.* 'I'd say excited . . . he's got awful hands; they are all soft . . .'

Again in flashback, we see Frank given his chance in a reserve-team trial, during which one of his supposed comrades won't pass him the ball, at the cost of a certain try. Team spirit is a secondary concern for someone who sees only a challenge to the pocket should this newcomer take his place. So Machin breaks his nose in a scrum, for which the opposing hooker is sent off. 'Not fit to be on a football field,' says the referee, while the real culprit smirks and his victim leaves the field. On the same side or not, the only common causes here are survival and cash.

Looking on from the stand are the club's directors, two-bit emperors at the Coliseum, thumbs at the ready. One, Slomer, notes that the wrong man was punished. 'It's a rough game, Charles,' says Weaver, his rival, with a lascivious leer. 'I like to see a man playing as if he really meant it.' Once signed, Frank and a teammate wrestle in the changing-room bath over a bottle of brown ale. 'Come on, you two fairies,' says a trainer. 'Let's have you out of there . . .'

Outside, in a Belle Vue stadium that is still recognizable today, Machin signs autographs for children. Mrs Weaver asks to meet him, so Weaver calls him over. 'Frank Machin,' she says, limp hand offered, eyebrow raised. 'You're one of the stars of the City according to my husband.' *We don't have stars in this game, Mrs Weaver; that's soccer.* 'What do you have then?' *People like me.*

On 'Super Thursday', as polling stations opened for council elections, Keegan Hirst reflected on a Batley campaign that had swung into its home straight. For the first time, Batley were out of the top four, replaced by Halifax, who overcame bottom side Workington 36–32. The Bulldogs' captain voted to stay positive.

'If you'd said that halfway through the season we'd be fifth, everyone would have said, "Yeah, we'll take that." It's a tough league with four full-time teams; your Halifaxes and Featherstones are good. Beating Leigh and then Halifax away, Sheffield at home and drawing with Bradford . . . but as you achieve, expectations change, don't they? Being fifth feels disappointing. Knowing we have beaten those teams and then lost to Swinton and Oldham . . . those were tough to swallow.' He admitted to having viewed them as easy-beats. 'I thought if there was two gimmes in this league, that would be them. Yet they turned us over, which says a lot about our attitude. If I thought that, less experienced players would have too. But that's sport, isn't it? If you don't turn up, you get caught out.'

As for 'the gay thing', as the season had unrolled so its status as a story had diminished. 'I am being asked to do stuff but, generally, people aren't asking about it any more. I've talked it to death.' With the exception of a couple of half-hearted comments at Halifax, crowds have responded with a shrug. 'No one actually cares now, do they?'

Keegan's personal life, though, is transformed. Out and about in Manchester people know who he is, most likely because he is a friend of Antony Cotton he thinks, though: 'I don't have an idea of myself as a kind of superstar. I'm a rugby player with Batley, not Sam Burgess. It might be easier to get carried away if the lads weren't so good at keeping my feet on the ground. Puff your chest out thinking you are Barry Big Bollocks and you get brought down a peg or two sharpish.'

The night after the Leigh defeat he went to Manchester United's Player of the Year awards, not from any love for football, just because 'how often do you get to go to something like that? It was all right. A fancy presentation night, we go in jeans and T-shirt, they wear black tie. Auction, raffle, awards . . . same but with a lot more money. A spa day fetched £8,000.' A season pass to Batley Baths won't get you that.

The decision to follow JK to Wakefield won't be official for another three months but, yes, it had been tricky, not least because the new Canadian team, Toronto, had also wanted him. 'I got caught up in the romance of it, international flights and all that. But do you know what, as a twelve-year-old boy watching my first match, Leeds against Bradford at Valley Parade, I knew that's what I wanted to be: a professional full-time rugby league player. Wakey will give me that opportunity. I wouldn't have been able to look in the mirror if someone in the future asked, "Did you have a chance to play Super League?" and I'd had to say I turned it down. That wouldn't have sat right. I went with my gut and then it was an easy decision to make.'

Though the step up will be large, former Championship players like Chris Hill at Warrington and St Helens' former Batley forward Alex Walmsley have made the transition in recent years, giving him confidence he can do the same. 'Five years ago, Chris was playing for Leigh and now he's a Super League captain. There are a lot of good players at this level – it gets undersold and overlooked.' Not that the move is much of a financial boost; dependent on how often he plays, he may be a little bit better off. 'I couldn't take a pay cut to go full-time. You've bills to pay and food to put on the table, haven't you? But it's the lifestyle. I was laying stone flags all day yesterday, sorting out doors today, tomorrow I'm plastering – not ideal game prep. At Wakefield, you get that ability to prepare properly and recover too. Rubs, massages and ice baths are hard to come by at our level. You've just to suck it up and get on with it.'

A scan confirmed Paddy's campaign was over, his shoulder needing an operation. In every player contract is a clause, rarely enforced. If he doesn't play for six months, then under medical advice the agreement can be terminated. Luckily for Paddy, that single match against Leigh re-bumped the clock, though he would be out of contract in November anyway. More immediately, he had a bright-red eyeball having had a first injection of three to remove fluid at the back of the socket. 'They clamp your eye open,' he said. 'It's hard to keep it still when they are coming at it with a needle . . .' Rugby league as directed by Luis Buñuel.

Nor would James Craven feature in the next eleven games that Kear, in the *Yorkshire Post*, called 'absolutely vital. The higher we finish, the more money we get. I want to leave the club in a really sound financial position to invest in further quality players.' Cravo popped in to see Iro and said his goodbyes with no fuss. A brief club statement confirmed that he had been released – frustrated by a lack of playing opportunities – with immediate effect. A regular in 2015, he was now off to play amateur rugby league at Thornhill. Zack McComb, just selected for England Students, would not be far behind.

There was better news for another former student player, Sam Scott, on Carl's bench having had his operation two weeks ago. Carl – a specialist in knees and shoulders – massaged the offending joint tenderly, stitched and scarred as it was. 'In six weeks, you will think it's getting better, then it will suddenly go backwards,' the physio said, advising him to chat with Cowling and Leaky, who had experienced knee reconstructions themselves. For a sales manager unable to drive, the past three months had not been ideal. Fortunately, the boss of the sportswear firm in Bolton is a keen rugby fan, so knew the risks and is very understanding. Scully, now embarking on six months of rehab, took the philosophical view. Yes, the injury was gutting and very nasty. 'But you've got to get on with it, haven't you? At least it's not my neck or back or anything serious.'

Keegan like Ainy was in the process of having a tattoo removed and the pair compared blisters. One tactic, apparently, is to cover the old one up. 'What with? A big arse with a rainbow coming out of it?'

Outside, the tackle shields were hammered with ferocity in the 'Gauntlet', a drill used to gruesome effect in *Gladiator*. 'Welcome to Bashville,' said Alex Brown as Cain took his turn. Two weeks ago, the strapping on Rowey's supposedly healing thumb had come loose, revealing part of the scar – 'about the size of a blob of jizz' – and it hurt like hell. He'd also nearly taken the end off a finger with a chisel at work, so that bothered him too. The big man was itching to get stuck into Halifax, in what would be his 100th game for Batley.

JK confirmed that the squad would not stay overnight in Workington next week: 'Lake District in summer, you can't get twenty-odd rooms, so we'll have to go up and win on the day.' The money would be spent on the players' winning bonuses this week instead. 'I'm not going to bang on about how important this is. If you don't know that, you don't look at league tables and if you don't look at league tables, you are not that fucking bothered.'

Again, training was intense, the players in vests, arms bared and glistening with sweat, those wrapped-up winter nights the stuff of memory, though Reitts still wore his woolly hat. And on a beautiful Saturday morning, the mood was surprisingly relaxed, though confidence-boosting clips of how they played at Halifax in game four had something to do with that.

Bev Nicholas called by. The Pink Weekend would be on 21 August and she proposed a nude fundraising calendar. In the first year, everyone took part but last year only five players came to the shoot and, of course, they'd not sold as well. Everyone agreed to join in.

Next day, after the warm-up, in the changing room all is agitation. Nerves are taught – tighter than Cropper's shorts, pulled nipple-high, shirt tucked in, wearer stone-faced. Brownie, 'Forever Young' tattooed on his lower back, paces about, pink as pork, shooting his rat-a-tat pellets of advice. Restless. Reitts calls for Deep Heat, which Cropper – Carl busy wrapping a bandage around Jimmy Davey's head – rubs into his teammate's legs. Players ask for tape or 'sniffy', spray the saline up their nose. Patch, calmer than most, wipes his hands on a training top. Dom talks out loud, though from deep in his own headspace. Student James massages Rowey, face down, legs akimbo, on a bench dragged into the shower area for the purpose. Keegan and Gleds pour bottled water into gumshields. Uce, who, like one or two others, had made his return in the Cup against Catalans, fidgets. 'How long we got?' someone asks. 'Have I got time for a shit?'

When the thump comes on the door, as usual JK asks them to take a seat. *We've only got a minute, boys. So hurry up.* 'It's all right, Brownie. They can't start without us. Listen, guys, I'll cut this short. You are ready to go, aren't you?' *Yeah! Yeah!* 'All I'm saying is, we know what the prize is at the fucking end of it, as long as we do the processes well. Keep things simple. Out-enthuse them. Be tougher. Outwork them and be smart, guys. Go out there and do them.'

Keegan calls the huddle. Hands anxious and determined meet at its centre. 'Bulldogs on three.' *One . . . two . . . three . . . Bulldogs!* And as they head toward the light, Kear again: 'Rip in! Rip in!'

There are days when you wonder how much of this is to do with team meetings, clips of strengths and weaknesses, tip sheets . . . and how much it's about muscle memory, instinct, layer upon layer of experience, the bounce of a ball, excitement, anticipation, luck, the thrill of the chase, riding a wave that is breaking your way.

After a minute's silence for Joyce Wood and Peter Walker, two supporters and volunteers who died in recent weeks, Joyce having worked on the turnstiles, Peter as a steward, Batley play uphill. What they do not want to do is trail 6–0 within the opening two minutes. It could have been worse. This past fortnight they have worked hard on scramble D and that pays off when Halifax tear down the touchline. Ainy tags the centre, Scotty tracks the runner and the last pass goes to ground. Moments later, when Cain forces a GLDO, the Bulldogs settle down and begin to go set for set as their coach requested.

Batley's first score, however, takes twenty-seven minutes to arrive, by which time they have spurned a kickable penalty in favour of building momentum, just as they had at Leigh. Dom's lovely cross-field kick is claimed and touched down by Reitts, the scrum-half's boot sure, steady and commanding, just as it will be all afternoon. Patch's conversion attempt hits an upright but Batley are now in the game and shortly before half-time, Ainy shimmies in from Uce's pass after more uncompromising defence forces the latest in a series of Halifax blunders. Even with the slope in their favour they look tired; Batley are getting stronger, though Ainy wastes a couple of late chances.

Behind closed doors, the Doggies are breathing hard but satisfied. Brownie is pumped. *We should be doing this; we shouldn't be doing that.* Keegan says to calm down, as Carl tends to a muscle on the captain's arm. 'Just keep doing what we are doing,' says Breth.

'We are flattening them, that's the top and bottom of this,' says JK. 'We've had twenty-three sets; they've had seventeen. That's why they are falling apart. They came out, threw everything at us, caught us cold, but we fucking weathered that storm, got back into it, went set for set, started to get some penalties, got the momentum and we've come out on the right side of the scoreboard, so well done. You were composed and you were fucking smart.' But, he warns, don't get caught this second half. 'We start strong. Complete the first five in O, first five in D. Okay? The other one, fellas . . . we've put some great kicks in, great chases, but when we get up there at marker, fucking namedrop and make the effort. A three-metre effort saves your mate eight metres up and ten metres back. But don't get caught offside. Be squeaky-clean. Get square. Work.' He asks Scotty how the numbering off is going at the back. 'Sweet? Good lad. It looks okay, let's maintain it; listen to what he's saying. Do we change anything? No. We play down there, field position, possession rugby . . . we let things unfold in front of us. Okay? Same commitment. Same effort. Same defence.'

The pack can sense blood and doesn't want to let this slip. 'Build pressure with good ends,' JK concludes. 'That's all it is. Relax now and get juiced up, fellas, for another big forty.' Patch tells everyone just to concentrate on their own role, Brownie that they should start strong. Keegan calls for the huddle. 'We've all said it. We've to go out there and do it. Don't get excited. Grind out the win, happy to get it in the seventy-eighth minute, yeah? Winners on three.' *One . . . two . . . three . . . winners!*

Again, though, they are caught cold. The try, three minutes in, comes via a midfield break and loose work at marker. Conversion kicked, the visitors lead again: 10–12. Ainy doesn't get the rub of the green when penalized for a ball-steal, but the Bulldogs get on with it and Reitts takes another kick in the corner to nudge the hosts back in front. Brownie is given a rest, with much slapping of hands in the dugout. *Nice, Brownie. Nice.* 'I could have carried on then,' he mutters.

Halifax press on but are denied by a superb double defensive feat from Breth and Patch on tackle four, forcing one of a number of turnovers. The view from the dugout is often a mirror image of how spectators see the game: focused on what players *don't* do as much as what they do. Little decisions – when to move a bit wider or back up and double back to make the next shape possible – it's those 'one-per-cent efforts' that catch the eye of coaches and teammates.

There's a worrying moment on the hour when Ulugia goes down having hurt his shoulder. He gets up and plays on for a while but is then substituted as Patch runs it on the last tackle and ducks under to score before adding the goal that makes it 20–12. Five minutes later, though, Fax claw their way back again. Blakey is judged to have dropped the ball after a surging midfield run before Reitts clouts a runner and goes on report. At the end of the set, Halifax score. The conversion is missed but at 20–16 there will be no relaxing.

To mark his centenary on the Mount, Alex Rowe detonates the most explosive hit seen on this or any ground in many a day. Adam Tangata is enormous but is felled by a blow fit to drop a Fred Dibnah chimney. Nevertheless, he is soon on his feet and pitching in for another carry. With ten minutes remaining, redoubtable second-rower Breth digs deep for a tackle that virtually wins the game, as Fax press hard on Batley's line. It's an astonishing effort from the oldest man on the field, particularly as he has been out there the entire match, without a break for a breather. As the seconds tick away, JK's advice to his half-backs that the Fax full-back isn't keen on spiralling kicks pays off. When the fumble results in a scrum, a pairs move is called and Dave Scott scampers past a couple of would-be defenders, Patch converting for 26–16.

There is still time for James Brown, back on the field, to make light of a gang of defenders from a Jimmy Davey crash ball and reach out to score with a couple of minutes remaining, Patch adding the goal in a game during which Batley had missed only fifteen tackles. Bang on target. At least two players missed none at all. *Doggies . . . Doggies . . . Doggies . . . Doggies!* The song could be sung again.

13

A DOUBLE OVER Halifax would be welcome in any season, but especially now. Although it doesn't get Batley back in the top four – Bradford were big home winners over Swinton, while Featherstone beat London – it suggests that they have what it takes to stay in the fight. Seventh-placed Sheffield's 30–37 home loss to Workington has seen a four-point gap confirmed between the Eagles and the top six that is destined only to widen as the race for the Qualifiers takes shape. A trip to Cumbria, though, is seldom straightforward and defeat there might see Batley's renewed confidence punctured.

The drive north is beautiful. Scree-scarred landscapes of caramel, green and grey; vertiginous peaks standing guard since prehistory beneath blue skies and billowing white clouds. It might be a setting for *Game of Thrones*. These smash-and-grab raiders, though, are interested in one prize alone: the two points.

Another new face, Frankie Mariano, is with them today, in like Minikin on a dual-reg deal from Castleford. The forward is a beast, huge, though has had a string of injuries to wrist, quads and knee.

The week's preparation had begun in gentle enough fashion with recovery in mind. A video review of the Fax game on Tuesday, then off to the T3 gym on Bradford Road for stretching and the like, John Heaton keen to get the muscles working. 'Muscles act as pumps. If you don't work the pump, whatever is in the muscle will stay in the muscle. So if lactic acid accumulates during the game and overnight, if you don't get rid of it, it's going to stay there.' Lactic acid is a waste product. At low levels, it is recycled, used by the body as a fuel, but if the intensity is hard enough for long enough, stiffness ensues, though it's not always to blame. 'In league, there is also the trauma of being bashed around for eighty minutes,' Heaton explains. 'It may not be lactic acid making you sore; it could be the impact or little tears in the muscles. Some of these lads do forty to fifty tackles – the equivalent of forty to fifty car crashes. Rugby is not always a lactic sport, like track cycling or a 2,000-metre row, which have different energy systems. A lot of the time, players ache because of the stopping and starting, twisting and turning, heavy impact.' And especially at Batley, where running down that slope causes a lot of muscle overload.

Overnight Wednesday, there was a break-in at the Fox's Biscuits Stadium. Iro discovered the burglary on Thursday morning. The offices were ransacked, files and stationery supplies thrown everywhere, by the evening piled in bin bags. Petty cash – takings for the Summer Bash, some Pink Weekend money – had been stolen, as had whatever was in the wooden War Chest that week on the bar in Ron's Lounge. Gloves and gauze in Carl's room had vanished, the intruders mindful of fingerprints presumably. Otherwise not much had gone, certainly no bottles of alcohol that might be expected to raise a few bob on any black market. The trophy cabinet too was left untouched.

The biggest mystery of all was how the intruders had gained entry, given that the only boarded-up window was downstairs in the physio room, one foot square at the most. A child could not squeeze through it. Interior alarm wiring was severed. Someone hiding in a toilet while the door was open for Wednesday-night tag, before a call to accomplices outside? The alarm bell too was broken, wires cut on the roof. No hope of identifying the culprits on the brand-new CCTV system either, since that had been stolen as well. Theories abounded. It was like 'CSI Batley'.

Was the alcohol thing a clue? Pottsy muttered grimly about anyone and everyone in the neighbourhood now knowing the interior layout of the club after that Communities United event at Easter; another chapter in the war of attrition perhaps? The burned-out Taverners' Bar, its roof timbers still charred and blackened after eight long months; the eggs and flour bombs hurled at the turnstiles – was it true that certain parts of the community didn't want the club there?

Not that the Batley directors exhibited such paranoia. It would take more than a half-cocked break-in to beat a club that had overcome far bigger threats to its existence down the years than this.

John Kear too had had a bit of trouble. His arm was scratched and bloodied. He'd been trying to push a heavy box into the slats of his garage roof at home, he said, when he'd tumbled from the step-ladders. Nothing broken 'aside from my phone and heart'.

In the tiny club gym, Keegan led by example, pumping hard on a landmine press. Seventy-five kilos of upward thrust in one-armed bursts, designed to replicate the pile driver fend of a hand-off. From there it was down to a rain-soaked field.

Groans were loud and prolonged at the sight of red tackle bags in a row down the K2 Stand touchline; Linners, drenched, had set it all up. Diskin had now confirmed that the club legend would not be required next year – he intends to bring in his own man – though Mokko, it later turned out, would stay. Pride wounded perhaps, Linners wasn't sure if he'd go up to Workington. It was a long haul and he would do fewer hours now, he reasoned. Nor did training proceed well. The session was scrappy, energy levels low. 'If you go with that attitude, you'll get beaten,' JK warned, as a soggy wet flan-nel of a sky dried up and a rainbow, unnoticed, straddled the valley. In fact, the evening very nearly ended in chaos, Cropper arguing with teammates and, worse, Linners, while the assistant coach was referee-ing, leading to a loose and ill-disciplined shift and the prop's removal from Sunday's team-sheet, with Breth, whom JK had hoped to rest, called back into service.

At least by Saturday morning 'Ken' Southernwood was over the effects of a collision with Chandler's thigh. Led from the field by John

Heaton, blood billowed from a wound above the eye sustained when he'd leaned in to tackle Jimmy. It needed stitches but neither Carl – absent due to a couple of punctures en route – or Doc Findlay were there, the only ones qualified to do it. A night in A&E was inevitable, though he'd have to wait for Scotty first, with whom he shared a car.

He'd done this before, he said, head bandaged in an otherwise empty changing room, coming round. 'That one was nasty.' Actually, he might go home for tea first, he reckoned, brightening. This was why his wife doesn't want their son playing rugby, although he reckoned it does a boy good. 'There's nothing better than that moment before you walk out to play, in here with all your mates. Nothing better than being part of a team.' He will miss that, he expected, when it's over. Two days later, it turned out he hadn't needed stitches at all. The hospital glued it up. 'Heal quick, don't I?'

Training had greater focus, the Tom Lillycrop scenario sending a message. 'He's copped it on the chin, has the individual, and I have set a precedent now,' said JK. 'If training goes that way again, you may well end up in the stand with me. That's how it's going to be, guys. We need quality training to produce quality performances.'

The physiotherapist too was as pumped as his tyres, showing off a new defibrillator. It was a Phillips 'Heartbeat', said Carl, and in its red zip-up case with a spare battery, scissors to cut through clothes and a plastic razor for shaving the chest, it was worth around £1,000. 'It's these you hear beeping during one-minute silences.'

Following the death of Keighley Cougars' half-back Danny Jones in May 2015, all Super League and Championship clubs must have one of these, an initiative driven by Danny's widow Lizzie. Players undergo an ECG, electrocardiogram, and are screened for abnormalities. If there is anything in the family history, they take a more advanced test – an echocardiogram – get an appointment with a cardiologist perhaps, results confidential. Consequently, a club may not be aware of the outcome; it is up to the individual to decide what to do with the information. Such pitch-side defibrillators, oxygen, emergency drugs and the like ensure hospital-standard care. Both Carl and

Doc Findlay must pass a course with practical exams every two years.

Batley, says Carl, are really lucky with their doctor, who is as much a fan as a part-time employee. He not only attends games, he is also available ad hoc for training sessions for little monetary gain, a valuable resource. 'I don't know what they will do if he leaves.' Not that the Doc intends leaving – other than to go to his property in Portugal from time to time. Beneath a shock of white hair, he is a gregarious and popular figure, and the Mount's second Scottish import to boot.

David Findlay, to give him his full name, wouldn't go so far as to call himself irreplaceable but qualified doctors like physiotherapists are scarce. He is often responsible for both teams and the crowd too. Other clubs rely heavily on Bucket and Sponge, an agency that farms medics out. 'Nobody wants to give up a Sunday any more,' sighs a man whose post-match medicine of choice is a pint of lager. And in league you must be ready for anything. Playing for French side Carcassonne in March, Aussie second-rower Haydn Peacock almost lost his penis, the force of a tackle reportedly tearing the appendage from his body. Remarkably, or maybe not in this game, he soldiered on till half-time. 'Eleven stitches later for the little fella, but she'll be right,' he tweeted. His coach, meanwhile, allegedly asked if the lad would be up for playing in a protective cup.

In May, there'd been a *Guardian* interview with England cricket all-rounder Ben Stokes, whose father Ged coached Workington Town from 2003 to 2007. Stokes, described by the paper as speaking in 'a gruff, northern monotone, even though he was born in New Zealand and lived there until he was twelve', grew up playing both cricket and league to a representative standard before settling on bat and ball.

In the piece, the men of the family were said to be 'ridiculously competitive', Ged in particular 'renowned for his steel, even in the macho world of rugby league. He used to tell Ben that he had lost a finger to a crocodile.' The truth was as dramatic. 'He kept dislocating the same finger,' Stokes told Simon Hattenstone. 'So he went to the doctor, who told him it needed surgery. But he couldn't afford not to play – he needed to pay the bills – so he just got it cut off.' His playing career ended eleven days after Ben's birth, due to a broken neck.

They like their players as tough as their coaches in Workington, and indeed down the road in Whitehaven, just five miles south, along the coast. Recent history, though, hasn't been kind. Founded in 1945 (local rivals Haven joined three years later), the club was the first from Cumberland to enter professional rugby league. Town were the outpost team of their day, since when it has been about survival mainly and neglect by administrations to the south. True, the years 1946–69 were healthy enough, with a Premiership win in 1950–51 followed by a Challenge Cup final victory the season after, under the leadership of iconic player-coach Gus Risman. But while the amateur game continues to produce talent in these parts, if not quite thrive, the two pro sides bump along almost through force of habit alone.

When a proposed 'Cumbria' merger with Whitehaven, Carlisle (thirty-odd miles inland) and Barrow (120 miles to the south) was scrapped in 1996, Workington actually lined up in the very first season of Super League but finished bottom and were relegated. That all seems a long time ago now and the Zebra Claims Stadium, capacity 10,000 but with only 681 rattling around today, looks like it hasn't changed much since Town moved here in 1956.

The pitch is small, dry and sandy, on an island in the middle of a speedway track. A covered main stand sits to the west, a smaller covered terrace opposite and there are two curved open ends, one in front of a church to the south and the other a grassy bank beneath electricity pylons stretching off in the direction of the Solway Firth.

Anyone watching from a terraced section at the foot of that main stand does so behind a wall with the pitch at eye level. Blue is the predominant colour. Blue seats. Blue paint. Blue mood. With here and there a smattering of rust. The changing-room walls too have the feel of post-war municipal austerity, tiled in patterns appropriate to public swimming baths. Enter Pottsy preceded by one of three green wheelie bins containing footwear and rolled-up kits, which he hands out to the players as they too come in and pick themselves a hook.

Up the tunnel, the players wander out into sunshine, gathering in groups, stretching legs, getting a feel for it. Leaky chats with the locals, some of whom he knows. Linners has made the trip after all – of course he has – and joins JK and Mokko for a chat with current town boss Phil Veivers, who has a full set of fingers. But with kick-off, camaraderie dissolves and a bruising tussle ensues in which Mariano, on his debut, concedes a penalty in the very first minute. Batley escape a scare on their goal line, Leaky is held up at the 'church end' towards which the Bulldogs are playing and then it goes set for set.

There aren't many in but they make plenty of noise, a chain around the dugout maintaining a five- or six-foot buffer zone. 'Good kick, Dom lad,' says JK. 'Well done, Blakey.' He and the players have arrived with a job to do and do not divert from the game plan. Town, though, score first. It is shaping into a rough tough game during which a yell comes from the main stand seats. *'Get off him, you faggot!'* A man in an orange bib walks up the terrace, asking folk to mind their language. The match commissioner has told him to, he adds almost apologetically, and a message goes out warning 'racist or homophobic abuse will not be tolerated'. Insults, if not opinions, are curtailed.

Meanwhile, on the field, Rowey has been felled illegally and Dom slots the penalty. The visiting defence moves up in a line and forces an error on the first tackle with Town in yardage. Luke Blake picks up the loose ball and a couple of tackles later is in between the posts, Dom's second goal giving Batley a 6–8 lead. That is improved to 6–14 just before the break, when Greg Minikin launches Reitts on a touchline run before taking the return and touching down, while Patch – on from a bench whose contribution is outstanding – adds the extras.

The second half, though, again starts poorly. Workington regain the ball from a short kick-off and when Jarrod Sammut, who Batley have again been warned about, sends up a steepler, no Bulldog claims it. Town regain possession, though when a try is scored way out on the left wing, video footage later reveals a double movement. Still, the touchline conversion is glorious and it's 12–14.

Workington may be propping up the rest of the Championship

but they are ebullient after victory over Sheffield last week and scent another win. In his 100th game for the club, Brownz dents those hopes a little by taking Patch's lofted kick after a line-break by Dom. *Nice!* And when Scotty scores a peach from a well-rehearsed pairs play, it allows Walker to kick the 500th goal of his career and make it 12–24 to the visitors. When man of the match Brownie is subbed, the prop is booed – a sign that the game is sewn up? Two tries in three minutes – including a split-second solo job from Sammut – suggest not; Town are level with a quarter still to go. And this after Batley failed to get in position for a drop-goal. It's a nervy time in a season full of them. Patience is required and a steady head. So who better to settle matters than Patch Walker? As the Bulldogs shape for another attack with five minutes remaining, Workington anticipate the ball going to Brambani. Batley's Daddy Cool, however, steps inside and calmly slots what may be a winning one-pointer.

Patch's goal increases the margin on the back of Leaky's late try, following more good work from Brownie with ball in hand. There is also time for Patch's penalty attempt from the halfway line to hit the post, when Town's restart doesn't make ten metres. No matter, it's 24–31, mission accomplished.

'That'll do for me,' says JK, heading for the changing room, where Brownie is already bouncing off the walls. *Get me some fucking beer!* 'Real chuffed with that, guys; this is a tough place to come. Your attitude was first class. There were some real smart plays out there; that's what brought the bacon home. Next training is Wednesday; make sure you do some recovery in the meantime. It's a tough period. The Summer Bash Dewsbury game is vital. It's on TV and it can continue us being upwardly mobile. But great stuff, have a few beers on the bus . . .'

And as it happened, the televised derby did continue Batley's upward trajectory, though not without an almighty scare in a season and at a club where narrow margins were again the norm.

The Heavy Woollen rivals took the field in Blackpool on day two of a weekend in which the Rams had been victorious in 2015.

Day one had been eventful, JK playing pundit on Sky Sports. Heavy spring bank holiday traffic on the M6 delayed Sheffield, who were then beaten by a London team that had the sense to travel up the day before. Whitehaven beat Workington, before Leigh edged Bradford in a thrilling finale.

The week before, a record aggregate crowd of 68,276 had been attracted to Super League's own two-day Magic Weekend at St James' Park, Newcastle. On the Fylde Coast, they were pleased with a 15,912 roll-up in total, as the Championship enjoyed its moment in the sun. The archetypal white working-class northern seaside resort was the ideal venue in which to showcase a tier of the sport with which it has so much in common. In its modern incarnation, Blackpool is scorned by time and 'upwardly mobile' sensibilities. Tatty round the edges, it is gaudy and prone to nostalgic sentimentalism. But there is also a fundamental honesty about a place that is too often dis-respected as a province of the great unwashed.

The Batley and Dewsbury clash began at 12.30 p.m., which neces-sitated the second 9 a.m. coach departure in a week. Before leaving, they filled up on lasagne: 'I know that's unusual for a Sunday morn-ing,' said JK, 'but it will carb you up and get you ready to play.'

Yet whatever the Rams had for breakfast pays dividends as they establish a 12–0 lead in as many minutes, snatching the initiative like seagulls scavenging chips. It is sixteen minutes before Batley complete a set. And this after Scotty concedes a penalty on halfway by booting the ball dead from the kick-off. Starts don't come any worse. Not for the first time, they have it all to do.

Having been hammered 31–0 at home by Featherstone in their last game, Dewsbury are fired up, while Batley seem distracted by the occasion. Beyond the roof of the Stanley Matthews Stand – his statue a reminder of a bygone era one day after Pepe's gamesmanship won Real Madrid the Champions League title – the famous tower stands in one-fingered salute. If the Doggies are to escape this pickle, they need to show similar defiance and fast. The sun is shining but the chill off the Irish Sea makes it cool in the shade and wind billows over banks of orange seats and out across the field to blight a mistake-ridden affair.

So when Cain, in the 100th appearance of his career, chips through with a bit of purpose and Uce is on hand to touch down, it is welcome. The Bulldogs' growl is back and, like trams and buses, the tries come in twos, Minikin nipping in from Dom's kick soon after, with Patch's single conversion and penalty goal drawing the sides level. Even so, Dewsbury have the final word of a half they end up leading 18–12.

All in all, it has been an atrocious 'advert' for Championship rugby league. Worse, Ainy, who twice went down with an ankle injury, will not return for the second period. So when stand-off Paul Sykes slots a penalty on the restart for an eight-point gap, the psychological blow could be mighty. No one reckoned with James Brown.

It had been a hell of a season for the gifted prop, eulogized by the pundits during Batley's previous TV appearances and generally in the game-changing mix. Dropped to the bench by his coach at Easter, he'd responded wonderfully. The first of a pair of ball-steals sees him barrel in after forty-nine minutes. Not long after, upon *his* return to the side, Cropper too scatters defenders like a hardwood ball in a coconut shy. Patch converts both tries and for the first time Batley lead, 24–20.

Score now and the Bulldogs might just get a roll on. But they have had two tries disallowed by the video ref – Leaky and Wayne Reittie denied – and when Dewsbury level it, after full-back Scotty needlessly concedes a dropout with the ball going dead anyway, the situation is again as sticky as Blackpool rock. A further Patch penalty edges his side in front, 26–24, but it does little to relieve the tension of a nail-biting final quarter. With six minutes remaining, he adds a one-pointer but still no one can relax, especially when Reitts is inches away from an interception and clear run to the line as the Rams press for the winner, only to knock on and relinquish a scrum twenty metres out. Batley's goal-line defence holds on with tenacity and when Brownie's second ball-steal is rewarded with a penalty at the other end, Dom Brambani adds a drop-goal of his own: 28–24.

The hooter sounds in tandem with an all-in brawl, during which Keegan is rebuked for running on from the bench and will later face an RFL charge. The points are Batley's and in Bloomfield Road's relatively luxurious changing rooms elation is tempered with relief. That injury-hit spell with four league games lost in a row can now be seen as just a bump on the track of a roller-coaster season, any suggestion of an early departure now surely put to rest.

'You weren't pretty,' says JK, 'but you kept grafting. When you are a good team with quality, you find a way to win. The middles were fucking gubbed to begin with, believe you me. But I'll tell you, in the other sixty-five you battered the fuck out of them. Well done.'

14

JUNE DAWNED WITH the smell of fresh-cut grass, the ground on the hill coming into its own. In winter, the landscape was often bleak and forbidding. With the rise up out of Soothill every shade of green, the view across the valley was indeed pleasant. Would Kev Nicholas, popping by, contemplate another site if the opportunity to move ever presented itself? 'No,' he said. 'If people watch a club, they will travel anywhere, won't they?'

John Kear had flown off to the Greek island of Rhodes for a week to attend his son's wedding. That left Mokko and Linners in charge and they presided over a more relaxed week than usual.

On Wednesday, Mokko studied clips on his PC in a darkened Ron's Lounge, face lit like a Bond villain in his lair. In the boardroom, led by Gleds, players quoted chunks of *Phoenix Nights* and *Max and Paddy*, as theatricals might recite Shakespeare. Pottsy, rarely in on training nights lately, was there tonight under another mod haircut. There was talk of a *Quadrophenia* remake and he hoped to land a role as an extra. He'd done that in 2001, he said, in a picture about hairdressers, *Blow Dry*, set in Keighley. One of its stars was the late Alan Rickman. When he died in January, Pottsy posted a message on the actor's social media account saying it had been a pleasure to work with him.

The team review went on a little longer, half an hour, Mokko adopting some of JK's flourishes, such as inviting comments from the floor. A 68 per cent completion rate made for a 'poor standard of game,' he said, taking them through the areas they must address this week: start; soft tries; fewer chiefs, more Indians. The former half-back wanted Cain and Dom to be more decisive. 'Don't dilly-dally and fuck about,' he said calmly. 'If you're going to go, go,' as unflappable and methodical as you'd want an airport fireman to be. He got the impression that some took JK's oft-repeated description of them as a good arm-wrestle team as a slur. 'It's not. That doesn't mean we can't play football. It means we have to get into the arm-wrestle to start with, win that, then take the shackles off and express ourselves.'

Batley's next opponents, Oldham, had been good in the first half of their Summer Bash game against Swinton, not so much in the second. Scott Naylor, their coach, questioned their desire, so they would be fired up here on Sunday. 'We've got to be ready, but we are going to give you a bit of freedom this week, fellas. You guys decide what you want to do [with ball in hand].' He showed a clip. 'I'd put all these men here, leave loads of space here,' he said. 'As defenders spread, attack that space, stay tight, skip, skip, skip and hit the lead on the edge. But there are a few options in a situation like that. We aren't going to reinvent the wheel, just play what you see, all right?'

On Friday, Linners slipped into the hot seat. In Carl's room, Keegan, charged with re-entering the field of play without permission – a grade B charge with a possible two-match ban – lay prostrate, a fallen oak on a plinth. The physio kneaded shoulders and a back that had been bothering the skipper for a while, grinding in an elbow and leaving red mottled marks. It didn't help. So Keegan moved to a couch along-side, less springy, and Carl had a go at cracking his back there, the big prop's face pushed deep into the cushioned headrest.

Having ebbed a little recently, injury concerns were again in full flow. James Brown and Gleds carried knocks but continued to battle away, and Rowey had today had a scan on a troublesome knee in Leeds amid strife over cancelled health insurance. He couldn't afford the monthly premium, he said, so if he needs an operation there isn't the money to pay for it. In any case, he would try to see the season out, although with obvious cartilage damage there is every chance it will go again. A big lad with the head of an Easter Island statue, he doesn't exactly turn on a sixpence when fully fit; his talents lie elsewhere. Would the call be courageous, daft or both?

There were no such doubts about Danny Cowling. His knee op put him on crutches for a month at least, likely gone for the year, while Ainy picked up that ankle strain in Blackpool. Gleds recalled a lad during his amateur days at Shaw Cross who dislocated a kneecap. The ambulance took so long to arrive his teammates had to use post-padding as a makeshift stretcher. He played again the next week.

Linners' team meeting lasted seven minutes. As Mokko mostly did D on Wednesday, Linners focused on O, 'offense'. At their place, Oldham caught them by surprise. 'We owe ourselves a reaction,' he said. 'We've got to dictate the tempo. Look up, see what the defence is doing and react accordingly. Mokko and me just want you to enjoy the game. Everybody plays better when they are doing that.'

'Hey, come on, boys,' said Blakey, as they trotted out on to the field on a still night ahead of a warm and sunny weekend. The windmill was immobile too, although its arm lurched in momentary spasm: the dying flap of a dragonfly's wing. 'Let's be good, eh?'

Batley owe Oldham one. But with JK away, it is imperative that they are dispatched as ruthlessly and comprehensively as possible. It would curtail further rumour – *a head coach absent at this stage of the season* – while confirming the round-nine away reverse as nothing but a blip. Nor would victory do the reputations of the stand-ins any harm, though neither is the type to make any reference to that.

On a beautiful day, the summer clothes are out, as smoke from what might be an allotment fire sweeps over the lower end of the ground. 'They don't want us here,' sighs one supporter, leaning on a crush barrier, though it is soon extinguished. The pitch is pretty, mown horizontal in stripes of lime and Sherwood by Jim Morley. It hosts an Under-16s curtain-raiser, Batley Boys versus Moldgreen, won by Batley's next generation, 36–16. At half-time in the main event, Carl and Doc Findlay will send one of those youngsters off to hospital by ambulance on a spinal stretcher. After hurting his neck, he will complain of pins and needles and an inability to grip yet is allowed to walk from Batley Boys' clubhouse to tell the professionals next door. Thankfully, there turns out to be no lasting damage.

The heat behind the Glen Tomlinson Stand could fry a Death Valley lizard; shirt sleeves, red necks, plastic bottles and pints of lager and cider, whose splashes turn to steam before hitting the ground. On the Ron Earnshaw Terrace, referee Robert Hicks – destined to officiate the Super League Grand Final at Old Trafford this year but now in T-shirt, shorts and sunglasses on a rare Sunday afternoon off – leans on a pram while sipping at a can of fizzy drink.

In the boardroom, club chaplain Derek says he doesn't want promotion. It would be the death of the club. They would have to go full-time and a lot of these players don't want to do that, so they would have to bring in players who don't have that bond with Batley. He would like to be in the top four, of course, with the money that brings, and get games against the big boys. But if they went up: 'Once we started losing, the supporters would soon be on their backs.' His is another voluntary role, the priority player welfare. 'I'm the one person here who's not concerned with performance but guys and their families.' He is here as a friend, somebody to talk to. 'When all's going well, I'm an encourager; when guys have problems, they can be confident those issues will go no further.' Actually, it all goes hand in hand. 'If your head isn't right, you can't perform, can you?'

Derek's fears about Super League appear moot when, after twenty minutes, Oldham lead 6–0 despite playing uphill. In the heat, both teams take on fluids at every opportunity. Breth was penalized for a ball-steal in the first minute and it got scrappier from there. Batley win a kickable penalty but opt to run it, points wasted.

When the fight-back comes, it is irrepressible. Luke Blake tears in from Keegan's burst, winger Wayne Reittie impressing in yard-age. Dom converts that score and Patch the next as Brownie, having another huge game, crashes in from close range. Half an hour gone, Batley lead 12–6 with more to come. It arrives after Cain leaves the field, hurting an ankle as Oldham camp on Batley's twenty-metre line. Play is held up for a while but once it restarts on the fifth and last, the ball is kicked to the far corner where it is collected by Reitts. What follows is one of the long-distance tries of the season, as he recalls later. 'Last time, our back three got a lot of things wrong, positioning-wise. We got mugged. We got together, said we had to be ready. You know in mid-air whether you are going to get the ball. The timing was perfect but my first thought was just to catch it, clean it up, get back into play and give our boys the chance to get rolling. The kick went over their centre's head and I caught it before the winger. As I've landed, I've handed off the centre and the winger kept chasing me but I just kept fending him. I kept going and kept going, thinking he's gonna get me, but as I kept running the gap got bigger between us. Once I passed halfway, I thought I'm going to get there.' After touching down, ever the showman, Reitts runs up the grass bank-ing, one arm raised in celebration, Patch converting. 'They always say score first then do your celebrating, but it's good to celebrate, isn't it? Middles only barge over from close range, but when you're an outside-back a chance to open your legs and run is great; it doesn't happen very often.' And when Brownie muscles in for a second on the hooter, Patch's fourth goal making it 24–6 at the break, it lifts Batley further.

'That came from our composure, that,' says Dom, as the players return to the changing room, lungs still pumping, flesh like streaky bacon. 'Stay focused; we need that attitude. Everybody on it.' Keegan warns them not to fall in love with themselves, because the game isn't won yet. They'll now be playing uphill in blistering temperatures for a start. Brownie suggests knocking the fucking fuck out of them.

This week it is Linners who takes over. 'Fellas, the talk's good. You're saying all the right stuff.' The start had needed to be good and it hadn't been. So it needed to be this half. Re goal-line D: 'Ball's the danger. Once it's gone, we can shut the gate and pan out.' Apart from that, all is fine but, 'Let's play the game at our pace. When we are in possession, we increase it; when they have the ball, we slow it down.'

Mokko joins in. 'Here's the challenge, fellas. We get into the grind right from the start and see how long they can stay with us.' In the huddle, Keegan reiterates that they don't have a right to win this game, just as the knock comes and the players prepare to jog out. They must go out there and earn it. But halfway up the corridor, one Oldham player can be heard telling another: 'We are downhill now . . .'

'We can't have a honeymoon next year,' says Heather Oates, twenty-six, who like her friend Katie Harwood, a year younger, is enjoying the sunshine after the Bulldogs complete the job 42–18, two days after the death of Muhammad Ali. Dom landed the opening blow of the second half, floating like a butterfly eight minutes in. Oldham scored two more, but so did Batley's scrum-half and Greg Minikin. Heather is due to marry Joe Chandler on 19 November, when the squad will be back in training. 'I don't think we'll get a day trip, would be nice if we did . . .'

Not that she resents it. She met Joe on a night out in Wakefield and knew what she was getting into. 'We could have postponed it until after he retired but I don't know when that will be. It will be a nice celebration and it will be our one-year anniversary as well, so . . .'

Joe and Katie's partner Luke Blake have been friends for ever. Both were raised in this part of West Yorkshire and, at sixteen, both lads joined the Leeds Rhinos academy, Chandler making a first-team appearance against Castleford in 2009. From there, though, his career trajectory was downward into the Championship. His younger brother, who has learning difficulties, is one of Joe's major motivations when it gets tough. 'He's never been able to play himself but is a really, really big Batley fan,' he says. 'Even when I was at other clubs it was "What about Batley, what about Batley, what about Batley?" So I got in touch, came across and have never looked back. My family love it and him being a massive Batley supporter just makes it that bit more special for me.' Last year the club did a thing for the charity Ambitions in which he got to run out with Joe. 'Well, actually, he didn't run out with me, he ran out with Blakey. He had a choice between him and me and chose Luke.' Outside rugby, Joe is doing a Masters and aims to be a social worker.

'You sign up for it, don't you?' says Katie, Heather's bridesmaid, while Blakey will be a groomsman. The girls are all organized, but the boys don't have their suits yet. Finding time for a fitting is tricky, but their size and shape can change too as the day gets closer, so it makes good practical sense to leave all that until later. With two more points in the bag, the field is alive with families and children, among them Keegan's, watched by their celebrity childminder Antony Cotton.

Katie, from Tingley, and Luke are not engaged yet, despite having been together for ten and a half years, having met at school, aged fourteen. Like his pal, Blakey too is bright and eloquent and also studying for a degree, in his case in construction management. See him away from the game and you might be dazzled by his smile. During training and in matches, three of those perfect front teeth are kept on a plate in his shoe. He lost the first two aged fourteen, slipping on ice in the school playground. The other was knocked out playing rugby with Joe. 'As a kid, he was much bigger than everyone else and ran with his knees up. You can imagine the rest.' He's not bothering to replace them until he retires, when he'll get some screwed in. In fact, Joe also has a front tooth missing, nothing to do with Blakey.

At nineteen, Luke signed for Wakefield under JK and made his first-team debut against Leeds. 'I didn't start, so wasn't too nervous, but all the shots going on, hearing the crowd and stuff, changed that. I only got about twenty minutes at the end, but it was good to play Leeds.' From Belle Vue, he was off for three seasons at Dewsbury but then, in 2012, decided to stop playing rugby all together and went travelling for about fourteen months with Katie. 'Before I came back, my dad was in contact with Iro, who asked if I was thinking about playing when I got home. I wasn't, to be honest. I was enjoying myself.'

The person who talked him into it was Joe Chandler, at the time also coaching at Shaw Cross. Their hooker got injured. 'He said he only needed me for three or four games; they were pushing for promotion. I hadn't played for well over a year and wasn't fit, but he persuaded me and that got my spark back.' He contacted Batley, who were still interested, and has been here ever since.

As for Katie, life with a rugby league player is all she's known. She too has been to university, while Luke will graduate in July. 'The only month you can go on holiday in is October, but we do what we can when we can. If he's got a Saturday game, we'll go out Saturday night. If he's got a weekend off, we'll book something last minute. Life revolves around fixtures but you make the most of it.'

If the boys are playing, the two women may go for a meal on a Sunday, close friends now too and adept at charting a course through the moods players are prone to, victory and defeat, apprehension and preparation shaping an average week at home. 'They can sulk for a while when they lose but it doesn't last long,' Katie says. 'It's not too bad through the week but when Luke starts to get mentally prepared on a Saturday afternoon, they go into themselves a bit then.'

How do they deal with injuries? 'Joe got injured last July and was out until January,' Heather says of a six-month absence. 'That got him down because he likes to play. He hates being on the sidelines.'

The urge to be on the field is powerful, like treading upon a theatre stage, you suspect, offering psychological refuge as much as it is physically testing. That was never more obvious than in 2009 when, as Katie recalls, Luke insisted on playing the following Friday even after the death of his twenty-year-old cousin Leon Walker. The young back-rower, Luke's teammate in Wakefield's reserve side during JK's spell there, died tragically during a game in South Wales having made his first senior-team start the previous Boxing Day following the death of another Trinity player, 31-year-old Adam Watene, some five months earlier. On that fateful day in Maesteg, Luke was on the field when his cousin fell before being airlifted to hospital in Swansea, where he later passed away. During the funeral at St Anthony's, Beeston, the then teenager had spoken movingly about his relative and friend, remembering how he had been the 'life and soul' of the journey down: 'He had everyone in stitches. Even at half-time I was laughing at him messing with his hair.' Leon, Luke said, had been an inspiration to him, adding that their late granddad, who would have been sixty-seven on the day Leon died, would be proud of him too. Days later, there was a game against St Helens that even coach Kear admits in his autobiography he had no stomach for. The reserve grade too had a match, in which Luke was determined to play. Katie wasn't keen at first but came around. 'It's their life, isn't it? They've grown up with the game and it helped him to cope. I would never make him quit.'

And how about when those playing careers are through? 'After ten years of rugby, I can't imagine it. I'll miss it, I think. We will have weekends obviously and be able to go away in the summer, but those are just things, aren't they? You can do them any time. Playing rugby league is something that means a lot to him now.'

For the third week in succession, Keegan can't get to the end of the song, forgetting the words mid flow. 'You're fired, big man,' says Brownie. 'I'm taking over.' To make the Oldham victory better still, Dewsbury have beaten Bradford, 16–14, the winning penalty kicked after the hooter. Batley's ambitions were already in their own hands, but the chances have widened considerably. With the achievements of Premier League champions Leicester City fresh in the memory – 5,000/1 outsiders and favourites for relegation at the start of the football season – will this be the year of the underdog in rugby league too? Batley's feat – if it comes to fruition – might be more impressive. The Foxes' total salary was only £23 million, the Bulldogs' £150,000.

On Monday, Keegan tweets that he is up at 5 a.m., his back 'in bits'. And on Tuesday night his neck is giving him gyp too. Having suffered pins and needles and been unable to lift his arm, a physio session has eased it, but you wouldn't know. Stiff as an upright, he is a whiplash victim without a neck brace. Handily, it is a light recovery session and two nights later he moves more freely. On Wednesday, an RFL hearing via Skype rules no case to answer for his Blackpool intrusion. He looks like he could have done with a guilty verdict just for the rest, but will be back in action tomorrow night.

Sheffield is the destination, although Linners won't be there. He'll be on a pre-arranged trip to Barcelona and looks devastated, though not about missing the game. He plans to turn the derelict land between the K2 Stand and terrace in his name into little garden plots, each to be donated to a local charity so they can plant flowers. It will look nice and tidy the place up, he says. If nothing else, make the garden shed feel at home. More seriously, he sees it as a focal point for the community. Linners spent three hours online yesterday filling in some fundraising application or other but it has now vanished completely. He will have to go through the whole tortuous process again before, later, the application is turned down.

Having returned on Thursday, JK turns to team matters. Leaky and Squiresy are eighteenth and nineteenth men. Tuna comes in on the bench and Jimmy Davey is to start at hooker. 'Playing Sheffield will inspire him,' the coach tells the little Cumbrian, who takes his demotion with magnanimity. JK thanks them all for their efforts in a game they handled well and which he has now seen on video. 'I've been concerned about the starts, and in the second half we got a bit loose, that would be my summary. But it was magnificent. All of a sudden, fellas, instead of me banging on about how good you are and what you can achieve, I can sense a bit of belief. When you do that, you get that inner resolve and mental strength that lets you prevail week in and week out. You know when to rest up, when to relax, and when to come ready to play. We are at that stage now and the next two games are absolutely vital – two away games; *winnable* games.' The Eagles, then Bradford, who play Workington away on Sunday, Oldham away on Wednesday and then Batley at Odsal. 'Button it tomorrow and we can have them two points, sit back, let them play two fucking games and then ambush the bastards on their own midden. It's a real important nine days. Let's not let it slip through us fingers.'

Sheffield's adoption of full-time status had not gone well. An understatement. A 60–22 reversal to Halifax last week left them in the bottom four. Nevertheless, as Batley's coach warned his players, on a big field like theirs they have more than enough talent to catch any team by surprise. The Doggies would need to be on their guard.

The venue, Hallam University Stadium, is an odd one. In 2013, demolition of Don Valley Stadium had sent the Eagles nomadic. To begin with, they returned to Owlerton Stadium, where their story began in 1984, but those facilities were now deemed unsuitable by the RFL, so in 2015 they shared the Keepmoat with South Yorkshire rivals Doncaster. A homecoming at Don Valley's redeveloped Olympic Legacy Park was anticipated a year later and when that stalled, Hallam Uni stepped in and offered to improve their 'sports park' on Bawtry Road, on the Rotherham border, a proposal that the Eagles were delighted – or more likely relieved – to accept. It would be short-lived, though; by 2017, they'd be forced to play home games thirty miles away in Wakefield.

The Batley directors stand on a balcony overlooking a pitch as wide as it is long, part of a clubhouse that houses the changing rooms. This viewing area backs on to a bar in which a television is show-ing France v Romania in the opening match of Euro 2016. Opposite, spectators lean on a railing, several under umbrellas on an evening of rain and fine drizzle, as though watching a park game in a single line. Otherwise, a tiny crowd sits in a narrow stand behind the posts, any realistic hope of building a lasting head of steam upon JK's Wembley achievement some eighteen years ago long since evaporated.

Scotty kicks off; despite the mammoth dimensions, he manages to boot it out on the full to concede an immediate penalty on halfway for the second time in a fortnight. The Bulldogs survive, just, but 'the pride of South Yorkshire', as Sheffield are optimistically called, take the lead after ten minutes. Full-back Quentin Laulu Togaga'e – QLT – is the scorer, a skilful and physical Pacific Islander of a type the Eagles seem traditionally to find. Batley protest defensive niggles – chicken-wing tackles, wherein a player's arm is locked awkwardly with raised elbows – but Sheffield won't go down without a fight. The mood on the directors' balcony is fraught, though skipper Keegan settles their nerves a little by barging over with five defenders on that back of his, before ex-Eagle Patch's conversion makes it 6–6.

The three ex-Sheffield men are playing well and when Dom Brambani is judged to have knocked on, a home fan shouts, *Thanks, Dom. We love you,* followed by a *Shut up, Dom,* when the scrum-half complains to a young referee making his Championship debut. Kev suggests he has come straight from school. These big and powerful opponents remain dangerous though, especially on the break, and the Bulldogs are forced to scramble a number of times. Their patient game plan pays off shortly before the break with a Patch penalty goal, but there is still time for more. When Walker then spirals a kick into the air, the otherwise dangerous QLT not only spills it – as predicted by JK in Thursday-night's team meeting – he as good as passes it straight to the lurking Greg Minikin, who needs only to fall over the line. Patch converts after the hooter for a half-time score of 6–14.

The young Castleford centre is proving a handy acquisition, with Adam Gledhill his nearest contender as man of the match. But for now there is a game to win and Batley begin the second half as poorly as the first. When Uce darts out of left-side defence, the Eagles swoop through the hole. Batley don't panic and six minutes later the eight-point margin is regained. A sweeping passing move on the end of Jimmy Davey's break puts Reitts in for a try too far out to convert. But when heavier rain turns the ball to soap in the final quarter, the entertainment deteriorates markedly.

If anything, the Eagles have the best of it; only desperate goal-line D keeps them at bay. They rip the shirt off captain Keegan's back. Some among the Batley board look ready to faint as first Reitts and then Brownz lose possession, while Brownie has a shocker after recent impressive performances. Daft penalties, coughing the ball up in yardage – all the cardinal sins are here as the Doggies play like they are chasing the game rather than eight points ahead.

Since that second-half fight-back in the 2013 Championship Grand Final, Batley have considered Sheffield a 'bogey side'; might they be so again? There is a particularly dangerous moment when the Eagles look certain scorers before conceding a penalty for tripping Alex Brown. But when Joe Chandler's leg-drive and determination make it 10–24 on the stroke of full-time, the second-rower changing his line to get outside the 'A' defender, all fears are put to rest. As the Hallam sound system blasts New Order's 'World in Motion' – well, rugby league is a *type* of football, isn't it? – Batley haven't stopped yet.

The nine-day interval is put to good use, although the Bulls do not trip on the road. Having beaten Workington in Cumbria, 22–29, they account for Oldham 48–4 in Stalybridge, watched by JK and old-boy Chris Ulugia from the stands. Never mind. If the Bulldogs go to Odsal tails up, after three games in seven days their hosts should be battered and vulnerable. Elsewhere, Halifax draw in Whitehaven – nudging Fax two points behind Batley, not one – and Fev lose narrowly at Leigh.

For Batley, five wins on the bounce . . . why not make it six?

Then tragedy.

15

BATLEY AND SPEN MP Jo Cox was one of the good guys; as familiar and friendly a face at Mount Pleasant as any other area of the constituency she represented so doggedly in Parliament. Places like Birstall where, on Thursday, 16 June, this much-loved 41-year-old mother of two, champion of many varied humanitarian causes, was brutally murdered outside the town library on Market Street after getting out of a car on her way to a lunchtime surgery.

Watched by horrified witnesses, Jo, born and raised in Batley and Heckmondwike, was repeatedly shot and stabbed by Thomas Mair, 52, an unemployed gardener and right-wing neo-Nazi terrorist who, as he attacked, was heard to shout 'Britain first', 'keep Britain independent' and 'this is for Britain,' one week ahead of an EU referendum in which the MP had been a vocal backer of the Remain camp.

In an increasingly poisonous political atmosphere, Jo, a Cambridge graduate whose family home was nowadays a houseboat near Tower Bridge, campaigned for those neglected communities – very often white, northern and working class – impacted most by immigration; a legitimate concern, she said, but not a valid reason to leave the EU. 'I very rarely agree with the Prime Minister, but on this he's right: we are stronger, safer and better off in.' And that position had at least partly inspired her white supremacist killer to shoot Jo twice in the head and once in the chest with a sawn-off .22 calibre rifle, before stabbing her fifteen times. Bystander Bernard

Carter-Kenny, 77, was also injured as he attempted to come to her rescue.

Co-chair of the All-Party Parliamentary Group for Friends of Syria, whose aim was to promote greater understanding of the ongoing conflict in the Middle East, Jo Cox was also a member of the All-Party Parliamentary Rugby League Group, and her influence had been put to good use in organizing last year's Batley Girls trip to Australia, for example; she was an admirable role model in so many ways.

By teatime, the centre of Batley was, if not quite a ghost town, hauntingly quiet. On another day, this might have been blamed on the pubs being full with people watching England v Wales in Euro 2016, but not now. Until 5 p.m., news bulletins reported that the MP was in hospital with life-threatening injuries. Then came confirmation from West Yorkshire Police. Despite emergency attention, Jo had died in the back of the ambulance, pronounced dead at 1.48 p.m.

The mood at the club was sombre, the players and coaches as shocked as anyone. Several knew Jo well. Coincidentally, an ITV film crew was there to collect footage of Keegan and teammates training – the local, national and international media descending on Birstall for weightier reasons. A forgotten town twenty-four hours ago was now in the spotlight. 'We'll do something,' Linners promised.

Keegs was filmed chatting around a boardroom table with Gleds, Rowey and Brownie, who praised and took the mickey out of their mate and club captain in equal measure, a welcome distraction. Off camera, they discussed the end-of-season run-in, bemoaning how if they had beaten Oldham and especially Swinton at home they would now be five points clear of Bradford not one. Defeat on Sunday would mean another fall from the top four if other results failed to go their way. Of course, the Championship Shield would still be there to play for were they not to make the Qualifiers but, as Keegan reflected, even in that: 'You can't rely on beating any side this year, can you?'

The team meeting was short and to the point, Kear reminding them that the Bulldogs were ranked fifteenth best club in the country, a nice way of looking at it. Bradford hooker Adam O'Brien was the big threat, he warned, particularly close to the line, from where he is apt to send in crash runners and fringe players alike. 'Be on your toes.'

The weekend, though, felt distant and – while perhaps pivotal – simultaneously trivial. On Friday, Prime Minister David Cameron and Labour leader Jeremy Corbyn placed wreaths by a statue of Joseph Priestley, born in 1733 in Birstall. The theologian and dissenter was a convert to the doctrine of universal salvation, which held that human souls, no matter how sinful or deviant, would be reconciled to God's eternal love and mercy. But by Saturday morning – with a tree-lined Purlwell Hall Road approach to Mount Pleasant in verdant bloom – the atrocity still hung like a migraine, the constituency bewildered.

'In Cold Blood – Whole Nation in Shock,' read the front page of *The Press*, as police and media presence in the town remained high. 'If that had been a Muslim, it would be terrorist this, terrorist that,' said JK, in the boardroom. 'Middle-aged white bloke and it's a loner with mental-health issues. It's as much terrorism as any Islamic attack, is that.' In court in London, meanwhile, the accused had given his name as 'Death to traitors, freedom for Britain'. No one knew how this slaying of a popular public servant would affect the EU referendum.

The mood brightened when Keegan arrived with his children. He gave them a glass of orange juice and got the Wi-Fi password for their gizmos. Soon they were playing outside, perfectly safely, while their dad and his teammates trained on the field alongside. A solid session it was, looked over too by John Miller, who, he revealed, plays guitar in a local band, Crème Brûlée. The game's not what it was.

Ainy's ankle scans were back: he would need two or three weeks more. And on a day when British astronaut Tim Peake opted surprisingly to return from space when he might have been better advised to stay there, Chris Ulugia laced up his boots, looking forward to tomorrow's match. Victory at Odsal would be Batley's first there in almost forty years and the centre was as keen as he had been in March to make a point.

*

An hour before kick-off, the vast bowl – only a decade or so ago packed with the in-crowd, colourful, vibrant and very much the place to be, supposedly a beacon for every club – is all but deserted.

It has been argued that the sport owed the initial success of Super League and the switch to summer to Bradford's reinvention as the Bulls and the gusto with which they embraced 'modernization'. Clubs like Leeds were dead set against seasonal change and to begin with did not care who knew it. At Odsal, the vision of late marketing wizard Peter Deakin (who would go on to similar success in union at Saracens and with Warrington), to introduce the sort of peripheral razzamatazz that originated up the road at Keighley, refashioned league as a family outing to the funfair. Music. Cheerleaders. Face paint. Bouncy castles. Mascots. A little radio-controlled truck that ran on and off with the kicking tee. The public responded with glee.

Nor did it do any harm that the Bulls had a formidable side coached by Brian Smith, father of new coach Rohan. There, though – aside from Robbie Hunter Paul in a suit – links to the glory days stall. This current Bradford team is a pale imitation of ones that, with St Helens, shared much of the available silverware in the first fifteen years. Since 2012, it has been a story of unremitting financial gloom and, in 2014, relegation when the club was deducted six points for entering administration. Despite changes in ownership, the Bulls are still full-time, by the skin of their teeth, but need to get back to the top flight or they will continue their slide towards obscurity. And in the 'new era', things have not gone well. Last October, they were pipped by Wakefield in the first ever Million Pound Game. In 2016, most fear it is now or never. For Bradford, the Qualifiers are a bare minimum and even reaching those may not be good enough.

Oh, there are still burger bars dotted around a venue that in more optimistic times has been dreamed of as a 'Wembley of the North'. Merchandise stalls. Mobile bars offering a 'Pie and a Pint'. In the Provident marquee, next to the Touchdown Bar, a bloke sings Amy Winehouse's 'Back To Black.' Rising behind the Rooley Avenue end is the Richard Dunn Sports Centre named for the heavyweight boxer who, in 1976, was the last knockout of Muhammad Ali's professional career. Its terraces are largely empty and stay that way as the game kicks off. 'The boys are working hard to hit some form in the run-up to the middle eights,' yells the PA announcer, attempting to drum up an atmosphere. The Bulls will have to reach them first.

There is a shared minute's silence for Jo Cox and seventeen-year-old Huddersfield player, Ronan Costello, who, following a serious injury in an abandoned Under-19s game against Salford, had tragically died in Leeds General Infirmary. After which, Batley are very much in it. The lessons of the midweek clips are taken on board, Jimmy Davey hammering O'Brien on the try-line. The Bulls, though, lead 8–0 through two unconverted tries. On the half hour, Cain gets his side on the scoreboard as the introduction of Brownie, Cropper and especially Patch off the bench does the trick. It's Patch who takes the ball to the line, interesting the 'A' and 'B' defenders, before passing to Uce. He now has space for a left-field break and feeds Brownz, who makes more yards before passing to the scorer inside. Scotty, in his 100th career appearance, is led off with a groin strain and Patch converts: 8–6. Five minutes before the break, it gets better. Uce barges over to score the try he hoped for, as the Bulldogs keep the ball alive well. Patch misses the conversion and a late drop-goal attempt, but Batley end a gritty first half 8–10 ahead.

The second forty starts with a scare when Scotty, back on the field, fluffs a clearance. Batley press on, their goal-line D drills serving them well as they read the Bulls' attacking intentions cannily. There is a worrying moment when Blakey takes a knee to the lower back. He plays on for a good ten minutes but is forced eventually to leave the field. Two minutes later, Dom, another with a point to prove to his hometown team perhaps, kicks his latest 40/20 and when Batley are awarded a fourth tackle penalty, Patch slots it over: 8–12.

The falling rain is getting heavier, leading to handling errors and slippery conditions. And when Scotty hacks a free play dead when he would have been better off falling on the ball and returning the action to where the original knock-on took place, it epitomizes Batley's under-the-pump plight. They cannot escape their forty-metre zone and, on seventy minutes, the pressure tells. Harried by the behemoth Epalahame Lauaki, Dom defuses a kick in-goal, the ball comes loose and Bulls second-rower Jay Pitts gets a hand on it, though too late. Referee Joe Cobb, however, interprets it differently – try. JK and his team are 'pig sick', as he will tell the media. The conversion is simple and the Bulls lead 14–12, all the more galling as Breth had a try in similar circumstances disallowed eight minutes after the break, the benefit of the doubt on that occasion going to the defender. And when Cain then drops a high ball to concede a scrum on Batley's ten-metre line, calls that he did so facing his own line are so vociferous the decision is changed to the penalty that makes it 16–12.

Batley, though, get the ball from a short restart and work their way towards Bradford's posts. On the last tackle, Walker's dab in-goal is fumbled and Cain grabs his second try. The kick is wide but it's 16–16 and a draw would suit Batley well, keeping them in third place. Uce, though, then spills the ball on halfway and it's Bradford's scrum. From there they easily build the field position that lets Kurt Haggerty kick a drop-goal five minutes from time. Yet even then, Batley almost snatch it. A penalty for ball-stripping moves the Bulldogs up the field but Keegan, never short of effort, knocks on playing the ball under the posts before a one-pointer, or better, can be popped over.

After a strong first half, Batley have completed only five sets in the last thirteen, when they needed to be at their strongest, mentally and technically. The relieved roar that greets the victory from a 5,000 crowd tells a story. Once there would have been 15,000-plus here and the six-times league, five-times Challenge Cup and three-times World Club Challenge winners celebrate as if they have beaten Brisbane Broncos. Bradford handled the rain better, a rankled JK tells the radio after the one-point defeat, his team now out of the top four.

By Tuesday, the steam is still billowing from Kear's ears. He has been on to the RFL's match officials department with twelve bones of contention but had no joy. Of the killer try he is told: 'Grounding has to be deliberate.' Though had that grounding been at the other end, the 'downward pressure' would have been sufficient to award a try – hardly logical. And without being a mind-reader, how can a ref know a player's intention anyway?

Luke Blake is in agony with his back. Blood tests have revealed his liver is fine but he is unlikely to be fit for Dewsbury. Patch and Cain picked up knocks too. Nor is Greg Minikin here. He will play for Cas against Wigan on Saturday in a Challenge Cup quarter-final. 'You can't blame the kid,' says JK. It's a big stage, a chance to impress, though Batley will miss him. Before Bradford, he was on a four-match scoring run and has made a big difference to the three-quarter line.

Clips are short. JK wants them to focus on the five remaining regular season games: Dewsbury at home on Sunday, then Whitehaven away, Featherstone and London at home topped off by a trip to Swinton. 'We need to buckle down.' After that, they can book a week's holiday if they wish. 'You deserve that time off because you've worked really hard and will hopefully maintain that standard.'

In a leadership group meeting prior, Rowey pointed out that last year they'd have been 'over the fucking moon with ourselves' at coming so close to victory at Odsal and JK nodded. 'That's where we are. But we need to nail this on Sunday.' The fixture is crucial because Bradford are to face Halifax. 'If we win, we'll go back into the top four, as one of them has to lose. So let's stay with it, fellas. We will have to be ruthless on the field and the coaches are going to have to be ruthless off it. If there's a decision that doesn't sit well, come chat with us by all means. But we've got a chance of doing something pretty special and we ain't gonna let anything distract us.'

When the rest arrive, he rolls the clips, complete with fancy new graphics inspired perhaps by those designed by Mokko during his week in charge. They can't feel sorry for themselves, he says. The evidence reveals they could have won the game anyway. 'These are where I thought we were a bit dumb, to tell you the truth. But rather than say "fucking dumb" at the top, I've put "negative smarts", okay?'

*

Heavy Woollen derbies are emotional and distracting affairs. As Blackpool had again shown, form books matter little. In November, JK said success meant finishing higher than Dewsbury. That seemed laughable now and distractions were a luxury Batley couldn't afford.

In which case, tough luck; the lead-in to the game was guaranteed to be tricky and match-day itself presented a minefield of diversion and obstacle, all of it unavoidable in the light of a much bigger picture.

Wednesday, 22 June would have been Jo Cox's forty-second birthday. Memorial events were staged worldwide, including a moving service attended by her family in Trafalgar Square. The tributes included a message from US President Barack Obama, who hailed the MP's work locally and globally. In Syria, a women's charity held a candlelit vigil.

There was a vigil too in Batley marketplace, where a thousand people turned up, coinciding with a press release from the rugby club outlining how they intended to honour Jo's memory at the weekend. Bernard Carter-Kenny, her attempted rescuer, thankfully discharged from hospital now, would be in attendance and a commemorative programme had been commissioned, production costs paid by Fox's Biscuits, with a target of £2,000 for Jo's charities. Fans of each club were to be asked to hold a photograph of her aloft during a minute's silence, sunflowers would be placed by both sets of players and other guests in the centre of the pitch before removal to the memorial garden. Birstall man Paul Egan was to sing 'Abide With Me' a cappella and, as Sunday was Armed Forces Day, the Yorkshire Regiment would form a guard of honour. 'The supporters, players and officials of Dewsbury and ourselves are huge rivals and nothing will change in this important game,' said Kevin Nicholas. 'However, we are united both as rugby league people and Heavy Woollen District friends.'

If that wasn't enough, the following day brought the EU referendum itself, with the stadium hosting a live broadcast from the press benches of the Glen Tomlinson Stand on BBC Radio Leeds, in which implications for civic harmony were discussed. Iro talked of the moment almost exactly one week ago when he and the club first heard the news in a state of disbelief. 'There was a rumour at first and you hoped that was all it was. But things unfolded; it was really sad. Jo was such a great part of the club.' He spoke of her fundraising activities, her visits to the Breakfast Club and the help she gave to the cheerleaders and Batley Girls. Iro told listeners about Bernard Carter-Kenny's links with the Bulldogs. 'It was eerie. Kevin rang me up about the incident and said, "I better ring my mate; his dad works in the library." Ten minutes have gone past and Kevin rings back, deeply upset. It's just horrific what's gone on.' Bernard had been waiting for his wife.

There was time to talk rugby too. After praising JK, 'who could have gone to a full-time job on a lot more money – it sums him up as a person that he was willing to turn [that] down to try and leave on a high note', he told presenter Richard Stead four more wins should do it. 'We've struggled for the last few years at the bottom, worrying about relegation. But this year . . . it's like doing a Leicester.'

Back at the ground that night, injury issues worsened. Most seriously, Blakey had fractured two vertebrae. Remarkably, he played on for fifteen minutes, as no one, including Luke himself, had realized the extent of his injury. Scans had shown the fractures to be stable and in need of no treatment but rest; however, his season was most likely over. If that wasn't enough, Leaky, not having played last week, felt rotten after training on Tuesday, took himself off to the gym and did his back in lifting weights. If unfit – and it didn't look good – Batley would be left with only one recognized hooker, Jimmy Davey, and he would need at least ten minutes' rest either side of half-time. Danny Cowling was off his crutches at least, ahead of a three-month rehab programme that would include a naked run since he hadn't scored a try other than the one against North Wales in preseason and friendlies don't count.

By the early hours of Friday morning, though, around half the nation needed painkillers as the referendum result became clear: victory for the Leave campaign by a margin of 51.9 to 48.1 per cent. A sifting of detail was revealing. On a day of political uproar, when sterling plunged to record lows, Prime Minister Cameron did a JK – announcing he would step down in October – and a motion of no-confidence was tabled in Labour leader Corbyn, it was clear that just about every rugby league town had voted for Brexit. Even Batley and Birstall, where the vote was 54.7 per cent Leave, 45.3 per cent Remain in a 70.7 per cent turnout, the death of Jo Cox notwithstanding. UK Independence Party leader Nigel Farage called the outcome a victory for 'ordinary, decent people', implying that those who wished to stay were not, the debate won 'without a single bullet being fired,' he said. Across the rest of England's north, people voted to 'get their country back'; towns with large white working-class populations mainly, lacking money, job security, identity and therefore with little, so they imagined, to lose. On the other hand, the big northern cities – Leeds, Newcastle, Manchester, Liverpool – voted narrowly for Remain.

It was the debate over rugby league's future magnified. Were the communities that had historically sustained rugby league holding it back nowadays and denying its potential? Should these big cities – in the north and elsewhere – be more aggressively targeted? Rugby league, like the nation, was at a fork in the road. Risk reaching out to cities that may not be interested – history suggesting that, with the exception of Leeds, they by and large are not – or hunker down in the dogged little communities that built and then sustained the sport through good times and bad? Dogged little communities like Batley?

As *Guardian* writer John Harris surmised: 'What defines these furies is often clear enough: a terrible shortage of homes, an impossibly precarious job market, a too-often overlooked sense that men (and men are particularly relevant here) who would once have been certain in their identity as miners, or steelworkers, now feel demeaned and ignored.' Might not a far-reaching RFL policy review be appropriate assuming the current governing body has sufficient will, intellect and ability to embark upon such an abstract though ultimately practical project? The signs weren't encouraging. High-level figures at Red Hall were said by staff to have openly advocated Leave in those same RFL offices. For that matter, Kevin Nicholas was open about his preference for Brexit, along with a number of players in a squad that, as in the rest of a divided nation, swung both ways on the issue.

Another distraction for the Bulldogs, perhaps, although their coach, in the Remain camp on account of practical matters such as what might happen to his pension, was confident otherwise. 'They aren't heavily politicized animals, rugby league players,' he reasoned. 'There'll be one or two bothered in each group, Leave or Remain, but generally they're not. Brownie admits he hasn't got a clue what it's about. I'd say 75 per cent are like that and the ones that aren't just get on with it. You can disagree over anything but once you go on that field . . . Same with prep: they might bicker and fall out but we have to come to some sort of agreement and fix it up.' Nor was there a policy of steering them off the subject. 'They can have political debates if they want them,' said JK. 'The referendum is a major issue; I just don't think these fellas are minded by it. They have differences and then get on with it. It's like with your missus. If you are going to make your marriage work, you've got to be right with each other.'

There was, however, no doubt about the views of Keegan Hirst. 'A person is smart but people are stupid,' he told his followers on social media. 'Blinded by ignorant rhetoric. Now even going to Spain is going to be a ball-ache.'

The Fox's Biscuits Stadium lies directly beneath the flight-path into Leeds-Bradford Airport. Sit on the relevant side of the plane and there it will be, splayed out in all its glory atop Mount Pleasant. What cannot be made out is the colour, faith or race of any of the dots in attendance. People are just people when viewed from up there. 'More in common,' as Jo Cox put it.

Come Sunday, Jimmy starts, Leaky doesn't, though JK praises him anyway. 'I know he has a bad back, but I'll give him a pat on it anyway because he's been very honest. He's desperate to play but hasn't said he'll take a painkiller and see how it is; he's admitted he can't play the forty or fifty minutes expected of him. That's why I like this group so much. You play like honest people and you behave like honest people off the field.' Scotty plays nine in attack and drops back to his usual spot in D, when one of the pivots will take over. JK is confident it will work without complication and is proven correct.

Training yesterday went well enough, though Keegan was an absentee. Sporting a red T-shirt – 'Some People Are Gay. Get Over It!' – he was in London, part of Pride 2016, a march through the capital to celebrate LGBT rights and remember people lost, such as the victims of recent shootings in Orlando. In Trafalgar Square, he spoke to a crowd far removed from those in front of whom he might normally be expected to perform. 'All this is about is education – teaching our kids what we are about. It's all right to be who you are.'

Meanwhile, back in Batley, Mokko, Linners and Mauny were missing too, so JK took the defensive drills and Dom the attacking. All went fine until the forwards began to bicker. 'Too many voices,' Dom said. 'If someone makes a fuck-up just get on with it, we go again . . . Come on, it's a massive game this'. In the huddle, JK, aware they only scraped past the Rams last time out with a penalty and couple of drop-goals, backed his key playmaker: 'If Dom says scratch your arse with your left hand and pick your nose with your right, that's what you do!'

On Sunday, a breezy day of sunshine, Batley town centre is reaching tentatively towards some sort of normality. Having turned up Branch Road – so known as it's where the ancient Dewsbury to Girlington turnpike used to diverge – on past the old Taylor's mill and bus station, now a supermarket and decorators' shop respectively, flowers and tributes to Jo Cox are still piled on the town hall steps. Up at the club, an hour and a half before kick-off, it is far busier than usual. A good-sized crowd builds, dotted with shirts and colours of other teams as the lads of Batley Boys and Dewsbury Celtic play. In the boardroom, chaplain Derek sighs that 'the country is broken', while chatting with a group of soldiers. Kev talks to Bernard Carter-Kenny and family, for whom the week has been a media whirl. As he points out a cordoned-off area of the Glen Tomlinson Stand, they tell him that a writer from the *New Yorker* has even been in touch. His name is Ed Caesar and in his piece he puts Jo's death into historical context – 'the first MP to be assassinated since Ian Gow, who was killed by the IRA, in 1990 [and] the first woman, and the first Labour MP, to be murdered in office' – one example among many of how Batley's story is, however tragically, being shared with an international audience.

Caesar quotes Jo's husband, Brendan Cox, telling the Trafalgar Square service beamed back to Batley that his wife would have spent her birthday 'dashing around the streets of her home town trying to convince people that Britain is stronger in Europe. She feared the consequences of Europe dividing again, hated the idea of building walls between us and worried about the dynamics [it] could unleash.' The writer goes on:

Many in Market Place wept openly as those words were spoken . . . it was difficult to imagine [how] anyone could have listened to that speech, and then voted to leave the European Union. But the next evening, as the polls closed, many told me they had done just that. At the Batley Conservative Club, a vast and formerly grand establishment at odds with its dwindling clientele of mostly old, white men, two members, named Darren and Stuart (they declined to offer their surnames), sat at the bar discussing how they had both voted Leave. Darren knew Jo Cox from school and said she was 'a lovely lass'. But both men spoke repeatedly about how they had been let down by politicians, particularly on the issue of immigration. Their complaint did not just concern the recent migrants from the EU but the older Muslim residents of Batley. Darren put his wish to leave the EU partly down to 'the change in the town and the feeling in the town. There are certain people who don't integrate.' Stuart said: 'It's a sad thing what happened last week,' but added, 'We just want our country back.' Both men expected the 'Jo Cox thing' to have 'skewed' the result toward Remain, but they still expected a majority in the district to have voted Leave. Darren and Stuart were right.

In the here and now, every club director, plus VIPs like RFL President Paul Morgan and Liberal MP for Leeds North West and chair of the All Party Parliamentary Rugby League Group Greg Mulholland (in a Batley shirt with 'Jo Cox MP' on the back), stand before a Van Gogh field's worth of sunflowers. Also paying their respects are the cheer-leaders of both clubs, members of the Yorkshire Regiment and the man who bravely intervened, along with two sides who have a derby to play. And with programmes waved (£800 raised for the Royal Voluntary Service), a moving John Miller speech given, the Last Post sounded and four TV crews on their way, play it those lads do, its outcome yet again decided by a slender margin.

Players are used to pre-match solemnities but most often they last one minute, not fifteen. After the waiting, the question arises – who will settle soonest? The answer: Dewsbury, 10–0 up in as many minutes. Too many missed tackles and poor ends costs Batley dear. They need inspiration from somewhere and frustration only grows when, in swift succession, Keegan, Brownie and Gleds are all tackled inches short of the line and Frankie Mariano – covering at centre in the absence of Greg Minikin – has a try disallowed for offside.

On a day for fighting spirit, even the referee has a story to tell and what a tale it is. Former Royal Marine commando Jack Smith served in Afghanistan and was shot on his first tour of duty by a Taliban sniper. The offending bullet entered his body at the base of his back, above his backside, put a couple of holes in his diaphragm too. As he lay at an angle on a rooftop under fire, the bullet also travelled through his liver and broke his right-side ribs (though some of that damage may have been the result of falling off the roof), busted the bottom lobe of his right lung and emerged below his collarbone. Before all of that, the bullet had already gone through the arm of a fellow Marine.

It's hardly comparing like with like but Batley too battle on and are rewarded when Brownz touches down for a try that Dom converts into a now swirling wind. Two minutes later, the half-back improves Uce's score, the centre barrelling over covered in defenders to make the most of Jimmy Davey's fine break. It has taken them half an hour to get ahead, but the Bulldogs lead 12–10.

They are, however, playing downhill, so further scores will be needed and, driven forward by rampaging replacement forwards Rowey and Cropper, Breth soon crosses out wide three minutes before the break. The goal is missed. Will 16–10 be enough?

The early indications are that it won't. Dewsbury only take two minutes this time to register, though they miss the conversion: 16–14. After which the action turns feverish. Alex Brown's lately faltering wide-kick D – practised diligently at JK's suggestion yesterday – is put to the test several times and the winger holds his nerve. There is a very dodgy moment when a Rams penalty goal attempt rebounds back into play off an upright, but Batley don't panic and react well before conceding a ten-metre scrum. This too is defended until another penalty is conceded and Dewsbury draw level.

The smart money now is on the visitors but only a minute later Batley win a penalty at the other end and Patch has no qualms about taking the two. It is 18–16 but there are still twenty-five minutes to go and what an eventful period that is. Cropper bounces over for a wonderful try that referee Smith, having arrived too late to spot the grounding, disallows. Nobody argues. But when Brownie too is soon denied, Reitts does complain and is dispatched to the sinbin for dissent. For ten minutes, uphill, Batley are reduced to twelve men.

The mood is tense as Dewsbury continue to press, helped by home transgressions. If they hang on here, it will be an against-the-odds scrap to remember. Gleds is tackled high on halfway and Batley have their first decent field position in an age, but play soon switches back downfield, where a Dewsbury cross-field kick to the spot where Reitts no longer is looks sure to be a match-winner, before the ball bounces harmlessly forward and the errant winger himself returns to see out the final three minutes.

Finally . . . finally . . . the hooter sounds and the elation is palpable. At the end of a week of enormous adversity, Batley are back on the winning trail, resilience personified. What's more, other results have gone their way – Featherstone suffering a shock defeat to Sheffield on Friday night and Bradford falling to Halifax in an equally surprising result at Odsal. They are back in the top four.

'Fellas, it's gonna be like that,' JK tells them in the changing room, as wrung through the mill as anyone. 'But if you show that grit, that determination, you'll come through and get it. Forget your fancy-Dan football – that was a win for heart and desire. Well done.'

And when the song is sung, Keegan once again remembers all the words. 'I'm back!' he roars, shirt off, soon swimming in chocolate milk. It must seem a very long way from London's famous Ivy, where, only last night, he dined on shepherd's pie.

16

IF A HARD-EARNED victory is to mean anything, the top-four impetus must be maintained. And where Batley head next is Whitehaven, second-bottom of the table but a Cumbrian trip where, like Workington, many a hope has come unstuck. It will be a Saturday-night match too, to disrupt the routine further.

Viewing the clips on Tuesday, JK remained concerned with how they were starting games: 'I don't know if it's me putting you to sleep or what it is . . .' Patch suggested that, to win, maybe Batley had to be up for it from the word go last year, whereas now they were more relaxed, confident in their ability to get out of it. Their opponents too arrived barred up. JK proposed no flashy remedy, just get to the end of the opening attacking set: 'Stay in "Cas"[code for the centre channel], one-out rugby, kick at the end, it'll settle us down.' And in the first defensive set: 'Tough but squeaky-clean and get the ball back. We just need to solve it.'

Next season's squad continued to take shape as Leaky – or 'Willow' now, on account of his supposed resemblance to the little farmer played by Warwick Davis in the fantasy film – and Tuna both agreed new two-year contracts, while Reitts extended his current agreement by a year. In May, Brownie and Rowey had signed up until the end of 2018; Matt Diskin inheriting a settled squad, sixteen of the class of 2016 by this stage committed. Elsewhere, London and Bradford both had a couple of NRL players flying in ahead of the big split.

London's made sense, 31-year-old playmaker Jamie Soward having played in the capital before. The Bulls' capture of 25-year-old Canterbury half-back Dane Chisholm, however, smacked of a last desperate toss of the coin with only four games left in which to stake a promotion claim.

On Thursday, Keegs had his first tabloid 'papping' by the *Sun*: pictured arm in arm with Antony Cotton outside The Box in Soho – 'Britain's seediest VIP club'. It gave his teammates a laugh and no one seemed much fussed, Cotton more annoyed he'd been snapped with a cigarette. 'The soap veteran, 40, and the 28-year-old Bately Bulldogs [sic] player were seen . . . holding hands,' it read. 'Not that a bit of seediness is enough to put off some of the most A-list of celebs, with clientele including Prince Harry, Zara Phillips, Kate Moss, Jude Law, Harry Styles and Mark Ronson.' Nor do the below-the-liners seem scandalized. 'Really interesting photo of two blokes walking,' read one online comment. Outside, Mauny watched the halves and wings practising kicks to the corner. 'Oh, I hope we get in the top four,' he muttered. 'I can't think of anything else.' Leaky was fit again; he wouldn't miss a trip home. And straight after a training session in which not a ball was dropped he drove up to visit his mum.

For the rest, another coach journey was in store that as on the Workington trip would stop for sustenance at Rheged, where they would meet Scotty, driving to Dundee after the game to his brother's stag do, and JK, having a few days up there at his holiday home. Trouble was afoot, though. Shortly after departure, Alex Brown had begun to feel unwell, Mauny told the waiting JK via his mobile phone on a bus delayed by M6 roadworks. On top of Greg Minikin's unexpected recall by Cas, it threw a king-sized spanner in the works.

Rheged is a consumer-friendly '21st century retail experience', but its name is steeped in history, a kingdom of the old north in the early Middle Ages with links to Wales. Were he an actor, JK would be ideal for the part of ruler Urien Rheged (son of Cynfarch the Dismal), but in any case, using all his monarchic acumen, he made a decision that might just have saved the day. Ainy had been tentatively back in training for a fortnight, though deemed not yet quite fit enough for contact. JK got him on the phone, at home in Wigan. Would he be able to give it a go? The winger, a couple of hours south, said yes he would zoom up; with a clear run he'd just about make it. His team-mates, unaware, munched through chicken, potatoes, salad and pasta. 'Don't let them know you are worried,' JK confided with a wink.

With the Championship's top two as good as sorted, Batley were in a four-club dogfight now for two spots. That evening's game was another crucial one, more than anyone knew since although Bradford were set to fall narrowly at Leigh the next day, Halifax and Featherstone would register easy wins. Whitehaven had run Batley close twice this year, losing by a single point at Mount Pleasant on both occasions, so would certainly be no pushovers here.

As the bus sweeps down into Whitehaven, the harbour tucked snug in its bay like a windbreak on a beach, the Recreation Ground – or Recre as it is known locally, 'r's rolled and purred in the Cumbrian twang – heaves into view. Blue skies bubble with cloud and threaten showers that turn heavy before drying up. It is chilly for the first week in July, the Irish or Manx Sea a forbidding grey as it fusses and broils beneath cliffs dotted with council and boarding houses.

As up the coast, the rugby league side here has not tasted much in the way of glory, although they did beat Australia in 1956. And as ever in Cumbria, there is wonder at how rugby league hangs on here like a hardy mountain goat. The answer is a once-vibrant amateur scene that has suffered diminishing numbers in recent times. Still, they battle on. Although 2016 has become yet another season of struggle, you take Haven lightly at your peril, especially on home soil.

Not uncommonly around here, their ground is partial to flooding, the river running behind the bottom end doing for London's aborted trip in April. Tonight, the Recre is a little damp underfoot, though firm. Open stone terracing lies at right angles on two sides, with a covered terrace at the clubhouse end and a small main stand behind the dugouts. Another deserted terrace abuts the changing rooms, the recreational pitches that give the place its name beyond that. Toilets lurk behind topless brick walls, grooves in bare earth a-stink and saturated with decades of piss. Not that any of it is put to much use. The official attendance is 571 and that may be pushing it. There may, however, be that many seagulls. After watching from the terrace stand roof, flocks descend from time to time, keen to join in.

'They were shouting, "Outside C . . . outside C" during ruck play,' JK told his side after watching Haven's preparations. Ainy had indeed arrived in time, trotting out of the sheds ten minutes into Batley's warm-up. 'Be aware of that. All I ask for is eighty minutes of intensity and focus, the little things done well. Make those fucking efforts. It will be an eighty-minute game, believe you me. Good luck, gents.'

Batley do as they promised their coach they would, completing their opening sets with and without the ball. Early on, Ainy is tackled in the air but lands unscathed and will last the pace, though admit to feeling sore. But yet again it's Batley's opponents who score first, Haven's half-back Grant Gore spotting a gap in the right-side defence, where Joe Chandler comes in for Minikin and Dom is momentarily wrong-footed. Otherwise, while the Bulldogs have the bulk of possession they are able to do little with it. Ends fizzle out due to over-reliance on kicks to the corner and, after spurning a kickable penalty, frustration sets in. Handily, a sinbinning diminishes Haven's numbers and Brownie takes advantage with the biff-and-barge try that makes it 4–4. Aside from low-flying seagulls, Whitehaven's chief threat is on the break and the hosts are almost in via that route after forcing a GLDO on the half hour. Prior to that, left-centre Jessie Joe Parker pulled up suddenly clutching a hamstring, the groan around the ground at the big Papua New Guinean's misfortune telling. It damages Haven where they are having most impact but they dig in anyway and put Batley's goal-line D under mighty pressure. As half-time approaches, they look certain scorers yet can't quite get through, as Batley's mad-dog defence comes into its own.

Having mulled it over, Scotty decided to play, as, 'If we lost this game and it cost us a place in the top four, I might regret it for ever.'

And as it turns out, he, Gleds and Frankie Mariano are the pick of the visiting crew. But saving the day before the break is Wayne Reittie who, in his 200th career game, races back to deny an interception try after Batley prod the Whitehaven line having forced a GLDO. JK said it would not be won in the first half and was correct. He reiterates the point. They need to end sets better, defend just as well, regroup.

Batley are first out for the second half, keen to finish the job. But when Scotty drops a high ball in the first set, it leads to a spell of sustained pressure just as another heavy shower descends. Somehow they survive the assault and are rewarded when a kick to the corner, Dom nudging it along the ground this time, finally pays off, Reitts showing composure to get his hand to the ball first. Patch converts and the visitors are ahead. There is still half an hour to navigate and on the hour Mariano pulls off another try-saving tackle, the gulls lined up in an admiring row. Its value is emphasized when Gleds then barges over, Patch again converting, to extend the lead, 4–16.

Heading into the final quarter, that really should be that, but handling errors help Haven back into the game. Brownie contributes one on his forty-metre line and hurls the ball at the turf in disgust. And at the end of the set, the home side scores in the corner, touch judge sent flying. The margin is now 8–16 with fourteen minutes remaining. Patch gets a chance to add two more points but only chews up the clock a little as another fraught match crawls toward its agonizing conclusion. See it out Batley do, though, and in the cramped shed JK is aglow with admiration.

'Joe, you did an excellent job in defence, son. Ainy, fucking hell, fella, I don't know if you had six pints at lunchtime, but well done . . . but that's what you need to achieve something. Sometimes it's about digging in deep and working hard. I'd have bitten anyone's hand off for an eight-point win here, I'm telling you. What we've done is pass the pressure to the rest: "Here you are. You fucking do it now."'

It's time to howl at the moon: *Doggies . . . Doggies . . . Doggies . . . Doggies . . .* but once all are fed and watered and – with the exception of Scotty, Ainy, Leaky and JK – set to clamber back aboard the bus, into a star-spangled velvet Cumbrian night sky drifts another familiar refrain from the clubhouse bar: Sammy King's 'Penny Arcade'.

> *Just ring the bell on the big bagatelle*
> *And you'll make all the coloured lights cascade.*

The tension is mounting. Pushed back into fourth by Halifax's 62–12 hammering of Swinton, Batley, like Fax, are three points clear of Bradford in fifth and sixth-placed Featherstone, with six points left to play for, three games to go. One worry is that in a season of close results the Bulldogs have a far inferior points difference to their rivals. League leaders Leigh and London are confirmed for the Qualifiers, as in Super League are Leeds, their home defeat to a Widnes drop-goal ensuring that the Rhinos too will be in the middle eight, a dream money-spinner for Championship clubs for whom the financial stakes could not be very much higher.

Take one game at a time. Don't worry about permutations. The outcome is in our hands. Do what we need to do and what others end up doing won't matter. Sound advice but easier to utter than follow.

On the bus ride home, Keegan, as captain, broached the subject of post-split payments with Kev, who aside from his usual quips declined the invitation. 'Let's get the London game out of the way and then we can discuss it,' he said, not wanting to jinx things. And training on Tuesday is again light, JK attempting to take as much heat out of the run-in as possible. Kev offers the players an extra £100 a man to beat Featherstone, next up, though that is kept in-house. No one wants to stoke Rovers' fire. Should Bradford lose to Whitehaven and the Bulldogs win, Batley will be confirmed in the top four, though no one seriously expects the first half of that equation to eventuate.

'We need to calm everyone down, focus on processes and what we do well,' JK tells the leadership group, who have the ears of the changing room. Anything else is enough to make your head spin. 'The more we get distracted, the worse it is. We all just need to pull in.'

The message is reiterated in the players' meeting. At Haven, he says, they looked like they wanted to win it in the first ten minutes. 'Well, we ain't going to be comfortable, guys, in any of the last three games. Each one is going to need us working our bollocks off.' They had shown great attitude, though, and the scramble was exceptional. Watching the clips, he tells Dom, 'You live or die by your decisions,' as one kick goes awry on the second tackle before another leads to Reittie's try. Good players show good judgement when it matters and have the skill to back those decisions up.

How do they feel as a group? Confident? Excited? 'Yeah, so you should be, so you should be. You've worked real hard to get here. How do we nail this next game then? Fuck the other two. How do we nail it? Good D. Tough. Composed. Completions. Good ends. As Leaky says, just do what we did in the Cup. It was 6–4, until sixty-odd minutes. Arm-wrestle, arm-wrestle . . . and they went. Well, I'd suggest we've got more reason to do that again, just do what we are good at. Complete, end well, chase well, defend tough. Be disciplined. Play our shapes, because we got loads of joy with that, didn't we? Two home games to come, guys, is a fucking great position to be in. But the only one that matters is Featherstone, the next one.'

On Thursday, the upholding of a six-point deduction for Salford for a salary cap breach means Super League's bottom four takes further shape, especially as the Red Devils fall 40–14 tonight at Warrington. Along with Leeds, they are confirmed in the Qualifiers. And despite JK's insistence that his squad should ignore the permutations, the 'ifs' and 'buts' persist. Rumours abound that Fev's players haven't been paid. Upset in the camp? Will Leigh Centurions, guaranteed the League Leaders' Shield, let Halifax win so as to deny Bradford Bulls, with whom the Leythers have fallen out this year?

On local radio, Iro can't resist looking forward. Yes, promotion to Super League would be a 'dream' but he can't rule it out. 'I fancy our team against anybody, and you get there and then who knows? It would be a great problem to have. I think we'd stay part-time, to be fair. Kevin and myself are looking at updating the ground. We're meeting all the requirements, which the money, if we get top four, will help us do. We'd definitely go to Super League.'

While Dom and company do extras in the sunshine, Rowey streams *Love Island* on his phone, top telly the big prop reckons. JK watches the group through the boardroom window: 'Got a lovely pass on him, Dom, hasn't he?' and they all laugh. Somebody wonders out loud whether Squiresy, also outside despite not being picked lately, has had a hair transplant. 'If so, he wants his money back,' says JK. 'It's like Keegan being gay. He should come out as bald.'

'Yeah,' agrees the captain. 'Take it on the chin. Hey, Mauny. You're metrosexual. Where do you get your eyebrows done?'

'Any hairdresser will do it for you.'

The humour masks anxiety. Various players admit to nerves. 'Why?' says Patch. 'Just beat all three and have done with it.'

'Nice, Patch,' says Brownie.

The clips are designed to give everyone a lift too – another look at the cup tie between the sides. The week before that game, Batley's right-edge was tested in London just as it was at Whitehaven. Having remedied those faults in training, it came up trumps in the Challenge Cup and the same must apply again, which is why they work on it outside tonight and on Saturday too. 'Keep coming forward . . . harass them. Take space, good contact, urgency to ground. Markers, work from the inside to pressure the pivots. Handle it together, map out or jam at the right time.' Neither Greg Minikin nor Frankie Mariano will be around any more, however, recalled by Castleford. Other players may be brought in before the 22 July deadline, although right now it's the ones at JK's current disposal that matter.

Scully, jogging up and down the touchline, chin like Dan Dare, isn't one of those, though the knee feels fine now, he says. It's just the joints that are a bit sore; he'll be ready for preseason. Having come back earlier than anticipated, Ainy will again be leapfrogged by the recovered Alex Brown, harsh reward for rushing to the rescue in Cumbria. After almost knocking the Wiganer out in one tackle, Rowey knees him in the next. Ice is applied but dead legs are notoriously worse after three days; they fill with blood and become virtually immobile. He has form with training injuries, does Rowey. Last year he got the blame for accidentally breaking the elbow of Anthony Nicholson – now at Swinton – in three places. The poor lad was out for three months.

In Super League, a 20–19 defeat to Hull Kingston Rovers consigns Huddersfield to the middle eight with Leeds and Salford, one team to come, most likely Hull KR. More ominously, Leeds beat league leaders Hull FC at the KC Stadium, 20–15, and are belatedly finding form.

Thursday-night training ends with sunshine bathing one half of the field and rain drenching the other in a glinting diamond spray, to produce another rainbow in the valley below, complete with pot of gold? By Saturday morning, it is bouncing it down. The clips show Featherstone's 44–22 beating of Workington last week, when they hadn't looked like a team on the wobble. Danger-men: Bostock, Taulapapa, Briggs, Channing, Roche – all handfuls but generally Rovers are low risk, big on completions, aggressive, direct, wrapping though sometimes folding, majoring in carrying and finding the floor. Yet with three or four in the tackle, they are bound to tire eventually if Batley can stay with them.

'What do we reckon, fellas? You tell me. At their place, they rolled us a bit. In the Cup, we learned from that. Fronted up. We've got to be smart. It's important we don't give away penalties and cheap position. What's the main test when they have the ball? The half-backs. Look after the shape and push through. Make it set for set. We need to challenge them with aggressive carries and quick play-the-balls. We need to execute our shapes well. We need to end our sets well. We need to be tough. We need to be high-energy and out-work them. If we do that, the reward comes. Don't think of the reward, think of how we *get* the reward. Okay, guys?'

And outside they trot, into the pouring rain.

Seventeen haunted faces betray the outcome, along with the devastated expressions of the non-playing squad and coaching staff. And this on the day of the big match, a game they so desperately needed to win, which had begun with such optimism.

Craig Taylor's Under-16s were bubbling, Girls Rugby League champions after a 28–6 beating of Huddersfield, their fourteenth win in fourteen games to crown an unbeaten league season; the bars behind the Glen Tomlinson Stand were well populated by flat-cappers and Doggies alike, though the weather hadn't known what to do with itself, one moment sunshine, next moment showers. 'It's do or die for us today,' confided one young Rovers player as the British Police met a Teachers Rugby League representative side, watched by both sets of players pre-match.

Both head coaches meanwhile, Featherstone's Jon Sharp and JK, the latter's wife Dawn up in the boardroom and here to support him as usual, affected inscrutability, calm and on the surface composed. In Kear's case, that Zen-like state was the product of routine. 'Same every match,' said Dawn. 'I take him a cup of tea in bed while he waits for the paper. When it arrives, he reads it with another cup of tea and a chunky Kit-Kat.' After which JK likes to be left on his own, taking his beloved dogs out for one hour and fifteen minutes on the dot. 'When he gets back, he has a full Monty breakfast and I leave him alone while he gets ready for the match.' It is rare for the couple to travel together; Dawn's father more often accompanies her.

By his own admission, if JK has a hobby outside rugby league, it is his hounds. He takes them out every morning for a couple of hours while Dawn is at work, and they are there to greet him win, lose or draw. Which is handy because the life of a professional sports coach can be stressful. 'Sometimes you walk on eggshells, especially on match-day.' Through the week there are matches to review, dead-lines to meet, preparation to do and games to see; it's just as well that his Chesterfield-born Myrtle – JK's name for everyone's wife or girlfriend – enjoys rugby league as much as she does. 'If I didn't, we'd be divorced.' The couple met in 1998, when Dawn and her dad were drawn to watch rugby league for the first time by Sheffield's Challenge Cup semi-final with Salford at Headingley, the first date coming two months after the Eagles' subsequent Wembley upset. 'He offered me free tickets to a St Helens Super League game at Don Valley. That shows how tight he is, doesn't it?'

Like Bev Nicholas, she tries to ignore outside criticism of her husband, though in the age of social media it can be tricky to avoid. 'John's quite thick-skinned; what he doesn't like is when it becomes personal, about his family or me. That's a different ball game.' For a while at least, next year's move to Wakefield had been contentious, though Dawn confirms that JK's focus is nowhere near there yet. No, she wouldn't recommend marrying a rugby league coach. 'Everybody thinks you've got a privileged life, but when John was at Wakefield before, I went to watch them play Catalan away, paid the plane fare, paid for my hotel, you don't get any perks whatsoever. I suppose the upside is that when the season's finished and his commitments to Wales are done, we spend three weeks together.' With the dogs too of course, who along with loyalty offer their owner valuable thinking time.

'Very much,' agrees JK, who has a Yorkshire Terrier (Arthur) and Labrador (Mollie), both rescue dogs. Prior to Arthur, they had another Yorkie, appropriately named Cassie. Arthur lived next door, until the neighbour fell pregnant and dog and baby didn't get on. 'Yorkshire Terriers are demanding, high maintenance, but very rewarding. They asked if we'd have Arthur for the weekend because they were going to put him in the RSPCA. So we got him and it's been the longest weekend since – about six and a half years – so he's done pretty well. The Labrador we got from Cliffe Kennels, near Barnsley. She'd been there for months, near to being put down. She didn't look well, as she'd been in a house with drug users. They'd been putting cigarettes out on her; that was their idea of fun. So she was scarred on one side of her body where she laid down. Obviously, the dog was emotionally affected and she used to cower in the kennels. So we took her on . . . well, it was Arthur who took her on because we were looking for another dog for company for him when Cassie died.' The two struck an immediate bond. 'There was no yapping. We took Molly out for a walk with Arthur and home for a trial fortnight and it just worked out. Arthur and Molly were like lovers in the sunset. I felt rewarded because I'd saved one dog from a rescue centre and one from an horrific four- or five-year life until we got hold of her.' JK loves dogs, having always been around them; his parents kept Alsatians on a long leash – no one nicked his dad's coal. 'I saw the other side. They might be guard dogs but they are loving dogs too.'

If only rugby league was so faithful. No sooner had Tracey Grundell roared her first 'Baaatttleeeeyyy' than Kear's Bulldogs, playing down-hill – Keegan having lost the toss – were already behind to a penalty. And when on seven minutes the man-of-the-match prop they'd been warned about, Andy Bostock, span over for a converted try, the arrears were 8–0. The calamity began when Scotty fumbled a bomb – high but of a variety he would normally pouch – worsening from there. As Batley's confidence drooped, so Featherstone's soared.

Effort was not the issue so much as lack of focus. Any luck went against them – bounce of the ball, refereeing decisions – and the cloud of victimhood descended. Rovers played well. Under no matter what pressure, their line was not breached. Players, dugout, home fans – all were tense. *Move the ball!* one frustrated cry at what its owner perceived as a lack of imagination. Batley, though, had a game plan and stuck resolutely by it, Featherstone's part going unnoticed.

Had the hosts been playing uphill, it's doubtful anyone would have been too concerned. Keep it tight in the first half, up it a gear in the second. But they weren't and Rovers dug in as if their existence depended upon it, which with finances in mind it very well might. As little things continued to conspire against Batley – Dom's attempted 40/20 inches short, for example – Rovers stifled their playbook and added a further penalty.

Batley's best chance came when Cropper took a bouncing Cain bomb on the half hour that Taulapapa didn't want to know about. Tearing towards the posts, he failed to notice his scrum-half along-side, the opportunity squandered. Trailing 10–0 at half-time had not been in the schedule and it might have been worse had Rovers not been bundled into touch with twenty-five seconds left. 'We are playing like a set of amateurs,' Patch said in the changing room. 'We are not getting to start points; we've got to take ownership . . .'

Brownie, emotional, interjected: 'Fucking hell, you've seen how long they're slowing us down, let's fucking slow them down. It's a million miles an hour for them, five for us. Get the fuck on the floor.'

'When we are coming out of yardage, they've a right fucking hard-on, haven't they?' said Keegan. 'Getting off the mark and belting us. We are getting them down there and letting them march out of yardage. Let's fight fire with fire.'

JK, pacing in silence and poring over Linners' stats, was less charitable. 'You're right, you're right. Keegan's called it. They've been more aggressive than you, more urgent than you, more enthusiastic. They deserve to be ten points up, believe you me. They fucking do. So what we need to do is re-address what we said we were going to do. We need to carry with some shit in us and some urgency to fight on the floor and try and play the fucking ball. We need to be assertive. There's too many fuckers tackling like this . . . [niminy-piminy grab at thin air]. Get your fucking shoulder in and sit them on their arse.'

Bostock was having a field day. 'He's played thirty-seven minutes. Thirty-fucking-seven minutes! Bostock! He ought to be fucked after twenty, I'll tell you. We've been fucking soft. Soft cocks . . . too bothered about the pats on the backs and plaudits. We ain't been prepared to earn it. So let's go back, complete high and get to points. Let's show every fucker we are a top-four team. Because we don't look it at the minute, agreed?' *Yeah!* 'In whose hands is it?' *Ours!* 'Let's buy time on the floor. Whack the cunts, stay tight, be nasty with them, I'm not bothered, so they know you mean business. Fuck the scoreboard; it's about attitudes and processes. Let's have some fire in us!'

And out they had run, reinvigorated, into a four-try blitz.

Again it began with an uncharacteristic error, full-back Scotty this time letting the ball bounce. When it didn't run dead as he'd hoped, a chasing Michael Channing patted it back into play for Kyle Briggs to score. Ian Hardman, Ashton Golding and Channing added the rest and Rovers were out of sight, 34–0, after thirteen minutes.

Thankfully, the floodgates slammed shut and Chris Ulugia's late try, converted by Patch, at least avoided a duck egg. But that was scant consolation for a second home defeat of the season – and the largest league loss so far – just when they needed it least. To make matters worse, Bradford clocked up fifty-two first-half points against Whitehaven on their way to a 64–18 victory. Along with Fev, the Bulls were now just a point behind Batley and Halifax – who mercifully had lost 58–18 at Leigh – with four points to play for.

As Featherstone celebrate, the Bulldogs wander back to the sheds, tails between legs. 'Tell you what, I read you wrong this week,' says JK, his tone softer now, more in sorrow than anger. 'I thought I'd have to calm you down, stop you getting too hyped up, over-aroused. You were awful. Tentative. Didn't want to play. They came here with desperation, intent to challenge you. And you fuckers backed down, rolled over and had your bellies tickled, I'll tell you. All that we have been doing all season, we stopped fucking doing it. That was the most unlike-Batley performance I've seen, and I've been here five years. It was soft as fuck. It really was. After all we say in here at half-time, four tries in five sets they get. We've white gloves on – "Come through, I don't want to tackle you . . ." Do you not understand, guys? We've used our get-out-of-jail card. To get in the top four, which we've worked for since November, we need to be desperate now. We've got to turn up and play, not pat each other on the back saying how good we are. We've achieved fuck all yet.'

They will train on Wednesday and Friday this week and by Wednesday he expects them to have watched the game. 'Have a look at yourselves, be critical.' He shakes his head. 'Fuck me. But it's gone. It's gone now. So we've got to look at that, dust ourselves down, train with intent, so when London come here we give them it in every single way. I don't mind losing, guys, so long as we look as if we've had a dig. We didn't today; you need to watch it. You need to see what everybody else saw from the sidelines.'

Keegan assesses the shell-shocked faces and says they need to ask themselves something. 'What we can do is go, "Oh, we've had a fucking good season. We nearly made top four and no one expected that. So fucking hell, that's all right, isn't it?" Or we can say, "That's not good enough. We've worked our bollocks off for eight or nine months, worked our fucking rocks off, to fall at the final hurdle?" How many games have we got under our belts? Twenty-one. Twenty-one games to throw it away in the last two? It's too easy to be a nearly man, to get there and fall short. No one fucking remembers nearly men. That's what we've got to ask ourselves between now and Wednesday, and on Wednesday we need to come with a fucking answer.'

'And it's no good being nervy,' adds his coach. 'You achieve by saying, "I'm good enough; I *am* going to do it." And every single one of us has to be good enough. There were people wanting to get off the field today, believe you me. Good call that, Keegan lad, good call.'

17

LONDON BRONCOS ARRIVE at the Mount having been turned over by Sheffield, 32–14, a surprise, and at the end of a week when Batley Variety Club was finally condemned to closure.

One year short of its fiftieth anniversary, the once iconic venue would shut up shop with a 'special event' on 30 July, a fortnight away ... *Golden days before they end, whisper secrets to the wind. It's over.* Manager Nick Westwell called it 'very sad' as April's hidden planning application came to pass: 'Change of use from nightclub/music venue to gymnasium (Class D2).'

'We are conscious that this will be quite emotive for many people and understand the loss of any significant entertainment space can be extremely damaging to small towns in particular,' he continued. But 'the commercial entertainment landscape has changed and the demands for larger arenas [as] opposed to smaller-style concert halls has been prevalent'.

A larger arena wouldn't be needed for London's visit – just over a thousand spectators turn up, very few from the capital – though the town has not staged such a game in decades. Once again, JK was forced to negotiate a tricky lead-up to a pivotal point in his five-year reign. How to lift a side whose confidence was so badly dented? Use last week's opposition as an example: 'They played with focus, intensity, desperation and channelled it in a very positive way – which is what we need to do this week.' Look on the bright side: 'If you would have told anyone we would be one point clear in fourth with two games to play . . .' Ensure that everyone's focus was fully on what lay ahead – no chance it would be otherwise there.

Again, though, the windmill kept turning. On Thursday came Keegan's appearance on the ITV strand *Real Lives*, filmed partly here in June. The 'Yorkshire man mountain' told a national audience that one unnamed teammate had been in tears: 'I can't believe you've gone through all of that on your own.' The skipper hadn't intended 'to go on any crusade. As long as I'm playing and I'm visible, it's certainly not detrimental to people who want to come out.'

Real Lives was broadcast at the same time as the beating of Hull KR by Hull FC, 36–12 on Sky, to confirm Super League's fourth middle-eight spot. The Hull derby also ensured there would no conflict of interest for Wakefield-bound JK. Other dubious scenarios were still in the offing, however, Featherstone on course to face dual-reg partners Leeds with a host of Rhinos players, for example.

On Friday, a funeral service for Jo Cox took the headlines, the public applauding and tossing flowers as the hearse went through Batley and Heckmondwike on its final journey, mourners carrying white roses. Posters read: 'Far more unites us than divides us' and 'Today I pledge to #LoveLikeJo. I will'. It was a respectful and low-key occasion, after which the Cox family was left to grieve in private and await an Old Bailey court case in November that culminated in a whole-life guilty sentence for Jo's cowardly murderer.

The training schedule had again been kept light. Midweek wasn't pleasant. Home truths were spoken. By Friday, though, the mood had lightened, a whiff of bacon sandwiches in the air in a show of gratitude for War Chest members. One hundred and ninety of them in total, though by no means all were present, the project exceeding its target comfortably and surpassing all original expectations. One man, Heinz Adler, had travelled from Switzerland for the London game and another, Will Linley, donated £100 won in the War Chest draw to its man of the match. The players and coaching staff were to attend, but first there was a team meeting and drills to get through.

There was another new face too, BARLA Player of the Year Mikey Hayward on trial until the end of the season. A full-back with amateur side Castleford Lock Lane, he impressed in his first session on Wednesday. Hope of bringing in Sam Smeaton, Halifax's outside-back currently on loan at York, seemed to have stalled. Another new arrival was Rowey's third son, born fit and healthy on Tuesday.

On the team-sheet, Cain was dropped, Patch taking over at stand-off. Shaun Squires would return at centre with Joe Chandler out of the side too, despite playing well in an unfamiliar position. The line-up: Scott; Reittie, Squires, Ulugia, Ainscough; Walker, Brambani; Hirst, Leak, Rowe, Day, Bretherton, Gledhill. Replacements: Davey, Lillycrop, J. Brown, Harrison. Three non-playing subs: Southernwood, Chandler and Alex Brown as eighteenth, nineteenth and twentieth men. New NRL signing Jamie Soward would make a second debut for the Broncos: 'Poor defender but a fucking good player with the ball,' according to JK. They will be challenged in the middles. 'If they bust us, we can't be as lazy as we were against Featherstone. I don't want us bullied again. They get excited in broken field. They are a very confident team at the minute, so expect anything. Play as a team, play us shapes and execute well. Let the occasion inspire you.'

Director John Miller, rushing around on a hot and humid July after-noon, greets 'Pie Man' Steve. *Nice day for it.* 'Be better at quarter to five with a win under us belt,' says Steve. 'I've been up since seven this morning.' John can raise him a few hours on that. Half past four.

What the Mount lacks in numbers it makes up for in tension, although a Broncos fan doing a Bernie Clifton on horseback in the Family Stand seems relaxed enough and there have been smaller crowds for London visits. Scott Leatherbarrow, a non-player today, is back among friends he left at the end of last season. A film crew from the BBC's *Songs of Praise* targets 84-year-old Jim McVeigh, last seen at the Breakfast Club and today manning the car park. Jim's son is a sponsor and brother Peter played for the Gallant Youths in the 1960s. It's via *Songs of Praise* that Jim, a Batley life member, will go

325

to Wembley this year, part of a choir of supporters from thirty-two clubs singing 'Abide With Me' at the Challenge Cup final. When not watching his beloved Batley – as he has done since the age of two – he entertains patients at Dewsbury District Hospital in the choir he helped to establish following a spell there with pneumonia.

Referee Jack Smith is here again and at the coin toss there is more bad news for the Bulldogs. Keegan loses the call and his side must start downhill, as they did against Featherstone. An ominous sign and the foreboding ratchets up further with the incremental riff of Led Zeppelin's 'Kashmir' blasting from the PA. Still, when Patch kicks off and London knock on in front of their own posts, hopes lift. In the dugout, Cropper yells, 'Yes!' as Tuna burrows his way over, but Smith signals 'held up'. Then Keegan is hauled down short on the last tackle.

Batley have at least begun with urgency, fighting on the floor, winning penalties, testing London's D. Keegan thinks he is in but the decision is again 'held up', before the ball is torn from Breth's grasp as he goes for the line. Soward's first contribution is a high kick to the corner that Ainy does well to take. Even when Batley concede their first penalty and GLDO, Ainy maintains his composure and the threat is defused.

Up front, Rowey leads the line bravely and takes several clouts to his head for the cause. Yet while Batley dominate possession, the opening quarter remains scoreless. Playing downhill, that must be a concern, especially when London claim the first try. It comes on the back of a Soward break that ought to have been finished off; the final pass knocked forward line begging. Soon after, from a ten-metre scrum, a Soward bomb has better luck. No one takes it at the first attempt, it bounces awkwardly and Elliot Kear – no relation – touches down, much to the annoyance of chairman Kevin Nicholas, who, watching from the boardroom window as he sorts out the raffle, throws the tickets in the air like confetti and rushes down to admonish a touch judge who has missed a knock-on. Soward fluffs the conversion and not long afterwards Brownie has the ball stripped at the other end.

'Keep going,' signals JK, not bothering with the two points. But the tap comes to nothing.

Although behind on the scoreboard, the Bulldogs continue to dominate play and a sustained spell of pressure before the half hour finally sees the home side in. After Reitts almost gets over, Brownie, injecting power from the bench, has the ball stripped again. The free play fizzles out and there is a twenty-metre scrum. After which another Patch kick hits a London boot and it's back to one. Batley go direct until, repulsed, they spin it left. Dom's long pass to Patch is shipped out to Uce and he feeds Ainy, who tears over on the corner, links in a chain. Patch can't add the conversion but the scores are level at 4–4.

Downhill, that might not be much of a return if not for the fact that the Bulldogs' completion rate is high, sapping juice from the opposition. It's hot enough to roast potatoes, the muddied entry to the field at the top of the tunnel baked with fag ends and stud-marks, London desperate for half-time. But better for Batley is to come. When Scotty is forced back over the line for a GLDO, Squiresy does well to regain possession from the kick. And at the other end, with six minutes to go, he puts his 6 ft 7 in. frame to even better use by climbing high to take Dom's cross-field kick. Patch's conversion hits the post on its way over for additional cheer. Maybe the rugby gods are with Batley after all. A minute before the break, the cushion is feathered further when Ainy takes a cross-kick from Dom in the opposite corner that, this time, Patch cannot convert – 14–4 it is.

Bursting into the changing room the players chat excitedly – the most talk there has been in a while. JK wanders around them individually, looks into each face and asks, 'Okay?' 'Okay?' 'Okay?' All of them nod, glad of a breather but eager to get back out there. Tuna sits silently on the floor, legs stretched before him at the end of one dividing wall, Chris Ulugia positioned likewise opposite. Keegan prowls the room, patrolling the space. Tenterhooks.

Dom: 'Boys. We know what we do now, don't we? We just catch, go boom, boom, boom, kick, chase the fucker and defend the set. That's what we do when we go uphill, don't we? And do it right.'

Keegan: 'Let's be really tight, because they are looking . . . let's plug, yeah? We've got to have line speed up this hill. They are a big set, aren't they?'

Brownie: 'Let's play it quick. They are short of petrol . . .'

'You've said it all,' JK interjects as Brownie retches phlegm in a toilet. 'We had twenty sets. Them? Fourteen. That's why they were fucking about coming up for the restart. They couldn't wait to get in, get some oxygen in the lungs, readdress and get the hill. We like what we face now, though, don't we? We like what we face.'

All they have to do, JK says, is kick and complete, just as Dom had suggested. 'But we fight aggressive, find your front, kick long, chase hard. At some stage, though, guys, your online D will be tested. It needs to be outstanding. It's absolutely in our hands. Look after the pill; keep charging up. They can have the fucking hill. Look after the ball, keep challenging them with carries and we'll be okay. But we've got to keep working. Don't think it'll just fucking happen. You've got to work harder than you've ever worked before. Happy to do that?' *Yes*, they echo as one. *We are.*

'It's the biggest test of our season this forty minutes,' says Dom.

'Okay, let's not talk it to death now,' says Keegan, calling for the huddle. 'On our toes – we do not let them roll us. Winners on three . . .'

London resume with a towering bomb that might have been dropped last week, but which this week Dom takes clean. And the set ends with a lovely kick that camps London in their ten-metre zone. But then Patch rips the ball as the Broncos reach halfway and from the penalty the first attack of the half leads to its first try. London go in at the corner as Batley's right-edge again backs off alarmingly. Soward's conversion is wide but the lead is one converted score.

It looks like being a long forty minutes as the Bulldogs' grip loosens. James Cunningham, their tormentor in Ealing, is on the field, Andy

Ackers causes problems and strong running out wide is giving the home defence and spectators palpitations. But when Brownie forces a knock-on on halfway, Batley are suddenly back in London's half, energized, where Dom's kick to the corner and a happy bounce allows Reitts to score a try that Patch converts: 20–8. Three minutes later, after the Broncos kick the restart out on the full, a short-side shift from the resulting penalty sees Dom twice jink back inside for a fine solo effort. That goal is missed but it's 24–8 with half an hour to go. The shift play was Brownie's idea; they'd stayed behind to practise it on Friday.

It must be doubtful that time has ever passed so leisurely, slower even than it had done in Whitehaven. Patch forces a GLDO but to no gain. Brownie goes off for a rest and then London score again. With the slope in their favour they are a dangerous side in open play. Livewire Soward converts and it is 24–14 entering the final quarter.

After his Featherstone nightmare, Dave Scott is 'reeling them in like an angler pond fishing', as his coach will later put it, directly into the glare of the sun. James Harrison jogs on from the bench and performs manfully, confirmed as a fine prospect. And when 'free-scoring Adam Gledhill' shows good feet and reaches over, all sing 'Hallelujah'. Let the songs of praise begin. Patch's extras make it 30–14 – they won't blow this now, will they? Yet when Batley nod off three minutes later, it seems they very well might. Awarded a penalty on his thirty-metre line, Soward taps and goes while the Bulldogs wander back to position or stand hands on hips, awaiting a controlled restart. Nothing lies before the scrum-capped wizard but open field, yet Scotty does just enough to delay him before a scrambling Uce hammers a support runner off the ball. Was it a shoulder charge – an illegal challenge nowadays? Uce is flat out for a while and receives treatment, the ref standing over him: sinbin or red card? Neither it turns out. A penalty. But despite determined goal-line D, London do power over belatedly through American international Mark Offerdahl. Soward converts: 30–20.

Keegan's return on seventy-one minutes lifts his side, but there are more nervy moments when Tuna knocks on in dangerous terrain. Batley, tackling with fury now, appear to be hanging on, though with a more comfortable margin than an audience with so much invested dares to accept. Rationally, the outcome is certain by the time Dom adds a 79th-minute drop-goal, but that doesn't stop everyone with cerise and fawn affiliation twitching along with each stretch of arm and jerk of a leg. In the dugout, Breth, who has spent the last ten minutes making every tackle in his seat and feeling every hit, can finally unleash those dimples. 'That's the game,' he grins as the scoreboard reads 31–20.

'You fucking beauty!' roars Brownie, the changing-room door again rocked on its hinges, hugs all round, smiles broad, the laying on of hands. 'Yes, Patch! Yes, Tuna! Whooooooo! One to go, boys! One to go!' Batley have now taken points off all four of the Championship's full-time teams – a draw with Bradford, a victory apiece over Leigh and London, and the double over Sheffield Eagles.

'Have a seat, guys,' says JK, fingers jumping but endgame in mind. Against Featherstone, they looked as if they couldn't handle the pressure. 'This week, we looked as if we relished it. That was fucking outstanding, fellas. Enjoy the victory but – I know I'm a boring fucker – we've got one more to go. Swinton is the most important game for this club in God knows how many years. We've got to come through.' JK points out that it's the six-year anniversary of the Northern Rail Cup final win, 'but next week we will go one fucking better. We are going to go over there and get into that top four . . .'

Doggies . . . Doggies . . . Doggies . . . Doggies . . . and DJ Brownz discovers that dustbin lids are satisfyingly noisy instruments of percussion.

The win moves Batley up to third, as Featherstone have beaten Halifax, 24–20, in a thriller at the Shay. Bradford, as expected, see off Oldham at home, to set up what will effectively be a sudden-death shoot-out between Bulls and Rovers for fourth, at the Big Fellas. Assuming it isn't drawn, Batley may even be able to afford to lose at Swinton if

Fax, now sixth, fall at home to London. A win will render all that irrelevant. Even a draw with the Lions would be sufficient. A remarkable season will go down to the wire, in true doggy style.

'We won't take Swinton for granted,' Kear tells the press. 'It's going to be tough. They came here and had an eight-point victory and were full value for it. But all we wanted was to go into the last game with it in our hands. It's up to you then. We'll prepare accordingly.'

Fortunately for the playing squad, Total Fitness was the venue on Tuesday once the team meeting was out of the way, at which Sam Smeaton appeared after all, signed just before the deadline on the hottest day of the year. His loan club York, it was reported, was in trouble and might not finish the season. Halifax approved and here he was. He couldn't play until the papers went through but would be available after that.

The London clips were pleasing. For Ainy's try, five London players were around the ruck, so throwing the ball wide was smart. Ditto with Squiresy's effort: 'When you've got a 6 ft 7 in. bloke out there, it's a good idea to kick to him,' said JK. It could be argued that when a team does a lot of kicking out wide, it is a good idea to have a 6 ft 7 in. bloke out there, but that suggestion later gets short shrift. 'What about the other five plays? It's not American Football. Do we send him on for special teams?' At one point, Leaky makes four tackles on the bounce from marker, summing up the effort in defence. Fighting on the floor for penalties – they had taken on board his criticisms of the previous week: 'We got to that middle channel and ripped in.' Do it again, he'd told them. Do it again. 'It's a cup final this, guys. All of you here, you can make history. You win on Sunday and you will be the best team this club has had since the early 1900s – that's over a hundred fucking years. It's a big thing, fellas.'

Thursday's clips made for more painful viewing – the home defeat to Swinton. JK was wary of them freezing, as they had against Featherstone, but could not risk complacency. The mindset, he said should be: 'If we win, we are third; if we draw, we are fourth; if we lose, we are out.' They should anticipate Halifax beating London. 'I do not want us going there thinking it's a done deal. Two Championship sides have beaten us here – Featherstone and Swinton – and it wasn't a fucking fluke. They are a good footballing team, capable of beating anybody. But we are better. Everybody plays their A game we'll beat them, believe you me. If we think we are there already, they'll get us.'

Swinton, lest they forget, went 18–0 ahead playing uphill, while Batley were defensively passive, lacked urgency, sloppy with ball in hand. 'I don't want to put you on a downer; you should be confident after that London game. But they can play. We have got to have our heads right, we really have. You've got history in the palm of your hands. It won't be given to us; we've got to take it.'

Come the weekend, Batley's backroom situation clarifies. Carl has met Matt Diskin and now thinks he will stay, though how a time-heavy ordered schedule – 5 to 9 p.m. on Monday, Wednesday and Friday – can be reconciled with his home life is unclear. Diskin's coaching partner at Odsal, Lee St Hilaire, will come too; Linners is out. Mokko will remain as per his part-time ad hoc arrangement; Mauny will be expected to focus on the commercial aspect primarily.

Saturday-morning training went much better after a Thursday-night session the coach labelled 'shit'. The worrisome right-edge was once again chief culprit – 'The ball's the danger, gents, the ball's the danger. Let's not fuck about, fellas, let's do what we ask you to do' – while Breth was forced from the field with a cut above the eye, sustained in a head clash with Leaky. Doc Findlay came to stitch the gash. Dom too was forced to sit things out, feeling a twinge in the tendon behind his right knee that Ally strapped up. 'It's just letting you know,' said Carl. 'Rest it.'

Yesterday, though, things had been brighter. Dom, up and running again, had worked with the right-edge to JK's satisfaction, the players voluntarily in for extra training. On a humid and hazy morning, the squad then marched in to the meeting dripping with sweat, Reitts fanning his face with a tip sheet. The coach left nothing to chance, the clips a double-bill of Swinton's most recent defeats. Every member of the squad sat rapt under the spell of a screen in a darkened room, Kear's preparations meticulous; each illustration judged to make explicit the point. Sermon preached, every man knew exactly what was expected of him and was inspired to go out and achieve it. At which point he warned, 'We are desperate, but we don't let our emotions run away with us.'

Swinton play in Greater Manchester, at Heywood Road, home to rugby union side Sale. Nowadays, the Sharks' first team ground-shares with Super League's Salford Red Devils at the AJ Bell Stadium, near the Trafford Centre, having moved from Stockport's Edgeley Park in 2012. Swinton, forced to depart their most recent venue in Whitefield (Park Lane, aka Sedgley Park) – on winning promotion last year, played home games at the AJ Bell themselves and in Widnes at the start of this season, the Lions another club who, since leaving famous old Station Road – and therefore the town of Swinton itself – in 1992, have put the 'no 'ome' into rugby league nomad. Gigg Lane, Bury, was the club's base camp until 2002, after which they went to Moor Lane, Salford, had an initial spell in Whitefield and shared Salford's first home, the Willows, deep in *Coronation Street* country, in 2011. They then did likewise at Leigh, went back to Park Lane and signed a deal to spend the rest of this current year at Heywood Road in March. Sale Jets, Sharks' junior side, are still resident here, though, necessitating training in – guess where – Salford, nine miles away.

Confused? Think of the poor supporters and a lost generation of potential fans. Little wonder crowds these days tend to be sparse, so coachfuls of noisy and excited Batley fans swelling the crowd to 1,147 are a welcome sight. And better days do appear to be on the horizon, the holy grail of a return to Swinton within tantalizing reach. A lease on a 7.3-acre site at Agecroft – inside the town's traditional boundaries – has been signed by the club, with plans to construct a new community stadium within three years there recently agreed.

Typically, JK's summation of the place is more succinct: 'It's a fucking big pitch, I'll tell you.' And so it is, a worry given that the Bulldogs thrive on close games and can come unstuck when teams get the ball in their hand with the time and space to chuck it around.

Throughout this Championship campaign, Batley's margins of victory have on the whole been slender, their off-season call to turn narrow defeats into narrow wins realized. Opponents have been kept close, worn down, set by set, before the killer blow applied. Amongst everything else, Batley are the only side to beat runaway League leaders Leigh all year – the Centurions' title confirmed with a thumping 58–0 win over Dewsbury today. That special opening-day victory at Mount Pleasant by two points set a pattern. Of seven defeats, only two might be deemed heavy – in London and at home to Featherstone with three games to go, though the sixteen-point loss at Oldham was a huge disappointment. The other four – by eight points, seven, two and one – could have gone either way.

And of the victories, only a couple approached blow-out status, the 24- and 32-point home wins over Oldham and Workington, with the Halifax 32–16 result next highest. Otherwise, history showed eight wins by fewer than ten points, three under fifteen points and a draw. Which made what came next all the more unexpected.

It must be a big game: the club has hired a luxury bus, a double-decker job that according to its driver, as hirsute as he is eccentric, once belonged to Glasgow Rangers. 'The road to Super League starts here,' says Kev, dapper as ever in club shirt and tie.

The team is unchanged from last week – Cain unable to regain a place – and Gleds is the first player aboard. 'Bit nervous,' he tells Mauny, and he's not alone. Halifax are rumoured to have had a whip-round to reward Swinton's players if they beat them. As in the sheds, players and coaching staff deal with pre-match anxiety differently. Squiresy took his dog for a walk. John Heaton shaved off his beard. Reitts climbs aboard with his beatbox for the journey back and the last three players, Rowey, Brownie and Tuna, arrive just a minute before departure. Ainy, the sole Lancastrian not counting Breth, goes straight there.

'Where do I know him from?' says the driver when Keegan climbs aboard, in an accent pure London yet with requisite northern glottal stop. 'Oh, I know! Off t' telly!' He further endears himself to a bridling JK by making an announcement re toilets, plug sockets and so on before departure, adding that they had better win or they will be walking home. Game heads must be handled with care.

The trip over the tops passes without incident but on arrival the vehicle is too big to access a part of the ground that lies at the end of a short cobbled street. The kit and equipment must be carted manually past a row of terraced red-bricked houses, bags carried, wheelie bins pulled. Through the turnstiles, the Steve Smith Bar and a stand run along one side, opposite a covered terrace shed in which the away supporters will congregate. A small car park is at the far open end, a large white building housing changing rooms, a gym and much else closest to hand.

The sun shines, though Batley's arrival coincides with the first of a couple of heavy showers. 'What a warm-up that was, not one ball down,' says Brownie, when the players come back into the cramped and stifling sheds and ask for dry towels, as the knock on the door looms. Great technique, Ainy agrees.

'Right, guys, I don't need to tell you what's on the line,' says JK. 'We achieve what we want to achieve by every fucker doing his job and doing it efficiently. I don't want us to start nervy – start early with aggression. Lay a marker down. If you're in an uncomfortable position, put it to one side and get back into play, because the team's the most important thing today. We handle it, then we can come back in here and have what we've achieved. Shake each other's hands. You can look each other in the eye and say well done for this season. But we only get to do that by going at it from minute one. Start strong. Start confident. Be good. Be aggressive. Work hard.'

'Eighty minutes' hard work, boys,' says Dom, veins twitching in his neck, seized by sacred vision. 'Leave nothing out there.'

Swinton score first. Winger Shaun Robinson goes in at the corner and Chris Atkin's touchline conversion makes it 6–0 in as many minutes, silencing the vocal Batley contingent. There then comes another sticky moment under a high kick, but the home side knocks on and the chance for a double-whammy is gone. It is one of those fixtures with which modern sports fans have become familiar: eyes on the field, smartphones trained elsewhere. Far too early to check on outcomes in Halifax and to a lesser extent Featherstone, but JK's fingers aren't the only body parts twitching – so much for a fast start.

Thankfully, Rowey is on hand to take one for the team – the first of many headshots that wins a penalty on halfway. Batley run it and the set ends with Leaky burrowing over from dummy-half, Patch converting to level the scores, and the day-trippers of Batley, who will henceforth act as eighteenth man, again find their voice. Six minutes later it's 6–16, two more high shots on Rowey and Gleds helping the Bulldogs up the field, where Tuna's half-break is shipped on to Patch and scorer Uce. Reitts then collects Dom's pinpoint kick wide after more punishing work from Leaky and Keegan in the build-up, as the middles start to dominate and Swinton's pack is out-classed. The Lions receive a team warning when Rowey's dome again attracts attention and when Gleds is interfered with in the tackle, so to speak, the sinbin reduces the hosts temporarily to twelve. Penalty kicked, it's 6–18.

Hirst's first-half display has been tireless and when more good work gives Dom the space to attempt an enormous 40/20, the ball doesn't quite reach touch but Reittie races up the line and somehow forces a GLDO. The Bulldogs are hungry. A high shot on Uce this time brings another penalty that Batley run, the right call with Swinton on the ropes, and Leaky is in for a fourth try that Patch converts. *Leaky, Leaky . . .* the travelling fans sing. Or is it: *Easy, easy . . . ?*

Phones may now be checked. Surprisingly, Featherstone lead Bradford 10–0, while Halifax and London share six points apiece.

Batley begin to get messy, their goal-line D put to the test. Having completed fourteen out of fourteen sets and scored twenty-four points in the opening quarter, in the second their rate is one in nine, which risks re-opening the gate for the Lions. It is a nervy spell but, six minutes before the break, Squiresy leaps high and extends his telescopic arms to take Dom's lofted kick and touch down for what ought to be a half-time lead of 30–6 to the Doggies. That it is not can't be blamed on Breth, working as hard as he has all year. The forward belies his age to save a certain try when Swinton find touch from the restart, a wonder-tackle in the corner, but there is still time for the hosts to capitalize when Batley cough up possession. The half ends 12–30, full-back Scotty held up between the posts.

Back in West Yorkshire, meanwhile, Fev reach half-time 18–0 ahead against Bradford; are the Bulls about to miss out on the Qualifiers? More pertinently from Batley's perspective, Halifax trail London 16–6, though no one in a packed and steamy changing room is aware of any of that.

The players are followed up the tunnel by the distant echo of their supporters' singing. Calm now, the usual excitable chitchat is absent, the mood studied and intense. Keegan says that when they are tight is when they are in control. Try little unpractised tricks and that's when Swinton start throwing shapes. 'Let's be happy to complete. To kick down there; play in their half.' Tuna, rarely one to speak at half-time, reminds them that, at Blackpool, Oldham battered Swinton 20–0 in the first half but Swinton came back 24–25. They can't switch off.

When the moment comes for JK to hold forth, he does so with his usual urgency and passion. 'Gents, we've to be smart, haven't we? We don't have to win the game twice; we need to get back to what we were doing. Let's be fucking smart. Carry aggressively. Push. But for fuck's sake, let's look after the ball. Once we are at the end of sets, we are controlling the game. That's the biggest thing we can learn.'

As for penalties: 'It's 7–2 to us. Well done, middle channel, you've fucking ripped in. But at some stage he's going to give them a few, isn't he? So we've to dig deep and be smart with regard to that too. Breth, that effort was brilliant. But I want that effort from every fucker. Let's ensure our standards remain high. We don't get fucking sloppy. Forget the fucking scoreboard. Forget the time on the clock. Play the game of rugby league. Keep getting to that middle channel.

Carry aggressively. Get to the end of the set. Kick. Chase like fucking Reitts did to get the double-deal, then defend tough. They will go, believe you me. They will go. They looked fucking tired when we did them completions, then all of a sudden we give them the ball and they get some energy. It's in our hands now, guys, isn't it? Big style.'

It only takes a minute to get the scoreboard moving again. Swinton drop the ball, Ainy twice hacks upfield, his second kick collected by scorer Uce Ulugia, and Patch converts. Take that. When Brownie is bundled into touch, the Lions lose possession, Keegan regains it and Tuna crashes over. Having fun now, the Bulldogs don't care what other teams are up to. Patch makes it 12–42.

There's a kerfuffle when Scotty pads the ball dead, his foot over the line, which the ref interprets as a GLDO; the ball stopped moving, he says. But a minute later, when the Scotsman makes amends by bringing the ball clear brilliantly as the defence again holds, Brownie romps in after Cropper softens Swinton up on their own line. 'This is not acceptable from our group,' says a member of Swinton's coaching staff in the huddle behind the sticks. As the game – and regular season – moves into its final quarter, Batley are ahead 46–12, Featherstone leading Bradford 18–0. London had the better of Halifax 22–6, but with fifteen minutes left Fax level it, 22–22, so Batley can't quite celebrate yet. And in fact Swinton score next, minutes after Squiresy puts in a try-saver almost on a par with Breth's. The conversion goes over but surely 18–46, a gap of twenty-eight points, will be enough whatever Halifax do?

It certainly looks that way when Swinton have a second player yellow-carded. And as London go back in front 22–28, word by now presumably reaching the field, the Bulldogs cut loose. First Ainy is on the end of Patch's dabbed kick, the latter's goal taking Batley's score past the half century for the first time this season, before the Wiganer picks up a dropped ball, sidesteps and goes in again, after the Lions find a gap among Batley's middles themselves. It's almost party time.

Fittingly, Keegs goes on for the last five minutes, though doesn't quite make the impact he'd like, the ball bouncing off his chest after Squiresy fields a short restart. But when a Swinton pass hits the deck, Batley feed a twenty-metre scrum. From Uce's break, Ainy almost completes a hat-trick, but Dom nips in for a deserved four-pointer, Patch adding the conversion after the hooter. The biggest win of the regular season in its very last game, eleven tries, nine goals: 62–24.

As the ball sails over, the Batley contingent erupts – fans, players, coaching staff, directors, family members and anyone else in cerise and fawn. Squad members rush on to the field. Photographs are taken that old men and women will gaze at, rheumy-eyed, in their dotage. In the here and now, though, satisfaction and relief eclipse ecstasy. In the days to come, stories will be written of an astonishing achievement on low resources, of part-timers doing it tough, all true enough. John Kear's already outstanding CV will carry another line – on balance his most impressive rugby league achievement of all.

Batley Bulldogs – Batley's *under*dogs – have bitten received wisdom in the arse. Living pay-cheque to pay-cheque in a sporting environment where money talks loudest, they have succeeded when they ought not to have been able to do so, and all of it without placing a precious 136-year-old community club at financial risk or breaking the bank . . . *woof, woof, woof, woof* . . . *hooowl!*

Featherstone leapfrog Bradford into fourth place – a financial boost for a club that needs one and a calamity for the once mighty Bulls, whose future is now cast in doubt. There are those who will go on questioning the sanity of the Super 8s system, convoluted as it is. Such critics, though, will hereafter be harder to find in Batley.

Doggies . . . Doggies . . . Doggies . . . Doggies . . .

The players are eventually persuaded off the field having performed a rousing rendition of the song for their travelling supporters, and in the tunnel one Swinton forward disgraces himself with a bitter tirade, dragged away by his embarrassed teammates and coaches. 'Bulldogs!' yells Brownie, as the door slams shut on that scene, before joining in with the loudest rendition of the song yet, doubtless heard in Halifax. And for once there is no need for JK to utter a word.

Believe what you see because we're not a fucking dream . . .

Prior to departure, the bar is packed with happy Batley folk, among them one former coach. 'It's not as good as the Northern Rail Cup win,' says big Karl Harrison. 'Never let it be forgot that I changed the culture at this club,' followed by a deadpan wink.

'Hey, Chris,' JK tells Uce Ulugia, as the bus driver agrees to let them back aboard. 'You should have stayed at Bradford. You could have come fifth.' Harrison's son James has a little smile to himself, too, given that the Bulls are the club who let him go. There are congratulations from celebrity fan Antony Cotton, who strolls jauntily up the Mancunian cobbles to the manor born, before heading off back to Weatherfield. Bottles of Kingstone Press cider take a hammering, Reitts' beatbox coming into its own.

Back at the Mount, Ron's Lounge is heaving and breaks into spontaneous applause as first the players and then JK enter a room where, eight months ago, he'd told them, 'We've got a great chance of kicking on and looking at the top six, if not frightening one or two in the top four.' An emotional Kevin Nicholas pats the wooden chest on the bar having promised '10p off a pint for every player!'

And as is the case every second, minute, hour and day of every week, month and year at the Fox's Biscuits Stadium, a little copper plate attached to a window ledge that, with shutters up, looks out upon a sloping field from a single unoccupied seat reads: 'Reserved for Ron Earnshaw. Our President.'

Regular season final Championship table – 24 July 2016

1	Leigh	23	21	1	1	881	410	43
2	London	23	17	0	6	702	444	34
3	Batley	23	15	1	7	589	485	31
4	Featherstone	23	15	0	8	595	384	30
5	Bradford	23	13	2	8	717	446	28
6	Halifax	23	13	1	9	615	484	27
7	Sheffield	23	8	0	15	583	617	16
8	Dewsbury	23	8	0	15	486	603	16
9	Swinton	23	7	1	15	449	813	15
10	Oldham	23	7	0	16	401	678	14
11	Workington (R)	23	5	1	17	455	756	11
12	Whitehaven (R)	23	5	1	17	367	720	11

Time Added On

I mean you have a gift for football. It raises you above the general level, don't you think?
     – *This Sporting Life*, David Storey, 1960

18

AND NOW FOR something completely different . . .

During episode eleven of *Monty Python's Flying Circus*, first broadcast in 1969, among such sketches as 'Dead Parrot', 'Nudge Nudge' and 'The Lumberjack Song', the Batley Townswomen's Guild staged a re-enactment of Pearl Harbor.

(*Cut to a muddy corner of a field . . .*)

'Well, we've always been extremely interested in modern drama,' the battle's director, Mrs Rita Fairbanks (Eric Idle) says to camera. 'We were of course the first Townswomen's Guild to perform *Camp on Blood Island*, and last year we did our extremely popular re-enactment of "Nazi War Atrocities". So this year we thought we'd like to do something in a lighter vein . . .'

(*A whistle blows and the two sides set about each other with handbags, speeded up 50 per cent just to give it a bit of edge . . .*)

And in episode twenty-two, during *Python*'s second series, the ladies were back, this time rolling around while re-enacting the first heart transplant, with Rita's sister Madge playing 'plucky little springbok pioneer Christiaan Barnard'.

In August 2016, meanwhile, with Huddersfield almost fifty points up at half-time of game three in what was proving to be a disastrous and embarrassing Super 8s campaign, the Townswomen's Guild pepper-pots may well have put up more of a fight.

*

It began with such optimism, though anxiety too. Reaching the Super League Qualifiers was historic, said Kev Nicholas, no doubt whatsoever about that. Part-timers against full-timers, or even part-timers against other part-timers who'd spent shedloads; Halifax, for example, began 2016 with a reported £800,000 banked.

Reaching the top four brought unprecedented media attention; even the national papers took notice. Imagine that. And it wasn't just Keegan they wanted to interview. Some of his teammates were getting a look-in too – Batley's high-achieving labourers, plumbers, joiners and rat-catcher, as at least one tabloid called the Bulldogs. With luck, the club's growing profile would spin off into bigger attendances and a resurgence of interest in the town itself. 'The following at Swinton was magnificent,' said the chairman. 'You just hope a few decided they can come more often.'

As for the financial benefits, they would be considerable, although the exact amount coming the Bulldogs' way was still to be settled, dependent upon where they now finished. Eighth would mean a payday of £450,000, compared to the £150,000 received this year, some of which, said Kev, would go to the players 'as a reward for their achievements'. Seventh would net half a million. In sixth, the figure would rise to £700,000. Above that and – assuming they weren't promoted automatically in the top three – the Million Pound Game awaited fourth and fifth, the losers getting £750,000, the winners promoted to an elite where a minimum £1.85 million had this year been available, with add-ons for international players, academy products and the like; Leeds, for example, bringing in around £2.1 million, or so it was reckoned.

The higher up Batley finished, the more the players stood to gain individually, although there too the amount of bonus was yet to be settled. 'I've put a proposal to them that hasn't been finalized. If the club benefits financially, I don't see why they shouldn't in some way.'

The players had been on a bonus at Swinton, rolled over from the one they hadn't earned against Featherstone. No bonus had been offered against London, as there would have been no point in beating London if they then went and lost at Swinton. Anyway, Kev wasn't sure about their influence. 'Players like them after the event, of course, but they were on a bonus against Featherstone and underachieved. They weren't on a bonus against London and over-achieved.'

As that rare thing in modern sport, a club without great debt, Batley under Nicholas attempt to balance the books as best they can annually, as the AGM confirmed. This year, there would be a surplus: 'it's just a matter of how we decide to spend it to improve the club'. Some of it seemed destined to go on the stadium, though whether that would be a significant amount or if the board would look at other things too had not yet been decided.

In any case, the money wouldn't arrive until January and only then in twelve monthly payments. 'It's not as though we are flooded with cash now. We've plenty of time to plan and have already planned for next year in many ways because most of our players are signed on. In itself, even before we got top four that is totally different for us. In the past when we've had good teams, some players have been picked off and we've had to start again. When we came third in 2011 and Karl Harrison left, we lost about five players, as we did when we were in the Grand Final.' One regularly voiced criticism of the middle eight is that it makes forward planning difficult, as no one knows the budget for the following year in advance. Perhaps Batley were emerging as the antidote.

There was, though, a potentially huge dilemma ahead, as voiced by Derek, the club chaplain, in the boardroom weeks before. Admittedly remote, it was the possibility that Batley would indeed gain promotion and be forced to deal with that, perhaps changing the club irrevocably. Contemplating the scenario, Kevin was guarded. After all, if you run a rugby club in a professional sport, it doesn't do to peddle common-sense practicality to supporters who demand glory and ambition.

'If we do over-achieve again and get in the Million Pound Game, we've then got a load of players signed on part-time contracts for the next two years, haven't we?' His preferred option was to remain part-time in the higher division. 'We'd have to have a think about it. I don't see how they could stop you. I don't know how we'd approach it, really. There would be hurdles to get over, that's for sure.'

Also a certainty was that he would instigate talks with the Rugby Football League and, he was keen to stress, the players. 'Batley is a bit different. I'm not saying we are the model other clubs should follow, but we do involve players in conversation because they are part of the club. In theory, the rules allow us to tear their part-time contracts up and go full-time – the same if you are promoted or relegated.' Kev didn't view that as honourable behaviour – it would get the club a bad reputation – and nor was it an argument for a franchise or licensing system. 'It's all right saying relegation is bad for full-time players as they'd lose their jobs and have mortgages to pay, I appreciate that. But that's just part and parcel of promotion and relegation in a full- and part-time game. The only way to solve that is with two full-time leagues.' Or two part-time leagues, a dispassionate onlooker might conclude, a more rational arrangement perhaps in a sport lacking enough large and self-sustaining clubs to fund such aspiration.

Still, in the asylum that is professional sport, when did common sense conquer hope and fervour? 'To be honest, I don't think we are quite ready yet, but we do want to build on this. With the stability we've now got with this team next year, we'll have a chance of getting into that middle eight again, won't we?'

Would the club invest in a reserve team, the better to retain the James Cravens and Zack McCombs of this world, Callum Casey having left now too? 'We'd like one, but it's got to be worthwhile. This year, what reserve set-up there has been was a joke – teams like Dewsbury pulled out for lack of fixtures. Only if there is a proper structure, or there's no point.' One possibility was JK's idea that dual-reg could work in reverse, junior partners' players getting a run in a Super League reserve team. In which case, Wakefield would be ideal. 'We'll see what can be resolved there.'

Finding ways to generate more income was another priority with, perhaps, Iro to have company on the full-time roster. For now the main thing was 'to enjoy the next two months and see how it pans out'.

Money issues, though, were not so easily to be put aside.

After Swinton, Mount Pleasant fell quiet. The only activity was the launch of the Super 8s at Old Trafford, host venue of the Super League Grand Final. Batley's representative was Keegan Hirst, the one Bulldog it seemed not on an overseas break. It was a low-key affair during which the fixtures across all three Super 8s groups – Super League, Qualifiers and Championship Shield – were displayed by PowerPoint, perfunctory rather than exciting, a waste of an impressive venue. And since those fixtures were already available online, a media presence whose numbers continue to shrink year on year took most interest in how long this latest 'new era' would last, especially if, as last year, no one won promotion. At least Keegan was as in demand as ever. Surveying the vista of the 'Theatre of Dreams', he remembered again the time he came to watch Bradford here as a boy.

A quarter of the campaign effectively remained to be played, though the impression at Batley was of the main target reached, mind and body relaxing accordingly. Jimmy Davey extended his contract to the end of 2018 and the remarkable Alex Bretherton – 'in great shape and enjoying my rugby' – agreed to stay for a further year: 'I want to send out a message that I will play for no other club.' Chris Ulugia would soon be on his way, though the hoped-for move to Wakefield was off. He signed a two-year deal at Featherstone instead. And come the weekend, with his teammates sipping their last Cuba Libres and no doubt trying to put an imminent Tuesday-night training session out of their minds, Keegan himself finally flew out to the sunshine island of Ibiza for a few days with Antony Cotton and friends.

After twenty-three gruelling games – without computing Challenge Cup ties and preseason friendlies – and coming down from a natural high of great achievement, returning to battle-mode on the back of nine days' rest and recuperation was always likely to be tough. Yet John Kear was determined his squad must do just that.

Three nights after Batley Variety Club finally shut its doors on

Saturday, 30 July – 'The Final Frontier' its one last party – the return to training was tough and physical: 'You'll get touched up and we'll see how your legs and lungs are from that.' No normal Tuesday this. No hydrotherapy pool at Total Fitness. JK called a meeting of the leadership group and coaching staff, including student rubbers Ally and James. 'Our best is yet to come,' he said, having fully digested a fixture list that, having kicked off at Hull KR, would roll on to London in week two, feature a pair of home matches with Huddersfield and Featherstone either side of another week off for the Challenge Cup final, and end with trips to Leeds and Leigh before a grand finale at home to Salford on Sunday, 25 September. Featherstone, JK reckoned, had relaxed, achieved all they wanted to do. Leigh had been aiming for this and had learned from a disappointing experience last year; London would take what comes. As for the four Super League sides: 'Shitting themselves, I'm telling you. Huge pressure.' If Batley kept doing what they had been doing, they could put the wobblers on them. 'We'll play the underdog card but need to make sure them fuckers downstairs don't think the season is over. This could be the most important part . . .' – 'them fuckers downstairs' being a term of endearment.

Having worked so hard for this, Rowey, Dom and Breth felt sure that everyone got the message: stick with the system that had brought them so far, no need to mess with it now. Brownie agreed but wanted to enjoy every match – visits to Headingley and Hull KR, big crowds at the Mount. Kear concurred but pointed out that the games they enjoyed most were against London and Swinton, when they played well and won. Hadn't enjoyed Featherstone so much, had they? 'Where we are strong is where the lower Super League teams are weakest,' he said. 'Down the middle.' There would be no pressure on Batley, just plenty on their opponents and they must exert it. 'It seems brutal to say it, but those players might lose their jobs. If that doesn't get your arse twitching, nothing will.'

Among the group, however, there was a glaring absence: Keegan. The captain should have been there but he had missed his flight home.

'I know we are mates and he is one of the lads,' said Rowey, 'but that's not acceptable. The boys need to see you deal with it fairly.' JK said he had already spoken to Keegs – who 'sounded like he'd had forty-eight pints' – on the phone and given him a bollocking. He would be fined and the coaching staff would discuss his place in the side ahead of the weekend trip to East Hull. Though he didn't say as much, it was just the sort of job-done-let's-relax attitude the coach was determined to avoid, all the more so since Keegan was the skipper.

The subject of player bonuses also remained to be dealt with, only days before the Qualifiers began. Again, Rowey put the players' case. This ought to have been sorted by now, he pointed out, aware that the issue had the potential to rock an otherwise steady ship. The players had earned the club a lot of money and felt they deserved a share in that good fortune. It had been mentioned that any bonuses from Super 8 games would go to the players who played in them but, given how these totals would be greater than usual, that wouldn't go down well with someone like the sidelined Luke Blake, for example, without whom they would likely not have made the top four at all. The primary problem seemed to be communication, not least because discussions on the subject had been between Keegan and Kevin, neither of whom were present.

When the club lacked a penny with which to scratch its arse, aside from the odd half-hearted grumble the players seemed happy with their lot. Now that was perceived as no longer the case, not so much. Kev's inclination to pull purse strings tight would need to be balanced with increased expectation from a squad for whom a share in the proceeds, aside from its practical purposes, symbolized proper appreciation of their effort and not being taken for a ride.

'No one loves money more than me,' said JK, promising to have a word with the chairman and set up a meeting that would, in fact, take place two nights later when Keegan too was back in the saddle.

Down the road at Odsal, the implications of missing out on the top four were being felt. A winding-up order had been issued at the Bulls, and owner Marc Green flew back from – somewhat ironically

– Ibiza on a fire-fighting exercise. Players and coaches had not been paid and CEO Steve Ferres resigned, general manager Robbie Hunter Paul destined to follow. The previous week, the RFL was forced to intercede to ensure that York completed the League 1 season; when the 2017 fixtures are revealed in October, the Minster city club will to begin with not be in them. Sheffield lost backers and were again in trouble, and Hemel Stags would soon announce that, after thirty-five years of existence, they would next year train 165 miles north in Dewsbury. With cracks widening in the very fabric of the sport, the importance of good housekeeping could hardly be starker.

'You have achieved a lot,' JK told his squad, in a briefer than usual team meeting before going down to the training field. 'But I was worried and have been assured that you won't now relax. I said to you at the start of the season that you didn't believe how good you were. Well, I think you're starting to believe it now. This is our fun time, guys, but you only have fun when you are prepared to put your balls on the line.' He showed them 2015's Qualifiers table, with Hull KR comfortably top on fourteen points after the seven-match campaign, Widnes and Salford in second and third on ten points each. In the Million Pound Game were Wakefield and Bradford, each on six points. Three victories ought to do it.

Training was indeed brutal. John Heaton arranged strenuous gym-style exercises on the pitch, but only after Mokko and Linners had patrolled up and down, throwing off stones and assorted rubble that children at a summer holiday rugby league camp had strewn everywhere.

Luke Blake took part, a good physical workout that in his case stopped short of full contact. As one of the few not to sign yet for next year, Blakey hadn't decided if he'd play at all, the idea always being to get a degree and play during the three years it took to attain it. When the Bradford injury hit, he'd just been awarded a 2:1 in construction management and was contemplating a Masters in design integration and building information modelling. Aged twenty-seven, there are things he and Katie would like to do while they have no children – live in America maybe. If he signs for anyone, 'It will be Batley.' Tuna too was thinking ahead, having begun a quantity-surveying apprenticeship in Leeds.

'We are getting flogged,' said Leaky, gulping like a landed salmon, as he completed part of a circuit dotted with weightlifting challenges, dumbbells, shot putt, push-ups, sprints and more besides. Brownie couldn't feel his fucking hamstrings. Mauny too joined in, doubled up after his first exercise in six weeks, a dripping jewel of snot and saliva hanging from his impeccably manicured chin. With ball in hand, the session had all the speed and intensity of a full-on game, JK twitching and making every tackle, head bobbing like a knobbly knee, the coach at least back in his element. Thursday training was equally ferocious, specially branded Super 8s balls now in use. *Hull KR will fight like fuck. Tight, guys, tight. Get tight! Run hard and hit with purpose.*

By then, Keegan had returned light of a third of a week's wages and been dropped for Joe Chandler in the opening game, both punishments taken with good grace. In the team meeting, though, there was money to discuss and JK ceded the floor to the chairman.

'If you are not happy with what I say, see Mauny,' said Kev with a half-hearted chuckle, back to the wall. The mood was awkward; Iro perched on a table alongside. Players should not be worse off, Kev, notes on knee, immediately conceded, than they would have been in the Championship Shield, where they would likely have won more games. 'So we have upped the amounts we initially arrived at. I don't know if people are going to be happy, but this is all we can get. Everyone is talking about us being millionaires now with a sudden cash cow, but it's not quite like that. All the players who've signed on for next year are better off as a result of reaching the middle eight. If anyone feels their contract has not made them better off, see me individually and I'll have a word with you about it. But I do feel that people have been rewarded with better finances next year, so that's the first point.'

What about those players who won't actually play in the Super 8s, yet who may have helped get them there? asked Rowey. In signing their contracts, some players agreed fixed amounts at the start, while others agreed to take a bit less but with a bonus worked in to reward finishing higher in the table. Rowey, it seemed, had opted for the first arrangement.

'We've tried to come up with something that is fair to the people who play most games,' said Kev, 'but is also fair to people who got us there and won't be playing in the majority because they are injured or haven't been picked or whatever. We don't want anyone losing out. Initially, we were going to give £500 for a win, £200 a loss, full stop. I do think we need to make some sort of provision but there is only a certain amount of money in the pot.'

One thing that had worked against them, said Kev, was failing to draw Leeds Rhinos at home, or to a lesser extent Hull KR. He pointed out that they could have made more money and got their hands on it quicker by finishing fourth. Featherstone host the Rhinos and Rovers and will therefore draw big away support to the Big Fellas. A real boost since home clubs in the Qualifiers keep their own gate receipts.

To some, such as Keegan, that suggestion was an affront, the implication being that the club would rather they had lost at Swinton and hoped for the best with regard to Halifax versus London. Not at all, said Kev, it was just the financial reality. 'That's not our problem, though, is it?' said Keegan. 'We've won the game as we were supposed to win and finished as high in the table as we could.'

Kev looked riled. His face, at the outset of an uncomfortable meeting not far off fawn, fast approached cerise. *Not our problem.* The comment narked him. 'Everyone wants more money in life,' he said, fighting to retain composure, 'but the truth is the truth, isn't it? I can't generate money that is not there, can I?' He reminded them that the money from the RFL wouldn't arrive until January and even then it would only be made in staged payments.

Rowey: 'I don't think anyone's arguing about that—'

Kev: 'Saying it's not my problem is arguing—'

Keegan: 'I don't think it is.' He pointed out – and Kev agreed –

that the first time they talked about match payments in this Super 8s period was on the bus back from Whitehaven. 'That's when it should have been sorted out, not now.'

Kev: 'I didn't feel comfortable talking about it then because we weren't there and I felt spooked. I didn't want to put the dampeners on it. But I accept that you did raise the issue, so that's a fair point. I don't see that the goalposts have been moved because we never said "you will get that" and now you won't. To say that not playing Leeds Rhinos is "our problem" is what's wound me up there, because it's a fact of life, isn't it? It is our problem that we haven't got five million pound in the bank, but that's where we are at, isn't it? The fact we get a 1,000 gate as opposed to a 5,000 gate – is that our problem? Probably it is, but we can't do anything about it, can we? We've got to live with what we've got. If we were playing Leeds Rhinos here, we'd be making a lot more money than if we were playing Salford: fact. It's just the way it's worked out.'

Brownie: 'Well, yes, but that's not our fault either, is it?'

John Heaton, set to confirm that he too would be staying as club conditioner in 2017, interjected. They were going around in circles without knowing exactly what was available. 'Let's hear the offer before we start arguing with it. Listen to what he's got to say.'

Kev had two proposals, both at great cost to the club, he said. Proposal one: for a win against a Super League club, £500; for a win against a Championship club, £400; for a loss against anyone, £200. 'What I want to do is this. Every player who ends up not playing any or many games but who has contributed towards us getting there should get a minimum £500, bottom line. Play one game and lose, you would get £200, but we'll top it up to £500 and so on. Nobody out of the twenty-two players we've now got will get less than £500. The other proposal is just to stick with match payments and you'll get a lump sum of £18,000 to split fairly between you. But I'd like the club to approve what you come up with; I don't want someone getting a load of money and someone getting nothing. We'd want to see that the deal is fair. Somebody told me Fev are getting three grand a man;

well, they're not.' A figure of £20,000 between them was mentioned.

Won't the second option be tough to work out? asked a voice in the gallery; Kev agreed that it would. 'What I'm trying to cover is to give as much on match-days as the club can afford while still covering those players who don't figure, so they still get a minimum of £500.'

There were other bonuses to contemplate too, dependent upon where Batley finish in the Qualifiers, which should also apply to all twenty-two players. 'So if we finish seventh, that's another £500; if we finish sixth, two grand in total; if we finish fifth, £3,000, because we get more money. These are just bonuses for getting there, but if you were in the Million Pound Game, the match payments for that will be different too and we share the gate.' Of the seven games, only three will be at home – 'Okay,' he held up his hands, 'our problem, I'm with that . . .' When they go to Headingley, for example, aside from the 10 per cent they will gain pre-selling tickets, they won't get a bean.

Brownie and Rowey pointed out that, from the players' point of view, going to Leeds and getting knocked about in front of a big crowd for £200 might also not be seen as much of a reward.

Kev: 'We are as pissed off as you, but it's just how it's worked out.' He reiterated that he was trying to cover the cost of five non-players getting £2,500. Iro interjected that anyone who had signed a contract for next year and beyond would also see a bonus on that.

Kev gave them an example of what might have happened in the Shield. 'If you'd won five games, lost one by more than twelve points and lost one by less than twelve points, you'd have got £1,400 in match payments [which is to say £250 a win, £100 a defeat by less than twelve, £50 a defeat by more than twelve]. Now, if you play seven games and lose them all, you'll get seven lots of £200 – £1,400. We've tried to work it out so you are not worse off from not being in the Championship Shield. You might not lose all the games in the Super 8s and you may not have won five games in the Shield, we don't know; we are trying to strike a balance. The cost over and above match terms is about £18,000 to the club, which is why I say if you want to share that out we can do it that way. But this system, if you win more we'll have to pay out more, but that will mean we will probably finish higher in the league and then the other bonuses are going to kick in, aren't they?'

Rowey again made the point that they were being asked to subsidize the non-players and, bearing in mind the profile of the games they would be playing in at Headingley and Hull in particular, and the physical toll, that did not seem fair. His argument was that the club should be finding that extra £2,500, not the players.

Kev further pointed out that some of this money, over and above contract, would not necessarily be paid over the next couple of months. The club would try to pay what it could but it might have to wait until January. 'It's better for us to admit that now than tell you "you'll get it next month" and then do a Bradford or a Fev.'

Rowey, an eye on the figures, continued the struggle for the £50, suggesting £250 a defeat. Keegan said he heard what Kev was saying but backed Rowey's view, as did Brownie; most of the other players letting them negotiate on their behalf. 'If people get injured, that's just part of rugby league,' said the latter. As players, they can't be held responsible for that or they are effectively being punished for staying fit. No one took offence. In fact, injured Danny Cowling, set to benefit from the £500 clause, made the helpful suggestion that any non-players could wait until January.

Kev: 'Is that the only bone of contention? I mean everyone wants more money, don't they, but—'

Rowey: 'Yeah, although it should be £500 a win against whoever we beat', since any points will ensure they finish higher in the table, with the extra finance that brings.

'I want everybody to enjoy these seven games,' said Kev, 'and for everybody to be in the right state of mind. Would that put it to bed, and also the understanding that if we haven't got the money in August, you'll get it eventually? I would like to pay up straight away and if we get a good gate against the Giants we might be able to do it. If we got 3,000, then 1,500 against Fev, 1,500 against Salford, we might just scrape through, I don't know. If we pushed it to £500 and £250 full stop – you've got them bonuses as well of £500, £2,000 and £3,000, haven't you? – and if we get to the Million Pound Game there'd be more, we'd have to look at who we played . . . can we concentrate on winning games and then you are even better off, aren't you?'

Meeting broken up, good humour was restored, superficially at least, the squad apparently content. Now all they had to do was apply the outcome to the field, more battles to be joined. *Do coaches get a bonus too?* Linners was asked. 'Do they fuck. Don't be stupid.'

On Sunday, a 58–18 shellacking spoke for itself – something was awry, the first dabble in the Qualifiers a reality check writ large.

As the cooling towers of Castleford, Wakefield and Pontefract gave way to wind farms, big skies and flatlands, expectations ran high. This was the big time. Hull, a city so steeped in rugby league that its main approach road, the A63, was renamed the Clive Sullivan Way in honour of the first black captain of any national British sporting side, glistened in August sunshine. Even the mudflats beneath the Humber Bridge were a-glint, idiosyncratic telephone boxes white as sharks' teeth. In 2017, a place that voted resolutely to leave the EU was due to become European City of Culture, further impetus to the area's reawakening self-confidence, as confirmed by the international flags that fluttered amid the spinnaker poles of a cosmopolitan marina.

But Rovers, it seemed, were there for the taking. It had not been a good season for a team denied its best talent by injury. If finishing second bottom in the Super League table wasn't bad enough, their neighbours and rivals in the west of the city, Hull FC, were in with a chance of the treble. Currently leading the table and favourites to reach Old Trafford, at the end of the month they would be off to Wembley, to meet Warrington in the Challenge Cup final. FC could actually win four titles if they then won the World Club Challenge at the start of next season. This being rugby league, though, there was as yet no confirmation of where or even if that game would take place.

Hull FC's parkland facilities at the KCOM Stadium – also home to Premier League football side Hull City, whose campaign was to kick off next weekend – put a ground east of the river in the shade, though a stand named for club legend Colin Hutton has perked up the former New Craven Park – now the KC Lightstream Stadium – no end. Smart and well proportioned, on a summer Sunday afternoon the view over the East Stand of rose-pink rooftops stretching off into a hazy distance was more Tuscany than Southcoates. The cranes of the Queen Elizabeth Dockyards assaulted the skyline to the right.

Whatever a divided city's achievements in black and white, the minds of its red and white citizens were concentrated purely on survival; the wish to secure a top-flight place regained in 2007 on the back of almost two decades of struggle in the lower divisions prior to that. Anything less than a commanding victory was unthinkable.

For a noisy Batley collective in a crowd of 6,684, this was the moment. Many wore specially manufactured kits: white mainly with a typical rugby league chevron on a fawn tint, cerise socks and trims. There was an away version too: black, with cerise and fawn touches reversed. Both versions had the head of a bulldog superimposed at the midriff, the only aspect of the design that chairman Kev wasn't keen on. For one thing, he'd noticed that when Cropper did his usual thing of tucking the shirt in and pulling his shorts high, 'You can only see its ears.'

Anyway, there'd been too much red in it and a colour clash meant that the players were forced to wear the regular away colours, black and lime, instead. As they jogged out, they were met with generous applause. The home allegiances were clear, the East Stand draped with banners – 'Hull Kingston Rovers – Our Religion'; 'Red Army'; 'Live, Love, Laugh and Be Happy' (the latter a line from Al Jolson's music-hall ditty long since adopted as the club anthem: '. . . *the red, red robin goes bob-bob-bobbing along*') – but few in rugby league had been anything other than impressed by Batley's achievement.

Keegan, named eighteenth man and therefore a non-player, warmed up with the team as giant flags bearing the Rovers and Batley crests were placed on the field either side of the players' entrance and dugouts beneath the towering West Stand, a pre-match routine before every Super 8s game from then onward. Rufus the Robin, Hull

KR's mascot, aimed a giant water pistol at John Kear's back, the Batley coach, his mind elsewhere, fortunately failing to notice.

As the heat rose, so did the sea breeze and anticipation. Dave Scott, a former Rovers player, settled his nerves by taking a few high balls and grubbers with Sam 'Smeats' Smeaton, debuting off the bench having now signed a one-year contract. Breth would make his 150th Batley appearance and it was he who led the team out in a commemorative shirt. Although the Doggies went well against full-time opposition in the Championship, this would be another matter. Super League has greater week-in, week-out intensity, Rovers all the more dangerous for being desperate. Against that, Oldham had already beaten them here in the Cup, though just how the Roughyeds had managed to do that was quite a conundrum.

It all began so brightly. Rovers kicked off, Batley brought the ball clear; the middles got an impressive roll on. First set in attack completed. In their first defensive set, Batley forced an error; scrum thirty-five metres out. The upshot: Leaky burrowed in from dummy-half, Patch with a simple conversion. It was a soft score to concede from the Robins' point of view, but 6–0 to the Bulldogs. The home fans fell silent; the away support dared to dream. There was nothing to this Super 8s lark, was there?

Optimism. Sweet optimism. Moments later, Rovers were level. Batley's markers were caught unawares, a familiar fault more likely to be punished by superior opposition, and Rovers poured through for the first of ten tries on the day. At 30–6, Batley looked bewildered, trans-fixed in defence. Rovers had kept the scoreboard ticking to the tune of a point a minute. Ball in hand, Bulldogs were lively enough, but they couldn't get ball in hand anywhere near often enough. Fatigue too began to tell, with injuries to Ainy and Patch further disruptions.

Still, even when Rovers went 36–6 up, Batley fought gamely on and were rewarded when Cropper went over from Brownie's tip-on near the line, Dom Brambani adding the goal. As written on a 'Mister Softee' ice cream van in the car park: 'Often licked, never beaten'. The visitors had at least scored the first and last points of the half.

At least one member of the Batley delegation had something to celebrate, Dan Winner living up to his name and collecting £100 for kicking a ball into a dustbin at half-time. And as the home fans settled back for a second-half points fest, the Bulldogs again began well, forcing a GLDO at the end of their first offensive set, with Leaky tackled short this time during Batley's best attacking spell. Yet a couple more tries by the hour mark made it 52–12 to the hosts.

With a quarter of the game to go and the sun merciless, it might have got really ugly but for the Bulldogs' obstinacy and the home side becoming loose. Comfortable now and preparing mentally for a more testing trip to Leeds, the crowd again fell silent – the only invitation Tracey Grundell in the Hutton Stand needed. 'C'mooooonnn, Batley!' she roared, competition for anything in the East Hull dockyards. And 'c'mon' Batley did, holding on until moments before the end, when winger Josh Mantellato added Rovers' final try and goal, the kick bouncing over off the crossbar, just to rub it in.

The previous day, Featherstone had also been walloped by Leeds, 62–6, at the Big Fellas, with opening-round wins for Leigh, 34–30, against London and Salford, 34–12, over Huddersfield. So Batley ended the first weekend in seventh, their negative points difference further reduced when Rowey crashed over for a late morale booster and Dom added the conversion four minutes into time added on.

The manner of the Hull KR defeat was disappointing, but at least they now knew the heights to be scaled. And a second trip to the capital beckoned, the first realistic chance of victory.

Within the group, Keegan's late return was put to rest. On Saturday morning, behind shutters in a darkened Ron's Lounge, the skipper had stood up and apologized. 'It was my fuck-up. All this shit that I binned everyone off is not the case. I slept in and missed the flight, that's all. I'm sorry and gutted I'm not playing tomorrow, but I'll be there, helping to support the team. I just wanted you to know.'

The shit in question was an outpouring of criticism and bile. When news that Keegan was dropped broke online, it led to conjecture on an independent fans' forum and a spat on social media where the chief culprit told the club captain: 'Stop retweeting everything to get likes [off] all the puffs who follow you.' At which Brownie and Rowey pitched in to defend him. 'We don't need fans like u why does [his] sexuality have to be brought into it? #bell'

'Great way to start on the middle eights,' wrote another, '. . . too bothered about all this pride nonsense. Rightly dropped.' According to this well-informed correspondent, Keegan missed training because he was 'a special guest at a big gay pride event apparently'.

Even less abusive posters turned angry. 'Nothing against the lad,' declared one forum post, 'but seems to me his form hasn't been the same since his new found "fame" for being gay. Could well be going to his head a bit and we only want players who are 100% committed to the cause and Kear is dead right to drop him for this.' The pundit added that: 'I would be tempted to drop him of [sic] the captaincy tbh, obviously he's no respect for his team mates, coach or even the fans if he can do what he's done at such an important stage for us as well, I would give it to young Dom Brambani, imo he calls all the shots anyway and is a very proven leader.'

Those closest to the club, of course, could sort the wheat from the chaff, though even among insiders there were concerns that the tightness of the group was undermined. Not so much by Keegan's absence, unwelcome though that had been, but more by the sudden attention shift to paid reward, where before all had been team spirit, a shared will to win and camaraderie. It was far too early to panic, but now players were guaranteed £250 for a defeat, any defeat, they were on the same money for losing as they had been previously for a win. Where was the motivation in that? Having got their way in Ron's Lounge, would they be content to be spanked seven weeks straight? The first result might suggest so, even as tries at the end of each half argued not. But when the London trip delivered an even heavier one-sided rout, the alarm bells really did start to clang.

Ahead of the trip south, the talk was constructive. Tongue in cheek,

Brownie reckoned that Hull KR had more players on the field. The injuries were a blow, Patch would be out with a groin strain, but otherwise rationality held sway. Eighteen points ought to have been enough to put them in the game and some of the yardage was very good. The ruck control, though, was poor and their attitude generally lacked edge, JK thought. 'For the first time this season, we were happy being jolly hockey sticks, good losers. Haven't they tried hard? Well, no. That was last year. This year we aren't accepting that. This year we've been fucking winners. We need that edge back.'

On Friday night, though, JK was privately concerned that the players had put their cues on the rack. Unusually, JK himself, Pottsy, Ally, Linners, John Heaton and Carl all rolled up before any squad member. Team revealed, Cain was back in the side, replacing Patch; Squiresy was dropped for Sam Smeaton and Brownz came in on the wing for Ainy, whose errant leg was temporarily in a brace. In the team meeting, JK stuck to the same theme. You can't take your eyes off them, he warned. The clips were of a narrow defeat to Leigh the week before. Trailing 34–8 with less than ten minutes to go, the Broncos somehow ran in four late tries and almost nicked it, all the more remarkable since Jamie Soward had just been sent off. Kick chase, markers, hard work, urgency, collision, control the ruck, get up, take space, work hard for one another.

'Has anyone been watching the Olympics?' he asked. 'Did anyone see the rugby sevens final yesterday? The camera panned to Fiji; they'd all got game faces: "We've got to the final but that ain't good enough, we want to win it." It panned on to the public fucking schoolboys [Great Britain] who were all laughing and joking and then got fifty points put on them. I'll tell you, guys, we need game faces. It's no good being satisfied with what we've done or else we are going to end up with seven games of fucking embarrassment. Something needs to inspire us and I hope that the inspiration is achievement.'

Yet in Ealing, where the sun was once again beating down on that artificial surface, the level of humiliation moved up a notch.

*

The highlight for John Kear was being picked up on a slip road nearer home, at junction 37 of the M1 motorway. 'Slept under t' bridge, John?' quipped Breth, the bus in good spirits. There and back in a day, no pyjamas needed.

All smiles disappeared, however, once the whistle blew. The mercurial Soward scored first, the hors d'oeuvres to a six-try first-half feast that left Batley down 32–0 at the break. They hadn't so much wilted in the heat as shrivelled completely, a great shame too for the large band of followers who had trailed them to the capital.

In the toilets at half-time, urinals shared on this occasion with a referee and touch judge, a handful of those paying punters reflected on the non-contest. One who'd claimed at the supporters' night in December, 'anywhere in the top eight I'd be happy with' now saw it differently. 'They've decided they've done enough, haven't they?' he told his equally disgruntled pal. 'Which is all right for them, but we've driven 800 miles for this.' And to compound those woes, hopes that a trademark JK team talk might instil some defiance were quashed by another couple of swift tries. It was 44–0 before the Bulldogs summoned a response, a close-range try apiece for Brownie and Rowey, with Dom adding the extras, before a further six tries from London in the last half hour completed a 76–16 rout. In between, Cropper was sinbinned for dissent – adding to his sending off here earlier in the year – and Uce Ulugia scrambled over for another score.

The result gave London their biggest win since 2006, an 82–8 Challenge Cup victory over Barrow. It was Batley's widest margin of defeat since the Cup thrashing by the Catalans, 74–12, in 2010. Quite a turnaround from that euphoric win just four short weeks ago.

In the changing room, Kear was mortified. Brownie threw his boots down in disgust. Calmly, the coach asked James, Ally and other members of staff to leave for a moment and took a pew. Before he could utter another word, however, Keegan got to his feet. 'Before we talk about the game, we are putting money in for them coming down to watch that fucking shower. They deserve better.'

'They do,' said JK. 'I am absolutely at a loss to know how we've gone from a team that could compete with anybody to a team that looks frightened of tackling. They scored eight tries in fourteen sets. Eight tries in fourteen fucking sets! I want to know – and I want you to say summat, because we'll all talk when it's about fucking money – why is it that we've gone from that competitive, tough, hard-working team to a team of fucking imposters? Let me know.'

Rowey mumbled something inaudible, staring uncomfortably at the floor. Brownie: 'Some people just didn't want to know, that's what I fucking think . . .'

Chandler: 'We came here thinking we were on a day out . . .'

Leaky: 'We look fucking unmotivated, don't we . . .'

Dom: 'We seemed to be on it in training and then . . .'

'Let's take Leaky's point,' said JK. 'Why aren't we motivated? Tell me. Do we think we've had enough? We've gone from what could be the best season in this club's history to the worst. I'm telling you, we could get eighty points put on us in every single game, the way we are going. Do you want that? They were taking the piss – offloading and skipping. Rhys Williams, he was fucking dancing around. Every single one of us needs to look at ourselves, guys. I need to look at myself, because something's obviously changed in the last two weeks. But you fellas who go out there need to look at yourselves as well. Now what are we gonna do about these fans?'

Someone suggested putting in £20. 'Twenty quid? We need more than that, fellas.' Kear suggested £50 each to pay for free transport to the next away game, but that meant Leeds, so the gesture was shifted to Leigh in September.

'What's going to happen next week, guys, that's what I want to know.'

'We are going to get dicked again, aren't we,' said Keegan, 'if we turn up like that.'

'It's at home,' said Leaky, 'so we need to step up, don't we, and play like we know we can.'

'You are playing a team who are fucking desperate,' their coach reminded them. 'And I'll tell you, they are a good team and if they get a sense that they can play with some confidence, they'll put a fucking hundred on us. They will, they'll fucking put a hundred on us.'

'If they get relegated, they are out of a job,' reiterated Keegan, 'selling their car, downsizing their house . . .'

'That's how desperate they'll be,' said JK. 'We are not desperate any more. We are not hungry. We are soft and comfortable. Somehow, guys . . . you don't want to look at individual clips, they tell lies. You need to watch that game as a whole. You were fucking disgraceful, guys, absolutely disgraceful. There's no other word for it. Not one of us can feel proud of what we've done – squad member, physio, fucking coach or player. Not one of us can take anything out of this.'

'At training, we need everyone on it,' said Dom. 'Positive as fuck, play how we know we can, because that wasn't us, me included. Skills, desire, everything – awful. I don't want to feel like that again.'

By the burger stand afterwards, waiting for the players to finish their post-match food, JK and the directors, Kev, Andy, John, Pauls Hull and Harrison, chatted in a group, the coach's fingers doing a Jerry Lee Lewis. What were they discussing? Could JK go early?

The higher up the eight Batley finished, the more they would make. At this rate, they were destined for the bottom, although Fev had helped out again by falling 62–16 at the Bulldogs' next opponents Huddersfield, so for now they remained seventh. Perhaps a new coach coming in would shake things up, give the players something to prove. It was hard to imagine Bradford, cash-strapped and running around in a Championship Shield they will win at a canter, standing in the way of Matt Diskin, wage bill in mind. The rumour mill cranked up again.

Viewed realistically, these opening two games on the road were always likely to be tough, though the manner of defeat was a shock. Next week's clash with the Giants might be make or break.

The drive back to Yorkshire was grim, especially up front where Doc Findlay, Jonny Potts, Kev, Sam Haigh and the coaching staff sat glumly. 'Too happy being underdogs, can't handle success,' muttered

JK, taking it personally. Approaching Lincolnshire, the coaches' gloom deepened when someone found cider and a group at the back began to howl Aerosmith's 'I Don't Want To Miss A Thing', though come South Yorkshire the repertoire had moved on to Al Green's 'Let's Stay Together'.

19

IT WAS OBVIOUS, wasn't it? Keegan's media profile was to blame. He'd taken his eye off the ball, become distracted by all this celebrity nonsense and let the side down. He had changed, got above himself, like Sammy King's mum and dad with their new settee. Forgotten his place. Never mind how, up to Swinton, he had actually been playing well, inspiring his teammates onward; that didn't fit the narrative.

In any case, the Batley captain's fifteen minutes weren't up yet, far from it. His growing fame burned more brightly than ever a year on. He'd popped up in papers, magazines and on television, brooding manfully in promotional photos at Mount Pleasant more often than not, having ended 2015 with a public pop at Tyson Fury's rant in the *Mail on Sunday*: 'There are only three things that need to be accomplished before the devil comes home: one of them is homosexuality being legal in countries, one of them is abortion and the other one's paedophilia. Who would have thought in the fifties and sixties that those first two would be legalized?'

During Stonewall's Equality Dinner at London's Hilton Hotel, Keegan told Premier League footballers: 'When you are ready to come out, we are here for you.' He recorded promotional clips for Lynx deodorant alongside boxer Anthony Joshua and footballer Bobby Petta, and in August his name turned up as a link on BBC2 quiz *Only Connect*. Rather more mainstream was his appearance the week before the Swinton denouement in an episode of Channel 4's

Celebrity First Dates, recorded on the first trip to London in April.

'Everything's a competition and I like to win,' Keegan said at the start of a show in which he shared celebrity status with floppy-haired Cain Southernwood lookalike Brad, twenty, lead singer with the Vamps. Another chap, Gary, who might have been from *The Only Way is Essex* and had a look of Joe Chandler, was matched with Natasha, thirty-three, from Cheshire: 'one third of Atomic Kitten'. Also on the pull was veteran northern comic Bernie Clifton, seventy-nine. 'Who's looking after the giraffe?' asked the maître d', before welcoming Keegan in off the red carpet: 'Have you been eating your greens?'

It's hard to find time to date, Keegs told the barman, who, to begin with, assumed he was meeting a girl: 'Beg your pardon, my bad . . .' Being a rugby league player must be pretty intense. *We've been playing today in London.* 'Did you win?' *No.* 'Better win tonight then.' But from the beginning it was obvious there was no chance of that in what he called his first time at the rodeo. His date was Paddy, twenty-six, from Stroud and an online fitness guru. Praising the asparagus as an opener, it all drooped into a nine 'oil from there.

'Kids aren't upset because their dad is gay; kids are upset because their dad's gone,' Keegan said in an attempt at seriousness, before it all turned embarrassing. Paddy flapped under the lights and began making ill-judged innuendos. He called Keegan a 'massive cuddle monster', which wouldn't have been so bad if he hadn't then remarked that spooning leads to forking, or so he'd heard. He even dusted off the old Phil Lynott line, 'Got any Irish in you? Would you like some?', his nerves and mouth running away with him.

In a more eloquent after-scene interview, Paddy noted that, 'So many people naturally form bonds and stuff at school. They date and kind of get a natural interaction with the opposite sex. When you are gay or lesbian and you are not out, you kind of miss out on that. You just kind of observe and kind of take notes on, like, how to behave.'

The internet being what it is, social media bristled with indignation on Keegan's behalf, the programme trending for a while. So much so that on the bus back from Swinton, he'd felt compelled to tweet:

'It was just a TV show, guys. He wasn't offensive or rude. Everyone chill out.' In the tabloids, though, Hirst was 'SLAMMED' for 'having a secret boyfriend' after ex-wife Sara tweeted: 'Aww @_Paddy_White_ maybe try to date lads without boyfriends next time they may be more interesting!' adding: '#awkward I should know I married him'.

'I would guess that everyone has been deceived by Keegan,' Paddy told *Mirror TV*. 'The show should be about two people meeting with genuine reason to invest time and energy in each other. He had no intention to ask me a question or make me feel comfortable – simply to be present for publicity reasons.' Meanwhile, a bear shat on the Pope in some woods.

Since his five-night stint on *Calendar* in February, it had been clear that if Keegan could forge a media identity, then he would – a rugby league playing career after all, and especially a part-time rugby league playing career, is simultaneously fragile and brief. He enjoyed the process of asking people questions for once, rather than the other way around, a natural in front of the camera. If he got the opportunity, then he'd like to do more. 'I'm a bit of an egotist or a narcissist. Saying that, I don't like watching myself on TV,' he'd said at the time. He got himself a more showbiz-oriented agent and now did corporate stuff, talking to big companies: 'They seem keen to get you in, but it's hard doing that with work, kids, rugby – all a bit much. I can't play rugby for ever, though, and it would be more interesting than a nine to five.' With the spotlight there, it would be daft not to step into it. Acting? 'I'd have a go. I like testing myself and being good at whatever I try my hand at.'

Recognition was widespread by now, even in the capital. He was meeting fellow high achievers like Olympian Nicola Adams and England and Arsenal Ladies' footballer Casey Stoney all the time, as thrilled to be in their company as they were to share his. Strangers might call him 'inspirational' while he was out for a couple of beers. 'Selfishly, I came out for me,' he smiled. 'But when you see how much of an effect it has, it's good for your soul.' In October, he would guest edit an edition of BBC Radio 5 Live's *Afternoon Edition*, 'Coming Out'.

'I've done things I never thought I would, met people I never dreamed I would meet; it's eye-opening. You just have to take it in your stride, embrace it.'

After the embarrassment of the opening pair of Qualifiers, preparation for Huddersfield's visit could scarcely have been more bruising or intense. Tuesday, Wednesday and Friday night, another emergency meeting of the Leadership Group before that first session, followed by a grim viewing of the London game in silence and in full. Stripped of goal kicks, kicks to touch and other assorted stoppages, it left a running time of forty-three minutes to endure. After which a list of questions was handed out that JK wanted them all – players and coaching staff included – to answer honestly and anonymously.

- Rate the team's performance on a scale of one to ten.
- Describe it in three words.
- Suggest reasons for the performance.
- What can we do to ensure we improve this week against Huddersfield?
- Is the team good enough to compete at this level?
- Rate your individual performance on a scale of one to ten.
- Describe your performance in three words.
- Suggest reasons for your performance.
- What can you do to ensure you compete at this level?
- Are you good enough to compete at this level?
- What motivates you to play rugby league?
- Any other comments.

'We need to correct this as a group,' JK had told the leadership meeting. 'One of the jobs as a coach is reading your players. See that photo there,' he pointed it out, taken at Swinton and already on the wall, everyone lined up, grinning in mutual achievement, a memory for the ages, 'they thought that was the end of the season. It's really important we give a good account of ourselves in these last five games

– every ruck, every tackle.' And so the soul-searching had continued. It wasn't about not caring, said Keegan. Himself, Cain and Brownz had only just come back into the team so cared a lot. Linners and Mokko reckoned it wasn't so much about technicalities, more a mental thing. Mauny said they weren't desperate any more.

'We are not going out there to lose, though,' said Rowey. No one is saying that, his coach went on, but they'd only had ten sets in the entire game. The worst thing, according to Keegan, had been all the bitching and backbiting. The worst it's been, agreed Dom. Couldn't stop it. Tell someone to shut up and a weed would pop up elsewhere. Everybody with something to say instead of just getting their head down and digging in. Negativity is infectious, Mokko thought. But when we are tight, tough and together, that's infectious too. 'Some people can't wait for the season to finish,' Chandler admitted.

And then Brownie arrived, held up late at work: 'A fucking laughing stock, aren't we?' he said, as Linners pointed out that in calculating losing money the club should have factored in margins of defeat. As it was, you might as well lose by sixty points as five. 'If people are doing that, they are in the game for the wrong reasons,' muttered Brownie. 'As soon as I put that shirt on . . .' He didn't need to finish.

'It's shit this, isn't it?' said JK, who, on Sunday, had gone home, watched the Olympics until the early hours, got up and watched the game again at 7 a.m. in dour reflection. 'We've got to be a team of action, not words. We've got to show up. We can't hide, can we?'

The next night, an apology detailing the free Leigh bus offer was published on the club website, just as the players themselves were bashing each other about with venom on the training field; a session that followed the outcome of Tuesday's questionnaires, JK and Linners alternately reading out fifteen minutes' worth of edited extracts.

- Team performance? . . . *not working together . . . directionless . . . soft . . . lacklustre . . . wank . . . disjointed . . . dominated . . . gutless . . . weak . . . lazy . . . disappointing . . . lethargic . . . amateur . . . poor . . . dishonest . . .*

- Reasons? . . . *mission complete . . . bitching . . . selfishness . . . money argument instigated by minority affected majority . . . foot off gas . . .*
- How to change? . . . *attitude . . . challenge ourselves . . . set goals . . . aggression . . . get back to arm-wrestle . . . be hungry . . . prepare like a Grand Final . . . leadership group practise what they preach . . .*
- Is the team good enough to perform at this level? . . . *yes, when everybody is on their game . . . yes, we didn't get here by being shit . . . people need to get out of their own arse and show some pride . . .*

'Brutal, wasn't it? But I'm really pleased with it, guys,' JK said, handing out sheets of paper on which he summarized the qualities he now expected to see:

- Honest – in all that we do. Be honest in words – no bullshit. Be honest in our actions – no short cuts.
- Respectful – to ourselves, to the opposition and to our teammates, so we always give of our best and turn up ready to play.
- Hard working – in our preparation but especially in our performance, as this is when we play to our best.
- Competitive – in training and on the playing field, so we challenge ourselves, our teammates and the opposition in every situation.
- Disciplined – in our preparation, in our roles within the team, in sticking to the game plan and with the officials.
- Action not words.
- Leaders LEAD!

After which, he said, he was drawing a line in the sand.

The players seemed better for it. Big hits. No holds barred. Teammates belted teammates. 'It's not a fucking youth club, is it? We are grown men. If we can't have a fall-out and then get on with it, we aren't fucking men, are we?' The mojo was back. 'Great contact, fellas. Great contact.' *Nice. Nice. Nice.*

Yet on Sunday here they were again, 48–2 down at half-time, blushing brighter than the shirts worn to mark the Pink Weekend.

At least the fundraising was going well. Last year's Freddie Mercury tribute act was back, along with Greg Minikin, here to say hello: 'A good lad,' said Linners. 'Got a head on him. Knows where he wants to go but knows where he's come from.' A 10k sponsored walk was completed the day before, tombola, stalls and a ducking stool on the day, upon which chaplain Derek took his turn – 'Normally, it's me doing the baptizing' – all of it helping to raise £9,500 and take the three-year total to £30,000. Less happily, on the field, the team too had been charitable. Apart from when Huddersfield strayed offside in the opening minutes and Dom's boot put Batley 2–0 up, it had again been excruciatingly one-sided.

In the press, JK said he wanted his team to regain their pride. 'I am expecting a response and will be very disappointed if I don't get one.' As for the Giants, they told their local paper they would treat the Heavy Woollen trip 'as a Grand Final'. And so they did, to begin with. Dom's penalty – in off the post – was followed by nine first-half tries and six goals as the Bulldogs completed only six defensive sets. Patch, clearly unfit, was a target and, after losing the toss and being asked to play uphill, every single one of his teammates was out-muscled and out-thought by far more physically imposing opponents.

A 3,000 crowd seemed philosophical, seeing it for what it was. Full-time players defending their livelihoods against part-timers who had given all that they could, expended every ounce of energy, blood and sweat simply to get this far. These lads had given Batley its best season in living memory, why let this closing stretch sour it? There was disappointment, though. No one could deny that. The remaining five weeks offered only the same torturous cycle of capitulation. And the coaching staff in particular knew that this Batley side was better than it realized. Once again, they had let themselves down.

In the sheds, JK, as stunned as anyone, stressed the need to be methodical. No panic. No histrionics. Just treat defensive sets like attacking ones, he said. Aim for completion. The game was gone, of course, but the imperative now was to regain some self-respect. If they did so, he told them, it could be the turning point of the season.

As the second half begins, a matter surely of damage control, Ainy watches from the dugout, itching to be out there, particularly as Brownz, in his 200th career appearance, is having a nightmare. On Wednesday, the injury-plagued winger had made another trip to Carl's treatment table, a contraption rescued from Dewsbury sexual health clinic. Carl could have it, they said, on the proviso he fixed it, though he'd had to sign a disclaimer in case anyone caught anything. If the physio's bedside manner was intended to cheer Ainy up, it hadn't worked. As the last of the evening sunshine made its way down the ground, the knee had gone again. It seemed permanently on ice. Carl – his future on the back burner once more, having offered Matt Diskin his services on fewer hours in a 'consultancy' role – had advised an X-ray. So off to hospital Ainy went, only to find the scanner broken. 'You take it out on the family,' he sighed, thoroughly miserable.

Even he, though, perks up when, in a season of remarkable turn-arounds, there suddenly comes another. Going downhill, Batley begin to fight in the tackle. They move the ball wide, win penalties and put a side that had after all finished bottom of Super League under extreme pressure. Squiresy – back for Sam Smeaton – soars high in a crowded in-goal area to touch down a lofted kick, after Cropper and Gleds have already gone close in the opening minutes. Batley's man of the match Dave Scott jinks in, Dom adding both conversions. An unexpected offload from Brownie gives Huddersfield the field position from which to score again on the hour, but the Bulldogs don't take long to reply; a second try for Squiresy and Dom's extras make it 20–52.

Thanks to sustained spells of possession, Batley can finally show what they are capable of with ball in hand, delivering the brand of entertainment a place in the Qualifiers was supposed to provide. And even when a wild Brownie pass sets the Giants away again for a length-of-the-field try, there is more left in these Gallant Youths.

First, Uce Ulugia conjures enough space to sidestep his way over for a try that is converted by Dom from far out. Not as far out as the score that comes a minute before time, however: one of the tries of this or any season. From the restart, Dom catches the ball and spins it with abandon across the line to Scotty, standing under his own posts. He ships the ball wider to Patch, who, on the first tackle, chips it over an approaching Huddersfield line, where it is collected by Brownz, who – having a much brighter second half – somehow stays in touch and hacks it on from halfway. As both teams stampede downfield, the ball bounces high in the Giants' ten-metre zone, where Scotty, smallest man on the field, reaches up and takes it at the second attempt before falling over the line. *We are not a side of fancy Dans . . .*

Final score, 28–58, avalanche averted. In fact, Batley have won the second half 26–10, the boost they were desperate for before once again facing Featherstone in a fortnight's time on the other side of Challenge Cup final weekend. Elsewhere, Rovers have produced a gutsy result of their own, falling only to a 30–18 home defeat to Leigh and dropping Batley to eighth in the Qualifiers table on points difference.

Confidence, nevertheless, is restored.

Although only JK – in the BBC commentary box – and Jim McVeigh were off to Wembley in any official capacity, the players were again given a few days off once a Tuesday-night session prior to the sport's annual pilgrimage south was concluded. Keegan took the middles and worked on peel, reset and marker issues, Patch and Dom the edges, addressing width, timing, shape and on-line D. Then it was down to the T3 gym with John Heaton and that was that.

Looking on was Luke Blake, in contact next week he said, having invested in a Velcro girdle. His back was fine under pressure. He could lift weights with no bother. The only problem that might arise, experts warned him, was another knock or knee to the back. There was a 95 per cent chance of him getting through a game unscathed, but if he's unlucky . . .

'I think we can take off from this, I really do,' JK told them in the team meeting. 'These Super 8s are new for us and what has struck me is how wound up the opposition are.' Look into the eyes of the Hull KR, London and Huddersfield players and it was clear to see they had a reason to play. 'We've to make sure we have a reason and the biggest is coming up.' If Batley want to be the top part-time team in the country, then the match with Featherstone would be the play-off final, wouldn't it? A week later, Hull having beaten Warrington in a Cup final thriller, preparations for that encounter began in earnest.

The only absentee was Chandler, stuck in Dubai after an emergency landing while returning from a pre-wedding 'honeymoon' in the Maldives, a better excuse than sleeping in. As for Keegan, he'd spent the weekend at Manchester Pride, a timely visit given the scoop in *League Weekly*. 'Blowing the whistle,' read a headline on rugby league's 121st birthday, above claims by two ex-referees that the RFL officials department was riddled with bullying and homophobia.

One of those referees, George Stokes, alleged that he had witnessed 'homophobic abuse being thrown about' on a Lake District team-bonding exercise 'by a very senior member of the match officials department', which he said had occurred in front of many witnesses.

> This is supposed to be a professional organization, yet here we are in a pub while somebody gets absolutely torn into about being gay – delving into his personal life and making a mockery of it, because he happened to be with another man. He sat there and took it for about half an hour. I reported this to [chief operating officer] Ralph Rimmer when I left, but nothing has happened about it.

It had taken the suicide of Chris Leatherbarrow – referee during Batley's final match of the season against Hunslet in 2015 – the report said, for referees' welfare to be taken seriously, though morale within the department was still low, with issues 'swept under the carpet'. For its part, the Rugby Football League – awarded the prestigious Stonewall Sports Award in 2012 but now condemned as 'the least professional organization in the world'– issued a quote from Rimmer: 'Whilst it might be true to say that the department has had some issues in previous years, we have undergone what at times has been a difficult journey. I believe the changes we have made are beginning to bear fruit.'

At Batley, meanwhile, victory that coming weekend felt crucial. If only to raise the spirits of a chairman still mithered and let down by the 'money night' meeting. To begin with, the players went up to the gym for an hour's cardiovascular work involving running down to the windmill, physical exercises and weights, past a Taverners' Club that now had only outer walls standing, its demolition finally under-way. Training on the field was also intense, though leavened as ever with Brownie one-liners: 'If that's ten metres, you can measure my dick.' Blakey too, back strapped tight, contributed fully. In a sport that takes no prisoners, that Rovers will know of his injury and target it despite potentially life-changing consequences can't be discounted, so the wisdom of his availability is questionable. Whatever, JK will pick him of course. He'd like seventeen Blakeys in the team if he could.

Uce Ulugia too was struggling, having snapped the screws that held in place his twice-dislocated shoulder. Another operation would be needed in the off-season, by which time he'll be Fev's concern. For now, he would just have to adjust a tackling style built on front-on power rather than strength-of-arm, and tough it out regardless.

Come Thursday, Chandler was back. After watching clips from the last heavy defeat to Rovers, the group set goals. Completions with ball in yardage: 95 per cent. In good ball, 'when you'll chuck it about a bit': 80 per cent. In D, yardage and good ball combined: 80 per cent. Against Huddersfield, they did eight sets out of twenty-one in the first half and the score was 48–2. In the second: eleven out of fourteen, the score 26–10 to Batley. 'Are we going to commit to that?' their coach asked. Yes, they said, they were. 'If you hit them targets, I'm not fucking bothered about the score. But I'll tell you what, if you hit them targets we'll win . . .'

And on Saturday morning, the seventeen running through moves did indeed contain Ulugia and Blake, the latter on the bench after having signed a disclaimer. Unexpectedly, Scotty limped off clutching a hamstring, injured in an innocuous bump in yardage. Carl diagnosed a grade-one tear, the least bad version, and packed it in ice as a precaution. At a push, the full-back could play – it is an important game after all, potentially worth £50,000 to the club – but if he stretched it and it worsened, he could be looking at a twelve-week absence, not good news for Batley and even worse news for Scotland, whom he hoped to represent in autumn's Four Nations. The physio went out to report to JK, who stood watching in the rain, and it was agreed that Scotty would undergo a fitness test the following morning.

It was a distraction they didn't need, though JK had already upped the psychological ante. The side above them was high in confidence, fast, hungry and full of energy. 'We need a performance from minute one. If we come lethargic, they'll get us. I would take massive pride, and I hope you would too, in being the best part-time side in British rugby league. I'm fucking sick of not winning in this competition, what about you? I want to come out of this game with something . . .'

The boy didn't know his father, a deserter who abandoned the family home in Harrow, north-west London, while the boy was still a toddler, leaving his mother to raise her son and newborn daughter alone. Nob head, gangster, idiot . . . not a pleasant person anyway, however you summed him up. Criminal, pretty naughty . . . he didn't want to know. The boy hadn't spoken to him since.

His mum is Christine, a brilliant woman from Leeds. When the boy was five, the three of them returned north, to Belle Isle. He liked living there, though admits it's not everyone's cup of tea, a bit rough to be honest. A vast sprawling council estate, Belle Isle was where he grew up and his mother still lives, a place he'll always regard fondly.

Already having family in Leeds helped, of course, but she was and is very independent, his mum, likes to keep her sen to her sen. She's always said she doesn't need anyone as long as she's got him and Mica, and that they are both healthy and in work. So it was just them – the boy, his mum and younger sister. It always had been.

Because Christine was a single parent, she worked 'every hour God sent' to provide for her kids, as a nurse, night after night, in A&E. To keep a roof over their heads, she grafted until she was borderline ill and the boy will forever be grateful for it as, despite her efforts, the trio never had anything but each other. He chokes up saying so.

They never enjoyed nice things or lush holidays, didn't travel, the focus was on getting by, heads above water. That was enough. Although when his own little 'un came along, the boy – now a man – realized that for her he wanted more. His mum still works those long shifts, days, night, twilights – getting by. She is an absolute diamond. He could not have achieved any of this without her.

At Belle Isle, the trio made their home near the roundabout in the middle of the estate, the Circus as it is known, though there are no lions and tigers, a few clowns maybe. A typical council house, really, in the mushroom style, bottom half pebble-dashed, top half slate; the Circus itself a big green where kids played morning, noon and night. The boy and his mates lit bonfires, made dens, smashed windows, climbed trees. When he goes back, the people he went to school with are still there. He would be too if his wife, who is from a more well-to-do part of Leeds, hadn't lifted him out of it.

He'd been an outdoor kid, pratting around, messing about, a bit cheeky, but always showed respect. You could play in the street in them days and nothing would happen, not like now. Their street was one where everybody knew everybody; walk in next door and no one batted an eyelid. The boy's best mate, who lived four doors up, is still there, having just got out of prison for armed robbery or something. He saw him two weeks ago when he went to decorate his mum's.

From time to time they played football, but mainly hung around, rode bikes, played kerby and the like. The boy began playing rugby league in Year 8 at Merlyn Rees High, a 'colourful' school, now flattened. Otherwise, the area was dominated by Hunslet Parkside ARLFC, the team with whom he would spend his amateur days.

The boy didn't like school and got kicked out, sent to an approved institution in Sweet Street, near the red-light area in downtown Leeds. The problem, he thinks now, is that he always thought he was older than his age. He was polite, would do anything for anyone, but thought he knew best, especially once it became clear that he was going to be good at rugby. At school, he just wanted to do PE. He quite liked art, woodwork, anything hands-on, otherwise no interest. By then, he'd been scouted by Leeds academy, on a contract, getting paid; only £500 per month, but enough to question the value of education. *What do I need to study for?*

It worried his mum, of course, though no matter how naughty he was at school, he always respected her. If he'd been swearing or being a twat, as soon as they said, 'I will ring your mum', it would be, 'Oh, don't.' It wasn't that he expected her to wallop him around the head; she would only have to say she was disappointed to hurt him more than any smack of the hand could do.

At Hunslet Parkside, the boy had been selected for trials with the Leeds and District Service Area and made the team four years on the trot. On that circuit, professional club scouts would watch and cherry-pick the best kids in the area. He was given four foundation games with the Rhinos as a further trial. *Play well and win a contract.* The last of those was against Bradford, at Odsal. He played his heart out, aware of what was at stake, remembers the rush when they said he'd been successful. He couldn't wait to tell his mum.

It was quite an achievement for a boy who, in his earliest years, packed rugby league in because he was cold, skinny, frail and timid. But then he began to put a bit of size on. He wasn't tall, though quite stocky, so they threw him into the back row with an equally young James Brown, the same ebullient character then as he is now. People called the boy bonkers. He wanted to smash everybody and it is true that, on the field, he has always been aggressive, but off it, not at all. He is a father, husband, brother, uncle, nephew.

He is also far from the only ex-Hunslet Parkside boy to have made the grade. Garry Schofield, Jason Robinson, James Lowes, Sonny Nickle – a list as long as your arm, several internationals, all went before him. Physically well developed in his teens, during his three years in the Leeds academy he was a regular in the pack until a positional switch. First-team appearances, though, never arrived.

In 2008, daughter Mya was born and Doncaster approached him with an offer to play in the Championship. He spent two happy seasons in South Yorkshire, scored nineteen tries, won promotion and, coached by Ellery Hanley, reached the Northern Rail Cup final against Salford, the Dons' first final in a fifty-seven-year history. It ended in a 60–0 defeat, the Cup presented by Kevin Nicholas, who was RFL President that year. Then Doncaster went into liquidation and he moved on, first to Hunslet then York, where he again won promotion in 2010. Karl Harrison was at that Championship One Grand Final and liked what he saw. 'Come to Batley,' growled Rhino, so that's what he did.

Just as the boy's mother Christine had been a lighthouse on the rocks, so it is with the man's wife. The product of a more comfortable upbringing, Kelly is from New Farnley, out Gildersome way, the posher end of town, and has shown him ways other than struggle.

It is in New Farnley that the couple now lives, to give the little 'un a better life. And away from the family home and rugby league, other young girls – and boys – gain the benefit of *his* experience too.

Leaving Leeds, he got a job in scaffolding – found by the Rhinos' then coach Tony Smith – as he and Kelly had just had their daughter. Aged seventeen, they were young, pretty and in need of money, like every other parent in this big ugly world. The company, APB Scaffolding, sponsored Leeds at the time and in fact he worked for them until 2015 before landing the role he now fills at Tong High School – a sports coach and specialist mentor. With challenging kids who find school hard, he conducts one-on-one chats, takes them out and generally shows interest. He wants to give them a good outlook on life, a service he would have given anything to have been provided

with himself. This reluctant schoolboy has been there, done that –
walked every step of their walk and several more miles besides.

Is Christine proud of her boy? Massively. It could have gone either
way. A lot of his friends are in jail. Through hard work, a strong
motherly influence and, yes, a chunk of good luck, he not only came
through a start in life that would derail a lesser man, a man like his
absent father perhaps, he earned the opportunity to build a world
around things he not only enjoys but excels at, things like family, a
sense of purpose, beatboxes, baseball caps, rugby league.

Batley is about kinship and it's his second time here. When Karl
Harrison left for Halifax, he went with him. Scaffolding, some weeks
busy others not, earned an inconsistent wage. Fax offered more cash
and he had to take it because, well, life is short, isn't it, and at the
end of the day you have to feed your family, don't you? But with
the high-school job came a steady income and when offered a return
to the Mount he took it in a flash. He is happy here, plays his best rugby.
They make him feel welcome. At the Bulldogs, he feels special.

His mum always wanted him to do better than his dad. What with
the job at Tong High, the rugby, his daughter, the boy is proving that
he isn't the idiot his father was. Four years ago, he got a message on
Facebook from a woman who turned out to be another sister by his
dad, someone he knew nothing about, roughly the same age as Mica.
That shows you what he was up to at the time, doesn't it?

But now here the boy is again, where he belongs, on a rugby field,
alive with it all, playing to the crowd, soaking up its noise, hunting
errors, sniffing out opportunities on the right wing. On some days
playing downhill at Mount Pleasant, that's not all you can sniff. The
touchline by the main stand often reeks of tobacco, enough to make
you gip, but there's no time to ponder any of that now.

His mate, Tuna, neck like a tree trunk, is wreaking havoc in the
opposition defence, running hard. Another, Patch Walker, has thrown
a daisy-cutter pass, too low for anyone to catch. Is the chance gone?
No, wait. Gleds, in at loose forward, gets his boot to it and hacks it on,
a weird unconventional kick but the ball is coming his way. There is

ground to make up but can he get to the thing first, get his hands on it, touch it down for the opening try? Yes, he knows he can. He'll make it now and once he does, it will be the best feeling ever. A try. *His* try! The crowd roars in vicarious approval. Swamped by teammates, he is a figure of respect, dignity – a contributor to a higher cause.

Wayne Reittie is somebody. He's doing all right for himself. You might not have been there but he, along with his mother and sister, struggling like fuck, is more of a man than you'll ever be.

He kisses the words 'MYA LOVE' on his wristband.

Patch's conversion attempt goes wide, but no matter. Since Gleds won a penalty in the first minute, it was clear the Bulldogs would not lack bite today. Scotty is declared fit and he too is involved from the start, defence key early doors. Prior to Reitts' try, though, Brownz had already been denied when Uce knocked on, playing uphill, near Featherstone's line. And at the end of the first quarter Rovers are level, gifted an unconverted four-pointer of their own; a lofted kick wide in a blustery rain shower spilled by Brownz.

Uce is having a busy time of it against a club he will represent next year, while the two starting props, Keegan and Rowey, and Tuna have been immense. Patient and methodical faced with opposition they do not hold in awe, Batley grind it out, back to basics. Replacement props too play forcefully – Cropper in his 100th career game and Brownie who, though he immediately knocks on thirty metres out, regains possession after the scrum with a degree of enthusiasm that sums up his side's attitude. Even so, three minutes before the break Fev go ahead. Patch pushes a player off the ball as Rovers tear down the field and the defence scrambles well, conceding a penalty. Fev run it and score a second try in the corner. When rampaging Tuna regains the restart with seconds on the clock, Batley are back in possession. As the half-time hooter sounds, Dom coolly slots a drop-goal: 5–8.

In the sheds, JK asks for more of the same and gets his wish. Playing downhill now, Batley force a GLDO and Scotty, who like Blakey is going well with seemingly no ill effects, is held up in-goal. But when the home side is penalized close to their line with half an hour left, Rovers this time opt to take the two and it's 5–10.

A contentious scrum decision then goes Batley's way after Rowey, back on the field, emerges from a ruck with the ball. He is clobbered to earn a penalty that Patch slots over, cat and mouse. One try in it, converted or not, whose concentration will crack first?

When Dom has a try disallowed on the hour, it gets fierier still. It's a pulsating match with enormous stakes but, four minutes later, when another kickable penalty gives Fev the chance to nudge further ahead, hubris or over-confidence or stupidity or whatever kicks in and they again elect to run it, this time unsuccessfully, Batley's rapid-reaction force standing firm against incoming artillery. Another penalty opportunity from further out this time goes exactly the same way.

Whatever their motivation, as the final minutes approach Rovers are made to rue those decisions. First Dom, with the skill to match his intelligence, kicks a 40/20. At the end of the set, Featherstone collect the kick to the corner but knock on in the tackle. Squiresy, reaching high, lands awkwardly and is led away by Doc Findlay, a damaged ACL ligament in his shoulder. But as one dejected actor leaves the stage, Reitts is taking a delightful back-of-the-hand pass from his replacement Smeats and completing a personal brace in the corner. Batley regain the lead, 11–10.

The conversion is missed and there is still a way to go, nervy moments to be endured. The Bulldogs hang on, though, and finish with a flourish as a superb Leaky break just lacks for support. After Dom forces another GLDO, Uce defuses it as the full-time hooter sounds.

The players have worked hard for this, any myth about their commitment exploded. An honest display, it is just the sort of game that would last year have unquestionably been lost, a tonic for Kevin Nicholas certainly, who, relieved and overjoyed, slaps each and every player's hand as they walk by and head up the tunnel. Should the next three games go as expected, the Bulldogs will be at least £50,000 better off than they might have been, though the expression on Kev's face speaks of a man for whom money is his least concern. Batley, the old Batley, the competitive Batley, the *true* Batley, are back.

In the changing room, the excited chatter led as usual by Brownie will soon give way to quiet satisfaction, but not yet. 'You should be proud of your effort there,' says JK, his own grin restored. 'Outstanding. I knew when we assembled there was a totally different attitude. The warm-up was different . . . that's the intent we need to take to Leeds on Friday. We achieved what we wanted to achieve, well done. Now let's go to Headingley and enjoy it. Let's not go there and lie down. Let's go challenge the arrogant millionaire bastards!'

Doggies . . . Doggies . . . Doggies . . . Doggies . . .

Upstairs, the Batley family pack ever more tightly into Ron's Lounge. They are going to need a bigger bar.

20

'I HONESTLY THINK we can win more, I really do. And I wouldn't be surprised if we win a couple. We had a shit two and a half games, guys, can't run away from that. But we've had a good one and a half since then and they've been enjoyable, haven't they?'

Training the following night was light: a team meeting followed by recovery at Total Fitness, part of a shorter turnaround. Leeds would go into the game having beaten Salford 30–8, while London lost 40–4 at Huddersfield and, the day before, unbeaten Leigh sprang their biggest surprise, a 25–18 away victory at Hull Kingston Rovers.

JK reckoned enthusiasm and smartness got them home against Featherstone. It would take a repeat and more to emerge with credit from their most formidable challenge yet. 'I don't know how many of us have played in front of 12,000-plus folk,' he said, knowing all too well the answer, 'but it's going to be a hell of an evening.'

Equally worth celebrating was Kear's inclusion, along with Leigh boss Neil Jukes and London's Andrew Henderson, on a three-man shortlist for the Championship Coach of the Year, winner to be announced at a dinner in Leeds the following Monday. Dom Brambani was in the mix for Player of the Year, heady days indeed.

Less welcome was the online homophobic abuse directed at Keegan Hirst and Antony Cotton. A first win in the Super 8s was not enough for the same online critic who had insulted the captain weeks before and had done so again last night on social media. On the club's website, the chairman confirmed that the culprit 'will no longer be allowed entrance to the Fox's Biscuit Stadium'. Since Keegan confirmed his sexual orientation, Kev continued, the club had been delighted by the response. The skipper would shortly be taking up a full-time career with Wakefield, having given great service, and ought to feel welcome and at home here, as should Cotton. 'There is no place in our sport for homophobic abuse or indeed any abuse [which] means we have to prevent individuals [from] making any of our friends feel uncomfortable in any way.'

Less offensive, though guaranteed to give the pot a stir, were the comments of former Leeds and Great Britain foreword Jamie Peacock on the BBC's *Super League Show*. After praising Batley's achievement this year on 'an extremely limited budget', the current Hull KR general manager cast doubt on the Bulldogs' right to the cash windfall that guaranteed their immediate future. 'I always question if it's money well spent within our game. No disrespect to Batley but we need to increase our spend up in the top division.'

Among the playing squad, the mood was upbeat. Physio Carl was asked by the coach to talk them through the play of the game, Dom's drop-goal on the stroke of half-time recommended to the scrum-half by the man in the orange bib as it turned out. 'I gave you a quick glance, John, and I've worked on my speed from earlier in the season after comments by Brownie,' he said, deadpan, to laughter. 'I think that's the quickest a physio has ever done forty metres.' *And what was the result, Carl?* 'A steady one-pointer that wins the game, John.'

'Good man.' More laughter from a group £500 each better off, egos once again intact. 'When you win a game, you feel great, don't you? Well, I want us to come away from Leeds feeling proud, I really do. I believe that with the people we've got in this room, we can go there, represent the club, but more importantly represent ourselves, our group, in a really positive manner.'

Which is exactly what they did.

By Wednesday, training was once again unrestrained, a full-on session that not even the first and only appearance of the year from the drug testers could disrupt. Ainy, Scotty, Gleds, Blakey, Jimmy Davey and Sam Smeaton were the lucky six selected, all passing water and the exercise without recrimination.

Less happily, a man who had been hoping for a Headingley trip all season was denied it at the last. The shoulder Brownie had carried all year finally got the better of him with only three games to go. 'It's a massive blow to us, but a big blow to James as well,' JK told the BBC. 'A Queens lad, he was looking forward to playing at Leeds. This was going to be one of the highlights.' One game short of a 100th career appearance too. Shaun Squires was also ruled out.

Rhinos coach Brian McDermott, while praising Batley and an eventual 15,135 attendance swelled by 10,000 season-ticket holders, admitted afterwards that it was 'not the highest profile game this club has been involved in', and he wasn't wrong. Yet for the Bulldogs, it was a night at the opera. Electronic ticket checks, the Friday-night-under-lights buzz of Headingley, its football stadium to one side, Test match cricket arena the other . . . it was another world, an occasion the club would never forget.

The first meeting of Batley and Leeds had been on St Stephen's Day 1890. The last, 1983, thirty-three years ago, a Yorkshire Cup first-round tie before 2,111 at Mount Pleasant won by Leeds, 30–14. Since the introduction of two divisions in 1973, Batley have not been in the top flight, Leeds winning that year too, 29–15. Batley's last visit to Headingley was for a Challenge Cup tie in 1977, the Loiners, as was, victorious again, 40–6. As for Batley wins, besides a purple patch in the 1920s, the one-time Mountaineers last got one over their big-city rivals in 1967, 13–12, a major surprise. The Gallant Youths' song was last sung at Headingley in 1954, after another Challenge Cup tie, their last league win on the sport's half-centenary, 29 August 1945. That a forty-nine-year losing 'run' was to be extended in 2016 was not in doubt, but what spirit they showed.

A match-up with last year's Super League treble winners, however disappointing a season they'd had, would be a handful at the best of times for a part-time side, several of whom had come straight from the day job prior to kick-off. And in the Qualifiers, the Rhinos were back in form, four wins from four. What say the pundits? Defeat by fifty points? Sixty? More? After all, London scored seventy.

With Leeds still not mathematically guaranteed a return to the top flight, coach McDermott was taking no chances. The line-up that walked out at Headingley with the Leeds United tune 'Marching On Together' blasting from the tannoy was the strongest team available. Were it not to be a very long night, extra-special effort was required.

The start was encouraging. Patch was narrowly denied a 40/20 at the end of set one and the line speed and scramble D that got them here was in evidence. They threatened with the ball, spurning two points in front of the posts early on, an up-and-at-'em attitude that come the hooter had the fans in the famous South Stand chanting their name. In one yardage set, they made ninety-five metres.

The Bulldogs couldn't quite cross the Leeds try-line, Alistair Leak coming closest on thirteen minutes only to discover that referee Joe Cobb had blown his whistle prematurely for a Leeds knock-on. But any space Leeds won they had to fight for, the home side playing predominantly up the middle with a view to wearing Batley down, presumably to capitalize as they tired. It didn't happen. The Rhinos were hustled and bustled as the Bulldogs, even out on their feet towards the end of both halves, thwarted the expected procession.

Three first-half tries and a couple of conversions that gave the hosts a 16–0 half-time advantage flattered Leeds, six of their points arriving a minute before the break. And although that had doubled to 32–0 by the end, the Doggies had contributed much to an entertaining game. With extra composure they may have troubled their illustrious adversaries even more. Four times the Bulldogs regained possession from restarts. They won the GLDO tally 3–1 and, up front, Alexes Rowe and Bretherton were two outstanding performances among many. As the players returned the applause of travelling followers on the western terrace and the South Stand found its voice – *Batley, Batley, Batley!* – the underdog had again had its day, or night, Brownie joining them at the end, arm in a sling. Leeds adores an underdog as much as anywhere else, just as long as the beast's bite is muzzled accordingly.

In the press conference, McDermott was impressed. Batley had put them under pressure and never let it drop off. JK said he was very proud indeed. A quality performance had been 'a reward for everybody at the club'. The players were buzzing, as they had been since half-time against Huddersfield in game three.

What's more, there was now the rare luxury of an eight-day turnaround in which to prepare for penultimate opponents Leigh. Tomorrow, that club's third victory over Super League opposition – a beating of Huddersfield by forty-eight points to forty – would guarantee the Championship leaders' ascendancy to the top flight.

Salford, embroiled in a Super 8s campaign from which they would be glad to escape unscathed, had done themselves and Batley a huge favour by beating Featherstone, 70–16. Which meant that, as well as having a win under their belt, the Bulldogs now had a superior points difference to Rovers: six (-161 to -167). Would it be enough to ensure seventh place? In London, the sixth-placed Broncos fell 18–58 to Hull KR, their stories too not quite finished yet.

At Mount Pleasant, a restful weekend exploded into life on Sunday night via a fuss stirred once again by social media. This time the target was a teenager exposed as a peddler of illicit tickets. The second fan banned in a week, he'd hit the pocket of a club he claimed to love, no more to loiter in the tunnel eager as a puppy. That he was allowed to get so close was partly because that's how Batley roll – open, family-friendly, if a little naïve and lackadaisical at times, vulnerable to malign intent. Either way, it was a sorry little episode, not least for the lad himself – seldom seen in anything but Bulldogs clothing – that might have had more serious repercussions. The club committed itself to examining all aspects of ticketing over the close season and sought to 'draw a line under an issue now dealt with. This is your club and we need to ensure every possible income comes to the club to help us prosper and improve. Please be vigilant.'

One match for which tickets could not be touted was the final away game. To celebrate promotion, Leigh owner Derek Beaumont, who had already spent at least a million in search of that very dream, announced that the gates would be open on Saturday as a gift to the town. Batley received 600 tickets to distribute as they wished. With transport paid for by the players in atonement for the London blitzkrieg, it meant a cheap weekend indeed.

And there was more good news on Monday night, at the annual Championships dinner, where JK was voted Kingstone Press Coach of the Year, beating off the challenge of Jukes and Henderson, no mean feat given the achievements of those sides too. A day later, JK thanked his squad for their contribution, with a nod also to Dom Brambani's Player of the Year nomination, that award ultimately going to Leigh's skipper, Micky Higham. 'It isn't about the individual, I've always said that; it's about the group. Every single one of you contributed to that and I was very proud. It was a shame Dom didn't pick it up, though he was in the top three and the winner is an outstanding player; to be in and amongst that was great stuff as well. I'm sure [Dom] wouldn't mind me saying that that's down to you guys as well, because like me he's just one part of the cog.'

After which the focus switched to game thirty-four of the year. Friday had been a buzz: 'you should be proud of your efforts', but improvements remained to be made. Leigh went on the piss until Monday; here was a chance to inflict a hangover. Eight thousand tickets had already gone, a large crowd and another great atmosphere was guaranteed. 'We need to go there with the same attitude we showed against Leeds.'

Clips. Gym. Field. Across the Pennines, Manchester was in the grip of rainstorms, a deluge so powerful it forced the postponement of City's Champions League clash with Borussia Mönchengladbach at the Etihad. No such surrender to the elements in Batley, where, as the skies turned black as coal after the hottest September day since 1949, the training drills carried on as planned, the sodden kit of players and coaches tinted blue by electrical flashes of thunder and lightning.

*

A chilly morning speaks of autumn, though come lunchtime sunshine breaks through as a hundred or so fans in red and white cluster out front at Leigh Sports Village. A half hour after noon, a statue in honour of Leigh's all-time record points scorer, John Woods, will be unveiled. One local paper predicts it will stand thirty feet high.

As the monument waits for its big moment under a sheet, like E.T. on Elliot's bike, it's clear that's a tall tale, even allowing for the pedestal. But two and a half hours before kick-off, the event is joyful. Several former teammates are in attendance and they join in a count-down from six, the great man's shirt number, to ensure it goes with a swing.

Among the guests is rugby league royalty, Alex Murphy OBE, widely held to be the best scrum-half ever, rendered in bronze with Gus Risman, Martin Offiah, Eric Ashton and Billy Boston at the top of Wembley Way. Murphy's friend and fellow one-time Leigh coach and hooker Kevin Ashcroft is also here; both were key figures when Leigh last brought home the Challenge Cup in 1971.

'Let me shake the hand of legends,' says one child of that era, now getting on a bit. He first addresses Murphy who, at seventy-seven, remains a typically gobby half-back associated with a list of Wildean witticisms longer than the East Lancs Road – 'If you want to know how good he was, ask him yourself . . .' the most famous. As for Ashcroft: 'The RAC had to get me out of bed this morning,' he half-jokes, having had two new knees fitted since his playing days and quite possibly a hip or two and other joints along the way. 'He's always been trouble, has Murph,' he confides. 'Two popes have resigned over him.'

Ceremony over, the crowd clears and the assorted VIPs head upstairs to the Premier Club pre-match luncheon, a giant TV screen above the LSV entrance flickering an advertisement for the reserves of Manchester United and Liverpool on Tuesday, 10 October. Derek Beaumont's parents and grandmother are present; his 65-year-old father one of the foremost Rod Stewart tribute acts in the country by all accounts, blond bouffant to match. During the meal, Beaumont himself arrives late on a neighbouring pitch via helicopter.

The Batley directors are seated at a table in the corner near the door, having 'successfully cleared passport control at Saddleworth,' quips MC Mike Latham. No, Kev says, he does not intend making a similar entry at the Mount next Sunday. Outnumbered, the group sits politely, though with a hint of disapproval manifested as dignity. Nice facilities these, if somewhat ostentatious, and ostentatiousness and Batley jar. It wouldn't do to be overly impressed.

As for Beaumont's other grand gesture, a colourful and noisy 10,556 crowd in a 12,000-capacity venue cuts a fine sight, the figure around a quarter of Leigh's total population. And though the players are denied entry to the bar afterwards, Batley are otherwise made welcome. Ahead of his penultimate game in charge and last on the road, JK is presented with an award in recognition of outstanding services to rugby league, a magnanimous gesture given how he had pipped Neil Jukes to the big prize. Similarly, Batley are first to enter the field of play before forming a guard of honour for Leigh's players as they emerge to a rapturous reception. Nineteenth win in a row today and only Leeds will stand in the way of an unbeaten Qualifiers campaign.

Luke Blake's withdrawal in the warm-up with a pelvic problem necessitates a late shake-up for the visitors. Chandler starts and eighteenth man James Harrison is on the bench. Ainy too is selected, having now given up on a leg scan. 'There's no point worrying about it,' he'd said, strolling up to the ground alone from nearby Wigan before his teammates arrived. He will soon be able to rest it for a few weeks in the off-season anyway.

As Kear predicted, though, a Leigh club still in party mood is vulnerable. Higham isn't playing and a handful of players return from injury absence, such as ex-Australia international centre Willie Tonga and the Toronto-bound Fui Fui Moi Moi, handfuls both, though maybe a little ring-rusty. Were Batley to win, a sixth-place finish is feasible, worth an extra £200,000. And while unlikely, nor would the Million Pound Game be mathematically impossible. For that to happen, though, not only do Batley need to win here but

London must dispatch Salford on the road. In which case, Batley, London and Salford would each go into the final game on four points; should Batley beat the Red Devils at the Mount and London then lose at home to Featherstone, the Bulldogs would be fifth. And as it turns out, the Broncos do produce a surprise, turning Salford over 19–16 this very afternoon, ensuring that the Red Devils' visit to the Mount will indeed carry must-win status. For one team at least.

First, though, there is this afternoon to get through and, after a bright start, the game frustrates. Leigh drop the ball from the kick-off and although nothing comes from that, on eight minutes Dave Scott scampers in on a swerving run, Patch adding the conversion for an early 6–0 lead. Soon, though, the Centurions assume control. Batley are dominated physically and a couple of home tries including one for the behemoth Moi Moi make it 12–6, in line with the run of play. Just as they have all season, the Bulldogs battle gamely and just before the half hour draw level through a trademark try by terrier Leaky. It's quite a day for pest control. John Woods – commended to eternity outside – is a 'rat-catcher' too. Patch kicks the goal and it's 12–12.

However, the Bulldogs then concede a GLDO from the restart when quicker thinking would have earned them a penalty; all Keegan needed to do was straddle the line and touch the ball in flight. Instead, the bounce is an inch short of going out on the full. Moments later, Leigh are back in front with the first of two tries, the game's turning point, that give them a 24–12 half-time lead.

For all their fight, Batley have been trying too hard, kicking out on the full, conceding needless penalties, handling errors galore, their set completion figures must be horrendous. Yet it's clear Leigh are there for the taking if their opponents could just tighten up.

The second half starts as the first ended – scrappily and with the Centurions on the scoreboard: 30–12. With half an hour to go, though, and Leigh having faded late numerous times in the Super 8s, Batley might still have a chance if they can conjure a few good ends. But the self-inflicted woes continue and opportunities go begging. Realistically for these part-time players, a fifth game against full-time opposition and sixth game in seven weeks must be taking its toll. Yet ask them and they will tell you those are excuses, and on this occasion at least it cannot be denied that they have brought the sheer volume of hard work upon themselves with too many wrong decisions. Exhaustion, though, isn't just about muscles and lungs; it will affect speed of thought too.

Cropper, Scotty and Tuna are praised by JK after a display in which he reckons his team was otherwise not only bettered but also 'battered'. Tonga, in a manful battle with Reitts to the winger's credit, displays his finishing prowess to notch Leigh's sixth, before Leaky's kick in-goal ping-pongs around several ankles and Keegan is first to the ball. It is likely his last ever try for Batley, Patch converting. Two minutes from the end, though, both sides cross again. When Batley recover a short restart, Reitts' sparkling footwork earns his team's last away try of the season, goaled by Patch, in a 42–24 result.

Effort has not been lacking and Dom, who ends the game with a black eye and blood pumping from an eyebrow, is that night triply recognized as Player of the Year by teammates, coaches and supporters at a player presentation evening in Ron's Lounge. Brownie wins 'Man of Steel'; Breth is voted Clubman of the Year; Top Try Scorer and Rear of the Year goes to Reitts. The winger now needs a solitary try to reach a century of career touchdowns. Can he score it against Salford?

Craig 'Linners' Lingard knows where he will be next year – at League 1 side Keighley Cougars, a successful interview last week in the face of stiff opposition earning him the hard-to-come-by head coach's role he had so coveted. Craig, wrote chairman Gary Fawcett, had been instrumental in Batley's campaign and would bring 'deep experience of coaching and extensive understanding of our game, having played or coached for over eighteen years'. Keighley hoped to 'emulate the successes Batley are currently enjoying'. Lingard's appointment 'might bring along with it some of that Batley luck!'

As for Linners himself, he was determined to give the Cougars fans 'a team that gives everything they have got'. A brand of rugby 'fast and exciting to watch'. The players would be given systems but within those 'will be encouraged to react to what is happening in front of them. As the game plan will be slightly more expansive, it will be unlikely that our completion rate will be 90 per cent-plus, so the players will have to enjoy the challenge of defending to play that way. Players need to enjoy playing without the ball as much as they enjoy playing with it.' JK, whom he has worked with since 2012, had offered his support, 'and his experience has been invaluable to me. Having John on the end of a phone is a massive positive for both myself and Keighley, and something that I will use.'

But first there was a final week to get through. At training on Thursday, Linners took one group on the field and Mauny oversaw another, both groups under the eye of the prowling master-coach. 'Don't be loose,' said JK, floodlights glinting in the twilight autumnal equinox, the squeals of Under-7s drifting over from the patch of grass behind the Glen Tomlinson Stand. 'If you're loose on Sunday, it will be sixty points, believe you me.' He was determined they finished well.

They practised the wrestle, pinning, just as they had done all year. 'Really challenge them,' said Mauny. 'These are big on the wrestle, aren't they?' *Straight in, straight in, turn him . . . turn . . . nice and tight. Make them work on the floor . . . squeeze. Nice. Nice. Nice.* They practised peeling off the tackle and getting back into line.

The last evening session done, JK gathered the squad around him. 'We can end up with a banquet or a sour taste,' he warned, having in the shortest team meeting of the year handed out slips of paper to players and coaching staff. 'Write three things you intend to improve upon this weekend and something that inspires you – to do with family, mates, a saying, anything . . . as long as it gets your heart pumping.' Unbeknown to all, he would return these on Sunday before the game, in envelopes to be opened there and then, which would also contain a personal note.

There had been a different tone two nights before, when a recovery session at Total Fitness followed a meeting in which the coach had laid it firmly on the line: 'We are not stroking the dog, we are kicking the fucking dog, unfortunately.' The Leigh clips made for ugly viewing – seven tries presented in procession. The half-backs were off point, not only kicking-wise but also skill-wise. Poor concentration: 'We need to be smart at all times' – substandard, in short. Dominated in the tackle: 'we killed ourselves because we wanted a nice steady afternoon.' An impartial observer might blame physical or mental fatigue at the end of a demanding campaign, or inevitable comedown from the exertions at Headingley. The reality of a part-time environment coupled with a lack of opportunity for squad rotation perhaps. But if he or she did, they had best not state the bleedin' obvious out loud.

Penalties were conceded because they were chasing shadows. 'Look at it, it's like they're on fast-forward and we are in slow motion. I want us to be hard on ourselves, fellas. Finish with shit performances after the season we've had and we are letting ourselves down.' For what must have been the 100th time this year, Carl turned the lights on. 'That isn't an ability problem, is it? And I would suggest it's not a structural or organizational problem, would you agree? What do we think the problem was then? How we approached the game, yes.' He nodded sadly. 'How we approached the game. The challenge now, guys, is for us to be fucking desperate, to be hungry, and for us to carry and make sure they can't put threes and fours in, to make sure we make good decisions, and make sure we play quick, and when they come running at us, we have good fucking contact so that we can trust in our techniques and systems and structures.' More so as Salford would be desperate, looking down the barrel of a smoking P45. 'These big guys [Rowey and Keegan were indicated] are vital. Forwards set platforms – the half-backs play off those platforms.'

Any other coach might have taken his foot off the gas a little by now – metaphorical pipe-and-slippers time. Not John Kear. He stood by what he told the media. 'They battered us, believe you me. Now we need to batter some other fucker and we've got one more chance to do it. I plead with you, this is the last week we are going to be here as a group. It's great that so many are staying. I'm chuffed because I think you'll have another good season next year. But I'd love us, I'd fucking love us, to finish on a massive high, guys, I really would. The guys who are moving on, we owe them that, don't we?'

The captain agreed. 'I want to sing that winners' song one more time, me,' said Keegan.

So here they are. It has come to this. An expectant Mount Pleasant on the last weekend of the season, the last weekend for the class of 2016 anyway. No Hunslet. No relief at relegation narrowly avoided. No slipping off quietly, crestfallen and knackered, after a campaign to forget. Instead, the visit of a Super League team at the end of the most successful year in living memory. Determination to bring the curtain down with the loudest song and dance act possible.

Doggies . . . Doggies . . . Doggies . . . Doggies . . .

Surprisingly, given what is at stake, the game isn't televised. Were Salford and their enigmatic owner Marwan Koukash to lose this fixture, unlikely on the face of it as that may be, and should London beat Featherstone in the capital, then their relegation to the Championship is assured. Leeds, having beaten Leigh at Headingley on Thursday, had topped the Qualifiers, the promoted Centurions taking the defeat philosophically in second. On 'Survival Saturday', a thriller at the KC Lightstream went Huddersfield's way, Hull KR losing to a disputed drop-goal, 22–23, to confirm safety for the Giants and fourth place for the Robins, who would therefore line up against the Red Devils – or London – in the Million Pound Game next weekend.

Rumours, fanned by the non-committal owner himself, are rife that Koukash will quit the club if Salford do go down. Yet on BBC 5 Live beforehand, unheard by the crowd, he had hinted it would be the other way around – relegation would see him stay. Television apart, the national media is out in force, Batley's tiny press box overflowing. Can the underdogs find their snarl for one last time and take advantage?

At the final training session on Saturday morning, JK had again ratcheted up the opportunity to finish in style. Players at the start of the week chatting amiably about a 'Mad Monday' or 'Silly Saturday' trip to Blackpool next weekend, super villains the theme – Keegan's Village People suggestion rebuffed: *It's supposed to be fancy dress, not your usual daywear* – were now focused absolutely. After tomorrow, it would become Batley Bulldogs 2017, 'which is different from our group. I want to be proud of what we put on. If there's one thing I've wanted to tick off in my time here, it's beating a Super League team. We've come *that* close three times in the Challenge Cup. I'd love us to do that then we can all shake hands and ride off into the fucking sunset.'

Twenty-four hours later, though, the Fox's Biscuits Stadium didn't know what to expect. Given the tight margin of the negative points differences, if Batley lost and Featherstone won, the Bulldogs might yet end the season bottom. JK too was a little off his stride, not knowing quite how to feel, though his fingers were a clue. According to Dawn, later presented with a bouquet and bottle of Bulldog gin by a grateful chairman – 'when you've drunk the gin, use the bottle as a vase for the flowers' – her husband spent twenty minutes that morning looking for his underpants. Yet as his troops returned from the warm-up, full of advice and chat, he regained his equilibrium.

'Listen, guys,' said JK. He'd been watching Salford go through their drills; they were tetchy, 'having more meetings than enough'. But what that meant is that they would come out like fuck and he did not want this to become another Huddersfield, okay? 'You starting thirteen have got a responsibility to get us in the game. The interchange bench, you stay with that. We are coming uphill. We are going to complete, kick long, we are going to chase hard. I don't want them to run harder than we've run, to hit harder, out-enthuse or out-work us. We just go out there and we give it absolutely everything for you guys, the band of brothers of two thousand and fucking sixteen. Let's make it a game to remember . . .'

Keegan called everyone together in a circle, in that instant the centre of the universe. All present – players, non-players, coaches, Carl, Doc Findlay, Mauny, John Heaton, Pottsy, Sam, Ally, James – brought here by chance or fate or heavenly provenance, in any case part of something bigger – *nice, Keegan, nice* – arms around shoulders, to hear the last exhortations of the pack's on-field leader.

'This is it, boys, innit, eh? It's been a fucking long year. It's been long and it's been tough, but it's been a privilege to be your captain. From them shitty horrible hills in winter, to losing away at Oldham, winning at Swinton and getting in the top four . . . a rollercoaster year and I'm proud of us all. But it's not fucking done yet. The ending isn't written. When it is, you become immortal. Either remembered for a damp squib or sending John away on a high and being immortalized as that. It's on us, this group of people, doing what we've fucking done all year. Doing it one more time, the best we've ever done it.'

One . . . two . . . three . . . Bulldogs!

Playing against the slope and into a strong breeze, Batley enjoyed the better of the opening minutes, defending doggedly, winning penalties and going set for set to establish a presence in the game. But when Salford crossed, they did so at the double. A side so much larger and more powerful began to make downfield yards, rucks were freed too swiftly and the Reds rolled, an avalanche hitting a hesitant defensive line. Still, if the half-time margin could be kept within reason, the hosts might still have a chance. And when Dom Brambani's clever kick touches giant three-quarter Junior Sa'u on the way into touch, a home scrum is formed. In the resulting set, quick hands and a shift create just enough space for Wayne Reittie to claim his century in suitably flamboyant style as word breaks that London are already beating Featherstone 10–0.

The touchline conversion attempt is missed but it's 4–12 – all to play for. Batley, though, concede a pair of penalties on last tackles, having muscled up well in defence. Upshot: another converted try. When Sam Smeaton's kick goes straight into touch, a fourth makes it

4–22 on the half hour. The centre has shown good touches in recent weeks, though that isn't one, and worse comes six minutes before the break when he injures an ankle trying to prevent a now rampaging Salford's fifth of the half, the Bulldogs outnumbered out wide. Two minutes before half-time, they are in again. At 4–34, the contest is as good as decided.

Straw-clutchers recall the visit of Huddersfield in August and that second-half 26–10 turnaround. In the sheds, the players are calm though red of face, having toiled hard against superior opponents. JK, not ready to throw in the towel, says they haven't helped themselves. He's unhappy with soft tries. 'Slow the ruck so we can number off – put some fucker on their arse. This last quarter of an hour they were taking the piss, believe you me. Let's rectify that, play field-position rugby. Make them fight to get upfield.' Salford are comfortable now and will chuck the ball out of their backsides. 'Errors will come, giving us an opportunity to camp down there. That's all I'm asking you to do. If we do that, things will happen for us. Are we happy with that? Let's make sure it's a good half. You can still emerge with a lot of credit.'

'Forty minutes, fellas, forty minutes,' Mokko reminds them as, after one last knock on the door, they head out and trot up the tunnel, onward towards the light.

This time Salford start with a tidy uphill set that ends with a kick to touch. It is clear they intend to set up camp at the top end. A well-drilled side who wouldn't even be in this position had they not had six points deducted earlier in the year for a breach of the salary cap, the match heralds a departure of their own. Director of football and ex-Australia coach Tim Sheens is set to coach Hull KR next term, by the look of it Salford's opponents in the do-or-die game next week. Were Salford not in the Qualifiers, Wakefield would be. In other words, JK and Keegan would now be attempting to condemn the club they were joining in 2017 to relegation. Whatever the outside forces conspiring against rugby league in its 121-year history, its own administration has all too often been chief culprit of opening the sport to ridicule.

Through it all, though, the athletes up and produce, as for Batley they do now, slope and wind finally at their backs. To the extent that the next score is another popular one, Reitts's 101st from Patch's pinpoint kick to the corner. *Easy, easy* . . . chant the wags on the Ron Earnshaw Terrace, though the conversion is wide. *Keep going, Batley,* comes a voice from the stand. The Bulldogs are almost in again when Blakey, making light of any back concerns, and Rowey are held up either side of a sixth Salford try. And when Patch forces a GLDO, Chris 'Uce' Ulugia powers in with six minutes to go for Batley's final try of the season. Patch's goal makes it 14–38. It's hard to imagine the quiet Samoan playing in Featherstone colours next year.

Batley don't quite have the last word, Salford scoring again to end the entertainment 14–42. But the conversion attempt is wide, ensuring these modern Gallant Youths 'win' the second half, 10–8, a season of slim victories in miniature.

The hooter is met with acclaim and generous applause, the team assembling before the Glen Tomlinson Stand for a final group photo. By the tunnel, chairman Kev congratulates the players of both teams, as he has done all year. A guard of honour, photo-bombed by Rowey, greets JK and Keegan as they depart the battlefield and, in the changing room, the mood is celebratory. Defeated on the scoreboard they may be, but underdogs to the end they have finished on a high.

'Featherstone lost then?' asks JK, once Reitts, stranded outside signing autographs, has fought his way in. 'Good. Good. Listen, guys, before we all break up, and this will be the last time officially that we will be here . . .' Emotion catches in his throat. 'Some, like Breth, have been here all the time and some, like Smeats, have just joined. But I'll tell you, I've had five good years and enjoyed every fucking minute. The enjoyment has come from the interaction with you fellas. This season is so, so special. Whenever I see you around the game, I'll shake your hand, look you in the eye and we will love every memory we've created. They go on about coaches, they go on about . . . I'll tell you what, the people who really matter are the ones who put the shirt on. You warriors. I've got the greatest respect for you. Thank you very much.' Glassy eyed, he shuts up while the going is good.

His players aren't done yet. *Be on your guard, stand firm in the faith, be men of courage, be strong.* As applause rings around the room, Danny Maun, next door last year – *Congratulations, kid. You've done yourself and your family proud* – steps up with a plaque bearing JK's favourite motivational quote: *Make the sacrifices, it's worth it.* 'I'll miss him,' Mauny says, handing the memento over as the boys look on, exhausted and contented. 'He's made us all better people.'

In Ron's Lounge, there are more speeches. Kev bids the leavers farewell in typical style – 'Here comes Keegan to blow his own trumpet' – the captain responding in kind: 'If I could, I would. Hopefully I'll do well at Wakefield,' he says, 'and give it a good crack, but I'll always be a Bulldog at heart.' He promises to come back and see everyone, although not Kevin, obviously. Not once he's been paid anyway.

And then it's JK's turn, when even Kev turns unexpectedly serious. 'It's great John is leaving in the circumstances he is – backing him mid season was one of the wisest decisions we ever made as a club, the wisest was setting him on in the first place. He's kept us in the Championship, got us to a Grand Final and now got us in the Qualifiers, a tremendous achievement given the budget we've got. It has been a privilege to have him as our coach.'

JK repeats his praise of the players, thanks the supportive directors and declares an emotional attachment to Batley that 'won't go away'. He'll be back to watch next year and hopes they get in the Qualifiers again, posting more than one victory next time. 'You do realize, don't you, that we are the number-one part-time team in this country?' It may be the most popular thing he has said. 'Thank you for making me and Dawn welcome . . .' and he is choking up again.

'No, thank *you*, John,' they shout. 'Thank *you*.'

When, eventually, the acclaim dies down, Kev reclaims the mic. 'Anyway, on to more important things,' he says, acknowledging the elderly lady who has waited patiently by his side. 'Gwen's raffle . . .'

Scenes at Cardigan Fields, Leeds, on the occasion of Batley's victory in the 1885 Yorkshire Cup final.

A Little Bit of History

EVERY CULTURE HAS its creation myths. Formed at the George Hotel, Huddersfield, on 29 August 1895, football's thirteen-a-side code was forged in indignation at the bullying toffs of Twickenham, whose refusal to sanction broken-time payments for working-class players then so prevalent in the north of England led to a breakaway that would be known as the Great Split. Twenty-seven years later, in 1922, that original Northern Union became rugby league, cementing an initial victory for common sense and moral righteousness over the class-driven hypocrisy of the Corinthian ideal: *This Sporting Life* triumphant over *Tom Brown's Schooldays*.

Although the facts and dates are clear enough – 1897: line-out abolished; 1906: reduction from fifteen to thirteen players, rucks replaced by play-the-balls and so on – as with any such tale, it was all rather more complex than that. With the advent of proper scholarly research into sport, a more nuanced not to say intriguing picture has emerged of those gas-lit days of creeping professionalism north and south, politicking, incompetence and muscular Christianity, much of it now written about and written about well. Suffice to say here that of the twenty-two who went their own way on a Victorian summer's evening – establishing 'the principle of payment for bona-fide broken time only' (and by the turn of the century being joined by just about every other rugby football club in Yorkshire, Lancashire and Cumbria) – Batley's Gallant Youths were the first names on the list.

There is no more comprehensive a review of Batley RLFC's first 100 years than *A 'Ton' Full of Memories*, self-published in 1986 by Brian E. Cartwright, though no longer in print. The book's author, a lifelong Batley devotee and 'equipment supervisor' to Great Britain in his time, details every up and down – though mainly down – in a history that prompts one contributor, the then RFL public-relations guru David Howes, to suggest that Batley typifies 'the northern heritage of the great game of rugby league . . . the Mount Pleasant club is an integral thread in the richly woven fabric of the oval ball sport.'

The Gallant Youths were a major success of the pioneer years, Challenge Cup winners in 1897, 1898 and 1901, Yorkshire Cup winners in 1912. They were founder members who finished eighteenth in that initial Northern Union season but who stayed the course far longer than original champions Manningham (nowadays Bradford City AFC), Broughton Rangers, Tyldesley, Runcorn, Stockport, Liversedge, Brighouse and the like.

Cartwright's book drips with the names of great old players like 'Wattie' Davies and Jackie Perry, John Etty, Billy Hudson, Eric Hesketh, Trevor Walker – superstars once upon a time but whose reputations are now fading among the younger generation, if not forgotten entirely.

Like many other fledgling football clubs of the era, Batley's roots lie in cricket. In 1880, Batley CC, then resident at evocatively named 'Owd Billy Wood's Cloise', sniffed the wind and became Batley Cricket Athletic and Football Club. However, setting a pattern of off-the-cuff eccentricity, the moniker was adopted before any such club – in an era when football in the north was more likely to mean 'rugger' than association 'soccer' – agreed to amalgamation. A group calling itself Batley Athletic was approached first, then Batley Mountaineers, who got the hump because they thought themselves a superior outfit. A challenge match was proposed to settle the matter.

Watched by a large crowd, it took place on 23 October 1880, though it resolved nothing as it ended up being abandoned with both sides asserting victory. The Mountaineers claimed to have won by one try and two touchdowns, to two Athletic touchdowns. Athletic said they had scored a 'try' via forward Albert Parker, though the referee ruled it a no-score, Athletic refusing to accept his decision. Confusion reigned, especially as the BCA&FC title insisted upon despite further protests from the Mountaineers (and a refusal on Athletic's part to countenance a rematch) was already in use three weeks earlier in what history now accepts as the first official game at Mount Pleasant. Bradford Zingari were the visitors, Batley winning by two goals, three touchdowns, two dead balls and a touch goal to Zingari's easier to untangle nil.

The new amalgamated club won its first cup tie too, scoring one try and two touchdowns to Harrogate's three touchdowns in the Yorkshire Challenge Cup, then just two years old, goals worth more back then since kicking was judged the greater skill. After that battle for 'T' owd Tin Pot', the whole town seems to have greeted the team at the station, along with a brass band that played Handel's 'See The Conquering Hero Comes'.

In those days, the changing rooms were in the Royal Hotel, an eight-minute stroll away at least, down on Bradford Road. By the end of that first twenty-six-game season, fifteen games were won, six lost and five drawn, a haul Brian Cartwright summarizes thus: twenty-one goals, forty-one tries, sixty-four minor points, two posters – to nine goals, fourteen tries, 102 minor against; a little esoteric now but a decent set of results at any rate. And the period between inauguration and the 1895 split was also marked by reasonable achievement, the second year better than the first. Players like Herbert 'Dodger' Simms took county honours, and in 1884–85 the club won its first silverware, beating Manningham in the Yorkshire Cup final by six minor points to two at Cardigan Fields, Leeds. The following year, however, Batley were disqualified when Yorkshire's county committee ordered a replay of a semi-final with Halifax that the Youths thought they had won. They were unable to raise a team for a rescheduled midweek fixture. As an aside, Herbert 'Dodger' Simms once raced a greyhound over a hundred yards for a bet, with the player given a twenty-yard start. It was ruled a draw.

Mount Pleasant hosted county games and a clash with a touring New Zealand Maori side, the latter prior to Christmas 1889. But as the decade turned, frustrations with an intransigent RFU simmered over. So much so that in 1892–93 ten of Yorkshire's biggest clubs formed an alliance that, after a struggle, won semi-autonomous sub-committee status with the Yorkshire Rugby Union. Batley were among that number, along with Bradford, Dewsbury, Liversedge, Hunslet, Halifax, Wakefield, Leeds, Brighouse and Huddersfield.

It heralded the launch of a Yorkshire Senior Competition that, for the first time, pitched the county's uppermost clubs together in a league structure, rather than ad hoc weekly 'friendlies' as previously. Worried about the RFU's reaction, Leeds in the end declined entry to the YSC in its first year and were replaced by Manningham, before coming in with Hull in 1893–94. Whoever topped the table won the Shield. Non-YSC matches might also be arranged with teams like Wigan, St Helens and Warrington. As one paper reported:

> A certain Yorkshire Rugby Football team – Batley to wit – have been enjoying themselves in Liverpool, having come into Lancashire to play a few fixtures. They are currently lodging in a local hotel and, Tuesday last, went for a little merriment – considerably astonishing city collars by their broadness of dialect and bluntness of speech.

In Batley's fourteenth year, 1893–94, a large stand was erected at the Mount, bought by the football committee after its use at the Yorkshire Agricultural Show in Dewsbury. This was the now fabled Long Stand and it ran along the whole length of one side of the field. Otherwise it was a season to forget. Batley finished second bottom and went out of the cup after a replay in round two with Halifax. Nor was the following season much better. And in the wider rugby world, political antagonisms that the formation of the Senior Competition had laid bare shifted ever more sharply into focus.

A hint that all was not entirely as has been portrayed on both sides of the rugby divide comes in the manner in which, during the lead-up to 1895–96, a 'modernized' and supposedly more democratic Yorkshire Rugby Union, formed in 1888 and now including smaller clubs as well as large (and thus riddled with political in-fighting), sought to persuade YSC clubs that the Senior Competition should feature promotion on merit. Amateurism's champions north and south warned that a commercial elite would be disastrous. Smaller clubs would be asset-stripped player-wise and swallowed up by ambitious larger neighbours. The senior clubs themselves risked insolvency down the line. In the hunt for profit and glory, however, not to mention a pragmatic need for cash with which to survive harsh economic times and in the face of a widespread RFU crackdown on 'professionalism' that, in Lancashire, used bans, points deductions and relegation from a similar league as a stealth tactic in the battle for control, the warning went ignored. The YSC stayed a closed shop, promotion and relegation as vexed an issue then as it is today. Not a little ironic too, given how just three of that 'Senior Football Alliance' of ten – Leeds, Wakefield and Huddersfield – are members of the YSC's modern-day equivalent Super League, while the rest – including Batley – are either outside looking in or folded as predicted. Another southern view was that northern players were too rough.

As the clubs in the north squabbled among themselves, the top teams growing ever stronger on the field but thought selfish off it by the minnows, Twickers doubled down, determined not to relinquish its grip on the reins. Until after more political jiggery-pokery, the historic decision at the George Hotel played out as it did. Whether a split was in rugby football's best interests or not long term – and of course most of those present thought it was, with the added pressure in some cases of player-strike threats if broken time payments were not in future permitted – the stubborn, proud and pathologically hard-headed north chose Twixit. The Rugby Football Union refused utterly to compromise, most likely calculating that the troublemakers would soon come begging for readmission, tails between legs.

It didn't happen. The north of England doesn't work that way. So over the next century the RFU instead adopted a policy of persecution, banning anyone who had any involvement or contact with the upstart code entirely. Whose game was 'rugby' anyway?

Batley's representative that August night was Jack Goodall, a notable player in his day. Although broken time was to the forefront, most contemporary statements revealed underlying dissatisfaction at the thwarting of what the clubs saw as their justifiable ambitions. The threat of soccer too was a consideration, as voiced by St Helens' F. Dennett in the *Clarion*:

> Less than ten years ago not a single association club could be found in either Manchester or district. Now both Newton Heath and Ardwick are high up and making big names for themselves at the dribbling code and have innumerable imitators. The conservatism evinced by the Lancashire Rugby Union is astounding – they are content to sit still whilst the tide of association football makes great inroads into the stronghold of the rugby game. The Northern Union will help to turn that tide.

In fact, the NU's first two decades were beset by problems. After initial noises of triumph and determination, the slog of making it work set in. Some clubs, already struggling financially before 1895, did go by the wayside, switched to soccer or chose loyalty to the RFU. Many of the junior ones vanished for ever, either unsustainable economically from the start or neglected by the NU elite, take your pick. Those who battled on evolved a more open entertaining handling code required to attract the level of attendance needed not only to survive but also thrive. Yet what ultimately assured league's future was the arrival of an international front in 1907–08 – New Zealand tourists nicknamed the 'All Golds' by a media keen to caricature them as mercenaries.

Led by Wellington postal clerk Albert Henry Baskerville, the party included an Australian – the genuinely iconic Dally Messenger – and staged Tests in Queensland and New South Wales on the return leg of a triumphant nine-month tour. Sadly, after a try-scoring Test debut on the wing in Sydney, and despite having survived winter in Rochdale, Hull and Merthyr Tydfil, Baskerville caught pneumonia en route to Brisbane by ship and died aged twenty-five. The first game of rugby league in New Zealand was played in his honour, raising a reported £300 for his widowed mother. Baskerville's contribution, if brief, was immense. Without him – and the life ban dished out by the NZRFU for his trouble – it is doubtful whether the Northern Union and therefore rugby league would have lasted as long as it has, still less blossomed as it went on to do, particularly on Australia's eastern seaboard.

Batley's first NU fixture was a 7–0 win at Mount Pleasant; Hull the visitors on 7 September 1895. They then went to Manningham, where 'Wilby' broke a collarbone, lost 5–0 and finished fifth-bottom in a 'combination league' of twenty-two. The following season saw a split into Yorkshire and Lancashire sections to save travel costs that, pre-cars and motorways, were considerable. Fifteen wins, five draws, ten losses: sixth. There is no doubt about Batley's finest achievement in these earliest rugby league years. In 1896–97, the Northern Union Challenge Cup was introduced, open to clubs in Yorkshire, Lancashire and Cheshire. Confirming the Northern Union's influence outside its elite competition, over fifty clubs entered, the prize a cup three feet high, cast in solid silver on a black ebony base, worth sixty guineas. The winning side would also receive fifteen-carat gold medals, inscribed with each county's coat of arms etched on a rugby ball.

Twelve clubs were given a round-one bye, Batley included. Their first Challenge Cup tie, therefore, came in the second round at Bramley, won 11–0 at Barley Mow. Brighouse were dispatched in round three in front of around 7,000 spectators at Mount Pleasant. A tighter home scrap with Widnes followed, by the end of which the Gallant Youths were in the semi-finals. Warrington were up next at neutral Fartown, usually home to Huddersfield. Those at that match endured terrible conditions, rain pouring relentlessly. It got so bad that, losing heavily, Warrington asked the referee if the second half could be cut short. He agreed, though that club's committee later had the cheek to request that the tie be replayed on account of it having been curtailed six minutes early. Cue £5 fine, objection overruled.

And so it was that Batley reached the first ever Challenge Cup final, where they were up against St Helens at Headingley. By half-time, they had built a 7–0 lead, having produced a display that earned praise from all present. 'A grand affair,' said one newspaper, calling it, 'a good classy exhibition of play, marvellous scrummaging and open football'. The try St Helens scored next was the first Batley had conceded in the entire competition and couldn't dent the delight at an eventual 10–3 win for a club hailed 'Champions of the North'.

Post-match celebrations were at the Exchange restaurant in Leeds, handy for the train home. And having made that journey, they emerged from Morley tunnel to the rousing – and one imagines startling – sound of 160 fog horns simultaneously discharged on the tracks, along with the roar of a crowd numbered in thousands stretching from Station Road to the town hall. After that, there was a procession in which congratulatory messages were read out. 'Our football side fought not only for the honour of the Borough,' said Alderman Wilson, 'but the whole county. This day will go down in the history of Northern Rugby Football with Batley's name entered for posterity – to be ever remembered as first ever winners of the cup for as long as it remains to be played for – and talked about.'

They won it the following year too, in a year when line-outs were replaced by a kick and the points system simplified to read: 'A try equals three points, a goal either placed or dropped, two. In cases of a goal from a try, the try to count in addition to the goal.' Fellow finalists last season, St Helens, were seen off 12–7 as an opener at Mount Pleasant. Afterwards, Walkden, Castleford and Oldham were dispatched before a semi-final with Salford at Oldham. Victory by a try and a goal to nil meant another visit to Leeds, against Bradford. Local legend has it that Batley's West Yorkshire neighbours erected a platform upon which to display the Cup outside the town hall the day before the game, impudence that enraged the Gallant Youths to such an extent they kept their opponents scoreless, 7–0.

A sign of how strong a hold the Corinthian impulse still had on the Northern Union, though, came in season 1898–99. NU players were by now deemed professional, but from the start a rule had been in place that they must also have legitimate employment away from the sport, the 'working clause' as it was known. And it was now, just before Christmas, that the NU chose to get tough and enforce the rule.

Batley had a Welsh centre, Dai Fitzgerald, a coal merchant when not on the field. An NU 'investigatory committee' found that he only worked in this role for three hours a day, earning three shillings and nine pence a week to go with the couple of quid paid for rugby services. This they said was 'not following employment in a bona-fide manner' and so they banned him for sixteen months. The club itself was fined £60, ostensibly for encouraging him to be work-shy. It was a large sum of money, though twice that amount was raised as an outraged public rallied around. The rest of the players, too, did their bit by winning a Championship, the Yorkshire Senior Competition, for the first time, a third trophy at Mount Pleasant in as many years.

Their Challenge Cup trail ended with resounding defeat to Leigh, but it wasn't long before Batley won it again, a couple of seasons in fact. The campaign of 1899–1900 had seen them pipped by a point in the league by Bradford and beaten in round three of the Cup by Leeds Parish Church. But as the century turned, Batley finished fourth in the league and were set for a year of – by previous standards – under-achievement. With the Cup on the horizon, extra training sessions were introduced.

This campaign began with a first-round bye and a second-round tie at Huddersfield, won 6–2. St Helens were then beaten, before a try and goal by 'Wattie' Davies at Runcorn meant semi-finals. At Fartown, they beat Oldham for another trip to Headingley, where in 1901 they vanquished Warrington, 6–0. That, though, would be as good as it got.

Batley had an aged squad and, one by one, their better players left for pastures new. A new combined Northern League also made life more difficult and by the end of 1901–02, they were third from bottom of that division, winning only eight out of twenty-six fixtures. In the Cup, though, they did enjoy one last big hurrah: a third-round visit from Bradford. Some 18,000 people packed into Mount Pleasant, the players taking to the field through spectators lined twelve rows deep. In the end, a ladder was called for and propped at the back of a small stand. The teams clambered over the supporters' heads as folk scrambled on to stones and bricks for a better view. An elevated patch of the cricket ground, some distance hence, was used as a makeshift grandstand. The game wasn't bad either. Trailing 10–0 at half-time, Batley fought back to level the scores midway through the second half. Unseen by the majority, when Batley were awarded a penalty kick, it is said that some in the home team asked 'Wattie' Davies to miss deliberately, in order to draw the game and give the visitors a thrashing at their own place. Whatever the truth of that, Davies sent it sailing through and Wilf Auty's late try confirmed the Gallant Youths' 15–10 victory.

Alas, they were beaten in the semi-finals by Salford and when further clubs joined the Northern Union at the start of 1902–03, two divisions were introduced. Although Batley were in the upper group, promotion and relegation, two-up and two-down, was now on the agenda. Suddenly, the future was less settled and assured.

In September 1904, the Mount Pleasant ground was suspended for a month by the NU after referee J. H. Smith of Widnes disallowed a late try by Wigan and was hit on the back of the head by a missile. In 1905–06, more structural changes were made to the competition, the tradition of change masked as innovation firmly established. Already, two divisions had reverted to an enormous Northern Union League, which also introduced top-four end-of-season play-offs. The sort of system, in fact, branded new and revolutionary by friends and foes of rugby league alike at the end of a third summer season in 1998, the year of Old Trafford's very first Super League Grand Final.

*

Batley's first thirteen-a-side match was at Salford on 31 August 1906. An omen perhaps of a rockier road ahead, they lost it 12–7. By the last week in November, they were in the top half of a table that boasted thirty-one clubs, yet a slump ensued. Every game was lost between Christmas and April Fool's Day 1907, a 220-point deficit against. Thirteen-a-side rugby wasn't going well.

After the touring 'All Golds' beat a combined Dewsbury-Batley side at the former's Crown Flatt in November 1907, the club saw off Australia's first tourists at Mount Pleasant in January 1909. Then again in 1912, before Batley's solitary NU Yorkshire Cup final win in 1912–13 against Hull. And although the Northern Union was just two decades old, there seems already to have been an appreciation of club history. In 1914, on St Valentine's Day, the 'old Gallant Youths', with the likes of 'Wattie' Davies, Wilf Auty and Joe Oakland, met the present-day side in an encounter of 'most entertaining character'. Fed on dinners of roast mutton, the old boys lost 12–8, but the young 'uns, so it was written, were frequently flattened in the scrummage, 'almost as though a steamroller had run over them'. After which novelty, of course, came the far more deadly adventures of the First World War.

Batley like others lost many a player to the killing fields of Europe, but the club soldiered on and a momentous double came in 1923–24. As Batley topped the Yorkshire section, thereby winning the Yorkshire League Trophy, they came second in the composite Northern Rugby League to earn a place in the Championship play-offs. There, they beat third-placed Oldham first up and Wigan, 13–7, in the decider at Broughton, Manchester, on Saturday, 3 May 1924. And so it was that Ike Fowler became and remains the only Batley captain to lift the Championship – nowadays Super League – Trophy.

The result sparked a record attendance in 1924–25 for a third-round Challenge Cup tie with Leeds. Some 23,889 folk ascended the Mount, an unimaginable figure today that, given a lack of electronic turnstiles, also likely went under-reported. Unfortunately for Batley, a one-point defeat encapsulated the season.

Season 1926–27 began with a surprise victory over the touring New Zealanders and a string of league defeats thereafter, a story that rolled on into and beyond the 1930s. War was again disruptive, with conscription doing its worst. Though as elsewhere, use was made of guest players billeted up and down the country in the forces.

With the war concluded, however, backs like John Etty and Bill Riches came to the fore, with pre-war forwards like Mick Foley, Jack Rhodes and George Brown resuming hostilities of a less dangerous nature. This early 'Brownie' too was quite the character, playing hard despite losing sight in one eye during fighting in South Africa. And it was in the 1946–47 season, incidentally, that the Rugby League put on an Easter Monday 'experimental game' featuring Batley and Dewsbury wherein a 'line-out' was reintroduced to cut down on scrums. The idea never gained traction. Come the 1950s, despite the talents of a team still fondly remembered in the town, and a number of impressive results and thrilling games, silverware remained stubbornly out of reach. Batley almost won the Yorkshire Cup in 1952 but were beaten by Huddersfield at Leeds in heavy fog.

As the decade progressed, underachievement was matched by financial woe. Directors struggled to keep the club afloat. Etty and Riches, among other popular figures, were sold to the disgruntlement of supporters. As Brian Cartwright writes in A 'Ton' Full of Memories: 'The overall changes at this time were hotly talked about on Saturday evenings among the Batley public, as they awaited their footballing Green, Pink and Buff sports papers from wee George Moyser's selling spot outside the Zion Chapel gate in Commercial Street.' Attendances fell.

Many locals took to watching soccer in nearby Huddersfield and Bradford. After finishing bottom of the table for the first time in 1955–56, Batley RLFC was at serious risk of extinction. Auctions, rag sales, wastepaper schemes, a Grand Ball and other fundraisers were launched before the immediate threat subsided. In 1958, Batley did get to the semi-finals of the County Cup, otherwise discouragement endured well into the 1960s, a decade of 'very thin bread and butter'.

Crowds declined further and the loyal hard core who did turn up were called 'wrong in the head' for 'watching yon lot'.

The cynics had a point. Batley scraped just twenty-seven wins and a draw from 1965 to 1968 – 108 matches – and finished bottom of the league twice. Facilities too were long past their best. A TV documentary that many felt took a perverse pleasure in decline portrayed a ground no longer cared for, overgrown with weeds, virtually derelict. Changing rooms, toilets and baths in the pavilion given over to cricket in the summer looked decrepit, as did the tea room, secretary's office and boardroom, rather grand titles for what was essentially an old hut.

The broadcast at least inspired a tidy-up operation from those supporters who still cared about the club deeply; it was a wake-up call, writes Cartwright, who experienced it first hand.

> It was not unusual to find players having a whip round to purchase coke for the boiler in order to assure heat and hot baths on match-days, especially when stocks appeared to quickly diminish following delivery to the coke shed, possibly through midnight marauders helping themselves while no one was around, the budget unable to replace it every time.

It was now that the ground, all but a century old, got a facelift. The Batley Miners Welfare Club – later Taverners' – was purchased for use as a social club. New headquarters were built beneath the short stand: 'officials, supporters and players whose employment outside of rugby league was as joiners, electricians, etc., and even directors' wives, sons and daughters, toiled together in the project.' Second World War era forward Mick Foley looked after the Pools.

In the early 1970s: optimism. An influx of international talent and experience, both in the playing and coaching ranks, hinted at good times around the corner. The BBC TV *Grandstand* cameras showed Batley against Wigan and St Helens. But while the decade did have its moments, such buoyancy was soon deflated. In 145 cup and league games from August 1974 to the end of 1978–79, only twenty-eight wins were recorded, of which just six were on the road. Money was tight as ever, crowds in the thousands in the old days averaging 630 in 1974–75. The reserve side was temporarily shelved. Any money for new signings came from the directors' own pockets, so, naturally perhaps, they took exception to supporters' club protest rallies. The club in question was 'shut down', though it carried on in secret.

There followed a brief rebirth of sorts in 1978–79, when the club returned to its ancestral cerise and flame livery ahead of the centenary year, 1980–81. A special committee oversaw activities that included the creation of special ties, clothing, plates and ashtrays in commemoration of the milestone. It was also marked by dinners, player reunions and a new lottery/prize draw, designed to earn cash. Hunslet's signing of a two-year co-tenancy agreement contributed further funds. But a season entered into with hope produced three wins from fifteen games to begin with, although at least Dewsbury were beaten, 13–5, on Boxing Day. The New Year saw a run of seven wins in nine games before the visit of the league's most recent entrants, Fulham, for the official centenary game. Batley had already lost that year at Craven Cottage to a London side containing many a grizzled northerner, yet cheered on by an attendance of 4,000 that included a hundred ex-players from Ike Fowler's 1920s to the late 1970s, the modern Gallant Youths won, 10–8.

Even then, however, joy met with tragedy. A town hall dinner dance designed to conclude the celebrations was held for 250 guests, among them current and former players. A deep overnight snowfall had failed to prevent a packed house, but there was one empty seat. It belonged to Batley director George Harwood, organizer-in-chief of the centenary calendar, who passed away suddenly the day before.

Through the 1980s, a journey marked by downs, ups and yet more downs continued as before, players and coaches coming in and out and back again to little lasting effect. Struggle was in Batley's DNA, though a record £50,000 transfer of GB international and Batley Boys product Carl Gibson to Leeds in January 1986 did help to pay the bills for a while.

In concluding his book at that point, Brian Cartwright saw the Gibson deal as a sign of a much brighter future, while sounding an elegiac note for those no longer around to share in it. How he would dearly love to have seen the pride of the late directors and players:

a chance of a playful boast perhaps from Alan Tonks, and even Ike Fowler . . . most certainly, the heartiest of joviality at Laura Walker's tearoom! As for Harry Beevers, his *Batley News* column would have been ecstasy to write! The past has been and gone. With it, memories tend to drift into oblivion. And although there have been a 'ton' of them to date, may many more follow [and] once again make Batley Rugby League's Gallant Youths a name to be proud of and feared!

Acknowledgements

No rugby league club could function without the help and devotion of a great many people – and indeed many great people – as the preceding pages have hopefully made clear. Nor would it have been possible to write this book without the generous access given.

To thank everyone who needs to be thanked at Batley Bulldogs RLFC is a task too formidable to attempt, so whether named directly in *Underdogs* or not please be assured of my appreciation for one of the most enjoyable – and stressful (in a good way) – years of my life. Among all the directors, players, supporters and coaching staff, however, three in particular must be singled out: the chairman, coach and captain. I doubt that I would have been made so welcome – or at least put up with – at any other club. So with due diligence to the idea that the team matters more than the individual, thank you Kevin Nicholas, John Kear and Keegan Hirst for your hospitality and candour.

I am grateful to Jim Etty for the loan of the late Brian F. Cartwright's *A 'Ton' Full of Memories*; Malcolm Haigh for his splendid tour and lunch; Daniel Spencer for statistical assistance; Gareth Walker for planting a seed; Ikram Butt for his useful introductions; John Dewhirst for permission to use the illustration from 1885; and my friend and publishing colleague Phil Caplan for his support as I immersed myself in this project. I am grateful also for the patience of Jacqui, my wife, who was in danger of forgetting what I looked like, though it is slightly worrying that she never once complained.

Gratitude too must go to my agent, Tim Bates, at Peters Fraser and Dunlop for his guidance and encouragement; Giles Elliott, my editor; Ailsa Bathgate, my eagle-eyed copy-editor, and everyone at Transworld for showing faith in a rugby league story – any errors, factual or otherwise, are entirely my own.

Before embarking on *Underdogs*, my appetite for a game that seemed hell-bent on losing touch with its roots felt under threat – a love affair that may have run its course. A year at Mount Pleasant changed that, the thing I am grateful for most. Rugby league must rise to the challenges of the future, but do so in the company of those who built and sustained it. Today's jazzy titfer is tomorrow's old hat.

If this book achieves anything worthwhile, I hope it persuades more people to support their community club – wherever that is and whatever the sport. A good place to start would be Mount Pleasant.

Believe you me.